W9-CMK-596

Hart Crane: The Contexts of *The Bridge*

Cambridge Studies in American Literature and Culture

Editor
Albert Gelpi, Stanford University

Advisory Board
Nina Baym, University of Illinois, Champaign-Urbana
Sacvan Bercovitch, Harvard University
Richard Bridgman, University of California, Berkeley
David Levin, University of Virginia
Joel Porte, Harvard University
Mike Weaver, Oxford University

Other books in the series
Robert Zaller: *The Cliffs of Solitude*
Peter Conn: *The Divided Mind*
Patricia Caldwell: *The Puritan Conversion Narrative*
Stephen Fredman: *Poet's Prose*
Charles Altieri: *Self and Sensibility in Contemporary American Poetry*
John McWilliams: *Hawthorne, Melville, and the American Character*
Barton St. Armand: *Emily Dickinson and Her Culture*
Mitchell Robert Breitwieser: *Cotton Mather and Benjamin Franklin*
Albert von Frank: *The Sacred Game*
Beth McKinsey: *Niagara Falls*
Marjorie Perloff: *The Dance of the Intellect*
Albert Gelpi: *Wallace Stevens*
Karen Rowe: *Saint and Singer*
Richard Gray: *Writing the South*

Hart Crane: The Contexts of *The Bridge*

PAUL GILES

ELMHURST COLLEGE LIBRARY

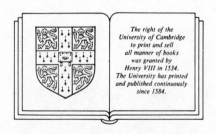

The right of the
University of Cambridge
to print and sell
all manner of books
was granted by
Henry VIII in 1534.
The University has printed
and published continuously
since 1584.

CAMBRIDGE UNIVERSITY PRESS

CAMBRIDGE
LONDON   NEW YORK   NEW ROCHELLE
MELBOURNE   SYDNEY

MAY   1987

Published by the Press Syndicate of the University of Cambridge
The Pitt Building, Trumpington Street, Cambridge CB2 1RP
32 East 57th Street, New York, NY 10022, USA
10 Stamford Road, Oakleigh, Melbourne 3166, Australia

© Cambridge University Press 1986

First published 1986

Printed in Great Britain at
the University Press, Cambridge

British Library cataloguing in publication data

Giles, Paul
Hart Crane: the contexts of The bridge. –
(Cambridge studies in American literature and culture)
1. Crane, Hart. Bridge, The
I. Title
811'.52   PS3505.R272B7

Library of Congress cataloging in publication data

Giles, Paul.
Hart Crane: the context of The bridge.
(Cambridge studies in American literature and culture)
Bibliography: p.
Includes index.
1. Crane, Hart, 1899–1932. Bridge. 2. Bridges in
literature. I. Title. II. Series.
PS3505.R272B734   1986   811'.52   85-19062

ISBN 0 521 32074 7

SE

Contents

Acknowledgements

I am glad to acknowledge first of all the Department of Education and Science and the Governing Body of Christ Church, Oxford, without whose financial support this work would never have come into existence. I should also like to thank Kenneth A. Lohf, Librarian for Rare Books and Manuscripts at the Columbia University Library, New York City, for making available to me Hart Crane's library, copies of the manuscripts of *The Bridge*, and other archive material; and for his patience in answering my queries. The Beinecke Rare Book and Manuscript Library at Yale University, the University of Delaware Library, the Pennsylvania State University Library, the Libraries of the University of Maryland at College Park, the Morris Library of Southern Illinois University at Carbondale, the Harry Ransom Humanities Research Center of the University of Texas at Austin, the Kent State University Libraries, Ohio, and the Brown University Library, Providence, Rhode Island, were all most helpful in supplying photocopies of Hart Crane's correspondence: I am grateful to the above libraries for permission to quote from unpublished manuscripts in their possession, and also to David Mann, Hart Crane's literary executor, for authorizing my use of this material. The British Library, the New York Public Library and the Bibliothèque Nationale in Paris were of great assistance in furnishing copies of various obscure magazine articles; and I should also like to acknowledge how my research was helped by several American libraries who sent me copies of documents relating to Crane: the Library of Congress, the Houghton Library at Harvard, the Lilly Library of Indiana University, the Alderman Library of the University of Virginia, the Van Pelt Library of the University of Pennsylvania, the Memorial Library of Marquette University at Milwaukee, the Golda Meir Library of the University of Wisconsin at Milwaukee, the Hamilton College Library at

Clinton, New York, the Library of the State University of New York at Stony Brook, the Poetry Collection of the State University of New York at Buffalo and the American Heritage Center of the University of Wyoming at Laramie.

Among Crane scholars, I am indebted to Sherman Paul, John Unterecker, Eric Sundquist, Alan Trachtenberg, Richard P. Sugg, Eugene Paul Nassar and (especially) Marc Simon for their interest and critical advice. I do not wish to implicate these distinguished academics in the findings of this book, merely to acknowledge that their comments helped me to bring my ideas into clearer focus. Although the controversial nature of my thesis sometimes involves me taking issue with various experts on Crane's work, I would like to underline the obvious fact that I could have done nothing without them. In England, John Bayley and Brian Lee also made helpful suggestions on points of detail when examining this text in its doctorate form. I must also express my gratitude to the late Dame Rebecca West, for answering questions in connection with her work on James Joyce; and the publishers and I are indebted to A. D. Peters and Company, representing the literary executors of Rebecca West, for permission to reproduce her essay "James Joyce and his Followers." I also extend my thanks to Selden Rodman, for allowing me to consult the letters written to him by Hart Crane; to Kenneth Burke, for permission to quote from an unpublished Crane letter; to Margaret Drabble, for permission to quote from her unpublished lecture on "The Future of the Novel"; and to London Weekend Television, for providing the transcript of an edition of *The South Bank Show* and allowing me to quote from it. At Cambridge University Press, I have been greatly assisted by Andrew Brown, Lesley Partridge and Albert Gelpi. Nigel Ledgerwood and Susan Berger both kindly surrendered part of their holiday in New York to track down for me vital books impossible to obtain in England. I am also grateful to Craig Raine, who first showed me how to read words before ideas; to Mike Weaver, who originally supervised this project; to Elsie Hinkes, who typed the manuscripts; and to Mike Temple, Roger Perrin, Peter Conrad and Nicola Mackie.

London
June 1985

. . . one should not think slightingly of the paradox; for the paradox is the source of the thinker's passion, and the thinker without a paradox is like a lover without feeling: a paltry mediocrity.

> Kierkegaard, *Philosophical Fragments*,
> 1844, trans. David Swenson

"Mother of heaven, regina of the clouds,
O sceptre of the sun, crown of the moon,
There is not nothing, no, no, never nothing,
Like the clashed edges of two words that kill."

> Wallace Stevens, "Le Monocle de
> mon oncle," 1918

Across the stacked partitions of the day –
Across the memoranda, baseball scores,
The stenographic smiles and stock quotations
Smutty wings flash out equivocations.

> Hart Crane, "For the Marriage
> of Faustus and Helen," 1923

Out of that dark, unstitched wound, that sink of abominations, that cradle of black-thronged cities where the music of ideas is drowned in cold fat, out of strangled Utopias is born a clown, a being divided between beauty and ugliness, between light and chaos, a clown who when he looks down and sidelong is Satan himself and when he looks upward sees a buttered angel, a snail with wings. When I look down into that crack I see an equation sign, the world at balance . . .

> Henry Miller, *Tropic of Cancer*,
> 1934

"'Have I got to *tell* you, after all these years and labours?'"

> Henry James, "The Figure in the
> Carpet," 1896

Introduction

The theme of this book is ambiguity in Hart Crane's long poem *The Bridge*. It proposes to demonstrate that the poem is constructed out of a series of puns and paradoxes: indeed that the pun, a bridge between alternative meanings, is the structural principle behind *The Bridge*. Concepts of irony, ambiguity and wordplay are familiar enough in recent Crane criticism, and this book is offered partly as a natural extension of the work of Eugene Paul Nassar, Richard P. Sugg, Roger Ramsey, Eric J. Sundquist and others. It is, however, striking out in a new direction in terms of the volume and intricacy of wordplay it finds in Crane's poetry. No attempt is made to be systematic or comprehensive: the massive task of annotating all of Crane's puns would require a longer and completely different book, whereas the first aim of this study must be to prove to the reader that puns are indeed essential to the construction of *The Bridge*. "Making out a case" is sometimes denigrated as a narrow and unbalanced form of academic writing, but this book assumes that a consideration of the technical basis of Crane's art is a *sine qua non* for any future study of the poet, and so the emphasis here is placed on an analytical rather than interpretative approach. The last section is a very modest attempt to summarize what this author sees as the poem's "meaning," but my hope is that readers may entirely disagree with this particular judgement and yet still admit the importance of puns and paradoxes within Crane's work.

My assumption is that Crane himself was quite well aware of the ambiguities written into his poem, and biographical and contextual evidence is produced to support this hypothesis. Of course it is impossible for either poet or critic to define with any precision the relationship between conscious and unconscious intentions in literary creation, and some of Crane's punning may have been purely instinctive and

1

unbeknown to him; but the essential concept of bridge as pun is so consistent throughout Crane's work that it breaks the bonds of credibility to imagine he was quite ignorant of his poem's designs. This is said mainly to emphasize what this book is not: it is not a post-structuralist "deconstruction" of Crane. The way in which the insecurities and machinations of an author's unconscious mind are expressed in literary punning has recently been a popular idea among many very interesting post-structuralist critics, notably Derrida, Riffaterre, Jakobson; and it is not difficult to understand how – say – the texts of Tennyson betray more uncertainty than that poet would have cared to admit. It is my contention, however, that the carefully engineered system of stresses and tensions in Crane's suspension Bridge is quite different in kind from a naïve Romanticism which is unaware of its own equivocations. On the contrary, the author to whom I see Crane as most closely related is that omniscient demon of ambiguity, James Joyce; and so it should be clearly stated at the outset that this book is concerned with Crane's authorial intentions. The fact that the earliest readers of *The Bridge* did not recognize these puns is no argument for believing Crane himself did not intend them: indeed, as I will show later, authorial silence and the consequent modification of meanings through time are part of the poem's integral shape. But this is not to deny that many admirable critics, to whom I am greatly indebted, have discussed the double-edged qualities of Crane's work within a theoretical framework similar to the one proposed by this book.

It would not be worth while to attempt to categorize at the start the kinds of pun used by Crane. He forces language into many different shapes, and although one may say any particular ambiguity is reminiscent of Cummings or Melville or the Surrealists or whoever, too much prior conceptualization would be not only arbitrary but misleading. There are, however, two things it might be useful to point out: first, that Crane specializes in the *visual* pun, where there is a discrepancy between what is heard when the words are conventionally pronounced and what is seen in the arrangement of letters on the page. This is consistent with the dialectic between *The Bridge* as public poem (one to be read aloud) and private poem (as it is apprehended by the solitary reader), a conflict that is put into perspective in Chapter 6. Very broadly, my argument is that often the poem *sounds* as if it is politely adhering to social convention, while the visual effect of the words is to reveal a plethora of alternative meanings; and so I see the poem's skilfully orchestrated aural effects as a kind of Platonic Noble Lie, whereby the poet-philosopher sanctions society's mythic illusions while inwardly acknowledging that all such arrangements are provisional and susceptible of contradiction. (Concern for poetry's typographical appearance was a familiar theme of the 1920s:

witness the fame of Cummings and Apollinaire.) My second point is that because it is one of the poem's functions to disturb grammatical logic, it is absurd to demand that every pun "fit in" with the sentence structure it is specifically out to disrupt. One might as well expect a thief to rob the bank only during office-hours. The thief may indeed choose to rob the bank during office-hours, but only if it happens to be more covenient for him to do so, for the standard convention of the bank's opening-hours is not one that outlaws recognize. Moreover, because Crane's puns are always threatening to dislocate what is pre-existent, it is not essential for every word of the poem to be a pun, for the non-puns form part of that pre-existent world which the puns themselves are reacting against. A great many of Crane's words are puns, but it has no effect on my essential argument to admit that some of them are not. *Finnegans Wake*, by contrast, is an absolute pun, and there one feels that every single word must have a punning significance; but *The Bridge* is quite different, being a relative pun where social decorum is to some extent maintained – although it always hovers on the brink of being overturned. As a corollary of this, it should be clear that Crane's puns will not be as pure as those of Cummings or Joyce. Because *Finnegans Wake* is concerned with the pun first and foremost, it can refuse entry to any ingenuity which seems below par; but because *The Bridge* embodies a perpetual opposition between subversive puns and the orthodox grammar of the everyday world, Crane's linguistic games necessarily embody more strain than those of Joyce – a strain which is, however, conceptually justified. For while it is true that some of Crane's puns and ambiguities may not be perfect by the rules of twentieth-century grammar, it is exactly this struggle between the world the right way up and the world upside down that forms the essential dialectic within *The Bridge*. From this, it will be evident that while Joyce's work created the historical context for Crane's writing, the literary and artistic tradition to which *The Bridge* relates is in many ways dissimilar. From Joyce, Crane derived much of his interest in the fluidity and etymological complexity of language; but whereas *Ulysses* strives to make visible and naturalize what might otherwise be considered unnatural and obscene, *The Bridge* moves in the opposite direction, seeking radically to dislocate and destabilize familiar objects and so reveal what the poet perceived as the sinister and dangerous forces latent within everyday life. Starting off from its Satanic epigraph, Crane's poem builds bridges between order and anarchy, between myth and sexuality, between financier and criminal; and in its transgression of the boundaries of social decorum, *The Bridge* may bring to a critic's mind any number of connected ideas and works of art: Gay's burlesque *Beggar's Opera*, for instance, or those Gothic extravaganzas analysed by Mario Praz in his famous exposition of *The Romantic Agony*. In this work

I have chosen to concentrate on Crane's poetic technique, because it is this technique which has, in my opinion, been largely misunderstood, and which can best be reilluminated in the contexts of the poet's own time; but it is not at all my intention to confine *The Bridge*'s genius to a purely formal issue, nor to deny Crane's conceptual associations with a great range of writers, from Emerson, Whitman and Poe through to Swinburne, Wilde and the other Decadents.

The shorter poems of Crane are worthy of a separate study in these linguistic contexts, but here I have been content to discuss them only in so far as they illuminate *The Bridge*. I have arranged this book into thematic sections because it seemed the best way to demonstrate the various forces at work inside Crane's long poem. To have gone through *The Bridge* from beginning to end would have been hopelessly unwieldy and repetitive, for the kinds of tricks used in the "Proem" recur again and again later on; and conversely, nearly all the poem's vast complexities are built into the "Proem," so that I might have found myself with a 300-page work on the poem's first eleven stanzas. Of course my divisions into "Relativity" and "Capitalism" and "Burlesque" are simply pragmatic, and because "Ave Maria," say, has been discussed as a burlesque poem, that does not mean it is not a Surrealist and capitalist poem as well. *The Bridge* cannot easily be divided up: it is all of a piece, and all its themes are in continual interpenetration. So my aim has been not all-inclusiveness but clarity of exposition, and I am quite well aware that much work still remains to be done on specific textual intricacies. I have attempted to make a contribution towards the art of reading *The Bridge*; I make no claim to finalize the poem. My last few chapters summarize the case for believing the particular view of Crane that I am putting forward, and any reader who finds his conviction wavering might like to look before time at Chapter 14 (where I discuss paradox), Chapter 16 (a summary of contextual arguments) and Appendix A (an analysis of the whole of the "Proem"). I have left these chapters at the end because they best make sense in the light of what has gone before, but my hope is they may also be seen as a bolster to the whole argument. No doubt specific readers will question the validity of specific puns, and I do not claim that any particular piece of wordplay is unquestionably "true," but I do believe the overall argument is coherent and convincing.

A frequent argument used against critical works of this kind is that once the floodgates have been opened, *any* possible pun might be permissible. Admittedly this is a problem, and there is always the danger for a pun-conscious critic that under his scrutiny the poem's text might degenerate into some kind of spiralling fantasy or psychedelic "freak-out." This is where critical judgement is important. There is no doubt that Crane used puns to some extent; the only question is to what extent, and I hope I have produced reasonable intellectual and contextual arguments to support the puns that I put forward. Of course this is a difficult and uncertain area, but we should not shy away from it because it is difficult and uncertain. The most dull-witted critic of John Donne might say: if you allow the pun on *die* as sexual orgasm, why not also say it's a pun about dyeing clothes? Such a use of "dye" was indeed available in the seventeenth century; but this line would be foolish, for the choice is not between a narrow literal-mindedness and "all possible meanings." The test must be whether any particular pun makes sense in the context in which the poet was writing, and whether it makes a feasible and useful contribution to the work of art. Crane's puns, I would suggest, do just that; and to ignore his puns completely on the grounds that we can't be "sure" about any of them does *The Bridge* a much greater disservice than to look out for puns and so run the risk of finding a few that Crane himself did not intend.

A note on dictionaries. Unless otherwise stated, all standard verbal definitions are quoted from the 1909 edition of Webster's *New International Dictionary of the English Language*, published by the Merriam Company of Springfield, Massachusetts. In these definitions, the following abbreviations are taken from Webster: *Obs.*, obsoletely; *Colloq.*, colloquially; *sl.*, slang; *esp.*, especially; *specif.*, specifically; *pl.*, plural. Slang definitions indicated "(f)" are from *The Dictionary of American Slang*, compiled by Harold Wentworth and Stuart Berg Flexner (2nd supplemented edition, New York: Crowell, 1975). The following abbreviations are taken from Wentworth and Flexner: *c.*, circa, approximately; *Orig.*, originally. We know Crane himself did use Webster (Malcolm Cowley said so: see Chapter 1) but the pitfalls for the critic involved in an over-mechanical deployment of this tool are obvious. It is by no means my assertion that, because Webster might list six possible definitions for one particular word, Crane was therefore intending six puns when he used that word in *The Bridge*. I have tried to use the dictionaries sparingly, and verbal definitions are quoted verbatim more in the interests of clarity and concision than in the belief that Crane had in mind any specific piece of lexicography at any given time. But my hope is that the dictionaries may have helped to recover the idiom of a particular time and place, for although *The Bridge* spans oceans and eras, it is also a poem rooted in the New York City of the 1920s.

Italicized words in quotations are usually my emphases; emphasis is specifically mentioned only when it occurs in the original text. Unless otherwise stated, all quotations from Crane's poetry are from the third edition of *The Complete Poems and Selected Letters and Prose of Hart Crane*, edited by Brom Weber (New York: Liveright, 1966).

1

Bridge as pun

In his 1924 essay "General Aims and Theories," Hart Crane declared that his poem "For the Marriage of Faustus and Helen" was an attempt "to embody in modern terms (words, symbols, metaphors) a contemporary approximation to an ancient human culture or mythology." Crane said that he was not interested in merely recording his own impressions of the twentieth-century environment, but was seeking to "go *through*" the materials of this visible world in order to uncover the "*causes* (metaphysical)" from which these impressions ultimately derived (emphases in original). In "Faustus and Helen," for instance, the way in which the New York flapper is related back to the Ancient Greek beauty serves to demonstrate the conjunction of mythological past and quotidian present, and so offers to make sense of the present by explaining it in terms of its imitation of the patterns of the past. Crane was, as he put it, "building a bridge between so-called classic experience and many divergent realities of our seething, confused cosmos of today, which has no formulated mythology yet."[1]

The analogy between flapper and Helen, while straining towards an objective account of social patterns, might seem to some readers unduly idiosyncratic, a link visible only to the fertile imagination of the poet himself; but Crane recognized this dilemma when he wrote in "General Aims and Theories" that while he "would like to establish [the poem] as free from my own personality," such an ambition was "of course, an impossibility." This admission did not make the poet's version of myth and history invalid, but rendered it provisional: it was, as Crane said, "at least a stab at a truth." The "truth" of poetry was dependent upon the reader putting into abeyance what he would otherwise think of as empirical and objective "facts":

6

It may not be possible to say that there is, strictly speaking, any "absolute" experience. But it seems evident that certain aesthetic experience (and this may for a time engross the total faculties of the spectator) can be called absolute, inasmuch as it approximates a formally convincing statement of a conception or apprehension of life that gains our unquestioning assent.[2]

Like "Faustus and Helen," Crane's long poem *The Bridge* functions on a system of analogies between past and present. Like "Faustus and Helen" again, it may not be possible to say that these analogies present any "absolute" truth, only to claim that they approximate to "a formally convincing statement." This daring kind of imagination which seeks to "go *through*" the visible world and posit its essential causes and patterns was celebrated by Emerson in the 1844 essay on "The Poet": "Banks and tariffs, the newspapers and caucus, Methodism and Unitarianism, are flat and dull to dull people, but rest on the same foundations of wonder as the town of Troy and the temple of Delphi, and are as swiftly passing away."[3] Emerson proposed a bridge between classical Greece and modern America; and the unity of Crane's *The Bridge*, both in philosophical terms and in terms of literary form, derives from this tendency to create affinities between apparently disparate objects. Thus, as so many critics have noticed, the smaller units of the poem involve a series of bridgings, which are synecdoches mirroring the larger design of the poem as a Bridge. Some of these bridges are designed to defeat space: in "Ave Maria," Columbus bridges the Old World and the New; in "Cape Hatteras," the aeroplane of the "Wright windwrestlers" bridges the earth and the sky; and in "Van Winkle," the macadamized roadway "Leaps from Far Rockaway to Golden Gate," bridging the American continent from East to West. But because these bridges span time as well as space, they also span the various sections of Crane's long poem, which are set in different historical eras. For example, in "Cape Hatteras," as R. W. Butterfield has said, "the aeroplanes break into a joyous dance among the clouds in preparation for the ritual sacrifice of a pilot, as the Indians had danced before the martyrdom of Maquokeeta [in "The Dance"]": in philosophical terms Crane is delineating the conjunction of Indian past and scientific present, but in literary terms he is also delineating the conjunction of "The Dance" and "Cape Hatteras."[4] Among other conceptual bridgings: the hurdy-gurdy in "Van Winkle" anticipates the escalator in "The Tunnel" which "lifts a serenade"; the paper wings in "Van Winkle" look forward to the aeroplanes of "Cape Hatteras"; and the song "Atlantis Rose" in "Cutty Sark" is a pre-echo of *The Bridge*'s final section, "Atlantis." Butterfield also saw the mention (in "The Tunnel") of New York City's Columbus Circle as "an ironic echo of Columbus' visionary ambition";[5] and in this light, the Genoese washerwoman's appearance in the same section could be seen as a bathetic recasting of the Admiral's elevated dream, for – as is mentioned in "Ave Maria" – Christopher Columbus himself originated from Genoa ("I thought of Genoa; and this truth, now proved, / That made me exile in her streets . . ."). When Crane sent typescript copies of "The Tunnel" and "Atlantis" to Yvor Winters in 1927, the poet himself stated: "I venture to think that you will like the various throwbacks to Part I, and the Columbus theme." Along the same lines, Sherman Paul commented on how the striptease in "National Winter Garden" is a shoddy counterpart to the ritual Indian dance in "Powhatan's Daughter," and how the shopgirl Mary in "Virginia" secularizes Columbus' "Ave Maria."[6]

The existence of these analogical links is a commonplace of Crane criticism. They are both literary bridges between one section of the poem and another, serving to impose a formal unity upon *The Bridge*, and also philosophical bridges blending past and present. Both constructions have a certain arbitrariness: the link between Christopher Columbus and Columbus Circle is claimed not necessarily as objective truth but – in Crane's words – "inasmuch as it approximates a formally convincing statement of a conception or apprehension of life." The fact that these literary bridges are not purely self-referential but imply the possibility of an actual, historical bridge between different eras was an idea Crane discussed in a letter to Allen Tate on 13 July 1930:

> I shall be humbly grateful if *The Bridge* can fulfil simply the metaphorical inferences of its title . . . You will admit our age (at least our predicament) to be one of transition. If *The Bridge*, embodying as many anomalies as you find in it, yet contains as much authentic poetry here and there as even Winters grants, – then perhaps it can serve as at least the function of a link connecting certain chains of the past to certain chains and tendencies of the future.[7]

In one of his essays on Crane, Tate called this tendency to create analogies "a philosophical pun."[8] Tate, of course, was using the phrase in a derogatory sense, indicating that because Crane lacked any orderly or educated sense of history he played nonsensically with ideas just as other people play nonsensically with words. Value-judgements are not our concern for the moment; what it is essential to stress is how Crane exploited actual, verbal puns to assist his verbal bridgings between different eras and between different sections of his long poem.

One clear example, which Stanley K. Coffman remarked upon in 1951, occurs in "Atlantis":

> The loft of vision, palladium helm of stars.

Here the poet perceives how the stars over the New York night are a re-embodiment of the statue of Pallas (*pallad*ium) Athene in the citadel of Ancient Troy, which was supposed to guarantee the safety of the city.

The chemical term *palladium* ostensibly refers to the silver metallic element which the stars visibly resemble (and there may also be overtones of the *stars* playing in the Palladium Theater); but Crane is slyly remarking how these silver stars of the twentieth century have a mythical status equivalent to the emblem of the Greek god in ages past. And this word itself, the pun *palladium*, is, quite literally, "The Bridge" between two different meanings.[9]

Another classical deity makes a surreptitious appearance in "Ave Maria." "Series on series, infinite," says Columbus, overtly describing the ocean-waves, but also punning on "Ceres," Latin goddess of corn and tillage, who watches over those images of harvest in "Ave Maria" ("gleaming fields," "pendant seething wheat"), and whose fructifying spirit epitomizes in a more general sense the cyclic notion of time embedded in *The Bridge*. In August 1926, three weeks after sending him the manuscript of "Ave Maria," Crane wrote to Waldo Frank: "to realize suddenly, as I seem to, how much of the past is living under only slightly altered forms . . . is extremely exciting."[10] The pun swinging between *series* and "Ceres" is the verbal unit which unites two separate eras. The same thing happens in "Cape Hatteras," where Walt Whitman is referred to as "Panis Angelicus," ecclesiastical Latin for "bread of angels," which covertly puns on the Greek god "Pan," and so emphasizes the way Whitman becomes an emblem of pagan fertility as well as being invested with a spiritual aura. One other quite clear classical pun occurs in "The Harbor Dawn":

> And you beside me, blessèd now while sirens
> Sing to us, stealthily weave us into day

These sirens, ostensibly the factory whistles which disturb the lovers' private idyll, pun on the singing *sirens* of the *Odyssey* who lured men to their doom. The allusion is indisputable, because it fits in with the description of "Cyclopean towers across Manhattan waters" eleven lines later (the Homeric "Cyclops," another hazard of Ulysses' voyage). This bridging of past and present is similar to the kind of technique Crane detected in the work of his friend the photographer Alfred Stieglitz, to whom Crane wrote in 1923 (emphasis in original): "You have the distinction of being classic and realistic at once. That, of course, is what *real* classicism means."[11] This was a pun by Crane on *real*: he had in mind "true" classicism, but also "realistic" classicism, which would make "*real* classicism" apparently oxymoronic, but exactly the style Crane intended by his yoking together of Homeric sirens and factory sirens. Like Crane's poetry, Stieglitz's photography appears at first sight solid and literal, but is in fact at the same time cleverly mirroring abstract patterns. In the fragment of a critical essay on Stieglitz putatively entitled "The Wires of the Acropolis," Crane noted how "we are thrown into ultimate harmonies by looking at these stationary, yet strangely moving pictures"; and Crane subsequently boasted to Charles Harris of how Stieglitz had responded by telling Crane he was "the first one to discover the secret of his marvelous photos." Three months later, on 4 July 1923, Crane wrote to Stieglitz: "I feel you as entering very strongly into certain developments in *The Bridge*."[12]

We remarked above on how this bridging of past and present is reflected in the formal links between earlier and later sections of Crane's poem. New York's "Columbus Circle" in "The Tunnel" exposes twentieth-century Manhattan as a reincarnation of Columbus' fifteenth-century America; but it also shows how, by the internal logic of *The Bridge*, "The Tunnel" is linked back to "Ave Maria." We should now extend this to see how Crane's actual language operates as the verbal correlative of this bridging:

> After the corridors are swept, the cuspidors –
> The gaunt sky-barracks cleanly now, and bare,
> O Genoese, do you bring mother eyes and hands
> Back home to children and to golden hair?

Just as the *Genoese* washerwoman echoes the nobleman from Genoa, so *cuspidors* is an echo of the line from "Ave Maria," "Sun-*cusped* and zoned with modulated fire." The "pointed end" of the sun (*cusped*) has been degraded into a spittoon (*cuspidors*). The philosophical pun has been transmuted into a verbal pun. In the same way, "the corridors are swept" harks back to the "troughing corridors" in "Ave Maria," the ocean-waves upon which Columbus sailed. These verbal links are examples of Crane's literary bridging, puns which preserve his long poem's organic unity, rather than *series* and *palladium* which simply bridge past and present.

Another sequence of verbal echoes which preserves *The Bridge*'s internal logic occurs at the end of "The Dance" as it merges into the beginning of "Indiana" (sections four and five of "Powhatan's Daughter"):

> "The Dance"
>
> High unto Labrador the sun strikes free
> Her speechless dream of snow, and stirred again,
> She is the torrent and the singing tree;
> And she is virgin to the last of men . . .
>
> West, west and south! winds over Cumberland
> And winds across the llano grass resume
> Her hair's warm sibilance. Her breasts are fanned
> O stream by slope and vineyard – into bloom!

And when the caribou slant down for salt
Do arrows thirst and leap? Do antlers shine
Alert, star-triggered in the listening vault
Of dusk? – And are her perfect brows to thine?

We danced, O Brave, we danced beyond their farms,
In cobalt desert closures mades our vows . . .
Now is the strong prayer folded in thine arms,
The serpent with the eagle in the boughs.

"Indiana"

The morning glory, climbing the morning long
    Over the lintel on its wiry vine,
Closes before the dusk, furls in its song
        As I close mine . . .

And bison thunder rends my dreams no more
    As once my womb was torn, my boy, when you
Yielded your first cry at the prairie's door . . .

What we have here is a thread of analogies which bridge the two poems.
The "wiry *vine*" in "Indiana" takes up "slope and *vineyard*" in "The
Dance." *Closes* ("Indiana") echoes "desert *closures*." The *dusk* ("Indiana") mirrors "the listening vault / Of dusk." And "furls in its *song*"
("Indiana") takes up the previous "*singing* tree." Because of these verbal
links, it is not speculative to associate "bison thunder rends my dreams no
more" ("Indiana") with the one word *torrent* in "The Dance." This
torrent can be split into "tor/rent," with "tor" punning on "Thor,"
Norse god of thunder, thereby making "thunder rends" and *torrent*
punning equivalents. The intricacy of the reflections, the manner in
which the poems closely mirror each other, suggests the analogical
affinities Crane perceived between these two standard American myths,
the Indian "Red Man" in "The Dance," and the gold-diggers of 1849,
the subject of "Indiana." Given the symmetry of the author's patterning
at this juncture, the possibility of *torrent* co-existing with "thunder
rends" by pure chance seems negligible; and so the principle that Crane
was consciously employing concealed puns must be admitted.

We should now move on to discover how the principle of the pun is
not confined to single isolated words, but is built in a more systematic
way into the very structure of *The Bridge*. Consider, for instance, the
significance of images of weaving in "Cape Hatteras":

The nasal whine of power whips a new universe . . .
Where spouting pillars spoor the evening sky,
Under the looming stacks of the gigantic power house
Stars prick the eyes with sharp ammoniac proverbs,

> New verities, new inklings in the velvet hummed
> Of dynamos, where hearing's leash is strummed . . .
> Power's script, – wound, bobbin-bound, refined –
> Is stropped to the slap of belts on booming spools . . .

Apparently these "spouting pillars" are the chimneys of the factory. But *looming* stacks, besides indicating the stacks looming into view, also puns on the weaver's loom, just as the *leash* can be "a string with a loop at the end for lifting warp threads," and *spools* and bobbins (*bobbin-bound*) were the cylinders employed by weavers to wind thread or yarn on. This series of weaving images is testimony to Crane's belief in how twentieth-century technology is essentially no more than a reincarnation of more primitive machines. The puns are the bridge between antiquated loom and modern factory. A few lines later, even the initial journey of the Wrights' aeroplane is described in weaving terminology:

> Warping the gale, the Wright windwrestlers veered
> Capeward, then blading the wind's flank, banked and spun

Warping is to arrange yarns in weaving; the blade (*blading*) is a spindle for winding on the yarn; and this spinning ("banked and *spun*"), which on one level suggests the aeroplane is spinning violently in mid-air, on another level implies the "windwrestlers" are skilfully manipulating their machine as though they were spinners at a loom. So the pun comes to have further conceptual importance, for it holds in balance active and passive moods: apparently the pilots are being spun, but in actual fact they may be actively spinning. A few lines later, the aerial pioneers are said to "ride / The blue's cloud-templed districts": and as a "temple" is a device in a loom for keeping the web stretched transversely, this emphasizes once again how the Wright brothers' flight is reconstituted within the terms of a weaving metaphor.

These kind of ambiguities persist all the way through *The Bridge*. In the "Proem," Brooklyn Bridge metamorphoses itself into a feudal chieftain ("Accolade thou dost bestow"), a Roman Catholic rosary ("Beading thy path"), a "harp and altar" and so on. Likewise, in "Atlantis" the Bridge is divested of its status as empirical object and becomes a "Psalm of Cathay," a "whitest Flower," and another weaving-machine for spinning yarns – "Pick biting way up towering looms," with a *Pick* in weaving being a cast or throw of the shuttle, suitable for the bridge's metaphorical *looms*. When Crane sent a version of "Atlantis" to Waldo Frank on 18 January 1926, he included a few remarks about his methods of composition:

> [The poem] is symphonic in including the convergence of all the strands separately detailed in antecedent sections of the poem – Columbus, conquests of water, land, etc., Pokahantus, subways, offices, etc., etc. I dare congratulate

myself a little, I think, in having found some liberation for my condensed metaphorical habit in a form so symphonic (at least so attempted) as this.

The bridge in becoming a ship, a world, a woman, a tremendous harp (as it does finally) seems to really have a career.[13]

As Butterfield has said, all Crane's themes are finally linked together in "Atlantis": seagulls, serpent, star, eagle – all these images the reader has come across earlier in *The Bridge* are now unified within this final vision. For example, the poem's penultimate line "The serpent with the eagle in the leaves . . .?" integrates the back-yard snakes in "Van Winkle" with the Indian totem in "The Dance" ("The serpent with the eagle in the boughs") and so provides both internal bridging, the coherence of literary form, and philosophical or external bridging, an acknowledgement of how different cultures reincarnate themselves in similar ways. Crane's friend Emil Opffer recalled how the poet would often make gnomic utterances along the lines "All of life is a bridge," "The whole world is a bridge"; and the form of Crane's long poem reflects exactly this conjunctive principle.[14]

BRIDGING HUMAN AND DIVINE

So in Crane pun and synecdoche work in tandem: Homeric sirens and factory sirens are cognate because the pun as a verbal bridge performs the same task as a synecdoche, which makes links between seemingly disparate objects by revealing that each is part of a greater whole. As R. W. B. Lewis put it, "Each version of the central experience, as we have had so many occasions to say, is a synecdoche; each stands for all the others, and taken together they accumulate into that same central experience the poem as a whole is enacting."[15] Most critics have seen Crane's use of synecdoche in Neoplatonic terms: that is to say, they have perceived the fragments of synecdoche to be emblems of a fallen, terrestrial world which is susceptible of being holistically reunified by the redemptive power of an Ideal state, of which "Atlantis" is the harbinger. The Platonic epigraph to "Atlantis" would support this reading: "Music is then the knowledge of that which relates to love in harmony and system," with the inference on our part that the poem's previous sections have manifested a less than perfect "harmony and system," that only at journey's end will the magic island of Atlantis rise out of the ocean within which it is concealed. Joseph N. Riddel is typical of this Neoplatonic outlook: "Crane's long poems do not develop; they recur. They pivot on the eternal event, which the poet is constantly reliving . . . History, for Crane, is simply the energy of the Word issuing into particular forms."[16] Riddel would see the back-yard snakes in "Van Winkle" as fragmented and imperfect emblems which must wait to be redeemed by the serpent in "Atlantis," totem of time, and so symbol of Man's conquest of the physical world.

This version of Crane ultimately depends upon an ideological premise. The Neoplatonist may wish to see Homeric sirens and factory sirens as "the broken pieces of the vast gestures," to quote Allen Grossman; while the secular anthropologist may prefer to acquiesce with Crane in the less intense notion that "to realize . . . how much of the past is living under only slightly altered forms, even in machinery and such-like, is extremely exciting."[17] It is not the intention here to decide among various possible interpretations of the poem, but rather to redress an imbalance in Crane criticism. Because Crane's evaluators have so much emphasized his straining after a state prior to or beyond language, they have lost sight of the tricks of this language itself. Grossman, for instance, saw Crane's work as an attempt to collapse the boundaries between life and art, Neoplatonic origin and its exile in language, with the result that Crane's ambiguities (according to Grossman) are ambiguities of means not ends, as his poetry is always searching for the perfection of final silence:

> This crowding of the frame came to constitute a trope peculiar to himself – not the modernist "ambiguity," which hierarchizes, or ironically totalizes, a plurality of meanings – but a singularly naïve rhetoric of shadowed wholeness (the impossible simultaneity of all the implications of desire) which struggles merely to include all meanings in the one space of appearance.[18]

This interaction between different levels of experience, between the human and divine, is the context within which those critics who have acknowledged (some of) Crane's puns have usually placed them. For instance, in a 1980 issue of *Twentieth Century Literature*, Roger Ramsey claimed "Crane's master" was Gerard Manley Hopkins, because, like the Jesuit, Crane used words in a "transubstantiative" way which transgresses the boundaries of common logic and so builds bridges between the material and the spiritual. Ramsey said that to search for some kind of Aristotelian unity in *The Bridge* was futile; rather we should look for a Longinian intensity – citing Northrop Frye's version of Longinus, "a series of ecstatic moments or points of expanding apprehension." Ramsey also quoted R. W. B. Lewis on how the pun "tries to say everything at once," and he noted that "This is the linguistic equivalent of transubstantiation."[19] Ramsey's article is admirable as far as it goes, and indeed there is an overt image of transubstantiation towards the end of "Quaker Hill":

> Yes, while the heart is wrung,
> Arise – yes, take this sheaf of dust upon your tongue!
> In one last angelus lift throbbing throat

As Sherman Paul noticed, this "sheaf of dust" is both the wafer of Holy
Communion and also the sheaf of paper, the poem, which the reader has
in front of him.[20] Crane is exhorting the reader to receive from him, the
authorial priest, this holy wafer of his poem, his pun, his Bridge. And, as
Ramsey said, by reading *The Bridge* and recognizing its punning
analogies the reader is participating in a sacramental act of integrating the
secular with the transcendental, for the idea of the pun is to transpose
once solid objects into another order of being. One clear example of this
kind of oscillation between material and spiritual planes is provided by
the last lines of "The River":

> Poised wholly on its dream, a mustard glow
> Tortured with history, its one will – flow!
> – The Passion spreads in wide tongues, choked and slow,
> Meeting the Gulf, hosannas silently below.

On a literal level, Crane is describing the Mississippi River's passage into
the Gulf of Mexico, which it meets at the mouth of the river – the
Mississippi Delta – where the river's main channel becomes divided into
several smaller tributaries (hence "spreads in wide tongues"). But
Crane's capitalization of *Passion* serves to emphasize the pun Eugene Paul
Nassar noted here swinging between "the river's passion to flow" and
"Christ's passion": so that "Meeting the Gulf" denotes not only the
Mississippi meeting the Gulf of Mexico, but also Christ's task of meeting
the gulf – bridging the gap – between God and the human race. This fits
in with those ecclesiastical *hosannas* in the last line; and it also transforms
"spreads in wide tongues" into another image of Holy Communion, the
worshippers opening their mouths wide to have placed upon their
tongues the divine host, in that act of transubstantiation which imitates
Christ by making the Word flesh. So in this stanza the American
landscape has become apotheosized, and the mouth of the Mississippi
punningly interacts with the mouth of a Communion suppliant. Given
this interest in metaphysical truths which might be immanent within our
quotidian world, it is not surprising that Crane was so fascinated by the
puns of Hopkins, for the Jesuit's "inscape" was similarly concerned to
probe the invisible centre of Man's visible existence: Crane wrote to
Samuel Loveman from California on 5 February 1928, "Winters loaned
me his copy recently (I had never read any of Hopkins before) and I have
discovered that I am not as original in some of my stylisms as I had
thought I was"; and four weeks after this, Crane told Waldo Frank that
Hopkins had come as "a revelation" to him. Crane's conception of his
own poetry as a form of revelation was an idea he had developed a year
earlier, in a 1927 letter to Yvor Winters: "I have a more or less religious
attitude toward creation and expression. I respond more to revelation –

or what seems revelation to me – than I do to what seems to me 'repetitious' – however classic and noble. That is one reason why [William Carlos] Williams probably means less to me than to you." So we can see that Crane, like Hopkins, preferred to exploit puns to (as he put it) "go *through*" this visible world, rather than acquiescing in what he saw as the "repetitious" photographic realism of William Carlos Williams.[21]

Nearly every critic has seen a few of the puns in *The Bridge*. It is very difficult to miss *curveship* in the "Proem" ("And of the curveship lend a myth to God") which linguistically blends the "inviolate curve" of Brooklyn Bridge with its metaphorical existence as a "ship": "secretes too ingenious a pun not to remark upon it," said R. W. B. Lewis. Lewis even went so far as to relate the word "ship" to a "nave" in religious architecture, asserting that both derive etymologically from the Latin *navis*, and that the implication here is of the *curveship* being equivalent in form to a church-nave across which the believer moves to approach the altar of God. The German word for a church-nave is "schiff," said Lewis, and he went on: "I have no doubt, myself, that Crane was intuiting all the possibilities of the suffix." Lewis similarly described *surfeitings* in "Ave Maria" as "an effective pun" ("Yet under tempest-lash and surfeitings / Some inmost sob, half-heard, dissuades the abyss"), and there the juxtaposition is of the ocean's "surf" with the astounding excess or "surfeit" of wealth ("delirium of jewels") to be gleaned from the new-found land.[22] Richard P. Sugg has also apprehended many puns in *The Bridge*, noting for instance that "Adams' auction" in "Quaker Hill" puns on Adam's action in eating the apple:

> . . . the ancient deal
> Table that Powitzky buys for only nine-
> Ty-five at Adams' auction . . .

Here the auction in the material world mirrors the primal event, the fall of Man, so that the pun becomes synecdochic of all human history.[23] In the context of this Metaphysical kind of punning, it is appropriate that Crane should have talked frequently of the desire he shared with poets like Donne to *condense* language, to employ verbal density as a means of transgressing the boundaries of formal logic so as to say many different things all at once. Writing to Selden Rodman in 1931, for instance, Crane criticized Rodman's poetry as "diffuse in patches, or at least susceptible of condensation" but he qualified his remarks by adding: "But when I speak of condensation I am presumably alluding as much to my own craze or weakness for that characteristic. For I've carried that element to the extreme point of unintelligibility more than once, as I well know."[24] Similarly, in his 1924 essay "General Aims and Theories" Crane talked of how poetic "terms of expression . . . are often selected less for their logical (literal) significance than for their associational meanings," and he ended by claiming that "the voice of the present, if it is to be known, must be caught at the risk of speaking in idioms and circumlocutions sometimes shocking to the scholar and historians of logic."[25]

Although this kind of density and associational idiom is quite compatible with the transcendental approach to Crane which we have outlined above, it is not self-evidently necessary to insert such poetic density into a Christian or Neoplatonic context; and the contention of this book will be that while Crane may or may not have been a mystic, he certainly was a wizard of words, a poet who manipulated language in a way approximating more to the magic of witchcraft than to the decorum and orthodoxies of well-made verse. Crane's distancing of himself from the exclusive demands of logic, his concern for verbal associations and circumlocutions, can be explained in terms of his interest in the apparently illogical and nonsensical pun, the bridge between two meanings, and the bridge between past and present. We know from biographical sources that Crane appeared to his friends to regard words as a form of black magic: Malcolm Cowley described Crane as "like the sorcerer of a primitive tribe," and he remembered that at parties Crane would vigorously imbibe alcohol as a means of attaining the kind of visions upon which his poems were based.[26] At a certain stage of Crane's drunkenness, said Cowley, "Everything reminded him of something else: landscapes, of musical compositions; poems, of skyrockets or waterfalls . . . Soon he was launched on a stream of words repeated more for their sound than for their meaning."[27] And, a little bit later on in the party, "he gave himself and others the illusion of completely painless brilliance; words poured out of him, puns, metaphors, epigrams."[28] Endowed with this temporary facility for discovering analogies and puns, Crane would dash off to record his ecstatic visions, and then spend many sober hours later on hammering his manuscript into shape. The drunkard formed the basis of the seer; and the seer would subsequently rely upon dictionaries to perfect his verbal visions. Cowley recalled that the kind of work Crane would have to hand when writing was "*Webster's Unabridged* and the big *Standard*," and that Crane would make long lists of words which might be used in a poem, "thesaurizing" them "like a magpie collecting bits of glass."[29] Crane's Vocabulary Notebook, recently reproduced by Kenneth A. Lohf, certainly shows groups of words arranged on criteria other than simple meaning: "forfeits" and "counterfeits" are aligned, for example; so are "agonist" and "antagonist"; and so are "paladin," "palfrey" and "palanquin," even though the Notebook maintains no kind of alphabetical order.[30] Susan Jenkins Brown was another of Crane's friends who mentioned in her reminiscences the poet's "constant use of an unabridged dictionary."[31]

To reiterate: I am not asserting that Crane was necessarily a Christian or divine poet, I am simply insisting that he was very familiar with the idea of pun as bridge and Bridge as pun. There may be a Neoplatonic side to Crane, but there is also a dark, sceptical, Nietzschean side; and while *The Bridge* sometimes seems to be reunifying the fragments of a fallen world, at other times it appears more like a self-parodic exercise, a confession of the arbitrary and ultimately invalid nature of all belief. The purpose of this critical work is not to impose any kind of dogmatic ideology upon Crane, but to reveal the technical basis of *The Bridge* and the intricacy of its wordplay.

2

Relativity

In the first chapter I introduced the problem of Neoplatonic as opposed to anthropological approaches towards Crane's verbal bridges. In terms of the culture of Crane's time, the Neoplatonic attitude was represented by the Russian mathematician and mystic P. D. Ouspensky, whose *Tertium Organum* Crane reported to Allen Tate that he was reading on 15 February 1923; and the anthropological or materialist attitude by A. N. Whitehead, whose *Science and the Modern World* Crane also knew.[1]

Ouspensky's *Tertium Organum* (1912) dismissed scientific positivism's obsession with the concrete world and historical progress, arguing that Man's apparently three-dimensional universe was no more than an optical illusion arising out of our bovine inability to perceive ulterior spheres. Everything that seems fragmented is actually part of some greater whole (emphasis in original): "If we put down the five fingers of one hand on the plane of the two-dimensional being they will be for him five separate *phenomena*," said Ouspensky, whereas evidently Man as a three-dimensional being can see that all five fingers are components of the same structure. Similarly, "it is impossible to convey to a dog the idea of the sphericality of the earth" because a dog is dull-witted and trusts only to the evidence of his senses; but Man, whose psyche is one degree more elevated, can understand what to the dog would be a fathomless mystery.[2] Ouspensky then proposed a superior zone which Man ignored only because he is in the same relation to this fourth dimension as the dog is to Man. Einstein said that space was a construction of the human mind, and Ouspensky applied the same criticism to time, claiming that we think time is passing because we are passing it, whereas actually past time does not disappear any more than a station ceases to exist once we have left it behind. The dog, said Ouspensky, thinks we are greeted with a new sun every morning, but Man knows it is only the old sun which the earth has gone round in a circle to meet again. By extension, Man talks about a "new" morning or a "new" spring, but the superior intelligence realizes it is only the old spring come round once more: nature seems to be in motion but is in fact at heart static. So, in the vision of *Tertium Organum*, time must be cyclic because it can go nowhere else; and Ouspensky quoted approvingly from Madame H. P. Blavatsky's *Isis Unveiled*: "all those great characters who tower like giants in the history of mankind . . . were but reflexed images of human types which had existed ten thousand years before."[3] Ouspensky's proximity to Emersonian Idealism is clear enough: the Russian's analogies between past and present resemble Emerson's affiliation of American Unitarianism with the temple of Delphi, which we saw in Chapter 1; but Ouspensky owed a more direct allegiance to Eastern thought, citing with approbation the Hindu notion of "Karma," where each phenomenon was seen as a link in an infinite and unbroken chain stretching from the past to the future and from one sphere to another. Metempsychosis, the transmigration of souls, was another aspect of the circular processes of time; and *"the faculty for perceiving analogies"* (Ouspensky's italics) between apparently different eras and dimensions was described as the starting-point for the wisdom the "superman" could achieve if he would only divest himself of the encumbrances and delusions of worldly personality. As on our limited plane such a state of purity was insusceptible of final attainment, the nearest approach to "truth" was to acknowledge that *"everything has an infinite variety of meanings"* (Ouspensky's italics); all objects known to us exist not only in those categories in which they are perceived by us, but also in an infinite number of other categories in which we cannot sense them. Ouspensky was concerned with the "invisible threads" which bind earthly objects together, and he believed that for the philosopher or artist to cultivate an inner eye capable of penetrating the "hidden meanings" latent in all things, *"New parts of speech"* are necessary, an infinite number of new words."[4] So the way in which Crane's factory sirens pun on Homeric sirens, and the transmutation of Brooklyn Bridge into a ship, a woman, a harp and so on, could be explained in terms of an Ouspenskian willingness to discover analogies (philosophical bridges) between one time and another, and so to move towards a higher dimension where all time would cease; and Crane's revolutionary punning language might be seen as fulfilling Ouspensky's desire for "new words" to uncover such invisible threads. Ouspensky's vision would provide a conceptual justification for those images of multi-layered constructions which persist throughout *The Bridge*, as in "Cape Hatteras," where the *Escadrille* (a unit of six aeroplanes) may be implying the different "planes" of reality to be found in the Ouspenskian universe of analogical links and within Crane's punning *Bridge*:

> Each plane a hurtling javelin of winged ordnance,
> Bristle the heights above a screeching gale to hover;
> Surely no eye that Sunward Escadrille can cover!

Similarly in "Quaker Hill" the narrator looks out over the three American states (New Jersey, Pennsylvania, Connecticut) visible from the top of the derelict Mizzentop Hotel; but these three states also come to connote the three-dimensional material world which the poet aspires to see beyond, as he claims for himself the perception of a fourth dimension:

> High from the central cupola, they say
> One's glance could cross the borders of three states;
> But I have seen death's stare in slow survey
> From four horizons that no one relates . . .

Hyatt Howe Waggoner has claimed that Ouspensky's work was actually "Crane's chief source of information about the new world pictured by Einsteinian physics"; and certainly Einstein's concern with the shifting nature of objects which had previously been thought fixed in space and time had many affinities with Ouspensky's ideas, the main difference of course being that the scientist's sceptical and materialist temper disregarded any possibility of higher consciousness or final truth.[5] But Crane is unlikely to have known Einstein only through Ouspensky, for although few people understood the Theory of Relativity (1905) except in its most generalized form, this did not stop Einstein becoming a familiar figure among music-hall comedians who espoused him as the champion of a world where appearance and reality never quite matched up. A popularized version of Einstein's ideas spread to all sections of society, so much so that in 1924 the Frenchman Maurice Sachs was complaining the bourgeoisie talked of nothing except golf and relativity.[6] And Einsteinian ideas were further disseminated by A. N. Whitehead's *Science and the Modern World* (1925), which put relativity into a broader philosophical context, and which had an important influence on several American poets. Crane mentioned to Gorham Munson that he was reading it on 5 March 1926, and William Carlos Williams also owned a copy in which he wrote: "Finished reading it at sea, Sept. 26., 1927 – A milestone surely in my career, should I have the force & imagination to go on with my work."[7]

Whitehead's project was to disestablish the "unimaginative empiricism" of "scientific materialism" which believed in "irreducible brute matter." He trenchantly deconstructed modern science and uncovered the ideological premises upon which it rested, the "one-eyed reason" of the eighteenth century.[8] This naïve belief in the autonomy of those natural processes institutionalized by science was identified by Whitehead as the "Fallacy of Misplaced Concreteness," and he pointed out that empirical "laws" had no more or less justification than the rationalistic geometry of the medieval schoolmen. In fact nothing was fixed, all was in motion: the Theory of Relativity was "a heavy blow at the classical scientific materialism, which presupposes a definite present instant at which all matter is simultaneously real."[9] Whitehead declared that earthly things were in a "prehensive" unity: that is to say, the totality consisted of parts which have a relative and constantly altering relationship to each other, and each of which modifies the other. Because "concrete fact is process," all objects become insubstantial and dependent for their existence upon the standpoint of the observer, who is obliged to "be content with a provisional realism in which nature is conceived as a complex of prehensive unifications."[10] And time is continuous process as well: Crane's belief in the simultaneity of past and present was backed up by Whitehead's refusal of historical demarcation, for Whitehead presented a philosophical vindication of Crane's visionary world where everything flows into everything else:

> space and time are simply abstractions from the totality of prehensive unifications as mutually patterned in each other . . . an event mirrors within itself the modes of its predecessors, as memories which are fused into its own content . . .
>
> In a certain sense, everything is everywhere at all times. For every location involves an aspect of itself in every other location. Thus every spatio-temporal standpoint mirrors the world.[11]

SYNTACTICAL AMBIGUITY

In linguistic terms, Whitehead's advocacy of the kinetic over the static has affinities with the grammatical ambiguities and puns of both Crane and William Carlos Williams, because – to use Whitehead's idiom – if "the aspect of B from A is the *mode* in which B enters into the composition of A," then the interaction of A with C must necessarily alter A's meaning.[12] One clear illustration is the end of Williams' "The Bitter World of Spring," from his 1948 collection *The Clouds*:

>   close
> under the bridge, the shad ascend,
>
> midway between the surface and the mud,
> and you can see their bodies
> red-finned in the dark
> water headed, unrelenting, upstream.[13]

The problem is whether *headed* in the last line refers to the *shad* or to the *water*. If the fish are the subject, they are actively propelling their way upstream. But if the "dark water" is the subject, then the fish have no choice except passive acquiescence in its currents. Relativity has displaced the fish from the centre of their world, and the ambiguity reveals how they have a perpetually shifting relationship to the forces acting upon them.

These kind of syntactical reversals were a common feature of Crane's work as well. Take an obvious example from "The Tunnel":

> For Gravesend Manor change at Chambers Street.
> The platform hurries along to a dead stop.

The passenger arriving in a train at a subway station may have the momentary illusion of the station platform being in motion rather than his train. "Common sense" would dismiss this idea as just that, a momentary illusion, no more; but the Theory of Relativity insists that station platform and train are in fact both constantly moving in relation to each other. So what seems here like mere pathetic fallacy actually becomes a moment where the schemes of science are revealed within the everyday world. (And if *platform* also refers to the boarding-platform of the train, then the pun would provide an even clearer explication of how train and station move relative to each other.) Exactly the same kind of syntactical inversion occurs in "Atlantis":

> We left the haven hanging in the night –
> Sheened harbor lanterns backward fled the keel.

In orthodox terms we would perceive the *keel* as fleeing rather than the *lanterns*. And similarly in "Ave Maria":

> The jellied weeds that drag the shore . . .

We would customarily see the *shore* as dragging the *weeds* closer, not the other way around. Of course Columbus' egocentric idiom implies the shore is coming closer to him, whereas in actual fact the Admiral himself must deign to move; but again, the pathetic fallacy merges into an exposition of the Theory of Relativity. We come across the same type of reversal once again when "Atlantis" depicts Jason's voyage with the Argonauts:

> And you, aloft there – Jason! hesting Shout!
> Still wrapping harness to the swarming air!
> Silvery the rushing wake, surpassing call

Like Columbus, Jason enjoys the illusion of being in control of the elements, "wrapping harness" to the air, so that he thinks of the ship's wake as rushing away into the distance at his command. But in sober truth it is Jason's ship which is actively rushing; and, to the naked eye at least, the silvery wake behind his ship remains static.

As in the Williams poem, this relativity of motion which becomes a relativity of syntax is an appropriate method of expressing a balance between active and passive moods in Crane's work. "The sea's green crying towers a-sway," says Columbus in "Ave Maria," referring to the ocean-waves, and we are left uncertain whether the waves are simply swaying up and down beneath the authority of Columbus' ship, or whether the waves are themselves the *sway*, the "Influence, weight, or authority that inclines to one side." That hyphen inside *a-sway*, absent in Crane's first draft of the poem, was not inserted accidentally.[14] If the waves are the authoritative sway, then the *towers* would become "towers," active forces which are towing or pulling the helpless Columbus. The conflict is between the Romantic hero who believes he can subjugate the world in his own person, and the ironic limitations imposed upon this hero by the external world. Epic voyager though he may be, Columbus is still dependent upon the favours of the earth's oscillating tides.

"Asway" or *a-sway*. It will be seen that the pun is a verbal counterpart to scientific relativity, for the "meaning" it denotes is in perpetual motion. The non-pun, by contrast, is a counterpart to the empirical science of the eighteenth century, Whitehead's "one-eyed reason," because the denotation of the non-pun is always static. (Hence the eighteenth-century Dr Johnson's famous derogation of Shakespeare's puns: "A quibble, poor and barren as it is, gave him such delight, that he was content to purchase it, by the sacrifice of reason, propriety, and truth.") In 1964 Harvey Gross offered to correct what he took to be the "misspelling" of *wrapt* in *Voyages* II ("the wrapt inflections of our love"); but although *wrapt* is not in the dictionary, the word comes up again in "Atlantis" ("wrapt inception and beatitude"), and with the same significance, a punning indication of how human ecstasy is both unique ("rapt") and circumscribed ("wrapped") at one and the same time. Man is both an active initiator and passive product of his environment. Melville uses the word in the same way in Chapter 84 of *Moby-Dick*: "wrapt in fleecy foam, the towing whale is forty feet ahead."[15] Again, the whale is rapt but wrapped.

The relativity of language and syntax is not at all the same as the simple punning accretions which many critics have found in *The Bridge*. Brom Weber, for instance, published in 1948 a fine pioneering study of Crane which pointed out how the poet's language is "fluid as well as solidified" and how it has a tendency towards "the plasticity of protoplasm, flowing in all directions with an enriching multiplicity of meanings." Weber picked on a phrase from "Cape Hatteras" – "Tellurian wind-sleuths on dawn patrol" – and described how *Tellurian* contains not only its dictionary-sense of a device to demonstrate that day and night are caused by the earth's rotation on its axis – thus implying how Crane conceived the planes as explorers of space in the same way as a tellurian probes into the spatial movements of the earth – but also "Tellus" (the earth-goddess) and "tellurium" (a silvery-white chemical element), so that Crane's image of the aeroplane is qualified on three levels.[16] For Weber, though, these were symbolic associations which expanded meaning without affecting the poem's philosophical logic. Indeed, Weber supposed that most of Crane's obscurity could be solved by the insertion of proper punctuation, and in an attempt to prove his point he selected two lines from "Ave Maria":

> And biassed by full sails, meridians reel
> Thy purpose – still one shore beyond desire!

Weber ascertained from Crane's manuscripts that there had originally been a comma and dash after *reel*, and its elimination, he said, had brought about confusion.[17] But in fact it brought about another constructive ambiguity, akin to the fusion of active and passive we saw in *wrapt*. For if a pause is supposed between these two lines, the *purpose* can go forward straight and true, with the *meridians* subservient to Columbus' forward thrust. But if there is no pause, then *purpose* becomes the object of *reel*, and those *meridians* are then active agents compromising Columbus' autonomy and revealing once again how human endeavour is ironically hedged in by forces beyond Man's knowledge or control. So this syntactical ambiguity which is a product of relativity does not just expand the poem's meaning, but significantly alters it.

Further proof that Crane was consciously exploiting ideas of relativity comes with his 1926 letter to Harriet Monroe about "At Melville's Tomb." Of the phrase "Compass, quadrant and sextant contrive / No farther tides" – a typical example of his syntactical inversions – Crane remarked (emphasis in original): "This little bit of 'relativity' ought not to be discredited in poetry now that scientists are proceeding to measure the universe on principles of pure *ratio*, quite as metaphorical, so far as previous standards of scientific methods extended, as some of the axioms in Job."[18] Of the platform hurrying along to a dead stop, we saw how the pathetic fallacy becomes the revelation of relativity; but in this letter Crane is reducing relativity itself to a form of pathetic fallacy, and declaring it to be merely a subjective and provisional way of imposing order upon the world. Just as Columbus in "Ave Maria" invents the world in terms of his "own cosmography" (as Crane said), picturing God as a medieval Catholic "Inquisitor," so the New York poet in 1926 depicts his world in terms of Einstein's scientific theories:[19]

> Now while thy petals spend the suns about us, hold –
> (O Thou whose radiance doth inherit me)

The "Thou" is Brooklyn Bridge itself, whose *petals* (Bridge as "whitest Flower") are overtly "spending" (using up, as to "spend" money) the *suns* which rotate around it. This is to elevate the Bridge to prime mover, as if to claim the Bridge is at the centre of the universe and the daily suns revolve in the orbit of the Bridge. But Crane's relativity of syntax reveals the fictitious nature of this myth: "Now while thy petals *spend*" (spend or exhaust *themselves*, as in the Victorian *spend*, the little death) – "the suns about us, hold": that is to say, the suns in fact hold fast and remain static. The Bridge actually revolves around the sun, not the sun around the Bridge. On the surface, *spend* is transitive, but the alternative intransitive mood ironically uncovers the provisionality of Crane's "myth to God." Similarly the "whitest Flower" which these petals make up can become a mere "flow-er," an image liable to flow away into nothing:

> Thy pardon for this history, whitest Flower

As a *Flower*, the Bridge is a figure of myth; but as a flow-er, it is a transitory worldly object. The pun is symptomatic of relativity in its refusal to be confined to a singular, fixed meaning; and it is relativity that will ultimately reveal the relative nature of all human constructions.

The syntactical reversal we saw above is in the same mode as a line earlier in "Atlantis":

> As though a god were issue of the strings. . . .

As though a god were the originator of the strings? Or, as though a god (object) were issue (object) of the strings (subject)? In the first reading, god issues the strings in his role as divine First Cause. But in the second reading, god has reduced to an expedient fiction, for if god did not exist he would have to be invented to justify the grand symbol of Brooklyn Bridge. This line wavers between belief and scepticism, and its initial two words "As though" should alert us to the ambiguities involved. God is not necessarily present, but it is "As though" he is.

Crane, then, was manipulating relativity to define his environment in terms of what he thought of as one of the most important myths of his age; and also as a means of subverting his own fictive creations, which slyly confess that they – like the social structures they mirror – are temporary edifices, not eternal absolutes. Take one more example from "Atlantis":

> In single chrysalis the many twain, –
> Of stars Thou art the stitch and stallion glow

Webster gives "ion" as "one of the electrified particles into which, according to the electrolytic dissociation theory, the molecules of electrolytes are divided by water and other solvents." In other words, the molecules of certain chemicals are broken down into ions by solution in water and this solution becomes a conductor of electricity. The derivation of "ion" (the present participle of the Greek *ienai*, to go) illustrates the idea of a current's perpetual motion. Crane's Bridge is dependent for its existence upon these movements of force, but wishes to eliminate any appearance of motion which would render the construction provisional rather than absolute. Hence "stall/ion" (*stallion*), arresting the ions into stasis: the form of the pun is the same as *torrent*, which we saw in the first chapter. Here Crane's pun is concealed just as the Bridge's material and earthbound nature is concealed, for its more grandiose function is to transmute such terrestrial interactions into an ostensibly more solid mythic symbol: to render "In single chrysalis the many twain."

To repeat, Crane quite specifically mentioned the Theory of Relativity in his letters. Remarking to Gorham Munson on 17 March 1926 that "truth has no name," he added: "Her latest one, of course, is 'relativity'"; and on 29 April 1927, he told Yvor Winters that "'Atlantis'" "contains a metaphysical synthesis of a number of things like aeronautics, telegraphy, psychoanalysis, atomic theory, *relativity*, and what not!"[20] Crane's interest in the subject might seem implausibly erudite, but the widespread popularity of Einstein's ideas among American artists of Crane's time cannot be emphasized too strongly. In 1929, the American poet Archibald MacLeish even published a long poem entitled *Einstein* with the Crosbys' Black Sun Press in Paris (who were to bring out *The Bridge* a year later), wherein MacLeish portrayed Einstein as presiding over the disintegration of the known objective world:

> Still he stands
> Watching the vortex widen and involve
> In swirling dissolution the whole earth
> And circle through the skies till swaying time
> Collapses . . .

MacLeish's poetic form is a counterpart to this "swirling dissolution," because here MacLeish, like Crane, employs ambiguity as the verbal correlative of a physical world that is always doubling back upon itself. Punctuation is conspicuous by its absence, and the confusions are deliberate. "Still he stands": Einstein may be still there (*Still* as "yet") but *Still* as motionless he certainly is not, for it is part of the premise of relativity that the subject cannot be detached from the world he observes; and so Einstein himself is caught up in the widening vortex. Crane certainly admired MacLeish, writing to Selden Rodman on 20 June 1931 that "MacLeish has a more flexible literary genius than anyone writing in America today, and he'll probably be the most noteworthy poet of our times."[21] But if MacLeish's *Einstein* was the most interesting work of the time overtly dealing with relativity, there were plenty of less ambitious efforts. Louis Untermeyer – an acquaintance of Crane's – even developed a line in comically rewriting modern poems in the light of Einstein's theories, and the first issue of the magazine *Broom* in November

1921 contained "The Sagging Bough" by "Rob–rt Fr–st" which outlined the subversive pressures of gravity on poetic flights of fancy.[22] Readers of *Vanity Fair* in the same year were treated to a "Rhyme and Relativity" feature by the same hand, including "Einstein among the Coffee-cups" by "T. S. Eliot" ("The night contracts. A warp in space / Has rumors of Correggio") and "The Ohm's Day-Book" by "Edgar Lee Masters":

> Succinctly, then, great men and little sparks
> Are all the same in some vast dynamo
> Of humming ether, ringed with unseen coils.
> Now here am I, the smallest unit of
> Electrical resistance.[23]

Crane himself can be seen to be dallying with ideas of relativity as early as 1922, when he wrote "For the Marriage of Faustus and Helen":

> . . . by strange harmonic laws
> All relatives, serene and cool,
> Sit rocked in patent armchairs.

(The rocking-chairs of family *relatives* punning on the rockings of relativity.) But by the time of *The Bridge* Crane had blended such ingenious Untermeyerian frivolities with a firm moral purpose, and he set out to institutionalize relativity as a fact of national myth. Whitehead said this century's task should be to "end the divorce of science from the affirmations of our aesthetic and ethical experiences"; and the goal Crane set himself in *The Bridge* was to maintain the technological adroitness of a modernist operator without losing sight of social and moral imperatives.[24]

In recent Crane criticism, an emphasis upon Crane's ambiguities has become commonplace. Herbert A. Leibowitz saw the shifting angles of Crane's poetry as "strengthened . . . by transposing nouns into verbs and verbs into nouns," and Leibowitz perceived that this use of language was "an attempt to face the truth of flux and to open up multiple perspectives."[25] This is certainly true. All that it is necessary to stress is how methodically Crane went about incorporating ambiguity within his work, and how the myths of relativity in the 1920s provided theoretical justification for this interchangeability of noun and verb, subject and object; and also how relativity's disestablishment of static and empirical "meaning" is a scientific counterpart to the verbal pun which refuses one single denotation and instead swings between alternatives.

3

Capitalism

Discussing the idea of relativity in the previous chapter, we saw how Crane deliberately made Columbus tell the story of "Ave Maria" "in the terms of [his] own cosmography" (as Crane said in a letter to Waldo Frank), casting Columbus' God in the rôle of medieval Catholic "Inquisitor" as a counterpart to Crane's own description of twentieth-century America within an Einsteinian idiom.[1] If relativity was the predominant intellectual force in 1920s New York, the predominant social force was capitalism, and Crane consequently addressed himself to the task of assimilating capitalist modes of thought into his *Bridge*. As a means of mapping out and ordering the world, Crane saw capitalism as equivalent in form to myths of earlier ages: factory sirens reincarnating Homeric sirens.

The American business world was a controversial topic among the cultural polemicists in Crane's circle. Waldo Frank, for instance, was constantly searching for a "medieval synthesis," that happy state where the artist was supposedly a celebrator of (and not a romantic protester against) the social conditions surrounding him; but Frank claimed that individual and social well-being would come about only by Man's reintegration of himself with the soil, and so he dismissed as decadent the myths of American commercialism. New Yorkers, said Frank, moved around as devitalized as "automata" on cinema-screens, "fathered by steel and broken by it."[2] One of the curious ironies of this time was that those intellectuals who stayed in the United States in the hope of building up their ethnic culture were often much less well disposed towards familiar aspects of American life than were the exiles who apprehended their native land through a Parisian lens. For Van Wyck Brooks, business was "the one profession which is wholly sordid"; but when Kenneth

Burke repeated Brooks' theme in a 1923 issue of *Vanity Fair*, Malcolm Cowley replied from Europe with a letter of what he said was "almost incoherent dissent," advising that "The only salvation for American literature is to BORROW A LITTLE PUNCH AND CONFIDENCE FROM AMERICAN BUSINESS."[3] In *Our America*, Waldo Frank approvingly quoted Maxim Gorki on how American amusement-parks were "the most mournful places he had ever seen"; whereas the cosmopolitan E. E. Cummings spent many happy hours on Coney Island's rollercoasters.[4] The explanation advanced by Cowley in *Exile's Return* was that the Parisians' version of America as a huge commercial fun-palace remained undisturbed by the brutal facts of capitalist life which actually set the merry-go-round in motion. For instance, in the November 1922 issue of *Broom*, a magazine edited from Rome by Harold Loeb, Matthew Josephson commended "The Great American Bill-Poster" as containing "a core of 'primitive' or folk poetry, both reflecting and appealing to the appetites, sentiments, and values of the common people"; but so keen was Josephson on the "fundamental attitude of aggression, humor, unequivocal affirmation which . . . comes most naturally from America" that he spent eighteen months in 1924 and 1925 wheeling-and-dealing on the New York Stock Exchange, an experience that brought about a mental breakdown and conversion to extreme left-wing politics.[5]

Crane's personal feelings about American commercialism were ambivalent. His family were staunch Republicans and his father was a highly successful businessman, owner of a maple-sugar cannery and subsequently founder of the Crane Chocolate Factory. Mr Crane senior's attitude to life could be summed up in Calvin Coolidge's dictum that "The business of America is business"; and while emotionally his son loathed some aspects of the capitalist world, Hart Crane was enough of a Midwesterner to perceive its centrality inside the American consciousness. In an interview with Alice Chamberlain printed in the *Akron Sunday Times* of 21 December 1919, Crane talked of how he disliked the "oily smugness" around him which he said the American poet must "fight against," but he admitted:

> the artist's creation is bound to be largely interpretive of his environment and his relation to it; and living as we do in an age of the most violent commercialism the world has ever known, the artist cannot remain aloof from the welters without losing the essential, imminent vitality of his vision.

Crane repeated this theme in a letter to Yvor Winters on 26 February 1927, and suggested that the capitalist world was not something a responsible American poet could ignore (emphasis in original):

> our vision of "eternity" is itself a product of the age we live in . . . I must conceive all or most of my poems under this process . . . I *must*, perforce, use

the materials of the time, or the terms of my material will lack edge, – reality;
one doesn't have to feel any great enthusiasm for one's age before utilizing the
immediate materials it proffers.

Crane discussed the relationship between romanticism and machinery,
heart and crane, in his 1923 poem "Recitative" – which he called a
"confession" – where the poet reluctantly admits the insufficiency of
self-enclosed imagination and so attempts to build a bridge between
himself and the decadent materialism of New York, "Wrenched gold of
Nineveh."[6] The grim paradox is that, in engaging with this commercial
world, the poet risks having his imaginative energy utterly eradicated by
the "shafts of steel that grant / The plummet heart, like Absalom, no
stream." The actual Hart had periods of drudgery working in
bookstores, and several spells as an advertising copywriter – for the
Corday and Gross agency in Cleveland from January 1922 until March
1923, and shorter interludes with J. Walter Thompson and Sweet's
Catalogue Service after his move to New York. He does not seem to
have particularly enjoyed this kind of work, although he was quite
efficient at it, but it was important that Crane had a practical and inside
knowledge of a business culture which the rich dilettante Josephson
applauded without really understanding.

BRIDGING MATERIALISM AND IDEALISM

The ideology of capitalism with its emphasis upon profit and debt
permeates "Ave Maria." "And later hurricanes may claim more pawn"
describes the ships on the ocean as mere implements of economic
exchange, to be traded in at will by the Almighty Father who
"Subscribest holocaust of ships." There is also the continual reminder
that Columbus' epic voyage was set in motion by the hope of material
gain:

> . . . this crescent ring
> Sun-cusped and zoned with modulated fire
> Like pearls that whisper through the Doge's hands
> – Yet no delirium of jewels! O Fernando,
> Take of that eastern shore, this western sea,
> Yet yield thy God's, thy Virgin's charity!
>
> – Rush down the plenitude, and you shall see
> Isaiah counting famine on this lee!

Columbus' caution to Fernando not to exhaust the new-found land's
wealth all at once reminds us that the Spanish monarchs Ferdinand and
Isabella backed Columbus' mission to uncover an alternative trade-route
to India only because of the promise of increased wealth for themselves if
Columbus were successful. The journey was an archetypal capitalist

venture: money invested in the hope of greater returns. Ferdinand and Isabella were the "angels" behind Columbus, the financial backers of his enterprise ("angel" is a familiar slang word, especially in political or theatrical contexts); and so when Columbus says "Some Angelus environs the cordage tree," we are to infer not only that the *Angelus* (the Roman Catholic devotional exercise which includes the Ave Maria) is protecting his ship (the "cordage tree"), but also that a sum of money from the angels env-*irons* it ("iron" being American slang for "silver coins" (f)). The puns on Angelus/angels and environs/env-irons are indicative of the oscillation between idealism and pragmatism inherent in Columbus' voyage, and of the way his heroic endeavour was mercilessly underpinned by material considerations. The concealment of these puns inside the poem reflects the way this hard profit motive is obscured by being wrapped up in the guise of altruism and respectability. Crane himself was recognizing this duality when he told Otto Kahn that in "Ave Maria" "The theme of 'Cathay' (its riches, etc.) ultimately is transmuted into a symbol of consciousness, knowledge, spiritual unity" – with *ultimately* being the key word.[7] Take another example:

> Urging through night our passage to the Chan;
> Te Deum laudamus, for thy teeming span!

We know that Columbus first thought he had landed in China, and even on his way back across the Atlantic he persisted in thinking he had found a new gateway to the Eastern Continent which would facilitate trade between China and Spain. Hence Columbus is not only thanking God for the "teeming span" of his ocean, but also thanking him for (as Columbus sees it) providing access to the "tea" offered by the "Ming" dynasty, whose reign or *span* in China lasted from 1368 to 1644. This punning redefinition of "Te Deum laudamus, for thy teeming span!" as "Te Deum laudamus, for thy tea/Ming span!" epitomizes once again the bridge which Crane's economic puns build between an idealistic surface and an underlying material reality. (And it is appropriate that later in history many of the buildings of Boston, citadel of American civilization, were indeed "built in the chastest Puritan style with profits from the trade in China tea.") Crane's pun also assists the internal logic of the whole poem, the analogies that are made between various sections of *The Bridge*, for commercial interaction with the Orient is the theme towards the end of "Cutty Sark," which concludes by mentioning *Taeping* and *Ariel*, those clippers which first brought back the China tea crop to America in 1866.[8]

Back in the "Proem," we find this kind of oscillation between materialism and idealism as early as the first two stanzas:

> How many dawns, chill from his rippling rest
> The seagull's wings shall dip and pivot him,

Shedding white rings of tumult, building high
Over the chained bay waters Liberty –

Then, with inviolate curve, forsake our eyes
As apparitional as sails that cross
Some page of figures to be filed away;
– Till elevators drop us from our day . . .

The symbolic grandeur of the first four lines is counterbalanced by the
world of work depicted in the second stanza, whose literal meaning is
that the seagull fades out of sight as quickly as boats pass the harbour, and
that the imaginative reveries inspired by the bird must be checked ("filed
away") in order to allow the business world to function. But this
opposition between a romantic desire to sail to far-off lands and an
acquiescence in humdrum clerical duties is also revealed by the tilting
between opposites inherent in the stanza's puns. The clue is *sails*, for,
given the context of figures and files and elevators, it would be more
predictable to find commercial "sales" rather than sailing-ships here.
Therefore we may see the "inviolate curve" of the Bridge as merging
into the "inviolate curve" of a sales-graph, for Bridge and sales-graph
become equivalent mythic forces which allow a renunciation of the
Romantic ego ("forsake our eyes," with a pun turning on "eye" and "I")
and which transmute the citizen into an item within the profit-and-loss
columns crossed off by this office-clerk, the "page of figures" (*page*: "a
man of humble birth or status").[9] Similarly, in the fourth line *Till* puns
on "a money drawer in a shop or store," which presents us with a
Surrealistic image of the New York office-workers being carried up and
down the city's skyscrapers as if on the levers of some gigantic cash-
register. Crane's intricacies extend even further, for *drop* is "to part with
or lose (money)," and "our day" puns on "oday," American slang for
"money" (f). Thus one cryptic version of this line would be: "Cash-
registers part us from our money." This testifies to the ceaseless orbit of
commercialism upon which New York revolves: the workers' wages are
exchanged for goods in shops, the sale of commodities enables businesses
to employ clerical workers – pages of figures – who in turn spend their
earnings to keep the cycle in motion.

The significance of these puns is to bridge the gap between ideal and
real, and also to reveal the material foundations upon which Crane's
American myth is based. Just as Columbus' teeeming span was also his
Ming span tea, so Brooklyn Bridge is not only "Terrific threshold of the
prophet's pledge" but also "Terrific threshold of the profits' pledge."
And the injunction in the last line of the "Proem" – "of the curveship *lend*
a myth to God" – involves this same capitalist idiom, the "lending" of a
myth from the *curveship* of the sales-graph, thereby offering the Bridge
enough financial capital to function successfully. Although Crane has the
(unfair) reputation of being exclusively a rhetorician, we know he was

not temperamentally averse to employing slang words like "oday" to bridge the various levels of his poetry, for after hearing D'Indy's Second Symphony in March 1923, Crane wrote to Gorham Munson that his

> hair stood on end at its revelations. To get those, and others of men like Strauss, Ravel, Scriabin, and Bloch into *words*, one needs to *ransack* the vocabularies of Shakespeare, Jonson, Webster (for theirs were the richest) and add our scientific, street and counter, and psychological terms, etc. Yet I claim that such things can be done![10]

Crane's mention of "street and counter" language is most interesting, suggesting as it does how commercial colloquialisms become intermingled with the high symbolism of mythic design. This is consistent as well with the great interest in slang, especially American slang, which many intellectual circles developed during the 1920s. The Parisian magazine *transition*, where several of Crane's poems were first published, was in the habit of printing long lists of current slang words, the magazine's editors believing that American slang (with its "richness and pliancy and nearness to life") could become a means of rejuvenating the ossified institution that was "British English."[11] As we shall see later, *transition* was the magazine most famous for Joycean experiments with language; and here we find the "Revolution of the Word" propagating itself at a more down-to-earth level.

This capitalist idiom is constant all the way through *The Bridge*. In "The Harbor Dawn," wailing factory sirens summon workers to produce profits for their employers:

> Gongs in white surplices, beshrouded wails,
> Far strum of fog horns . . . signals dispersed in veils.

Crane's concealed puns reveal the commercial infrastructure underpinning American society. The *surplices* pun on those financial "surpluses" the capitalists hope to produce; *veils* puns on "vails," an obsolete term for "avails; profit; return; proceeds"; and *dispersed* is just what all this profit-making relies upon, consumers dis-pursing, extracting money from their purses and transforming it into entrepreneurs' vails. The way in which Crane's overt religious imagery interacts here with capitalist puns cleverly suggests the American tendency to invest its business ethos with spiritual grandeur. The slogans from advertising at the beginning of "The River" are an obvious continuation of this capitalist idiom; but later in "The River," the narrator persists in employing financial figures of speech to make sense of his landscape:

> But some men take their liquor slow — and *count*
> — Though they'll confess no rosary nor clue —
> The river's minute by the far brook's year. . . .

> Time's rendings, time's blendings they construe
> As final *reckonings* of fire and snow;
> Strange bird-wit, like the elemental gist
> Of unwalled winds they *offer* . . .

This mode of perception is also prevalent in "Indiana" – not surprisingly, for that poem deals with the abortive search for wealth on the gold-trail of 1849. This places it firmly within the line of American capitalist enterprises which make up Crane's *Bridge*: "Indiana," like "Ave Maria," is the chronicle of an expedition for material gain. The narrator tells her son Larry, who is on the point of leaving home for a life at sea, "How we, too, Prodigal, once rode off, too." Here the capitalized *Prodigal* denotes the Prodigal Son which Larry's mother takes him to be, saying she will "always wait" for his return; but it also punningly suggests the prodigal, spendthrift, tendencies of the narrator and her husband Jim when they set off confidently on their quest for "Eldorado," the land rich in gold:

> The pebbles sang, the firecat slunk away
> And glistening through the sluggard freshets came
> In golden syllables loosed from the clay
> His gleaming name.

Wentworth and Flexner's *Dictionary of American Slang* says that "slug" has been used to mean "dollar" since about 1875; and so the adjective *sluggard* here is a pun on "slug," which cleverly ensures that the verbal unit signifying dollar is buried inside this stanza just as the gold and material wealth itself was concealed inside the ground. The capitalist idiom informs everything; the widow bemoans her husband's "lost bones" – not only his physical bones, but also the cash he was cheated out of, *bones* being another American slang word for "dollars":

> Back on the gold trail – then his lost bones stirred . . .

– and she enjoins her son Larry to keep his *pledge*, as if his promise to write home were a form of financial guarantee:

> Write me from Rio . . . and you'll keep your pledge;
> I know your word!

"Indiana" vacillates between sweet sentiment and hard material fact, and "Cape Hatteras" is similarly "surcharged / With sweetness," the capitalist image (*surcharged*) once again suggesting how this American world is defined in financial terms. In this section, however, the discrepancy between sentimentality and bathos, an elevated ideal as opposed to a capitalist real, becomes an immediate social and political danger. The implication of "Cape Hatteras" is that the First World War was at bottom a capitalist enterprise which became justified and sanctified by the layers of sentimentality superimposed upon it. Crane's punning language subverts the complacent images which conceal war's true horror:

> Remember, Falcon-Ace,
> Thou hast there in thy wrist a Sanskrit charge
> To conjugate infinity's dim marge –
> Anew . . . !
>
> But first, here at this height receive
> The benediction of the shell's deep, sure reprieve!
> Lead-perforated fuselage, escutcheoned wings
> Lift agonized quittance, tilting from the invisible brink
> Now eagle-bright, now
>
> quarry-hid, twist-
>
> ing, sink with
> Enormous repercussive list-
>
> ings down
> Giddily spiralled
>
> gauntlets, upturned, unlooping

This passage manifests once again our philosophical bridges between past and present, in that the fighter planes are *tilting* as if engaged in a medieval joust, and their "escutcheoned wings" hark back to the "escutcheon" of the Middle Ages, a shield with armorial bearings. The *fuselage*, besides being the body of the aeroplane, also punningly signifies the fusing or bringing together of different historical ages or eras ("fuse/l'age"). The images of medieval tilting expand the poem's symbolism without affecting its logic; but a more subversive *tilting* is the oscillation between opposites built into these lines. The meanings see-saw between high and low, the elevation of "eagle-bright" contrasted with the depths of "quarry-hid." And what is *hid* in the *quarry* of the poem is a series of financial puns:

> Falcon-*Ace* (a fighter pilot, but also slang for a one-dollar bill)
> a Sanskrit *charge* (a dash or gallop, but also the price demanded)
> infinity's dim *marge* (the margin of infinity, but also the profit-margin)
> benediction of the *shell's* deep, sure reprieve! (the shell as an explosive weapon,
>   but also "shells" as slang for coins, money, as in "to shell out")
> Now *eagle*-bright (*eagle* is slang for "a fighter pilot who has shot down many
>   enemy planes" (f), but also means a ten-dollar coin)

"The benediction of the shell's deep, sure reprieve!" implies on the surface that death by shelling is something to be welcomed: *dulce et decorum est pro patria mori*. But the pun on "shells" as money insidiously expands this to suggest that death in war is to be welcomed because it helps to safeguard the interests of financial shells: the disconcerting suggestion is that it is the shells of the American capitalist economy which really provide justification and "benediction" for these fighter pilots' death. The standard criticism of the First World War made by American radicals was that its chief motivation was trade markets and commercial profits; and here Crane is echoing this viewpoint, asserting that the battle seems glorious and splendid only because we see its "eagle-bright" rather than "quarry-hid" aspect. The line "War's fiery kennel masked in downy offings" summarizes this principle: the violence seems *downy*, placid and harmless, only because we see it from so far away, just as *offings* indicates the distant part of the sea visible to an observer on the shore. Crane's poem is similarly "masked in downy offings": it seems pleasant and harmless from a long way off; but the challenge to the reader in this section is to "upturn" the "Giddily spiralled gauntlets" that are the poem's verbal puns (*gauntlets* both in the figurative sense of challenge, and also in the literal sense of a glove, an object designed to cover something else). For if we take up Crane's gauntlet and uncover his puns, the "Giddily spiralled" words which build bridges between orthodox ideal and subversive real, then Crane's meaning becomes anything other than the "fierce and joyous rant" which R. W. B. Lewis saw in "Cape Hatteras."[12] Crane laments the folly of the First World War in the same way as Whitman mourned the loss of life in the American Civil War:

> What memories of vigils, bloody, by that Cape, –
> Ghoul-mound of man's perversity at balk
> And fraternal massacre! Thou, pallid there as chalk,
> Has kept of wounds, O Mourner, all that sum
> That then from Appomattox stretched to Somme!

These lines from "Cape Hatteras" are unusual in their unequivocal moral impact, and it is not at all the intention to claim that Crane invariably takes a hostile attitude towards capitalist ideologies. In fact, earlier in "Cape Hatteras" he salutes Whitman for

> Confronting the Exchange,
> Surviving in a world of stocks . . .

Crane admired Whitman's ability to embrace the Stock Exchange, Wall Street, within his poetry. Whitman did not scorn as irredeemably vulgar the urban world of money and machinery, but attempted to assimilate it within his mythopoeic art. Whitman survived not only in a world of stocks and shares but also in a world of stock phrases and ideas, for both he and Crane were intent upon incorporating inside their work a "divine average." *Song of Myself* and *The Bridge* both search for mythic status by attempting to mirror the dreams of average Americans, and in Crane's case this led to his elaborate metaphors of the capitalism which he deemed the most vital force in 1920s America. The most frequently noted direct source for *The Bridge* is Emerson's essay on Plato, in which Emerson was making exactly this point, that Platonic myth should be all-inclusive and provide a mirror in which the populace see their aspirations reflected:

> [Plato] is a great average man; one who, to the best thinking, adds a proportion and equality in his faculties, so that men see in him their own dreams and glimpses made available and made to pass for what they are . . . He has reason, as all the philosophic and poetic class have: but he has also what they have not, – this strong solving sense to reconcile his poetry with the appearances of the world, and build a bridge from the streets of the cities to the Atlantis.

For Emerson, Plato represented the "balanced soul" able to reconcile the immediate realities of daily existence with a more abstract vision of life's overall unity.[13] Hart Crane's bridge to the Atlantis pulls off the same feat by its recasting of philosophical essences in terms of the accidents of capitalism.

In "Quaker Hill," the concept of mutability is defined by an economic metaphor:

> The woodlouse *mortgages* the ancient deal
> Table . . .

So is the idea of millennial triumph:

> Who holds the *lease* on time and on disgrace?

And the dilapidated state of the "old Mizzentop" Hotel on Quaker Hill is arousing the interest of financiers intent upon extracting profits from the land:

> This was the Promised Land, and still it is
> To the persuasive suburban land agent

Again, the "natural" landscape has been refracted through a capitalist perspective:

> . . . loose panes crown the hill and gleam
> At sunset with a silent, cobwebbed patience . . .
> See them, like eyes that still uphold some dream
> Through mapled vistas, cancelled reservations!

On the surface, these lines simply describe the forlorn and run-down condition of the Mizzentop Hotel. But, as if by a trick-mirror, Crane's puns rotate this literal fact into an image of the hotel as it appears in the mind of the capitalist entrepreneur. Overtly, the hotel's "loose panes crown the hill" because its window-panes have fallen out; but for the opportunist agent, these loose panes fill the hill with gold "crowns" or coins as he envisages all the money he can make from selling off the land which the hotel will vacate. Those "cancelled reservations" are on one

hand the reservations cancelled by guests whom the Mizzentop Hotel
now fails to attract; but the entrepreneur is far more interested in the
hotel's owners cancelling their *reservations* or title-deeds to the land,
thereby allowing him to set about his business. The sad old hotel might
proudly try to "uphold some dream," but its unprofitable life is doomed,
for *uphold* puns on "upholder," in an obsolete sense "one who holds
things up for sale; a broker or auctioneer." Thus the hotel upholds some
nostalgic dream, but, by a syntactical reversal, the greedy upholder
dreams of a "sum" of money (a pun on *some*): cash-registers are ringing in
this land agent's head. So while the Mizzentop Hotel is *cobwebbed* in the
sense of being in a state of fusty disrepair, capitalist America is "cob/
webbed" in a more mercenary way: a latent "web" ("any complicated
fabrication, arrangement or contrivance") made up of interlocking
threads of "cob" (in obsolete senses, "the old Spanish dollar" and "a rich
covetous person"). These rich covetous cobs lend their myth to God by
turning the countryside into real estate. The pastoral world becomes
redefined within a commercial idiom.

"Atlantis," "Deity's glittering *Pledge*," is similarly a capitalist haven.
Its "glistening *fins* of light" ("fin" being slang for a five-dollar bill (f)) are
dependent upon "black em*bank*ments," businesses running in the *black*
with plenty of money in the "bank." "In the black," of course, is slang
for "operating at a profit" (f):

> – From black embankments, moveless soundings hailed

In "Atlantis," the capitalist metaphors merge into pathetic fallacy and
become a means of imposing provisional order upon the world:

> Now while thy petals *spend* the suns about us, hold –
> . . .
> Like spears ensanguined of one *tolling* star
> That *bleeds* infinity . . .

It is as if the star were "bleeding" (extorting money from) infinity,
imposing a charge or "toll" upon the infinite darkness and so requiring
infinite darkness to bow to the star's financial demands. The fictive aspect
of this metaphor would have been well known to Crane, with his interest
in Einsteinian relativity; and indeed there is a pun on *tolling* as the tolling
of a death-knell, suggesting how this mythic capitalist system will
eventually wear itself away to nought. Construction and deconstruction
are thereby fused together inside one punning word.

CAPITALISM AND IMPERSONALITY

The same kinds of metaphorical impositions are evident at the end of
"The Tunnel," but here there is also an interesting comment on the

relationship between subjective freedom and the objectifications of myth:

> Tossed from the coil of ticking towers. . . .
>   Tomorrow,
> And to be. . . . Here by the River that is East –
> Here at the waters' edge the hands drop memory;
> Shadowless in that abyss they unaccounting lie.
> How far away the star has pooled the sea –
> Or shall the hands be drawn away, to die?

By a natural interaction of physical forces, the star would "pull" the sea and control its tides; but here the sea has been *pooled*, as if it were a business firm forced to throw in its lot with other public companies. Similarly the "ticking towers" contain overtones of New York City's financial *towers*, its money-making skyscrapers, with "tick" being slang for "to buy or sell on credit." Of course these *towers* are ostensibly clock-towers – hence the *ticking* of the *hands* – but the *hands* also have sexual connotations; and it is as if in the "dropping" of memory they are attempting to divest themselves of the encumbrances of the material world in order that they might attain an extra-temporal dimension where they would be *unaccounting*. This dimension would liberate the lover's hands from the constrictions of capitalism and from the world in general. But the pun on *lie* signifies the illusory, or at least ambiguous, nature of this private ecstasy. As Eric J. Sundquist excellently put it in his essay on "Magic, Lies, and Silence in Hart Crane,"

> The hands of memory slide away to yield a moment of apparently unobstructed vision, one without veiling shadows and one which has to make no *account* – yet they again *lie*, and the oppressive realization instantly returns that they have still to pay homage to the greater "Hand of Fire," the most inaccessible ancestral god to whom the whole of *The Bridge* must constantly account.[14]

This "Hand of Fire" which appears at the end of "The Tunnel" builds a formal bridge back to the "Hand of Fire" Columbus prays to in "Ave Maria," a capitalist god who "Subscribest holocaust of ships" and who manipulates his subjects as if they were profit-and-loss items on his Almighty ledger. So here the lover's hands cannot escape from their pun on the hands of the clock, nor from their involvement with the systems of capitalist America: the subjective dream cannot flee from objective myth. The pun on *lie* gives this phrase two contrary directions: the hands either lie in blissful unaccounting ignorance, or their unaccounting subjectivity is a mere illusion, a lie, because everyone must finally "account" to the great god of capitalist myth. It is the same oscillation between freedom and circumscription that we saw in *wrapt* ("wrapt

inception and beatitude"), and it demonstrates once more the sophisticated logic behind Crane's wordplay.

The economic machine that Crane delineates in *The Bridge* has some
affinities with the Darwinian version of life that Crane would have found
in Theodore Dreiser's work, and also in D. H. Lawrence's *The Plumed
Serpent*, which Crane mentioned in a letter to Munson on 5 March 1926,
soon after the novel had appeared. Kate Leslie in *The Plumed Serpent* feels
that "As long as time lasts, [America] will be the continent divided
between Victims and Victimizers"; and the novel goes on to lament the
oppressive nature of the American landscape which plucks out "the
created soul in a man," leaving him merely "a creature of mechanism and
automatic reaction."[15] It certainly is true that the Bridge as "Terrific
threshold of the prophet's/profits' pledge" subjugates Romantic freedom by refusing any unfettered individuality: the hands in "The
Tunnel" believe they lie unaccounting, but their unaccounting turns out
to be a lie because the Bridge has conscripted all the forsaken eyes into the
"inviolate curve" of its sales-graph, and the "Accolade" it bestows is one
"Of anonymity." However, the abstractions involved in Crane's version
of capitalist America are not necessarily imbued with the gloomy
fatalism of Darwinian thought. The myth does have its negative
underside, as in "Cape Hatteras," but it also espouses the more positive
acceptance of capitalist impersonality propagated by the zany Surrealists.
In September 1922, Harold A. Loeb (never short of a spare dollar
himself) wrote an article in his magazine *Broom* where he defended "The
Mysticism of Money," claiming financial affairs had defined the
American state since the days of "No Taxation Without Representa-
tion," and that money was now "the measuring staff of all values." In
moral terms, Loeb recognized that this could be "the most cruel of recent
religions" which "has put into practice systems of torture that . . . stunt
the body and shorten and embitter life"; but Loeb found aesthetic
pleasure in steel and concrete buildings which he declared greatly
preferable to the pseudo-Classicism of libraries and churches, and he
criticized intellectuals who found nothing of value in modern commercialism. The cash-nexus formed the geometry which bound America
together: for Loeb it was the basis of a classical myth because
"Differentiation of individuals is not a faculty of archaic periods, in fact
only in times of decadence is it emphasized."[16] If he had been able to
understand *The Bridge*, Crane's poem would surely have found favour
with Loeb, for Crane exploits the mysticism of money prevalent in
Twenties America to disintegrate the autonomy of individual human
and verbal units, and to transpose them into ciphers manipulated by New
York City's economic machine: "O caught like pennies beneath soot and
steam," as "The Tunnel" puts it.

To summarize: Crane sees capitalism as the most vital force in contemporary America, and so presents his *Bridge* within a capitalist idiom. The puns in the "Proem," "Ave Maria" and "Atlantis" reveal the economic infrastructure underpinning the poem's symbolic Idealism. In "Indiana" the puns are buried inside the verse just as gold is buried inside the ground; but in "Cape Hatteras" the palliative layers of sentimentality superimposed upon the commercial puns suggest in a more sinister way how political skill and social conventions concealed the economic motives underlying the First World War. In this capitalist context, it is interesting to note that when in 1921 Crane's friend William Lescaze made a sketch of the poet wherein his right eye is the focus of the composition and heavily emphasized, Crane himself chose to interpret this picture in accordance with the dictum of the German mystic Jacob Boehme, who claimed that a man's right eye looks forward into eternity while his left eye looks backward into time. Boehme said that a man will not achieve unity of vision until his eye of time and eye of eternity are brought into alignment; and Crane's puns manage to produce exactly this synthesis of vision: for by praising God for his teeming span and his Ming span tea both at once, Crane's puns bridge idealism with materialism, and so allow *The Bridge* to keep one eye on eternity and the other firmly on the main chance.[17]

4

Capitalism and the underworld

"NATIONAL WINTER GARDEN"

There have grown up in the city certain so-called cabaret places which in a measure have taken the place of such resorts as were on 29th Street, although the evidences of immorality instead of being open and flagrant are very much concealed and would not be observed by the casual visitor. This makes it easy for the management to present many witnesses who will testify to the good character of the place.   (U.S. Government Report on Prostitution, 1914)[1]

In the early years of this century, vice rings in American cities became increasingly well organized and harder to crack. Things became particularly bad after the introduction of Prohibition in 1919, because the enormous profits which the bootleggers stood to make depended upon the successful veiling of their illegal activities under the guise of decorum and social respectability. The cloak-and-dagger world of bootlegging became a very familiar scenario in the national newspapers, whose readers would follow with great gusto the exploits of the famous New York agent Izzy Einstein as he attempted to run the bootleggers to ground. Einstein would visit Harlem in blackface or pose as a cosmopolitan gourmet ordering his dinner in French if he thought this would help to catch the vendors of alcohol off their guard. St Patrick's Day was a particularly fruitful time for Einstein, who used to festoon himself with shamrocks and go round shouting "Begorra!" In this respect, New York in the 1920s was a place of deceit and disguises, for Prohibition agents were concerned not just to track down secret drinkers but to expose the shady organizations whose business was to supply alcohol. The mysterious telephone call that Jay Gatsby receives in the middle of one of his glittering parties, with its suggestion of some corrupt financial transaction, is typical of the discrepancy between base fact and guileful illusion that prevailed at this time. The criminals were all the more difficult to uncover because their operation of the law of freedom of choice for the consumer seemed to be so firmly within the established American capitalist ethic ("Prohibition is a business," said Al Capone. "All I do is supply a public demand"); and so to the public at large these racketeers took on the rôle of glamorous figures evading the clutches of a petty-minded bureaucracy.[2] Susan Jenkins Brown remembered how around 1925 Hart and his friends used to drink speakeasy rum at the Poncino Palazzo, "a grim six-by-eight hole behind a delicatessen on West Fourth Street"; and Malcolm Cowley similarly recalled that Crane was accustomed to drink bootleg liquor in "Village speakeasies and Brooklyn waterfront dives," on which occasions Crane's "high spirits would be mingled with obsessions" that the authorities were watching them. "'See that man staring at us,'" Crane used to say, "'I think he's a detective.'"[3]

We have seen how capitalism permeates the imagery of *The Bridge*, and if we look just a little harder we can perceive how the devious forces of this criminal underworld come to exercise a similar influence inside the poem. There is one overt reference to bootlegging in "Quaker Hill":

> This was the Promised Land, and still it is
> To the persuasive suburban land agent
> In bootleg roadhouses where the gin fizz
> Bubbles in time to Hollywood's new love-nest pageant.

But after this open identification, we might care to take a second glance at that seemingly innocuous hotel described sixteen lines earlier:

> Above them old Mizzentop, palatial white
> Hostelry . . .

According to Wentworth and Flexner, *white* was the 1920s term for bootleg gin; and so we may surmise that the "white / Hostelry" of this Mizzentop Hotel served the same important function as these new "bootleg roadhouses" which sell bubbling "gin fizz": both Mizzentop and roadhouses being, in fact, handy resorts for furtive drinkers. The verbal concealment of the gin through a pun is analogous to its necessary concealment from the police at the time Crane was writing. (And indeed on 27 June 1928, Crane wrote to Yvor Winters from Patterson, New York – where this "Quaker Hill" poem is set – mentioning "a cashiered army officer turned bootlegger over on Birch Hill, who makes very good applejack.")[4]

A more systematic treatment of this theme of deception occurs in "National Winter Garden," the title of which derives from a New York vaudeville theatre popular in the 1920s:

> Outspoken buttocks in pink beads
> Invite the necessary cloudy clinch

> Of bandy eyes . . . No extra mufflings here:
> The world's one flagrant, sweating cinch.

Outspoken attributes to this row of girls' buttocks a sense of defiance and daring as they parodically re-embody the traffic-lights, described as "Beading thy path" in the "Proem," with overtones there of the *beads* of a Christian rosary. This strip-show demonstrates how the world seems to turn on an axis of dehumanized lust: that *cinch* could be "a strong girth for a pack or saddle," and so, by extension, the G-strings encircling the waists of these women who have been demoted to the status of animals. The adjectives *flagrant* (literally "on fire," hence "burning; ardent") and *sweating* could both indicate the sexual excitement of the audience as they watch this striptease; and *cinch* as a Portnoyesque "tight grip" is highly suggestive in this voyeuristic context. "No extra mufflings" may refer to the girls' lack of superfluous clothing; but "muffle" also carries the idea of concealment in a more general sense, and "to muffle" can be "to speak indistinctly, or without clear articulation." So it could be that we as readers are being urged to "know" (*No*) "extra mufflings": to be aware of echoes hidden beneath the surface of the poem, and to invite into our minds what is here a necessarily *cloudy* ("indistinct; obscure") *clinch* ("a play upon words; pun"). So, to recap, we have: (a) *No* extra mufflings – no clothes for the girls, but also (b) *Know* extra mufflings – an injunction to the reader to apprehend the layers of deception inherent in the poem. This directs us towards the sleazy capitalist or criminal gangs lurking in the poem's back-room: for, as we have seen, a *cinch* can be a "tight grip"; and by derivation from this, Webster's slang definition of "to cinch" is "to get a sure hold upon; to get into a tight place, as for forcing submission." The implication is of the burlesque dancers being under the thumb, not to say the cosh, of the nightclub owners. This neatly complements the muffled connotations of *sweating*: "to sweat" is "to get advantage, as of money, property, or labor from (any one) by exaction or oppression"; and a "sweating system" is one specifically designed to exploit employees for low wages. This would turn *flagrant* into its more normal meaning of "glaringly wicked" or "heinous." So we can see that this phrase "flagrant, sweating cinch" could refer to the activities of the theatre's owners (extortionate), or of its employees (dehumanized), or of its customers (masturbating). Again, Crane's language depicts a world in constant interpenetration.

From these shady dealings going on behind the poem's façade, we must infer that the capitalist owners have reduced both strippers and audience to statistics on the cash-nexus. These stealthy manipulators have wormed their way into a knowledge of basic human requirements which they have then rearranged to suit their own bank-accounts, preying on the men's lust and the women's need of money. The images in "National

Winter Garden" are of violence and oppression: "Pearls *whip* her hips" (the pearls of her own garment, but also each pearl, "pupil of the eye," of the audience); "the lewd *trounce* of a final muted *beat*." This musical *beat*, the accompaniment to which the woman gyrates, punningly symbolizes her domination by the capitalist economy which compels her to produce this fraudulently glamorous image of herself. There is a more optimistic side to this burlesque show, which we can examine later, but here we need to stress its affinities with that criminal underworld which is itself a parodic exaggeration of certain aspects of the American capitalist system:

> Then you, the burlesque of our lust – and faith,
> Lug us back lifeward – bone by infant bone.

"National Winter Garden" is indeed a *burlesque* of the *faith* Crane places in his mythic vision of capitalist America, the terrific threshold of the profits' pledge. *Lug* is a slang term used in the underworld to mean "money . . . paid for police protection" (f): and *bone* as slang for "a dollar" suggests not only the bones paid by the nightclub owners as protection money, but also the bones paid by the audience to gain entry to the show. So we can see how the "National Winter Garden" is as much a hard-headed capitalist enterprise as the voyage of Columbus or the gold-trail of 1849 or any of the other scenes described in *The Bridge*.

"VIRGINIA"

Bleecker Street, in the lower East side of Manhattan, was one of the areas these sinister racketeers used to operate from during the 1920s, and they make another subversive appearance in "Virginia," the last of Crane's "Three Songs":

> It's high carillon
> From the popcorn bells!
> Pigeons by the million –
> And Spring in Prince Street
> Where green figs gleam
> By oyster shells!

> O Mary, leaning from the high wheat tower,
> Let down your golden hair!

> High in the noon of May
> On cornices of daffodils
> The slender violets stray.
> Crap-shooting gangs in Bleecker reign,
> Peonies with pony manes –
> Forget-me-nots at windowpanes:

Out of the way-up nickel-dime tower shine,
>Cathedral Mary,
>> shine! –

At first glance this is a pleasantly inoffensive if rather sentimental evocation of springtime in New York City. Sherman Paul is representative of the attitude critics have taken towards this poem:

> Its queen is Mary, the good country girl whom the city cannot sully (her smile protects her) and who like the flowers in the window boxes of tenements, fills the daylight world of this poem with the fragrance, color, and radiance of springtime innocence . . . The flowers of this lovely verse evoke young love, the shy girls and the still-uncertain boys of some *West Side Story*. "Pony manes" summons the world of childhood and recalls the frisking Pocahontas of the Strachey epigraph. Raised to nobility by "reign" and "Prince Street," the crap-shooters are lovely boys . . . an innocent homosexuality.[5]

But no other section of *The Bridge* has been so radically misunderstood, for the puns in "Virginia" tilt the poem back to reveal beneath this sentimentality a lurid and criminal underside. The most obvious puns in the poem are what I have called its internal verbal bridges which create a coherent formal pattern between one section of *The Bridge* and another: hence "High in the noon of *May*" looks back to "virgin May" in "The Dance" ("There was a veil upon you, Pocahontas, bride – / O Princess whose brown lap was virgin May"); and so this "Cathedral Mary" has links both with Columbus' "Ave Maria" and also with the Pocahontas legend which, as R. W. Butterfield has reminded us, "was most closely associated with that region of America which became the state of Virginia."[6] The title "Virginia" suggests a corporeal and sexual side to Mary, as if she were more than a spiritual "virgin"; and in fact the first stanza quoted above reveals images of Spring's physical fecundity: for the *figs* and *oysters*, as Sherman Paul noted, are sexual symbols, and Mary's "golden hair" suggests "the plenty of Ceres' blessing."[7] Figs, of course, are notorious for making their consumers excrete, so it may be possible to detect a pun swinging between the modern verb *gleam* and the archaic falconry term *gleam*: "to disgorge filth, as a hawk." This latter reading of *gleam* would give the images of springtime a more animalistic foundation; and if *Pigeons* plays on its slang meaning of "a girl or young woman," then this vision of Spring becomes less picturesque and more down to earth, less like virgin and more like Virginia.

But the pun on *gleam* also links up with the "Crap-shooting gangs" in the next stanza, who are shooting all kinds of shit as well as dice, for the polite covering up of Man's animalistic behaviour becomes analogous to the layers of placid euphemism superimposed upon distasteful financial and criminal dealings. A "pigeon" ("Pigeons by the million") has another slang connotation: "a victim of a swindle; one who has been duped; an innocent or naïve person, one easy to dupe or take advantage of" (f); and what we must infer here is that these New Yorkers are blind to the devious ways in which Bleecker Street gangs have infiltrated and rearranged the city's institutions, just as Crane's readers have not appreciated how this poem's subversive puns unmask the pastoral illusions so pleasantly put forward. The "Crap-shooting gangs" are not innocent boys (though they may like to portray themselves as such) but hard-headed racketeers who "reign over," keep under strict control, their "Peonies with pony manes." On the surface, "peony" is a pretty flower, but there is a pun on "peon," a word of Mexican origin denoting "common laborer"; and, says Webster, the word "implies bondage or serfage." Similarly a *pony* is here not so much an innocent animal as "a chorus girl, burlesque dancer" (f). It was a slang term popular in the 1920s: a character in Dos Passos' *Manhattan Transfer* (1925) takes his friend to a nightclub and tells him to "Look out for the Pony Ballet."[8] Thus these "Peonies with pony manes" are the reluctant employees of the capitalist underworld; and with *manes* punning on the anglicized Latin word *manes*, "spirits of the dead and gods of the lower world," we can see how these infernal deities of the burlesque stage have been manipulated and dehumanized by underworld gangs in the interests of financial profit. The "slender *violets*" are not just nice-looking plants, for the pun also suggests the "violation" or transgression of the boundaries of polite life. These "Crap-shooting gangs" violate social decorum in the same way as Crane's puns violate the decorum of the text; but the seeming impregnability of such social respectability offers a most convenient façade behind which the capitalist criminals can carry out their dirty work. When we hear the "high carillon / From the popcorn bells," we do not immediately realize that the popcorn and ice-cream stands are in fact being skilfully controlled by the Bleecker Street gangs:

> On cornices of daffodils
> The slender violets stray.

But split *cornices* into "corn/ices," and we can see how far the racketeers' interests extend. The slender violets stray into fields of corn and ices, and to them the jangle of these "popcorn bells" would suggest that business is booming. The *daffodils* (slang for "a homily, proverb or aphorism") demonstrate how the brutal self-interest of these commercial organizations is concealed behind cloaks of gentility and self-justification. How admirable for the "Forget-me-nots at windowpanes" to talk of the rejuvenation of the Spring, and how vulgar of them to be punningly reminding us that they too have a commercial context, "forget-me-not" being exactly the exhortation of advertisements at "windowpanes" to casual passers-by. Now the "green figs" which "gleam / By oyster shells" come to have a financial face to them, with the colour *green* punning on *green* as slang for money ("money, esp. paper money" say Wentworth and Flexner, "Since c. 1920. Orig. sporting and underworld use"). And *figs* puns on "figures," the cash-figures which are brought about by the extraction of *shells*, coins, from New York customers who obligingly "shell out" for consumer fodder such as popcorn and ice-cream.

So Crane's commercial puns serve to undermine the pastoral illusions in "Virginia." The puns bridge a high world of social respectability with a low world of mercantile transaction. Might it even be that "Cathedral Mary" is actually engaged in bootlegging, and that the assignation for which the poem's narrator waits is one designed for the reception of smuggled alcohol? This was a familiar enough theme in the New York of the Twenties: compare Ellen in Dos Passos' *Manhattan Transfer*:

> From under the blanket that was wrapped round the baby she produced a brown paper package . . .
> "Two quarts of our special cognac . . ."

To which Hildebrand responds, "Of course what you kids don't realize . . . is that the difficulty under prohibition is keeping sober."[9] So could

> O blue-eyed Mary with the claret scarf

be suggesting that Mary has wrapped her *scarf* around a bottle of *claret*? And could

> Out of the way-up nickel-dime tower shine,
> Cathedral Mary,
> shine! –

be a secret injunction to Mary to smuggle *shine* (slang for "whisky; esp. bootleg whisky or moonshine" (f)) out of this "nickel-dime tower" in which she works? "Nick" is "a play on a likeness in words; a pun"; and out of this nickel-dime tower of Crane's *Bridge*, cheap puns bring forth concealed goods.

At any rate, the disguises and deceptions brought about by bootlegging and other dubious commercial activities in the New York City of the 1920s are faithfully mirrored in the form of Crane's poem, with its punning oscillation between ideal illusion and base reality. As we have seen, the capitalist ideologies in *The Bridge* are sometimes fairly overt, and Crane makes no secret of his definition of America in terms of the most vital force of his day. But "Virginia" is more concerned with the way capitalism, at least in its less respectable aspects, is Janus-faced: just as the green figs "gleam," eject waste matter, as well as luminously *gleam*, so the "Crap-shooting gangs in Bleecker" are not simply playing dice, but also shooting the crap of commerce, engaging with the squalid processes of money-making that underlie this seemingly innocuous city landscape. Through Crane's use of puns, capitalism pushes its way up through the masks of social sentimentality and idealism, just as the poem's sexual imagery relates spirit back to the obdurate necessity of the body.

"THE RIVER"

Let us now turn back to see the way similar deceptions operate in "The River." At the beginning of the poem the infiltrations of capitalism are quite obvious, as Crane begins with a *mélange* of phrases drawn from contemporary advertising:

> Stick your patent name on a signboard
> brother – all over – going west – young man
> Tintex – Japalac – Certain-teed Overalls ads
> and lands sakes . . .
>   . . . if it isn't
> Erie it ain't for miles around a
> Mazda – and the telegraphic night coming on Thomas
>
> a Ediford . . .

Crane's commercial sources for this passage have been tracked down by John Baker, who pointed out how "Jap-A-Lac" was the "trade-mark for varnishes, stains, and enamels made by the Glidden Company, Cleveland"; how *Certain-teed* was a similar "trade-mark for products manufactured by the Certain-teed Products Corporation – asphalt shingles, paints, varnishes, linoleum, oil cloth, and plaster of Paris"; how *Erie* was the Erie railroad running through Cleveland; how "Thomas a Ediford," punningly conflating Edison with Henry Ford, fits in with the Edison *Mazda* lamps popular at the time.[10] A few lines later in the poem, there is a reference to the radio contact established between America and Richard E. Byrd, whose aeroplanes flew over the North Pole in 1926:

RADIO ROARS IN EVERY HOME WE HAVE THE NORTHPOLE

By defining his environment in terms of all these technological miracles of the 1920s, Crane seems to be positing a dichotomy between the modernistic world of industrial capitalism and the older, slower world of hobo life which is portrayed later in this poem:

> So the 20th Century – so
> whizzed the Limited – roared by and left
> three men, still hungry on the tracks . . .

(The "20th Century Limited" was a Pullman sleeper train running between New York and Chicago.) Commenting on "The River,"

Richard P. Sugg talked of "the imprisoning nature of this hypocritical, even insane, belief in the superiority of abstractions, machines and reason to the processes of the universe"; but the problem with this reading is that it ignores the elaborate analogies Crane goes on to make between the operation of the natural world, Sugg's "processes of the universe," and the all-embracing machine of capitalism.[11] Take for instance *sumac-stained*:

> They lurk across her, knowing her yonder breast
> Snow-silvered, sumac-stained or smoky blue

Sumac is a shrub yielding material for tanning and dyeing: and so this natural object, the pastoral shrub, is related back to the *Tintex* in the poem's third line, which in the 1920s was the brand name for a domestic dye.[12] Importunate capitalism invades the rural world. Take another example:

> Papooses crying on the wind's long mane
> Screamed redskin dynasties that fled the brain

John Unterecker has pointed out that *Papooses* and *redskin dynasties* were at this time the names of Pullman cars on the railroad service.[13] The trains were named after Indian mythology, of course; but this redefining of an apparently "natural" world through the lens of technological culture is characteristic of the way in which "The River," like "Virginia," unmasks its pastoral illusions as it proceeds. Crane employs puns to disestablish the possibility of belief in any naïve or simple "description" of the world:

> . . . you, too, feed the River timelessly.
> And few evade full measure of their fate;
> Always they smile out eerily what they seem.

Here *eerily* puns on the Erie railroad, referred to, as we saw, at the beginning of "The River." The substance of these lines is that even the hoboes who believe themselves to be "free" are swallowed up by the gargantuan appetite of a capitalist monster which devours everything in its sight. The hoboes are not allowed the freedom to be "eerie," for the pun on *Erie* catches up with them and compromises their autonomy. The pun is a means of transposing active into passive. Similarly, the next two lines tell of the legendary hobo Dan Midland who was killed while hitching a ride on a railroad freight car:

> I could believe he joked at heaven's gate –
> Dan Midland – jolted from the cold brake-beam.

Dan Midland attempted to realize his liberty, but the machine-world revenged itself upon him by bringing about his death. All these hoboes try to be the arrangers of their own destiny, but the tentacles of capitalism are always threatening to render them no more than passive instruments of its own will. The "Pullman breakfasters" are pulling men ("Pull/man") into line, breaking down their attempts to stand fast and assert their own individuality ("break/fasters"):

> And Pullman breakfasters glide glistening steel

The hoboes are thus turned into "blind baggage," mere ciphers on the economic merry-go-round.

Let us take two longer examples from "The River" to show how syntactical ambiguity and its verbal equivalent, the pun, make these bridges between opposite significations:

> Behind
> My father's cannery works I used to see
> Rail-squatters ranged in nomad raillery,
> The ancient men – wifeless or runaway
> Hobo-trekkers that forever search
> An empire wilderness of freight and rails.
> Each seemed a child, like me, on a loose perch,
> Holding to childhood like some termless play.
> John, Jake or Charley, hopping the slow freight
> – Memphis to Tallahassee – riding the rods,
> Blind fists of nothing, humpty-dumpty clods.
>
> Yet they touch something like a key perhaps.
> From pole to pole across the hills, the states
> – They know a body under the wide rain

Here the first four lines bring into play Crane's typical interchangeability of subject and object, with its thematic consequence of the reversal of active and passive. If *ancient* is denoting the old wisdom of folklore, then these hoboes, "Rail-squatters," are engaged in good-humoured banter or *raillery* against the world. But the rail-squatters might also be the possessions of an *ancient*, "an elder in his capacity as a dignitary," with the implication that a capitalist *ancient* or business-mogul is a reincarnation of the old feudal chief. In this case the "Rail-squatters" would not range over the world with their humorous raillery, but rather be "arranged" (*ranged*) inside the capitalist organization of the railroad industry (a pun on *raillery*, as Sherman Paul noticed).[14] The subsequent lines support this ambiguity: the hobo-trekkers may be forever searching for the wilderness of freight and rails, but the business empire of freight and rails is similarly forever searching for them, because it knows that runaway hobo-trekkers can be easily exploited as cheap labour, and also that the hoboes pose less of a threat to the smooth running of the system once they have been integrated inside it. "Cannery" (in "My father's cannery works") puns on *cannery* as slang for jail (f), and the economic system is attempting to enclose these vagabonds within its own kind of prison. Meanwhile the aim of the hoboes is to preserve their romantic freedom by collapsing the way social landscapes are traditionally demarcated in terms of rod, pole and perch ("on a loose *perch*," "riding the *rods*," "from *pole* to *pole*"). But even while these hoboes are attempting to ride over or ignore the rods, they are at the same time being conscripted as passive riders along the rods of pre-existent structures. The pun builds a bridge between romantic freedom and classical circumscription, for even the hoboes find they cannot "evade full measure of their fate" (with *measure*, a pun on rhythm or metre, being another image of determinism).

Three stanzas from the final section of "The River" reveal more of Crane's punning demonstration of the capitalist infrastructure beneath this pastoral landscape:

> Down, down – born pioneers in time's despite,
> Grimed tributaries to an ancient flow –
> They win no frontier by their wayward plight,
> But drift in stillness, as from Jordan's brow.
>
> You will not hear it as the sea; even stone
> Is not more hushed by gravity . . . But slow,
> As loth to take more tribute – sliding prone
> Like one whose eyes were buried long ago
>
> The River, spreading, flows – and spends your dream.
> What are you, lost within this tideless spell?
> You are your father's father, and the stream –
> A liquid theme that floating niggers swell.

In these lines there is an equation between *tributaries* (streams) and *tribute* (the cash-payment); and one of Webster's offerings for "tributary" is "paying tribute to another, either from compulsion, as an acknowledge-ment of submission, or to secure protection," a double meaning which would make the equation between the flowing of water and the flowing of money even more marked. Once again we come across the *ancient* in the second line, not just an adjective advising us of the river's longevity, but also a noun signifying "an elder in his capacity as a dignitary"; and if we switch *flow* from noun to verb, we can see how the money "flows" to him, as in a cash-flow. This *ancient* subsumes the *pioneers* into his financial system: they are "bourne" rather than *born*, passive not active. The "pioneer" may be an individualist and explorer, but may also be a subordinate: "one of the soldiers, esp. of an engineer corps, detailed to remove obstructions, form roads, dig trenches, make bridges, etc." The etymology is the same as a "pawn" in chess, the common root being the Old French *peon*, a foot-soldier, which is relevant because the capitalist *ancient* is an analogue to the feudal chief of olden times who used to treat all his vassals as pawns. The hoboes, while they try to ignore time and act in its *despite*, are nevertheless continually threatened by the pun on "despot" which will force them to acquiesce in the despotic, tyrannous nature of the world around them. "They win no frontier by their wayward plight": because *plight* is not only a dilemma, but also a "pledge," as in plighting one's troth to a lord, the hoboes must renounce their romantic dreams, for they can "win no frontier" themselves but must instead "drift in stillness," give way to the circumstances of the world around them.

In the third stanza *spreading* includes "spread," a jargon-word of speculators on American money-markets ("an arbitrage transaction operated by buying and selling simultaneously in two separate markets, as Chicago and New York, when there is an abnormal difference in price between the two markets"). The word suggests how the labourers are manipulated by capitalist financiers, as though the conscripted hoboes themselves are sales that cross some page of figures to be filed away.[15] The adjective *liquid* denotes assets that "can be promptly converted into cash"; and *floating* has a similar meaning, "to establish in currency, as bonds." From the picturesque and sentimental angle, these *niggers* are obligingly crooning the "liquid theme" of the Negro spiritual "Deep River," a Disneyesque image of the jovial workers heigh-hoing as they toil.[16] However, the monetary angle is more menacing: the *niggers* are actually the basis of this capitalist state, ironically it is they, and not the speculators, who are *floating* it (to float: "to support, as a commercial scheme or a joint-stock company, so as to enable it to go into, or continue in, operation"); but nevertheless the nigger labourers are themselves likely to be "floated" (liquidated or cashiered) at any moment. "Float" in this sense of "make redundant" was very common in Crane's time. The phrase "sliding prone / Like one whose eyes were buried long ago" is an apt intimation of the Negro's condition, the way his wages are *prone* (liable) to be established on a "*sliding*-scale" ("under which the wages depend, more or less, upon the selling price of the product, the rate of pay rising and falling with the price according to a certain scale"); and also of the way his individuality ("eye" or I) has been submerged (*buried*) by the system. And it is appropriate that the river *spends* dreams, turning them into implements of economic exchange. When Crane sent "The River" to Yvor Winters on 1 July 1927, he mentioned his "long struggle with an attempt to tell the pioneer achievement backward"; and we can see that not only does the poem's overt chronology move backwards, from technological decadence in the opening lines to Mississippi primitivism at the end, but also the willed self-determination of the pioneer is reversed: he becomes a passive agent of capitalist forces.[17]

These stanzas are themselves "sliding prone," *prone* or liable to slide between different levels of meaning. As in "Virginia," the surface meaning is socially respectable, while the concealed puns indicate the more brutal realities upon which such social respectability is superimposed:

> You will not hear it as the sea; even stone
> Is not more hushed by gravity . . .

"You will not hear it as the sea" refers ostensibly to the river, with the implication that the river's movement is as silent and remorseless as a stone's attraction by *gravity* to the centre of the earth. The river is no more likely to cease flowing than a stone is to start leaping around in mid-air. But this first phrase can also become: "You will not hear it as thee see" – in other words, you can appreciate the poem's verbal games when you see them on the page in your private act of reading, but they are not audible when the poem is read aloud. ("Thee" might seem implausibly archaic, but remember Crane addresses Brooklyn Bridge in this form throughout the "Proem" and "Atlantis.") So in this context *gravity* puns on solemnity: "even stone," even the most conventional stony-faced prig, is not more anxious to maintain a posture of frigid dignity than is *The Bridge* itself. The poem's hidden jokes and inversions must be repressed into underground channels (*hushed*) for the sake of society's Noble Lie.

There are many other examples of this tendency of Crane's capitalist world to mask itself in subtle disguises. In the fifth verse of "The River," for instance, a sinister member of the road-gang offers the following advice:

> "There's no place like Booneville though, Buddy,"
> One said, excising a last burr from his vest,
> " – For early trouting."

Ostensibly he is simply *excising*, taking out, a thistle (*burr*) from his jacket (*vest*). But when we know that "on the burrole" is slang for "to live the life of a drifter," a "hobo or beggar" (f), we can see that this devious agent is concerned to clear the hoboes out of this piece of land in which he has a vested financial interest (*vest*). This is why he is excising the burrs, recommending that the hoboes move on to "Booneville" which he advocates as a town of plenty; and *excising*, punning on the charging of "excise," a tax-payment, surreptitiously defines his hard-headed eviction of these hoboes in the terms of a capitalist idiom. There may even be a further pun between *burr* and "burrole," which was at this time a slang underworld expression for "an eavesdropper; one who seeks information; a stool pigeon" (f), for it is just this duplicitous world of concealed motives that Crane is dealing with.

The way in which high capitalism and the low criminal underworld come together in *The Bridge* is symptomatic of the way Crane's poem canonizes the commercial era it inhabits while at the same time subversively undercutting its idealistic pretensions. The poem's "myth to God" is thereby revealed as nothing more than a mercenary fiction:

> Under the Ozarks, domed by Iron Mountain,
> The old gods of the rain lie wrapped in pools

The "old gods" have been relocated inside the technological context of our twentieth-century "Iron" age. The gods are "wrapped in pools" as if to indicate how they have been reinvented in capitalist terms (a business "pool" or company: compare "The Tunnel," "How far away the star has *pooled* the sea"). The gods are of course a *lie*, an expedient and expendable image, but they impose upon the world a vision of coherence. Crane preserved an ambivalent attitude towards the American money-machine, for, although he recognized its brutalities, he delineated in "Atlantis" a world whose "harmony and system" was the aggrandizement of capitalism to a godhead, "Deity's glittering Pledge"; and it is precisely because of its disintegration of the individualistic and non-conformist world of the hoboes in "The River" that *The Bridge* can finally bring forth such a deliverance.

It may seem to us incredible, sixty years later, that *The Bridge* could so deviously secrete hidden meanings within itself. But the 1920s was an era when deception was all the rage: when bootlegging and crooked business deals were everyday facts of life, when undercover agents were heroes and when Prohibition was, as Ring Lardner put it, one better than no liquor. Part of the falsity of Crane's poem derives from its being very much a poem of its time. For Crane himself to have methodically pointed out how these disguises work would not only have taken the fun out of his poem, but would also have invalidated one side of *The Bridge's* raison d'être.

5

Burlesque

THE POCAHONTAS LEGEND

Burlesque plays were very popular in the United States, particularly in New York City, throughout the nineteenth century. The most celebrated exponent of this art was John Brougham (1810–80), an Irish wit skilled in all kinds of parody. The characteristic of these burlesques was their inclination to stand the established world on its head: to recast *Medea* as *My-Deary*, as was done in 1857.[1] Brougham was essentially an iconoclast, and his 1855 burlesque *Po-Ca-Hon-Tas; or, The Gentle Savage* travestied and so exposed the pretentious sentimentality that had accrued to the Indian legend during the nineteenth century. Brougham's play was constructed out of a huge number of emphasized puns (italicized in the printed text) which had the effect of undermining the dignity of his dramatis personae. Here, for instance, is Captain Smith promising Pocahontas he will keep his tale brief:

> I shall be *curt*, un*court*eous beauty, and *curt*ail it;
> *Begin*ning with the *end* I had in view,
> Which, upon my *soul*, was *sole*ly to see you, –
> When from the *verge* of yon *Virginny* fence
> I *saw* and *heard* a *sordid herd* advance!
> From the *spot* I would have turned to flee
> But one of the Chief's savages *spotted* me,
> And at his *back* the savage, at whose *beck*
> They have a *knack* of tightening one's *neck*![2]

And so on. Brougham kept up his punning throughout two long acts. Discussing the Pocahontas legend, Philip Young has said: "Brougham's burlesque was extremely well-received . . . and it performed a service for our drama that nothing has adequately performed for our poetry . . . Most nineteenth-century Pocahontas poems seem to begin either with some silly sylvan scene or with 'Descend O Muse, and this poor pen . . .'"3

But in fact Hart Crane's version of the Indian legend, "The Dance" section of *The Bridge*, does perform such a service, for it punningly refurbishes Pocahontas as a capitalist production of the 1920s. Indeed, the poet explicitly admits that the images we are presented with there are fraudulently manufactured:

> Lie to us – dance us back the tribal morn!

The passion for Pocahontas was, as R. W. B. Lewis has said, a "cliché of popular culture" in the 1920s, when the physical bounty of the "Red Man" was held up as an antidote to the cerebral agitations of a nervous Protestant civilization.4 Of course, the fact that this Indian myth could be reconstituted only through a commercialized and jazz-tinted lens did not invalidate its usefulness: indeed, the anthropomorphic images built into "The Dance" – the "Mythical *brows*" of the god of winter, the "Steep, inaccessible *smile*" of the Appalachian mountain range, the "sleek boat *nibbling* margin grass" – all these imply how any kind of mythology must necessarily be a linguistic and cultural fiction; but Crane's poem takes this anthropological perception one stage further to suggest how every era rewrites history in its own idiom to bolster its own beliefs. Crane was recognizing how "The Dance" of Pocahontas was more a dream of the capitalist 1920s than any kind of objective "truth" when he told Otto Kahn he was concerned in "Powhatan's Daughter" "to work backward through the pioneer period, *always in terms of the present*"; and when Yvor Winters claimed "The Dance" had failed in its attempt to become a spiritual apotheosis, Crane retorted that "mapping out heaven" was none of his business: "Here," Crane told Winters, "as often elsewhere, you confuse the intentionally relative with some interpolated 'absolute' of your own."5 This idea of an "intentionally relative" creative misreading is also given expression by the author's intentional puns inside "The Dance":

> There was a bed of leaves, and broken play;
> There was a veil upon you, Pocahontas, bride –
> O Princess whose brown lap was virgin May;
> And bridal flanks and eyes hid tawny pride.

Ho ho, a deceptive *veil* indeed: for what should we find behind "a veil" but "avail," "profit; return; proceeds." There was money to be made out of Pocahontas in the 1920s by redefining her in terms of packaged popular culture. The "bed of *leaves*" puns on the leaves of a book: Pocahontas has been transposed from natural object into cultural artefact; and so "broken *play*" is the poet's verbal play (punning) as well as the woman's sexual play. And if the "bridal flanks and eyes" thematically hide "tawny pride," they also verbally conceal the American slang "taw," "enough money to finance an enterprise; a stake" (f). No less than Columbus' voyage to America, the idealistic claims of the Pocahontas legend gloss over its origin as a pragmatic capitalist proposition:

> Now lie incorrigibly what years between . . .

What years between the objective truth of Pocahontas, and the *lie* or falsehood of this poem. And what *years* – "a banknote; a dollar" (f) – as well!

Similarly subversive puns occur a few lines later:

> A cyclone threshes in the turbine crest,
> Swooping in eagle feathers down your back

Crane mentioned in a letter to Yvor Winters how he had deliberately used "the turbine engine" to describe the *crest* of "the warrior's headdress," seeing this as an example of the bridging of past and present, "the currency of Indian symbolism in whatever is most real in our little native culture."[6] But currency is the right word, for the next line in Crane's poem reveals how Pocahontas has been redefined within a modern capitalist idiom. The *eagle* appears on American banknotes and coins, and in its own right specifically means a gold coin worth ten dollars; and so Crane suggests here that the "swopping" (a pun on *Swooping*) of the *eagle*, the processes of commercial transaction to which Pocahontas gives rise, *feathers* the *back* of a capitalist merchant with *down* (soft fluffy feathers). In other words, the money made from exploiting the Indian legend will provide the entrepreneur with a comfortable material living. Four stanzas later the same theme recurs:

> Spears and assemblies: black drums thrusting on –
> O yelling battlements, – I, too, was liege
> To rainbows currying each pulsant bone

The oscillation here is between an actual physical reality (the raining of bows, the arrows which the narrator "could not pick" from his side) and the distortion of this reality into something artificial and picturesque, the intangible *rainbows* which make up the commercial version of Indian legend. In this idyllic refraction, the *drums* become the tom-toms of glossy advertising ("drumming up" enthusiasm for Pocahontas), as the cunning capitalist world seeks to ingratiate itself (*currying* favour) with its market in order to extract from the consumer "each pulsant bone" (*bone* being American slang for "dollar").

In "The Dance," then, Crane's puns undermine the pastoral pretensions of Indian ritual as it was romanticized in the 1920s. There is indeed "Smoke swirling through the yellow chestnut glade," a deceptive smokescreen swirling around the hoary old *chestnut* of Pocahontas; but by transgressing the boundaries of decorous grammar, Crane's verbal play reveals the noble savage in a more mercenary light. Specific evidence that Crane was consciously exploiting burlesque forms in "The Dance" comes from a surviving piece of paper (E9 in Lohf, *Literary Manuscripts of Hart Crane*) upon which Crane has scrawled the titles of what seem to be comic songs on an Indian theme.[7] The full manuscript reads as follows:

Title

Pipe down, Pocohontas (name of comedy)
I'd like to Warm Your Wampum
Who Pokes your Hontas when I'm Gone
Wig Wagging in a Wigwam ("for two")
Who put the tea in Tepee
Tea in a Tepee

An Esquimaux Opera

I'm Happy in your happy Hunting Ground
Tommy-Hawk Tommy
I've got those Gichigume Blues (dance and song)
Naughty Nikomis (theme-song)
A Piece of your Peacepipe (waltz)
Katzenjammer-Saskatchewan (clog-dance)
Siskiyou-Sue (character-villain)
Sitting Bull Blues
Rain-in-the-face Rag (hit song)
Who Peaks your Pike while I Poke

A Kenneth Lohf said, Crane's titles "seem to have been for a comic opera about Indians"; and these songs appear to be Crane's original inventions, although Indian numbers along the same lines were rife during the 1920s: "Hiawatha's Melody of Love" was a hit record in 1920, for instance, as was "Indian Love Call (Rose Marie)" in 1924. Lohf added that the poet "used none of [these song titles] in his surviving work, but they offer evidence of at least his good-natured humor"; but now we can see that this humour is essential to the poem, for "The Dance" is not so much the "passionate native sacrificial" offering which Lohf applauded as the kind of burlesque performance that could have been acted out on the stage like one of Brougham's comic operas.[8] Crane's reference to "Katzenjammer-Saskatchewan" further emphasizes his recasting of the Indian myth in lowbrow terms, for the Katzenjammer kids were a gang of roguish children whose exploits used to be featured in a syndicated strip-cartoon in the Sunday newspapers. All those puns in the list above ("Who *Pokes* your *Hontas*," "*Tea* in a *Tepee*") suggest just the sort of popular comedy Brougham would have admired, and they also mirror the punning iconoclasm of "The Dance." The irreverence of Crane's attitude towards the past is further demonstrated by the way he selected the name of his unlikely Indian chieftain – "Know, Maquokeeta, greeting" – "merely from the hearsay of a NY taxi driver who was obviously of Indian extraction (and a splendid fire-drinker by the way) who said that his Indian name was 'Maquokeeta.'" Crane subsequently told this story to Yvor Winters and asked him whether Maquokeeta had any obviously "jarring connotations," but Crane then felt guilty about the otiose scholarly investigations which ensued. "Even if it has no existence as a name it's quite practical for my purposes, as it certainly *sounds* Indian enough to apply to a redskin," wrote Crane to Winters a month later; and in March 1927, he concluded: "I think that the Indian chieftain's name is all the better for not being particularly definite . . . I shall continue to depend on taxi drivers for all matters of folklore."[9] So Crane was concerned to rework the Indian legend in terms of the clichés of his own era; and while Crane's purpose – unlike Brougham's – was not straightforwardly comic, the burlesque element within "The Dance" is crucial to its meaning.

THE WORLD UPSIDE DOWN

Another offering of Brougham's was *Columbus El Filibustero!!*, produced at Burton's Theater, New York, in 1858. Here the heroic purpose of Columbus' voyage was undercut by its depiction as nothing more than "a gold-grabbing affair," as Constance Rourke put it.[10] The Almighty Dollar appears "in regal robes, promiscuously attended"; and the King of Spain is interested only in the material profits to be gained from the venture:

> If to our realm you'll add some foreign nation,
> Rich and disposed to stand extreme taxation . . .[11]

This is a forerunner of the bathetic commercial imagery we noticed in Crane's "Ave Maria," where Columbus ostensibly thanks God for his "teeming span" but is really more appreciative of the Ming span's tea (erroneously supposing he has uncovered a new trade-route between Spain and China). A few lines later Crane's hero talks of:

> White toil of heaven's cordons, mustering
> In holy rings all sails charged to the far
> Hushed gleaming fields . . .

Here Columbus is punningly anticipating how his voyage will eventually lead to "sales" (*sails*) being *charged* up on the "holy rings" of American cash-registers. The financial motivation behind this initial enterprise sets the pattern for the capitalist idiom of twentieth-century America. As Crane remarked to Waldo Frank, "the past is living under only slightly altered forms."[12] A further example of Crane's commercial idiom burlesquing the solemnity of Columbus' quest occurs in the lines

> Into thy steep savannahs, burning blue,
> Utter to loneliness the sail is true.

Here *burning* may be an adjectival participle – denoting the *burning* heat of the *blue* sea – or it may be a verbal participle, indicating Columbus' determined motion through the water: his ship consumes the *blue* ocean, *burning* it up as the ship sails for home. By extension from this, we have a Whiteheadian ambiguity: Columbus believes his *sail* is moving straight ahead with *true* purpose through the *blue* waves, but once we know that *blue* also designates "the south (south-seeking) pole of a magnet," we can see that the direction of Columbus' sail is not as self-willed as he himself imagines. So in the line "Utter to loneliness the sail is true" we find a dramatic irony revenging itself upon the Admiral, for his ship is quite clearly not utterly alone, as its movement is partially dependent upon the interaction of all kinds of impersonal forces – magnetism, the rotation of the earth and so on. Here, then, *true* is false; but if by a pun on *sail* we project forward to the "sales" on which the America of the 1920s depended, then we uncover a similar falsity, because to *Utter* can be "to put in circulation . . . counterfeit notes or coins." "Uttering false notes" is a jesting phrase used by Brougham in *Po-Ca-Hon-Tas* with the puns swinging between the uttering of speech and the uttering of money, and there it is quite clear from the context that Brougham intended *uttering* to denote fraud:

> KING: Here he comes; no *counterfeit* is he
> Like Smith, whose very name's a *forgery* . . .
> POCAHONTAS: I heard him *uttering false notes*, just now![13]

So in Crane's "Utter to loneliness the sail is true," the luckless Columbus finds not only his sail not true, but his sale not true either. Crane's commercial homophone equates the duplicities of financial dealing with those duplicities of magnetism and relativity which displace Columbus from the centre of his world; and this is typical of burlesque's tendency to compromise the dignity of the world into which it irrupts.

The inversions of burlesque are in the first place, of course, farcically comic; but in her book on *American Humor*, Constance Rourke portrayed burlesque as a particularly appropriate American art-form because of its propensity to destroy what was old, rigid and lofty. Rourke saw burlesque as a levelling and democratic mode which concerned itself with bringing to light the self-interested motives underpinning even the most elevated people. In the world of burlesque, nobody is allowed any moral superiority over anybody else. By extension from this, the tendency of burlesque to stand the established world on its head is a counterpart to the American Romantic dream which refuses to accept its environment as a *fait accompli*. American Romanticism's constant search for "New thresholds, new anatomies," as Crane put it in "The Wine Menagerie," runs parallel to the iconoclasm of burlesque which desires the overhauling of what is pre-existent. In Brougham's play, the King of Spain initially rejects Columbus' vision of "a corresponding half-world":

> What, turned upside down!
> Strange kind of man, to think mankind, like flies,
> Could in such strange position stand – he lies.

The King cannot believe anything could be so radically "turned upside down."[14] But the style of Brougham's burlesque is doing just that, inverting the King's royal dignity by transposing him into a comic clown; and this reversal of decorous form inherent in burlesque merges here into a reversal of the decorous philosophical precepts of the old medieval world. Columbus' voyage of discovery is itself a burlesque, an overturning, of the established world:

> FONESCA: So please you sire, the Vigilance Committee
> A foolish foreigner this day has found,
> Who swears, confound him, that the world is round,
> And swings, on what the fellow calls its *axis*,
> Just once a year.
> KING: He's thinking of the taxes.
> FONESCA: It taxes both credulity and patience.
> To listen to the mountebank's relations.
> QUEEN: Perhaps he's right – let's ask him here to sup,
> There may be something in –
> KING: My love, shut up.[15]

Crane's Columbus experiences exactly this sense of displacement as he returns from his voyage of discovery after having redrawn the map of the world:

> . . . lo, here
> Bewilderment and mutiny heap whelming
> Laughter . . .

The obsolescent adjective *whelming* means "turned upside down." In this sense, burlesque is an equivalent to the image of the hurricane, which comes up in "Ave Maria" ("And later hurricanes may claim more pawn") and, as Allen Grossman has noted, recurs throughout Crane's work ("Eternity," "O Carib Isle," "The Hurricane").[16] For the

hurricane also is symptomatic of this continual threat of inversion posed
to the visible world:

> Nought stayeth, nought now bideth
> But's smithereened apart!
>
> ("The Hurricane")

> Everything gone – or strewn in riddled grace –
> Long tropic roots high in the air, like lace.
>
> ("Eternity")

The hurricane, like burlesque, overhauls; and Crane's hurricane or
burlesque imagination was always hovering on the verge of destroying
the world's solid constructions. His Brooklyn Bridge is itself a burlesque
object, one that always faces the possibility of being reversed, for the way
in which creation and ironic destruction go hand in hand in *The Bridge*
(the "whitest Flower" flow-ing away into nought) is commensurate
with the insubstantial universe which Crane's burlesque presents.
Burlesque, like the hurricane, turns the world upside down. And it is
significant that Brougham should have italicized paradoxical contraries
as well as puns in his burlesque plays, because the effect of such linguistic
reversals and oppositions is to re-emphasize the propensity of burlesque
to turn established constructions on their head. In Brougham's burlesque
imagination, anything that can be said can be contradicted:

> But here you shall remain till you've resigned
> To settle *down* as I've made *up* my mind!

> *Single*, ere this, and now thus *doubly*-mated!

> Your voice all*owed*, but has your heart re*lent*ed?

> There's not a red marauder in the land
> But henceforth *seeks* your *hide* to have it tanned!

> You must *die early* so you can't *dilate!*[17]

As we shall see later, in Chapter 14, the poetry of Hart Crane is imbued
(slightly less obviously) with exactly the same kind of paradoxical
oppositions – "Toward *endless terminals*, Easters of speeding light," for
instance; and Crane's oxymorons serve a similar purpose, the burlesquing or overturning of objects' pretensions to solid autonomy.

Burlesque shows were very popular again in the 1920s. The Ziegfeld
Follies and the National Winter Garden were the two most famous
theatres; and in his 1924 book *The Seven Lively Arts*, Gilbert Seldes
polemically celebrated the "low" arts (of which burlesque was one) and
attacked what he saw as the false solemnity of opera and drama inside a
desiccated genteel tradition. In "The River," Crane mentions Bert

Williams, the Negro comedian who frequently appeared at the National
Winter Garden before his death in 1922:

> . . . under the new playbill ripped
> in the guaranteed corner – see Bert Williams what?

We are left in ignorance of "what" Williams proposed to do because his
name simply peeps out from the corner of an old playbill which has had a
more up-to-date poster pasted on top of it. But *corner* puns on "corn-er,"
one who produces "corn," slang for sentimentality; and Williams' stage-
act, like *The Bridge* itself, is a "guaranteed corner," a vaudeville turn
which goes through its comic and slushy repertoire while being at the
same time ironically aware of its own performance. The pun here on *corn*
is the same as in "Atlantis":

> Pacific here at time's end, bearing corn

William H. Pritchard naïvely criticized "the idea, say, of 'getting under
the skin' of a 'glorious and dying Indian'" as "the least attractive and the
corniest aspect of *The Bridge*"; but one of the essential points about
burlesque was its own consciousness of inhabiting this world of
sentimentality and illusion.[18] Fanny Brice singing "My Man" in the
1921 Ziegfeld Follies was liable to find Joseph Urban's flimsy stage-sets
of the Eiffel Tower crumbling about her shoulders, for the clichés of
Parisian romance were deliberately presented tongue in cheek. In
burlesque, emotional reaction is not cancelled, but sentimentality and
irony go hand in hand; and *The Bridge* extends this principle to imply the
ultimately fictive nature of all myth. Crane's poem conjures up the
sentimental emotions inherent in myth while at the same time ironizing
those sentiments, as in these typical "corny" lines from "The River":

> And if it's summer and the sun's in dusk
> Maybe the breeze will lift the River's musk
> – As though the waters breathed that you might know
> *Memphis Johnny, Steamboat Bill, Missouri Joe.*
> Oh, lean from the window, if the train slows down,
> As though you touched hands with some ancient clown,
> – A little while gaze absently below
> And hum *Deep River* with them while they go.

This highly implausible scenario depends upon a series of picturesque
coincidences ("*if* it's summer *and* the sun's in dusk," "*Maybe* the breeze,"
"*if* the train slows down") and even then its fulfilment would rely upon
the vivid daydreams of the onlooker ("*As though* the waters breathed,"
"*As though* you touched hands"). This "ancient clown," if not actually a
concoction of some advertising agency, is part of that American popular
mythology which is hardly to be distinguished from pure fiction. This is

not necessarily derogatory: the gently parodic and Disneyesque ambience of "ancient clown" suggests how the rhetorical imagination can spin fictions out of mid-air, fictions which exist provisionally without being accredited as final "truth." Crane himself worked intermittently for advertising firms, and the chimerical fictions of advertising formed as much a part of Crane's cast of mind as, say, the medical doctor's life infiltrated the mental landscape of William Carlos Williams. Appropriately enough, Crane wrote to Waldo Frank in 1926: "A bridge will be written in some kind of style and form, at worst it will be something as good as advertising copy."[19]

So the sentimentality of "Indiana," "Van Winkle" and so on is part of Crane's deliberate design. Crane's subjects in *The Bridge* are the clichés of American history: Columbus and Pocahontas were actually burlesqued by Brougham, as we have seen, and Ring Lardner created a sketch about Rip Van Winkle for the Ziegfeld Follies of 1923.[20] In one of his letters to Kahn, Crane specifically stated that the beginning of "The River" was "an international burlesque on the cultural confusion of the present," and the word *burlesque* here should not be taken as a synonym for satire.[21] For the function of burlesque, like the function of the pun, is essentially iconoclastic: it presents the audience with a stereotyped image, at the same time as subversively disrupting that image, so that the spectator is compelled to observe the object from two different angles at once. "Some Angelus environs the cordage tree" puts Columbus forward as epic voyager and mercenary adventurer both at once. "There was a veil [avail] upon you, Pocahontas, bride" similarly burlesques the Indian Queen through an iconoclastic commercial pun. The idea of burlesque goes back as far as Shakespeare: the "rural fellow" who brings Cleopatra figs ensures she is seen as childish clown as well as heroic queen, and this pivots her between tragic dignity and mere pathos by demonstrating how her "immortal longings" are rooted in an irredeemably human environment. We see all sides of Cleopatra and not just the noble façade she would wish her audience to see. The best theorist of burlesque in the 1920s was Crane's friend E. E. Cummings, who wrote an essay on the subject for a 1925 issue of *Vanity Fair* (emphasis in original):

> in burlesk . . . "opposites" occur *together*. For that reason, burlesk enables us to (so to speak) *know around* a thing, character or situation. To put it a little differently: if the art of common-or-garden painting were like the art of burlesk, we should be able to see – impossibly enough – all the way around a solid tree, instead of merely seeing a little more than half of the tree (thanks to binocular parallax or whatever it is) and imagining the rest. This impossible knowing around, or nonimagining, quality, constitutes the essence of burlesk and differentiates it from certain better-understood arts.[22]

This fusion of opposites which Cummings saw as central to burlesque is also central to *The Bridge*, a burlesque poem which bridges opposites through its use of puns.

The link between pun and burlesque is emphasized by the way New York's National Winter Garden was the home of the pun during the 1920s. Edmund Wilson quoted one citizen as saying "when he wanted to hear 'dubble-entenders'" he would rather go to the Winter Garden than anywhere else, because "here's where you get burlesque as you like it, without any camouflage – sincere dubble-entenders."[23] We have already seen how Crane's "National Winter Garden," the second of his "Three Songs," contains punning indications of the theatre's involvement with the machinery of capitalism, and we have noted the dehumanizing tendencies in the poem. But Crane's attitude towards the striptease is double-edged, and part of the fascination the place holds for him lies in the way it overturns human individuality by sending all the participants in its ritual, strippers and audience alike, spinning on an axis of lust and money. Capitalism is the agent which breaks down false ideas of gentility. In this respect capitalism resembles burlesque, for nothing can escape the spikes of its iconoclasm. Just as Columbus' altruistic romantic heroism is undermined by the puns which point out his material greed, so Crane's "National Winter Garden" conjoins capitalism, pun and burlesque in its effort to decompose the autonomy of human character – which eventually becomes reconstituted in a new form. The dehumanizing cash-nexus is the means of this transition, for after conscripting all the forsaken "eyes" into the "inviolate curve" of profit-and-loss, the poet can then proceed to invest these algebraic equations with mythological significance by accrediting them with Platonic harmony, as we see in the epigraph to the last section of *The Bridge*, "Atlantis" ("Music is then the knowledge of that which relates to love in harmony and system"). America's financial system becomes a kind of mystical mathematics, and the profits' pledge of Brooklyn Bridge a "myth to God."

So although the strippers and their admirers seem to become ciphers in "National Winter Garden," and although this is certainly the negative pole of Crane's mechanical paradise, it is surely wrong to take such a sanctimonious attitude as have previous critics of the poem, who have been unanimous in their disgust at this "shoddy, sleazy world" (R. W. Butterfield), this "modern lapse from the erotic universe represented in vegetative myth" (Sherman Paul).[24] We should notice that the last stanza compares the stripper to Mary Magdalene – not a saint turned prostitute, but a prostitute turned saint, and the woman who discovered Christ after he had risen from the tomb. Crane's striptease artist is similarly the harbinger of a resurrection; and thematically there is an important comma at the end of this poem's penultimate line:

> Yet to the empty trapeze of your flesh,
> O Magdalene, each comes back to die alone.
> Then you, the burlesque of our lust − and faith,
> Lug us back lifeward − bone by infant bone.

It is not faith which lugs us back, it is Magdalene. Magdalene is the burlesque of human lust and of human faith. Although it is possible to read *faith* as the redemptive agent, which would secularize the process of renewal and make it more dependent on an effort of human will, this romantic freedom is balanced by reliance on a more impersonal power, in the same way as Columbus' epic discovery of America was balanced and made possible by the financial backing of the Spanish court. And so how very appropriate it is that *infant* should be an obsolete form of "infanta," "any legitimate daughter of a king of Spain or Portugal" or "a young lady likened to a Spanish or Portuguese infanta," for symbolically the striptease-artist Magdalene is the offspring of the Spanish nobleman Columbus. Just as the Spanish court sponsored Columbus' quest to the New World, Magdalene will sponsor Crane's quest to Atlantis. Equally ingenious is the fact of *bone* being American slang for a dollar, for just as Columbus required gold to finance his voyage, Crane requires dollars to symbolize the financial bonds of his Platonic continent. And nothing could be more proper than that this burlesque poem should sign off with a pair of "bones" (*bone*: "one of the end men in a negro minstrel performance"). Bert Williams, mentioned in the opening lines of "The River" (as we have seen), was one of these bones, a Negro vaudevillean who often used to feature at the National Winter Garden. As Williams' stage-character was that of the perpetual loser, his appearance anticipates the exploited Negro labourers humming "Deep River" later in "The River"; and this implies how the whole of *The Bridge* is and is intended to be a burlesque performance. On the surface, "bone by infant bone" carries grim overtones of the hard epic struggle involved in rejuvenating the human body; but the alternative readings indicate how the means towards this freedom is the comedy of the cash-nexus and the facility to become part of this seemingly childish (*infant*) burlesque world.

So Crane's quest is less a journey towards self-knowledge than towards self-parody. The assimilation of burlesque forms becomes a moral imperative. This was a familiar theme of E. E. Cummings' *Vanity Fair* essays in the 1920s, where Cummings celebrated menageries, circuses and burlesque theatres as looking-glasses inclined to disburden Cambridge ladies of the self-sufficiency of their furnished souls. By seeing themselves travestied in this way, thought Cummings, the audience would become sufficiently deprived of their customary identities to acquiesce in a cheerful lower-case anonymity inside time. For Cummings, burlesque, like Freudian therapy, was an agent of

impersonality to whom men could confess their lack of uniqueness; and
he opined that four-fifths of American hospitals, jails and insane-asylums
would close down if every adult were compelled to visit the circus twice
a year.[25] In this context, we should notice as well how the form of
"National Winter Garden," with its rhyme-scheme patterned so that the
first half of each stanza mirrors the second, is a technical counterpart to
Crane's thematic impulse: something we can appreciate most clearly by
contrasting "National Winter Garden" with its immediate predecessor,
"Southern Cross," the first of the "Three Songs":

> Whatever call – falls vainly on the wave.
> O simian Venus, homeless Eve,
> Unwedded, stumbling gardenless to grieve
> Windswept guitars on lonely decks forever;
> Finally to answer all within one grave!

The discordant half-rhymes here – "wave," "Eve," "for*ever*" – are a
formal corollary of the idea of isolation prevalent within "Southern
Cross." These sounds fall "vainly on the wave" and are "Unwedded";
and the lack of perfect rhymes reflects the lonely state of the protagonist,
for he too is "Unwedded" – both lover and vowel are searching for their
perfect mate. In "National Winter Garden," however, singular has
become plural, for the second and fourth lines respond directly to each
other:

> Always and last, before the final ring
> When all the fireworks blare, begins
> A tom-tom scrimmage with a somewhere violin,
> Some cheapest echo of them all – begins.

This is one of Crane's clever jokes: *begins* in the fourth line is indeed the
"cheapest echo of them all," for its purpose is to chime with *begins* in the
second, and when the poet needs a rhyme, he can't have an echo cheaper
than the same word again! (Crane's dash in the fourth line demonstrates
how that *begins* is supposed to be emphasized.) But this is especially
interesting, because it shows Crane consciously foregrounding the play
of language: in a more traditional conceptual sense, of course, "National
Winter Garden" is a cheap echo of the Pocahontas theme; but the
comedy of burlesque, where audience (and, in this case, vowel-forms)
find themselves reflected in mirrors, was also crucial to Crane's meaning
in this poem – and indeed throughout the rest of *The Bridge*.

"CUTTY SARK"

The centrality of burlesque to Crane's mythic design is emphasized by
the intrusion of capitalist and theatrical enterprises into the seafaring

"Cutty Sark" section. The failed quest of the previous poem, "Indiana," and the redundancy of the whaler introduced in the opening lines of "Cutty Sark" signify the exhaustion of a pioneering, frontier mentality; and the imagery in "Cutty Sark" turns upon a transmutation of epic into pastoral, linear into circular. Thus: "*Heave, weave |* those bright designs the trade winds drive . . ." (the exhaustion of "heaving" becoming the pattern-making of "weaving"); "*Pennants, parabolas*" (the sharp point of a pennant becoming a parabolic curve); "It's S.S. *Ala*–Antwerp . . ." (the epic connotations of *Ala*, Latin for "wing," transferred into *Antwerp*, a Belgian homing-pigeon). "Cutty Sark" epitomizes the withdrawal from a Romantic clash with the unknowable whiteness of the ocean, and moves instead towards the ocean's domestication within forms of myth, illusion and Noble Lie.

One of the ways in which the ocean becomes anaesthetized is through commerce, and the last part of "Cutty Sark" describes American ships racing home with the first of the China tea-crop, as if to imply how the seas may become regulated into a corporate plaything rather than remaining obstinately inhuman (emphasis in original):

> *Sweet opium and tea, Yo-ho!*
> *Pennies for porpoises that bank the keel!*
> *Fins whip the breeze around Japan!*

The porpoises or small whales "bank the keel" in the sense of skirting around these whaling ships, but – by a typical Craneian reversal of subject and object – the keels also *bank* them, convert them into items of economic profit (hence the "*Pennies* for porpoises"). The grammatical metamorphosis is an equivalent to the poem's thematic metamorphosis, for Crane's transposition of epic freedom into corporate system is reflected in the way these subjects are verbally displaced from the centre of their world, to become mere objects that are controlled by the forces they thought they were controlling. And it is also highly apt that *Fins* should "whip the breeze around Japan": for the "fin" is a fish's steering organ, of course, but it is also a slang word for a five-dollar bill (f). Crane's puns comically puncture the seafaring world and redefine it in terms of a capitalist perspective (emphasis in original):

> *at Java Head freshened the nip*
> *(sweet opium and tea!)*

Apparently *nip* as breeze: but also *nip* as slang for the Japanese man who is "freshened" not so much by healthy breezes as by the "sweet opium and tea" whose allure permits this cycle of trade to continue. Here is another of our grammatical reversals: "sweet opium and tea freshened the nip!"

With all this interest in things Oriental, nothing could be more appropriate than an echo from *The Mikado*, an opera by Gilbert and

Sullivan (two of the favourite artists of Gilbert Seldes, the great
champion of "lively arts") which is actually set in Japan! *The Mikado* is a
burlesque performance which, like commerce, imposes a playful order
upon the world:

> Blithe Yankee vanities, turreted sprites, winged
> > British repartees, skil-
> ful savage sea-girls
> that bloomed in the spring – Heave, weave
> those bright designs the trade winds drive . . .

In *The Mikado*, the Lord High Executioner Ko-Ko finds Nanki-Poo
inveigling him into marriage with Katisha as the only way to save his life.
"When Katisha is married," she assures him, "existence will be as
welcome as the flowers in spring." As they contemplate the forthcoming
nuptials, Ko-Ko and Nanki-Poo sing a duet:

> The flowers that bloom in the spring,
> Tra la,
> > Breathe promise of merry sunshine –
> As we merrily dance and we sing,
> Tra la,
> We welcome the hope that they bring,
> Tra la,
> > Of a summer of roses and wine;
> > And that's what we mean when we say that a thing
> > Is welcome as flowers that bloom in the spring
> Tra la la la la la &c.[26]

R. W. B. Lewis complained of how "Crane's cross references get
muddled incongruously with Gilbert and Sullivan." But "winged
British repartees" should have convinced Lewis that these references
were not accidental: *winged* ("swift") *repartees* ("a clever, ready, and
witty reply or retort") are exactly what Gilbert and Sullivan's *British*
productions specialize in, with the repartees being a lowbrow form of
Atlantean antiphonal whispers swinging to and fro. Lewis professed
himself disconcerted by these lines: "British clippers," he said, "are
envisioned, surprisingly, as 'savage sea-girls / that bloomed in the
spring'"; but again what we have here is the aesthetic re-production of the
functional world, its transposition into burlesque and myth.[27] Those
sprites (sprite: "a shade; ghost; spirit") are in the first place the hulks of
old-fashioned ships like the British man-of-war the *Temeraire*, celebrated
by Melville in an elegy quoted as epigraph to "Cutty Sark":

> O, the navies old and oaken
> O, the Temeraire no more!

In this case, "turrets" would be those revolving towers "within which heavy guns are mounted . . . on vessels of war." But as if to demonstrate how the epic conflict of war has been metamorphosed into the pastoral play of theatre, those *sprites* can also be the elf-like girls of a Gilbert and Sullivan chorus, with "turrets" becoming the cute little towers ("often a merely ornamental structure") which make up the stage-set. So the "bright designs the trade winds drive," as well as being ornamental ensigns blown about on the ocean-waves, are also theatrical colours subject to the harsh winds of trade; and there is a similar punning analogy involved in "Bright skysails ticketing the Line": on one hand a line of sailing-ships in the distance, on the other hand a bright outlook for the commercial "sales" (*sails*) of theatre-tickets which the customers in this *Line* are queuing for. Like the whaling trade, Broadway is obliged to work within a capitalist system and pander to economic necessity, and this capitalist system is capable of domesticating the terrifying emptiness of the ocean (emphasis in original):

> the star floats burning in a gulf of tears
> and sleep another thousand –

As Crane told Otto Kahn, " 'Cutty Sark' is built on the plan of a *fugue*," and "Two 'voices' – that of the world of Time, and that of the world of Eternity – are interwoven in the action."[28] The eternal *star* floating in the heavens may burn patiently for a thousand years; but the temporal *star* in the *floats* or footlights of this Broadway stage has a more immediate purpose, to act as a cathartic agent which "burns in" the tears of the audience, thereby putting "another thousand" of the citizens to "sleep." If the audience discharge their emotional energy upon manufactured entertainment, they will have less inclination to worry themselves about the grim realities of life and death that so perturbed the alienated old whaler. So his poem's puns are the means by which Crane interweaves alternative meanings and alternative worlds.

The structure of "Cutty Sark," then, is a structure of reversal:

> or are there frontiers – running sands sometimes
> running sands – somewhere – sands running . . .
> Or they may start some white machine that sings.
> Then you may laugh and dance the axletree –

The frontiersman has always been concerned with *running* the *sands* of the sea, but now in his old age he finds that for him the *sands* of time are *running* out. This verbal inversion of "running sands" into "sands running" is indicative of the tendency within "Cutty Sark" to burlesque or turn upside down; and death, of course, is the supreme burlesque, the levelling of all human schemes and constructions. Like Melville's Ahab, Crane's mariner in "Cutty Sark" has attempted to conquer the physical world, but has subsequently found the ineluctable physical world revenging itself upon him. So at this point "Cutty Sark" turns away from transcendence towards immanence: the inhospitable white ocean is transmuted into a sociable juke-box, "some white machine that sings"; and these revellers in South Street "dance the axletree" as if to manifest their acquiescence in human limitation and contentment. The phrase "I started walking home across the Bridge . . ." which concludes the first part of the poem signifies once again Crane's modification of the pioneering ethic into a harmonic pastoral dance; and the lines immediately preceding this recapitulate earlier sections of *The Bridge*:

> interminably
> long since somebody's nickel – stopped –
> playing –
>
> A wind worried those wicker-neat lapels, the
> swinging summer entrances to cooler hells . . .
> Outside a wharf truck nearly ran him down
> – he lunged up Bowery way while the dawn
> was putting the Statue of Liberty out – that
> torch of hers you know –
>
> I started walking home across the Bridge . . .

The phrase "somebody's nickel" echoes "Van Winkle" ("Keep hold of that nickel for car-change, Rip"); "wharf truck" takes us back to "The Harbor Dawn" ("And then a truck will lumber past the wharves"); and with "dawn . . . putting the Statue of Liberty out" we are back in the world of the "Proem." The effect is something like a film rewinding, an appropriate device for a poem which will end where it began, and whose "philosophy" revolves upon the idea of time going round in a circle to reincarnate itself in slightly different forms.

So in "Cutty Sark" everything "progresses backwards," as Crane told Otto Kahn; and the pun is the agent of this reversal, for by turning the "sails" of ships into the "sales" of theatre-tickets, and by turning the *Fins* of porpoises into the five-dollar *Fins* traders gain for catching those porpoises, Crane's puns are deliberately rewriting an epic world as a mock-epic world.[29] In his essay on "The Comic," Emerson defined comedy as the discrepancy between high-minded idealism and "the crooked, lying, thieving fact"; and he said that the failure to realize an idea's full potential, "an honest or well-intended halfness," epitomized that inextinguishably comic side of human nature which, by mocking the transcendental ego, preserved that ego's sanity and its sense of sympathy with other men.[30] This acquiescence in limitation is exactly what we have in "Cutty Sark": the punning transposition of ocean-going vessels into a Gilbert and Sullivan jest indicates the irruption of burlesque into quotidian existence. But this irruption comes to have mythopoeic importance, for burlesque, pun and capitalism are the iconoclastic agents which distintegrate objects' claims to independent self-sufficiency; and by metamorphosing these once solid objects into components within its own rules of "harmony and system," *The Bridge* can thereby succeed in proposing its capitalist "myth to God." Crane's inversion of epic into mock-epic is comic, but not merely comic, for burlesque uncovers those mercenary interests which all human beings have in common. The world upside down is a world where everyone is on the same level. Nobody can step outside the frame of capitalism. In this way, burlesque becomes a levelling device which reveals how the capitalist myth of Brooklyn Bridge is able to subsume everyone under its benign providence.

6

Bridge as myth

In one of his essays on *The Bridge*, Allen Tate suggested that Crane's sentimental approach to American history, especially in "Powhatan's Daughter," formed part of the poet's deliberate design. The skilfully manipulated simplicity of Crane's approach was, said Tate, "the history of the motion picture, of naïve patriotism. This is sound; for it ignores the scientific ideal of historical truth-in-itself, and looks for a cultural truth which might win the spontaneous allegiance of the people."[1] The idea of "spontaneous allegiance" was one of Tate's feudalisms, of course; Tate, like Eliot, cherished a reactionary vision of the ordered community. Nevertheless, as we have seen, *The Bridge* is a poem quite consciously "bearing corn," delivering sentimentality while at the same time ironizing that sentimentality; and this kind of deliberate deception is given theoretical justification as early as the third stanza of the "Proem":

> I think of cinemas, panoramic sleights
> With multitudes bent toward some flashing scene
> Never disclosed, but hastened to again,
> Foretold to other eyes on the same screen

As Joseph J. Arpad has noted, this refers to the cave-allegory in Plato's *Republic*, where the stupefied masses are depicted as prisoners able to see only the shadows of things on their cave-wall, in contrast to the heroic philosopher who stands outside the cave and perceives ideal forms. Contemporary commentators such as R. H. S. Crossman in *Plato Today* (1937) have seen in this a model for social engineering: the Noble Lies on the cave-wall appeal to the emotions of "the stupid majority" and stimulate them into obeying the law.[2] Crane may not have been as coldly cynical as this, and he may have believed myths tend to grow organically inside a civilization rather than being simply the impositions of external authorities, but the point remains that myth creates internal logic but not absolute truth. Crane was an assiduous reader of the old father of lies, and he recognized his own connection with Plato in a letter to Gorham Munson on 17 March 1926:

> What you admire in Plato as "divine sanity" is the architecture of his logic. Plato doesn't live today because of the intrinsic "truth" of his statements: their only living truth today consists in the "fact" of their harmonious relationship to each other in the context of his organization of them. This grace partakes of poetry.[3]

The sense of the stanza from the "Proem" quoted above is that the cinema-screen interposes itself to defend Man against untutored nature, and so both reflects and creates the illusions society bases itself upon. The massive popularity of the cinema in America during the 1920s ensured that the fictions of Fairbanks, Pickford, Chaplin and other stars of the silver screen were rapidly acquiring mythic status. Indeed, Otto H. Kahn, the banker who subsidized Crane's *Bridge*, was at this time also one of the major financiers behind the Paramount motion picture company, and this sense of official patronage may have reinforced Crane's desire to write a public poem inscribing the legends of America rather than one chronicling simply the legends of his own soul.[4]

We have seen how Crane exploits capitalist metaphors to create his "myth to God"; but we have also seen how he acknowledges that relativity ironically circumscribes all myths, rendering them provisional rather than absolute. The kind of irony that breaks down poetic form is a familiar aspect of Crane's lyric style in the *White Buildings* collection:

> What fountains did I hear? what icy speeches?
> Memory, committed to the page, had broke.
>
> ("Passage")

> Scatter these well-meant idioms
> Into the smoky spring that fills
> The suburbs, where they will be lost.
> They are no trophies of the sun.
>
> ("Praise for an Urn")

In both these poems the artistic creation is presented as a temporary moment of vision, soon to be retracted. Similarly in *The Bridge* the mythic symbols of America become temporary creations, expedient fictions, hedged around by irony and relativity. The conflict is between land and water, with Brooklyn Bridge attempting to conquer the sea both literally and figuratively. As Crane wrote to Yvor Winters on 15 November 1926, his long poem was designed to arrange the Western world "in chronological and organic order, out of which you get a kind of bridge, the quest of which bridge is – nothing less ambitious than the annihilation of time and space, the prime myth of the modern world."[5] The "prime *myth* of the modern world." The Bridge will "*lend* a myth to God," posit a Platonic Noble Lie rather than demand that its myth become objective truth. And Crane manipulates his puns and syntactical ambiguities to propose and dispose of myth at one and the same time:

> Thy cables breathe the North Atlantic still.

The Bridge's cables attempt to superimpose themselves on the ocean's tides, to render them *still* or quiescent; but this idea of order is ironically undercut by the knowledge that even now (*still* as adverb) the Bridge is compelled to gather its life-giving substance from those waters that will eventually wear it away to nought. This pun from the "Proem" was spotted by Eugene Paul Nassar, who discussed Crane's ironies in his book *The Rape of Cinderella* and concluded that "the building of delightful, necessary illusions is the core-definition of myth-making with which Hart Crane works."[6] Nassar saw *The Bridge* as turning upon the conflict between transcendental belief and a sceptical undercutting of such belief, and he was sympathetic to the idea of the pun as an expression of this dualism. Of "Ave Maria," Nassar wrote,

> The pun on "through thy mantle's ageless blue" is quite conscious, referring to the Catholic concept of Mary's power of intercession but also to the blank blue of the heavens under which man lives. Crane wants this ambivalence of attitude, this poise between Columbus' faith and the poet's doubt.[7]

Certainly. And the way that in the same stanza the dumbfounded Indians hail Columbus' ships as "The Great White Birds," divinities descended from the heavens, is an implicit comment upon Columbus' invocation of "Madre Maria," for – like the Indians – Columbus must explain to himself in supernatural terms a material world he cannot fully understand. In this way a dramatic irony subverts Columbus' dignity, because he becomes equated with the Indians:

> And lowered. And they came out to us crying,
> "The Great White Birds!" (O Madre Maria, still
> One ship of these thou grantest safe returning;
> Assure us through thy mantle's ageless blue!)

And it is also apposite that Mary's blue cloak or *mantle* of Catholic iconography should pun on *mantle* as "in birds, the back together with the folded wings." Crane's pun once more equates Christianity with the "White Birds" of pagan anthropomorphism, and produces an ontological ambivalence: in both cases the picturesque image may be mythopoeically necessary, but is nevertheless exposed as an illusion. The telling of fables to protect oneself against overwhelming darkness was a familiar theme of modernism, of course, and Nassar compared Crane to Wallace Stevens, whose ideas of order similarly superimpose language upon the ironic sea. Nassar found all kinds of thematic ironies in *The Bridge* and saw Crane's puns as ancillary to this, whereas the argument here is that Crane's ironies are more verbally centred, with the pun as bridge being at the very heart of the matter.

We see this in the very first stanza of the "Proem":

> How many dawns, chill from his rippling rest
> The seagull's wings shall dip and pivot him,
> Shedding white rings of tumult, building high
> Over the chained bay waters Liberty —

The last line presents us with an image of the New York harbour mapping out nature, the "bay waters" being *chained* to allow the flourishing of *Liberty*, which is both the Statue and – by extension – the American constitution. But this optimism has a negative underside: *waters* may become a verb, suggesting that *Liberty* will be gradually eroded, watered away into nothing. It is the kind of Whiteheadian reversal of noun and verb so typical of Crane. A similar inversion, this time of subject and object, is used in "Atlantis" to reveal the ambiguities inherent in myth:

> Of inchling aeons silence rivets Troy.

During its lifetime *Troy* (active subject) rivets silence (demands its citizens' acquiescence in common beliefs); but all these constructions must be provisional, for eventually *silence* (active subject) rivets Troy: time grinds the city into the dust of oblivion, as a famous passage in the second book of the *Aeneid* laments. We have already noted how the pun inside "palladium helm of stars" links the silver stars surrounding the New York night back to the protection granted by Pallas Athene to the citadel of Troy, and Crane's ambiguities are consistent with the way in which early twentieth-century anthropologists were continually emphasizing the impermanence and relativity of human systems. But the anthropologists also pointed out how each civilization established itself by transposing concrete history into imaginative myth, something appreciated by Ezra Pound when he wrote in 1909 that one of the prerequisites for the creation of an American epic poem was a "damn long time for the story to lose its garish detail and get encrusted with a bunch of beautiful lies."[8] During the 1920s Freud was working in the area of society and religion, and in his essays *Group Psychology and the Analysis of the Ego* (1921) and *The Future of an Illusion* (1927) Freud signalled his disapproval of mythological fictions which in his opinion tended to frustrate the development of individual responsibility and maturity. Nevertheless Freud did recognize the powerful allure of religion or of any organized group which acted as some kind of substitute father inside whose security infants could repose. Crane's own copy of *Group Psychology* still exists (signed inside "Hart Crane '26"); but, unlike Freud, Crane seems to have apprehended myth as an inevitable and necessary social control, a form of order no less valid for being illusory and temporary.

It will be clear that Crane's riddling juxtapositions of positive and negative polarities are most apparent in "Proem" and "Atlantis," those sections of *The Bridge* where the land does indeed meet the sea. This is not to say that other kinds of puns and ambiguities do not persist throughout Crane's long poem, but the direct oscillation between order and chaos is most obvious here. Take four lines from "Atlantis":

> Up the index of night, granite and steel –
> Transparent meshes – fleckless the gleaming staves –
> Sibylline voices flicker, waveringly stream
> As though a god were issue of the strings. . . .

On the surface the geometry of Brooklyn Bridge portions out the night, but, as we saw in our discussion of relativity, the last line performs Crane's familiar trick of pulling in contrary direction: is it the god who "issues" the strings, or is he "issued" by them? That is to say, is he a First Cause, or merely a consolatory fiction? We may indeed wonder if *The Bridge* has not been "stringing" us along all the time (string: "a hoax; a trumped-up or 'fake' story. *Slang*"). If we should settle for a positive interpretation, those *staves* will signify the integration of the Bridge into a harmonious relationship with the American landscape (stave: "the five horizontal lines, with their spaces, on which music is written"). This is the Bridge as a harp, and it can also be a ship guarding itself against ("staving off") the surrounding waters (stave: "to render impervious or solid by driving with a calking iron; as, to *stave* lead"). The pessimistic reader, however, will surmise that *staves* may also be negative (stave: "to break in a stave or the staves of; to break a hole in . . . as, to *stave* in a boat"); and this line then begins to imply that the *night* which is *gleaming* through the "Transparent meshes" of the Bridge is a perpetual reminder of the fragility of human institutions. Melville uses *stave* in a similarly double-edged way in *Moby-Dick*: "and come a stove boat and stove body when they will, for stave my soul, Jove himself cannot."[9] Ishmael's "stave my soul" could imply either Jove's failure to save his soul, to render it impervious, or Jove's failure to stave in Ishmael's proud soul and crush it into nought. In Crane's poem, *staves* participates in a demonic Whiteheadian reversal: is the poet celebrating the exuberant *gleaming* (adjective) *staves* (noun) of Brooklyn Bridge? Or is it the night's *gleaming* (noun) that *staves* (verb) the Bridge and collapses it into nothing? In this latter case, the Bridge's machinery would not be *fleckless* (blemishless) but rather "feckless" ("spiritless; weak; worthless"); and the *Sibylline* ("prophetical; mysterious; occult") voices would not whisper temptingly, but give up the ghost altogether (*flicker*: "to fail; flunk. Local, U.S."). The Bridge can be maintained as a credible myth only by a defensive process of shutting off the night, the sea and certain areas of forbidden knowledge; and this proscription exactly resembles the papal *index*, which here (transmogrified into the lights of the Bridge) appropriately remains *Up*. The pun is similar to that noted by R. W. B. Lewis in "Chaplinesque," where the *index* suggests those literary ideas outlawed in philistine America.[10] In "Atlantis" Crane is more sympathetic to censorship, and "index of night" is a cunning paradox: the brightness of the New York lights indicates how dark the literal night is; but the symbolic night of nihilism must be repressively placed on the index so that the symbolic lights of mythic poetry are able to shine through. Everything about this passage does indeed "waveringly stream," vacillate uncertainly between one possibility and another.

The pun on *strings* as hoax or trumped-up story also appears in the "Proem":

> (How could mere toil align thy choiring strings!)

The conflict is between the toil of the sea (*mere*, a pun on *mer*, Latin and French for sea) as opposed to "a lie in" (*align*) the hoax or *strings* of the poem, for *choiring* puns on "quire-ing," the quires or sheets of paper upon which Crane's mythic poem is inscribed. The pun on "mere" as sea is a frequent device of Crane's, employed most obviously in his four line poem "The Return," which considers the concept of regression to a primal source:

> The sea raised up a campanile . . . The wind I heard
> Of brine partaking, whirling spout in shower
> Of column kiss – that breakers spouted, sheared
> Back into bosom–me-her, into natal power . . .[11]

Here the "bosom" of sea and mother are explicitly equated. The sea becomes analogous to "natal power." And this analogy finds its verbal counterpart in the fusion of "me-her" into "mere": French *mère*, mother, and *mer*, sea. Although Crane tended to be self-deprecatory about his knowledge of languages, pointing out he never even finished high school, he cannot have been entirely ignorant of French because twenty-four books in that language have survived from his library, many of them with annotations and the occasional word translated in the margin. Certainly it is unlikely *mer* and *mère* would have been beyond him. And indeed absolute proof that Crane was conversant with the idea of bilingual punning comes with a letter Crane sent to Kenneth Burke on 16 November 1923 which started off "Dear Butter-Tail," for when Burke sold this letter to Pennsylvania State University Library, he added an explanatory note at the bottom of the page: "To save my honor I must make haste to explain the epithet. Bill Brown used to write me as 'Beurre-que,' a kind of 'French' for 'Burke.' From that the joke developed in bilingual punning to 'butter-that.' And Hart added a further development, as per the epithet." So: Burke to "Beurre-que," butter that; and "Beurre-que" to "Beurre-queue," butter-tail ("queue" as French for tail). Crane simply could not have made this joke if he had been ignorant of French or uninterested in wordplay.[12]

As I have said, The Bridge is concerned to conquer the sea, to superimpose a myth upon it ("One arc synoptic of all tides below," arc punning on Noah's "ark"; "pyramids of silver sequel," sequel becoming "sea/quell"); and so the erection of human constructions over the mere, the sea, becomes of paramount importance:

> the suns
> And synergy of waters ever fuse, recast
> In myriad syllables, – Psalm of Cathay.

A "sill" (syllables) is "the basis or foundation of a thing; esp., a horizontal piece, as a timber, which forms the lowest member of a frame, or supports a structure; as, the sill or sills of a house, of a bridge, of a loom, a mine set, and the like"; and to this is added "label" (syllables), a technical word in architecture: "that part of a cornice, sill course, or any other horizontal member, which projects beyond the rest, and is of such section as to throw off the rainwater." So upon the "sill" or foundation of his Bridge, Crane constructs a gigantic "label": just as the label or dripstone outside a house protects the building against the intrusion of the elements, so by projecting itself out to sea the Bridge defends the land (and human society) against the threat of a more inveterate aquatic foe. "Atlantis" unequivocally declares that the sun and synergy of waters fuse and recast in myriad syllables, and "In myriad syllables" can itself be fused and recast as "In mere I add sill labels." Jason and the Argonauts are mentioned just a few lines before, and Crane's poem is imitating these nautical pioneers by skilfully protecting itself against hostile waters. (Compare the fog leaning "on the sill" in "The Harbor Dawn," where there is a similar conflict between human edifices and external impingements.) Also apparent here is the huge burden of responsibility Crane imposes upon his language: Bridge and syllables become cognate and interchangeable in all senses, for the syllables punningly erect the sill labels of a Bridge over the water, just as the bridge as pun constructs its myth of America out of the syllables of language. Crane is in fact collapsing the gap between life and art: demanding that his punning bridge become a mythopoeic Bridge, that his verbal syllables become mythopoeic sill labels, that his language accept the task of imposing order upon the world.

So Crane is indeed constructing a bridge over troubled water, for images of domesticating the hostile sea are always balanced by images of the sea infiltrating and washing away human edifices; and this ambiguous interaction between land and water is especially apparent in "Ave Maria," where Columbus' words of revelation are in the shadow of an uncharted ocean which constantly threatens to overturn his frail craft:

> For here, between two worlds, another, harsh,
> This third, of water, tests the word . . .

(In Columbus' time, of course, it was thought that the seas covered a *third* of the earth's surface.) This last line contains Crane's favourite kind of syntactical ambiguity: the *water* puts the *word* to the test, or examination; but, by a Whiteheadian reversal of subject and object, the *word* also *tests* the *water*, metamorphoses nature into the precious metal of prophetic art (test: "to refine, as gold or silver, in a test, or cupel; to subject to cupellation"). This pun on *tests* typifies the reciprocal interaction between language and ocean in Crane's poem; and the "galleries of watergutted lava" in "Cutty Sark" are part of this same theme, with the exclamation of the sailor there that "life's a geyser" being synecdochic of the whole *Bridge*, for the purpose of a geyser is to metamorphose water into steam, nature into art. (Crane told Yvor Winters he was pleased that "Cutty Sark," "symbolically touching . . . on the sea," should come "about midway in the poem," thereby reflecting the sea's "presence under the center of the bridge.")[13] In ancient times it was believed that the gods demanded the sacrifice of a human life as recompense for the hubristic exercise of transgressing against nature by daring to construct a bridge – a pattern imitated by the fate of Brooklyn Bridge's designer, John Augustus Roebling, who was accidentally killed while supervising Brooklyn Bridge's construction, leaving the task to be concluded by his son Washington; and the various insecurities inherent within the artifice of Hart Crane's *Bridge* should not be overlooked.

So one of the functions of Crane's puns is to bridge positive and negative polarities and to exploit wordplay as a way of assimilating irony into his apparently monolithic edifice. In this context, nothing could be more appropriate than that the curve of the actual Brooklyn Bridge, the Roeblings' triumph of engineering, is maintained by cables hanging freely between two fixed points of support. The extended cables are in tension, while the towers, resting on their foundations on each bank, are in compression. "Viewed theoretically," as Alan Trachtenberg has said, "the structure was a unity of opposite forces, harmonizing tension and compression." Brooklyn Bridge demonstrates how "a constant play of energies and movements" produces a construction that is apparently, but only apparently, in stasis: "By balancing all its forces in a harmonious system, the universe appeared to be in equilibrium. But in truth, all appearances of rest were illusions."[14] Trachtenberg went on to distinguish between Roebling's equation of fact and symbol as opposed to the ultimate disembodied idealism of Crane's "Atlantis"; but this interpretation is debatable, for we can see that suspensions are built into Crane's structure as surely as they are into Roebling's. The engineering of the Brooklyn suspension bridge depends upon "stays," parts in tension holding the structure together; and in Crane's masterpiece, as in Roebling's, these stresses are implicit not explicit, concealed from public view:

> Implicitly thy freedom staying thee!

BLINDNESS AND VISION

As an example of these tensions, let us take this stanza from the "Proem" which starts off with an ambitious theology and then brings us down to earth with a bump:

> And Thee, across the harbor, silver-paced
> As though the sun took step of thee, yet left
> Some motion ever unspent in thy stride, –
> Implicitly thy freedom staying thee!

The Bridge is here described in such grandiose terms that it is as if it were not only crossing the harbour but also harbouring a cross, assuming upon its shoulders – like Christ – the burden of redeeming the race. For "pace" (*silver-paced*), Webster gives the first meaning as "a movement from one foot to the other in walking," and we can see that the literal – slightly Surreal – image is of a giant hero bestriding the harbour, a personification that fits in with the poet's salutation of the Bridge in the second person. But Webster also gives an architectural context for "pace": "a broad step or platform; any raised part of a floor, as around an altar"; and as in visual terms Brooklyn Bridge is indeed a platform raised above the rest of New York City, the religious connotations of the word are unlikely to have been lost on Crane as he tried to persuade his Bridge to harbour its cross and "lend a myth to God." Webster also offers a weaving context for "pace" ("a device in a loom, to maintain tension on the warp in pacing the web"), and with the "bound cable strands" of the Bridge pictorially resembling a loom ("Taut miles of shuttling moonlight"), we can see that the appropriate symbolic connotations are of an ancient Homeric poet weaving the myth of his race. All these are symbolic accretions which expand the possibilities of the image without impinging upon its logic; but, as Crane knows, this myth may also be simply the evanescent product of a dream-factory: following on from the cinema's "panoramic sleights" in stanza three, *silver-paced* performs its own sleight-of-hand trick to become "silver-paste," thereby bringing this image of Brooklyn Bridge down to a papier-mâché Hollywood prop. So the Bridge becomes one of those trick-mirrors which give a different reflection according to the angle they are seen from – it may be religious artefact, epic opportunity or merely false glitter. Since myths are equivalent and Hollywood reincarnates certain aspects of previous ages, the "silver-paste" possibility would suggest the hollowness not only of modern myths but of all myths; and this would infuse the whole poem with a sceptical light.

The second and third lines contain a similar tilting between opposites, for they indulge in the religious fiction that Brooklyn Bridge is the centre of the universe, around which the sun revolves:

> As though the sun took step of thee, yet left
> Some motion ever unspent in thy stride

This would be a renewal of the Rationalist theology of the Middle Ages, where the earth was deemed to be the centre of a cosmos mapped out by the geometry of the schoolmen. Because such claims for a ponticentric universe are so obviously a nonsense, the reader should be alerted to the irony built into the elision "motio*n ever un*spent." The sun, actually, is static: it *never runs*. Webster's musical context for motion – "change of pitch in the successive tones of a voice part" – gives another clue to the vacillations inherent in this stanza. So these lines are secretly admitting that the Bridge is only arbitrarily requisitioned as a fountain of grace; and here is the discrepancy I discussed in my Introduction between the sound of Crane's public poem and the sight of that poem for the individual reader. The myth is socially validated, but privately retracted. This fable that Brooklyn Bridge is at the centre of the universe is repeated in "Atlantis," and there again it is unmasked, as we saw when considering Einstein in Chapter 2:

> Now while thy petals spend the suns about us, hold –

In actual fact the petals of the Bridge do not spend the sun: by a syntactical reversal, the suns *hold* while the Bridge's petals *spend* themselves. Crane knew all about the shifting angles of relativity, and here he expands its modes of thought into philosophical significance.

So irony is built into the verbal structure of Crane's *Bridge*. Pun and paradox are the bridges swinging between opposite possibilities and covert admissions of the fictive nature of the poet's "myth to God." The inference to be made is that, as in Plato's Noble Lie, blindness becomes a form of social vision, for the manner in which Crane conceals his subversive puns from the reader is akin to the way in which Plato's cave represses forbidden knowledge: the audience's ignorance of anything except shadows on the cave-wall becomes a way of operating success-fully within the necessarily illusory world of society. Crane's Noble Lie is that Brooklyn Bridge is at the centre of the universe, and this "blindness" is socially acceptable. The alternative possibility, that the Bridge is stranded in space and time, that the sun never runs, while being a heroically disinterested philosophical "vision," is nevertheless a form of symbolic blindness or social incapability. (Prophets are traditionally blind, and ostracized by society.) Two lines from "The Dance" illustrate Crane's awareness of this paradoxical opposition between blindness and vision:

> Flame cataracts of heaven in seething swarms
> Fed down your anklets to the sunset's moat.

On the surface we have no more than *cataracts*, waterfalls, tumbling down from the heavens. But this pleasant refraction of Indian myth through a jazz-tinted 1920s lens is exploded by the double pun on *cataracts*, blindness, and *seething*, "see/thing." The subversive suggestion is that to believe in this Indian myth is actually a form of cataracts, blindness; but that the uncovering of these illusions must be continually repressed for human life to continue, just as the puns on *cataracts* and *seething* are quite literally repressed by the decorous surface of the poetry. Of course the sun in its apparent daily journey across the sky does not in truth create anything like the *moat* which the next line proposes: that would be to suppose the earth is static with the sun rotating to form a circle around it, a conception which, as Galileo pointed out, is very far from being correct. But this picturesque image of the sun's moat has a mythopoeic significance: it is a conscious fabrication, a benign blindness (*cataracts*) which alert readers will realize the falsity of ("see/thing"). *Flame*, with its overtones of illumination and sight (Latin *flamen*, a god's priest) is commensurate with the reference in this first line to *heaven*, for men traditionally attempt to elevate their own mythopoeic fictions by ascribing them to divine powers. But the punning oxymoron between *Flame* and *cataracts* re-emphasizes the paradoxical nature of these lines: *Flame* and *heaven* are proposing a "myth to God," while *cataracts* and *seething* subversively dispose of that myth. Robert Combs has said that Crane's mythical tableaux are designed to be seen *through*, and here pun and paradox are the means of rendering these tableaux transparent.[15] So we can say that tensions are incorporated into Crane's *Bridge* without being allowed to rise to the surface, for, as in Roebling's masterpiece of engineering, what seems to be static is actually in perpetual motion. Architectural fact and devious poem are both truly suspension bridges.

Besides the reference in the "Proem" to Plato's cave, there are a great many other classical allusions in *The Bridge*, especially in "Atlantis," which mentions, Troy, Tyre, Aeolus and Jason's Argonauts as well as the

Sibylline Oracle ("Sibylline voices flicker, waveringly stream"); and it is probable that Crane was aware of how his riddling juxtapositions of positive and negative are imitating models in Ancient Greek culture.[16] For although classical Greece has more traditionally been associated with humanistic, Socratic wisdom, American critics in the 1920s – under the influence of Nietzsche – were beginning to develop theories of a savage clash between Apollonian order and Dionysian disturbance in ancient culture; and Marcel Detienne and Jean-Pierre Vernant have recently extended this idea to demonstrate how Greece set great store by *metis*, the idea of devious intelligence or cunning. *Metis* manifested itself in many forms, from the tricks of the crafty Hermes and Odysseus, to the "beguiling rhetorical illusionism of the sophists," to the technical know-how of Olympians like Hephaestus and Athena who were responsible for skills such as metallurgy and weaving by which the civilization came to grips with its environment. Detienne and Vernant claimed "the shifting net is the most perfect of images for *metis*"; the idea is of a net closing upon its prey, like Brooklyn Bridge closing upon the dark night.[17] In the Delphic Oracle this *metis* merges into a means of social control, for the riddling poems the Delphic priests produced in response to the utterances of the Holy Chasm would often surrender their last secrets only at the expense of chaos and dissolution. When Oedipus uncovers the true meaning of the Delphic riddle he is blind and disgraced, and though for the hero this physical blindness is symbolic sight, there is, as in Crane, an implication that social order is preserved only by physical sight and symbolic blindness, the Noble Lie whereby the tantalizing enigmas of the Oracle remain unanswered. Like many other Greek tragedies, *Oedipus Rex* is erected upon a structure of paradox and ambiguity, with certain phrases having respectable surface-meanings but dark subversive undercurrents. When he says *ego phano*, for instance, Oedipus thinks he means "it is I who will bring the criminal to light," but by a gruesome irony the phrase could also mean "I shall discover myself to be the criminal." Crane did himself possess a copy of Sophocles' tragedies, but it does not seem to have been a particularly treasured possession because the book rests at present in Columbia University Library with fourteen pairs of pages still uncut. Nevertheless, at this time Greece was not at all an unorthodox prototype, as we see from Gorham Munson's 1927 book on Robert Frost (also in Crane's library) which celebrated the New Englander as "the purest classical poet of America today" and one who, like the Greeks, was interested in common sense as the sense of a common or communal world.[18] And it is also interesting to note that Crane's nickname for Emil Opffer, his most constant lover, was "Phoebus Apollo."[19] Of course this would have been a tribute to Opffer's Grecian beauty, and many artists particularly in the late nineteenth century used motifs from Ancient Greece to justify their own homosexuality; but considering Crane's interest in aligning personal fulfilment with social control, and considering that Phoebus Apollo was the god who spoke in riddles at the Delphic Oracle, we can only regret the apparent destruction of Crane's letters to his lover. Crane fell in love with Opffer in 1923 and wrote the *Voyages* sequence for him, and the two men continued to see each other until 1930. In an interview with Helge Normann Nilsen in 1978, Opffer, now living in Denmark, claimed he never bothered to keep any of Crane's letters although he remembered "they were long and full of intense sentiments and large-scale poetic visions." In a letter to me in August 1983, the eighty-seven-year-old Opffer wrote: "I am sorry that I can be of no help to you about Hart Crane. All our mutual friends are gone, – and I have nothing that could be of any value to you . . . My books by Hart were left in Spain."[20]

To conclude: pun and paradox are Crane's means of pivoting his *Bridge* between decorous blindness and subversive sight. If we read the poem from inside Plato's cave, Brooklyn Bridge is a grand symbol of America; if we read it from outside the cave, the Bridge is no more than a tawdry deception. The tension between these opposite polarities puts the suspension in suspension bridge. We know that the fabrication of belief as a momentary stay against confusion was a subject close to Crane's heart, for when he visited the hard-headed rationalist Yvor Winters in 1927, the conversation turned to Emerson's conception of a man remaining immortal even after relinquishing his personal identity in death, a Romantic idea that Winters opposed, but Crane supported, though with the rider, "Well, if we can't believe it, we'll have to kid ourselves into believing it."[21]

7

Abstraction and the city

The impalpable sustenance of me from all things at all hours of the day,
The simple, compact, well-join'd scheme, myself disintegrated, every one
disintegrated yet part of the scheme
(Whitman, "Crossing Brooklyn Ferry")

THE FRAGMENTATION OF IDENTITY

One of the tasks burlesque performs in Crane's work is to fracture and disintegrate identity, and the image of the city in his poetry has a similar function. Some of Crane's early letters from New York testify to his apprehension of the metropolis as a kind of gigantic vaudeville performance, and the very first of them all – to his father on 31 December 1916 – talked of how "It is a great shock, but a good tonic, to come down here as I have and view the countless multitudes. It seems sometimes almost as though you had lost yourself, and were trying vainly to find somewhere in this sea of humanity, your lost identity."[1] Crane's attitude towards New York City has been the subject of some dispute. Jean Guiguet talked of Crane's "provincial enthusiasm for the city," but Brom Weber thought "Crane's feeling about the city in his life and in his poetry appears to be almost exclusively one of negation."[2] Both attitudes are misleading. As with capitalism, Crane may himself have disliked many aspects of urban life, but that was – as Gatsby would say – just personal, and did not prevent him from judging the necessarily structural relationships of the city as artistic image (and actual vehicle) of Platonic harmony. "The Tunnel" describes how, in familiar epic fashion, Man must be broken down or submerged before he can be redefined "as an inclusive attribute of the universal," to use a characteristic phrase of Crane's friend Waldo Frank.

In his books like *Our America* (1919) and *The Re-discovery of America*

(1929), Waldo Frank developed his idea of balancing subjective and objective worlds into "Wholeness," "the masterful, conscious fusion of the strong ego with life."[3] In this, Frank was reflecting the reaction against individualism which was typical of the 1920s. Both T. S. Eliot's work and T. E. Hulme's famous essay "Romanticism and Classicism," published in 1924, epitomized the prevalent hostility towards Shelleyan flights of the imagination. So Waldo Frank's anticipation of a future time when Man "disappears from the snug centre of the universe he had for so long occupied. But he reappears in a far more powerful modification: as an inclusive attribute of the universal" is symptomatic of the urge towards impersonality and towards the abstraction of social systems which was an important theme in intellectual life during the 1920s.[4]

In the cases of Eliot and Hulme, this reaction against Romanticism expressed itself in a dedication to traditional hierarchical values; but in Crane, the agent of depersonalization was the city. In historical terms, the Twenties was indeed the decade when the American population became more urban than rural. In 1920, 50 per cent of Americans lived in towns and cities; by 1930, the figure had increased to 69 per cent.[5] Many of the novels of Sherwood Anderson, among others, deal with this migration from God-fearing countryside to scurrilous big city. (The son leaving his rural homestead behind is, of course, the subject of "Indiana.") In The Bridge, Crane exploits the city as an image of the shift in consciousness that urban landscapes helped to bring about: a transition from a puritanical and romantic individualism, where character was sacrosanct and each man communed privately with his God, towards a classical harmony where character is protoplasmic and Man is defined in terms of his relationship to others. In Emersonian terms, what was once opaque becomes now transparent. So in the city world of "The Tunnel," as Richard Combs has said, "Crane uses the sense of anonymity one gets in a crowd on a busy street to shatter the circumscribed and protected sense of self," for Crane's subways and revolving glass-doors engender that world of "hysterical classicism" Malcolm Cowley mentioned in a letter to Kenneth Burke to describe how the automatism of New York life expresses itself "in terms of geometry and mechanics."[6] Cowley disliked such dehumanization, as he saw it, distinguishing it from "the classicism of the Mediterranean, which results from sympathy with one's environment instead of rebellion against it"; and he believed New Yorkers did not willingly submit themselves to the landscape, but found instead the city coercing them into co-operating with its rigid disciplines. In Exile's Return, Cowley elaborated: "Its people have a purely numerical function: they are counted as units that daily pass a given point. Their emotions are coefficients in calculating the probability of trade."[7] Crane's theme in "The Tunnel" is to reveal the negative and debilitating aspects of this disintegration of personality, those aspects that Cowley found so disheartening; but also to demonstrate how this disintegration is a necessary preliminary to the world of "Atlantis," where the "gleaming staves" come together in perfect harmony and order.

The images in this poem of tunnels and subways are highly appropriate externalizations of the punning underground passages inside Crane's verse. The visible poetry implies the invisible: "of cities you bespeak / subways." But the pun is also thematically crucial to "The Tunnel" in so far as a pun is the verbal correlative of this shattering of a "circumscribed and protected sense of self," as Combs put it. In the pun, swinging between opposites, singular becomes plural. The word's selfhood, its one meaning, is broken down. An image of this sundering process occurs in "Atlantis":

> And you, aloft there – Jason! hesting Shout!
> Still wrapping harness to the swarming air!
> Silvery the rushing wake, surpassing call,
> Beams yelling Aeolus! splintered in the straits!

On his quest for the Golden Fleece, Jason was obliged to sail through the Symplegades, unfriendly rocks guarding the entrance to the Bosphorus, which would drive together and crush any ship attempting to pass between them. To help Jason evade this hazard, Pallas Athene fitted an oracular beam into the prow of the *Argo*: another punning justification for the "palladium helm" thirteen lines previously, and a form of divine protection which directs us towards Crane's pun between *hesting*, obsolescent for "command," and the Greek deity Hestia, "Goddess of the hearth, whether of the home or city." So here we find Jason favoured by the gods and subjugating the natural elements of wind and water; but the implication is that, like the mariner's ship, and like individual identity, the individual word is constantly liable to be "splintered in the straits," shattered into the duality that is the pun. (In the version of this story which Crane would have known, the Symplegades clashed together behind the *Argo*, slightly damaging the ship's stern.)[8] So while in "Atlantis" it may be possible to navigate beyond such hazardous duality and discover harmony, this kind of fracturing and fragmentation nevertheless remains the current earthly condition. Just as Aeolus, god of winds, splits ships in twain, so the Aeolian harp of Crane's *Bridge* splits words in twain. Another image of sundering straits comes up in "Cutty Sark":

> *Thermopylae, Black Prince, Flying Cloud* through Sunda

Sunda, the Sunda Strait in Indonesia through which these trading vessels must pass, is an image of division both literally and linguistically: for

Sunda itself puns on the "sunder," the sundering of the poetic word, that is the central principle behind *The Bridge*.

However, in "The Tunnel" the punning processes of swing and exchange have resulted in a loss of human dignity and will. Language and identity have been fractured to no apparent purpose (emphasis in original):

> Our tongues recant like beaten weather vanes.
> This answer lives like verdigris, like hair
> Beyond extinction, surcease of the bone;
> And repetition freezes – "What
>
> "what do you want? getting weak on the links?
> fandaddle daddy don't ask for change – IS THIS
> FOURTEENTH? it's half past six she said – if
> you don't like my gate why did you
> swing on it, why *didja*
> swing on it
> anyhow –"
>
> And somehow anyhow swing –

The word *recant*, as Nassar said, is a pun: literally "sing again," but also "take back."[9] So this recanting of the *tongues* suggests that a concept is no sooner proposed than retracted. The human mind spins about aimlessly like a weather vane, with its "whethers," its ambiguities, all in "vain." The processes of *repetition*, *links* and *change*, the punning analogies between one era and another, have now been reduced into mere financial exchange (the *change* which this prostitute refuses to give) and the equally mundane *change* of subway trains necessary at Fourteenth Street. The poem's internal bridges reveal the bathos of "The Tunnel": just as heroic Columbus degenerates into New York's banal Columbus Circle, so the exuberant links and exchanges of puns have degenerated into the banal business of exchanging money and subway trains. And the swinging between different points which is the glory of the pun has here been relegated to a tawdry sexual context, the "fandaddle daddy" "swinging" on the prostitute's "gate."

Swinging is a persistent image in *The Bridge* for vacillation between opposites, from the seagull oscillating its wings in the second line of the "Proem" to the last line of "Atlantis" where "Whispers antiphonal in azure swing." But here in "The Tunnel" one of the chief connotations of this swinging is the fracturing of mind and body, the quite literal disintegration of identity, which is the hazardous counterpart to Crane's dream of "Atlantis." Whereas "Atlantis" moves "Upward, veering with light," "The Tunnel" descends into darkness to parody and thus reveal the sombre underside of that final triumph; and so Crane's juxtaposition of "The Tunnel" with "Atlantis" itself makes for an oscillation, a swinging between opposites. In "The Tunnel" the hapless Edgar Allan Poe appears to the narrator on the subway train, and Poe's headless ghost becomes the ghoulish corollary to Crane's purposeful fracturing of selfhood:

> Whose head is swinging from the swollen strap?
> Whose body smokes along the bitten rails,
> Bursts from a smoldering bundle far behind
> In back forks of the chasms of the brain, –
> Puffs from a riven stump far out behind
> In interborough fissures of the mind . . . ?

Poe's head is hanging from a strap in the subway car, while his body has been left behind on the railway-line. But conceptually, this image of decapitation introduces the *swinging* between mind and body which Crane depicts as the kernel of Poe's problem. The body *smokes* and is *smoldering* ("to burn and smoke without flame; to waste away by a slow and suppressed combustion") because it has despaired of matching external circumstances with inward desire and has accordingly repressed physical sexuality into a mental fantasy. *Bursts* ("to fly apart or in pieces; to break open") implies Poe's fragmentation, the pulling of his mind and body in opposite directions. As a noun, a "burst" is also "a broken place . . . specif., a rupture or hernia"; and Webster gives an intriguing historical usage for *bundle* which continues this theme of the Puritans' timorous distancing of physical recreation (emphases in original):

> To sleep or lie on the same bed without undressing; – said of a man and woman, esp. lovers. According to G. E. Howard ("History of Matrimonial Institutions"), the custom of *bundling*, and the similar Dutch custom of *queesting*, prevailed in the less sophisticated portions of New England, New York, New Jersey, and Pennsylvania, and also in Wales, Ireland, and Scotland. As a custom it was found in remote localities in New York in 1804 and in Pennsylvania in 1845.

An example is given from Washington Irving: "Van Corlear stopped occasionally in the villages to eat pumpkin pies . . . and *bundle* with the Yankee lassies." So Crane is suggesting that Poe's genius might be reducible simply to the expression of frustrated sexuality. Was Poe merely a "smoldering bundle," and his literary work nothing but "Puffs from a riven stump"? *Puffs* could be "any of various objects inflated, or appearing as if inflated"; while *stump* suggests that some integral bodily part has been removed. The imagery of this description in "The Tunnel" is all to do with division: the "back *forks* ["the place where a division or a union occurs"] of the *chasms* ["a cleft; a fissure"] of the brain"; the "*riven* stump" (rive: "to rend asunder; to split; to cleave"); the "interborough *fissures* of the mind." "Fissure" has a specific medical sense of "a bone

fractured without complete separation of the parts," and this exemplifies
the way all kinds of dualities are swinging on hinges here. Poe's head is
dissociated from his body, but it is the fact that it is not completely
severed which brings about his agony.

The analogy we have already seen between this *swinging* and the
swinging of commercial and social exchange is exploited by Crane to
demonstrate how, literally as well as figuratively, Poe was destroyed by
division. The adjective *interborough* (ostensibly referring to Poe's mental
discords) makes this link between public and private schizophrenia, for
Crane finds symbolic significance in Poe's death being caused by the kind
of gang of party workers who would use violent means to persuade
voters to endorse their electoral "ticket":

> And when they dragged your retching flesh,
> Your trembling hands that night through Baltimore –
> That last night on the ballot rounds, did you
> Shaking, did you deny the ticket, Poe?

Shaking is another of Crane's punning relativities: Poe is *Shaking* with
fear, but only because the gang of workers are *Shaking* him ("shake"
being slang for "the act of blackmailing; a shake-down" (f)). The word
Shaking itself "shakes," oscillates between different syntactic positions;
just as the next line transmogrifies this electoral *ticket* into that subway
ticket the narrator must purchase to travel to Gravesend Manor (on the
IRT, the Interborough Rapid Transit system, which is itself a linguistic
and conceptual metamorphosis of these "*interborough* fissures of the
mind"):

> For Gravesend Manor change at Chambers Street.
> The platform hurries along to a dead stop.

The city becomes a Whiteheadian field of relativity where nothing is
static, all is in perpetual motion: for New York City's processes of barter
and exchange, where every commodity has its recognized equivalent,
are another manifestation of the interaction of different forces which the
political game depends upon. A political candidate is defined by his
relation to the other candidates as surely as a subway ticket is defined by
the distance it will carry its passenger. Neither candidate nor ticket can
exist as a unique and isolated entity. And the pun, verbal emblem of
division, is the stylistic equivalent to this thematic interaction between
oppositions.

URBAN RITUAL IN "THE TUNNEL"

In some ways the commercial transactions of the urban jungle may be as
destructive for Crane as all these divisions were for Poe; but, as we have

seen, the final triumph of "Atlantis" is a capitalist haven where the ritual of buying and selling delineates its own kind of myth. So Poe's determined alienation of himself from society is treated equivocally in *The Bridge*

> And why do I often meet your visage here,
> Your eyes like agate lanterns – on and on
> Below the toothpaste and the dandruff ads?
> – And did their riding eyes right through your side,
> And did their eyes like unwashed platters ride?

The adjective *agate* is one of Crane's internal verbal bridges, punning on the prostitute's swinging *gate* a few lines earlier. But the really interesting line is

> – And did their riding eyes right through your side

On the surface this is the *eyes* of the passengers *riding* on the subway train. These eyes pierce "right through" Poe's "side" and so elevate him to a victimized Christ-like figure. In this reading, Poe's search for supreme beauty and his scorn for the business world bring about his martyrdom. But if Crane's grammatical aim had been straightforward, he could have omitted *right* altogether, for it adds nothing to the logical sense, only prevents him from using a verb which might have clarified his expression. Crane's design, however, was not straightforward: for, in the alternative reading, *riding* and *ride* take up *fissures* four lines earlier, to "ride" in a surgical context being "to overlap (each other); – said of bones or fractured fragments." And if we also allow a pun swinging between *right* and "rite," then the scene here comes to echo "Ave Maria," where the eyes of Columbus' crew accrete upon the image of the new-found land. In this way, the rites and rituals of society, in which *eyes ride* or overlap, serve to undermine the arrogance whereby Poe asserted himself as superior to his society: *through* puns on "throw" as "to cause to fall; to prostrate"; and *side* is slang for "swagger; conceit; pretentiousness." So the meaning of this line cuts two ways: either Poe is a martyr with oppressive eyes piercing right through his side, or he is an arrogant outsider whose side is overthrown by society's necessary rituals:

> And did their riding eyes [pierce] right through your side *or*
> And did their riding eyes rite throw your side [conceit]

The image in the next line of eyes as *platters* – not just large circular plates, but also instruments which plait or braid different strands into one band – effectively re-emphasizes this corporate nature of social identity.

The same pun on *ride* also appears in the third verse of "The Tunnel":

> Or can't you quite make up your mind to ride

The initial meaning is the dilemma of whether or not to take the subway train. The narrator's indecision here, his eventual rejection of the idea of a brisk walk and weary acquiescence in the subway that "yawns the quickest promise home," is characteristic of the failure of willed self-determination which the swing, the pun, the ambiguity, can bring about. But from the citizen's viewpoint, *ride* also implies the visionary ability to see oneself overlapped and so to apprehend oneself as an adjunct of the corporate state. And from the reader's viewpoint, the counterpart of this is to understand how Crane's words themselves *ride*, overlap into magical puns. The deliverance of "Atlantis" implies a world where linguistic units, like social units, are in a continually interpenetrating harmony:

> Be minimum, then, to swim the hiving swarms
> Out of the Square, the Circle burning bright –
> Avoid the glass doors gyring at your right,
> Where boxed alone a second, eyes take fright
> – Quite unprepared rush naked back to light:
> And down beside the turnstile press the coin
> Into the slot. The gongs already rattle.

Like *Square* and *Circle*, *alone* and *a second* are opposites. It is not so much the moment of isolation that terrifies the eyes of the pedestrians as the fact that each "lone" self finds itself confronted with a mirror-image in the glass door: "a/lone boxed (sparred with) a second." It is a Dostoyevskian image of doubling and division. Crane's mirror here is the embodiment of a pun: it fragments singular into plural; and because they try to guard against this fragmentation, the scared *eyes* (each solitary "I") box against their subversive shadows and hurry swiftly back to the light of day. This hint of disintegration has made them only too *naked* or defenceless. But the magic island of Atlantis will require such disintegration as a precondition of the citizens' admission into its mystical mathematics: the injunction at the end of "Quaker Hill" ("break off, / descend – / descend –") must be fulfilled. So the effect of this ordeal is to reveal how the "hiving swarms" are not yet fit to enter into the ideal state of Platonic redemption. The frightened New Yorkers cling to their protective sense of self and evade the ritualistic wholeness suggested by this image of revolving mirrors ("Avoid the glass doors gyring at your right," with *right* punning on "rite"). We can see how the four consecutive end-rhymes (*bright, right, fright, light*) imitate the revolution of the door; but the pedestrians fail to respond to the promise of this "burning bright" *Circle*, despite the Blakeian intimation of riches hidden in the darkness ("Tyger tyger *burning bright* / In the forests of the night"), which takes up Blake's exhortatory maxim that Crane placed as epigraph to "The

Tunnel" ("To Find the Western path / Right thro' the Gates of Wrath").
So while in a mundane and everyday sense the solid citizens "rush naked
back to light," in a visionary sense they have their *back* to the *light* because
they continue to resist the dazzling illumination ("glittering Pledge") of
Atlantis. The puns and syntactical ambiguities here, the pulling of
language in two different directions, become a linguistic correlative to
that more general process of sundering which is presented in this poem as
a moral imperative.

The essence of this passage, then, is transmutation and exchange. Just as
coins can be pressed into slots and transformed into tickets, so the mirrors
of this glass door serve to fragment personality, but its revolving magic
Circle also promises to metamorphose human beings into a new ideal
unity, of which New York City's subway alarm-bells – a modern
reincarnation of the noble oriental gongs – are the harbinger. Again, the
city's commercial and ritualistic processes of exchange are the manifestation in a lower order of that Universal Exchange, the cosmic pun,
which forms the "timeless laugh" of "Atlantis"; and so it is appropriate
that "Atlantis" should acknowledge the specific importance of urban
ritual to Crane's *Bridge*:

> Sustained in tears the cities are endowed
> And justified conclamant with ripe fields
> Revolving through their harvests in sweet torment.

The cities are "endowed / And justified" with a mythic status equivalent
to the "ripe fields" of the American countryside eulogized so often by
nineteenth-century writers like Emerson and Thoreau. And just as the
rural harvests revolve upon the oxymoron of "sweet torment," so the
cities are oxymoronically "Sustained in tears": for *tears* not only suggests
the laureate weeping over his beloved city, but also puns on *tears* as "state
of being torn; a rent": demonstrating thereby how America's cities are
mythically *Sustained* (held up "without failing or yielding") by the
holistic vision of this epic poet, even though the cities themselves
engender disintegration, fragmentation, tearing asunder. (We might
compare Crane's images of New York City's divisions and "stacked
partitions" in "Faustus and Helen.") So, for all his apparent apathy
towards this modern world, the narrator in "The Tunnel" inwardly
acknowledges how in fact the city is not isolated in space and time; how,
on the contrary, its tomorrows are engaged in a perennial reincarnation
of yesteryear; how, for instance, Old French *verte-di-Grice* – green of
Greece – has been culturally and etymologically transformed into urban
verdigris, a greenish deposit formed on metal as a rust:[10]

> This answer lives like verdigris, like hair
> Beyond extinction . . .

The puns manifest Crane's ecstatic apprehension of the interpenetration of different eras, the past living under only slightly altered forms within the skeins of the present. As "Atlantis" implies, the "cipher-script" of Crane's poem brings "Tomorrows into yesteryear" through the "timeless laugh" of a global pun:

> – Tomorrows into yesteryear – and link
> What cipher-script of time no traveller reads
> But who, through smoking pyres of love and death,
> Searches the timeless laugh of mythic spears.

The Bridge translates time into the forms of a huge Verb whose syllables are recast or inflected as the waters of the earth revolve:

> . . . O Choir, translating time
> Into what multitudinous Verb the suns
> And synergy of waters ever fuse, recast
> In myriad syllables . . .

and the puns in Crane's poem are no more than another version of this recasting or transformation of one object into another.

In his essay on Edgar Allan Poe, D. H. Lawrence claimed that "the rhythm of American art-activity is dual," and Lawrence said this was:

1. A disintegrating and sloughing of the old consciousness.
2. The forming of a new consciousness underneath.

Poe's quandary, suggested Lawrence, was to have "only the disintegrative vibration."[11] In this context Poe's appearance in "The Tunnel" is most appropriate, because "The Tunnel" and "Atlantis" are formal counterparts: "The Tunnel" descends and disintegrates, and "Atlantis" then ascends to construct a new consciousness out of the ruins. In "The Tunnel," New York City's geometry and structural relationships become an image of the fragmentation of identity; and the pun, the splintering of words in the straits so that singular becomes plural, is the linguistic equivalent of this fragmentation, which results in an apathetic swinging between opposites and the surrender of selfhood to the city's processes of barter and exchange. But in "Atlantis," these processes of exchange are redeemed by the capitalist godhead, "Deity's glittering Pledge"; and its verbal counterpart, the exchange inherent in the pun, is similarly sanctified by the "multitudinous Verb" which fuses and recasts in myriad syllables.

8

Music

SYNCOPATION

The relationship between high and low culture was a controversial topic among the literati of the 1920s. Crane's friend Matthew Josephson, with his zany and Surrealistic *joie de vivre*, whole-heartedly embraced the machine as "our magnificent slave" and declared that art should seek to celebrate rather than exclude the material world, "the brilliant minutiae of . . . daily existence in the big cities, in the great industrial regions."[1] The critic Paul Rosenfeld, on the other hand, derogated Gershwin's "pink world of received ideas and sentiments," and said the gaudy commercialism of American jazz and machinery were not suitable subjects for art.[2] Gorham Munson suggested that "culture must now work out a harmony between three factors, man, nature and Machinery"; but in 1929 the obdurate Waldo Frank was dismissing T. S. Eliot as a "meagre modern soul" imbued with all the degrading aspects of the jazz-age: "Aesthetically and culturally," said Frank, "there is little to choose between the best of [Irving] Berlin and 'Mr. Prufrock' or 'The Waste Land.'"[3]

Hart Crane built his customary bridge between these polarities, reconciling modern technology into a traditional idealistic whole. He did not swallow all of Josephson's rhetoric about the supremacy of popular culture, but he did aim to "invent an idiom for the proper transposition of jazz into words! Something clean, sparkling, elusive!"[4] This was Crane writing to Allen Tate in 1922, while contemplating "For the Marriage of Faustus and Helen," and the second section of that poem is an attempt to assimilate the syncopated rhythms of jazz into formal verse:

> White shadows slip across the floor
> Splayed like cards from a loose hand;

98

> Rhythmic ellipses lead into canters
> Until somewhere a rooster banters.

Jazz syncopation is a slurring of the notes to give them the excited feel of running headlong into one another rather than being static or predetermined entities. Webster defines "syncopation" as "the commencing of a tone on an unaccented part of a measure, and continuing it through the time of the following accent, which is thereby at least apparently shifted back." Because the "Rhythmic ellipses" of syncopation disestablish the solidity and autonomy of individual musical notes, it is analogous to the fluidity of language represented in the pun, for the pun is another kind of syncopation, the slurring of meanings to give them the excited feel of running headlong into one another. Hence the *rooster* that banters in the lines quoted above is a verbal equivalent to syncopation, for, as Leibowitz noted, *rooster* – as well as denoting the cock who heralds the coming of the dawn – puns on the dancing man as a "peacock" who asks for a change of partner.[5] Similarly in the poem's first lines:

> Brazen hypnotics glitter here;
> Glee shifts from foot to foot

Here *Glee* is not only "joy," but also a "song of English origin for three or more solo voices, and usually in two or more contrasted movements." It is, notes Webster, "not necessarily gleesome." Thus the *Glee*, the song, "shifts from foot to foot" between its various levels; and so the movement of the dancers, the "Rhythmic ellipses" of the syncopated style and the rocking motion of the poem's verbal puns all become cognate.

There is an overt reference to jazz syncopation in the "Atlantis" section of *The Bridge*:

> Taut miles of shuttling moonlight syncopate
> The whispered rush, telepathy of wires.

And if we rhythmically syncopate or elide the verbal units within one line of the "Proem," we can see in operation that thematic syncopation which is a slurring or overlapping of meanings:

> Foretold to other eyes on the same screen

Brooklyn Bridge is unusual in having four main cables rather than two, and these "four" confront the "horizon" with the same kind of *screen* as Plato's cave and the cinema: a device to avoid or screen off areas of darkness. The conventional syllabic pattern of "other eyes on" is altered to "horizon" by syncopation:

> Four told to the horizon the same screen

Just as disparate meanings accrete inside the pun, so these alternative syntactical arrangements suggest how the accidents of the fallen world reflect its one central essence, Brooklyn Bridge. The *screen* of this New York cinema is linked, thematically and verbally, with its pontifical master. The syncopated variations, "other eyes on"/"the horizon," indicate this oscillation between accident and essence (or real and ideal) that is at the heart of *The Bridge*. But Crane's syncopated elision also reveals the ironic underside of his Platonic myth: the way in which cinema and Bridge are both engaged in keeping up the index of night and thus screening off the forbidden darkness beyond.

HARMONY DAWNS

This integration of the mundane world into an overarching harmony is, as Michael Sharp has suggested, a theme of *The Bridge* which can be explicated in terms of the poem's musical motifs. Sharp noted that there are in *The Bridge* "nearly two hundred direct or indirect references to sound and music," including the "harp" ("Proem"), the *Te Deum* ("Ave Maria"), the "hurdy-gurdy" and "grind-organ" ("Van Winkle"), the "black drums" ("The Dance"), the "nickel-in-the-slot piano" ("Cutty Sark"), the "choristers" ("Cape Hatteras"), the "windswept guitars" ("Southern Cross"), the "somewhere violin" ("National Winter Garden"), the "popcorn bells" ("Virginia") and the "phonographs of hades" ("The Tunnel"). All these come together, said Sharp, in the "One Song" of "Atlantis":

> . . . the orphic strings,
> Sidereal phalanxes, leap and converge:
> – One Song, one Bridge of Fire!

Those "orphic strings" imply Orpheus, mythological lutanist who accompanied Jason on his quest to the Golden Fleece; so that this song signals, as Sharp put it,

> the ultimate harmony of *The Bridge* . . . Just as Atlantis's circle of islands was bridged so that all the inhabitants could be in communion with the citadel, so the poet used Brooklyn Bridge as his sacred object, his "palladium helm of stars," to harmonize the sounds of the past and the present into a polyphonic whole.[6]

In the light of this kind of harmony, Stanley Coffman saw the aptness of Crane's exploitation of the fact that the cables of Brooklyn Bridge cause the structure to physically resemble a harp: "Crane reveals a correspondence between his symbol and an Aeolian harp whose music by its harmony recalls the harmony between man and his universe, the harmony within the universal plan."[7] And indeed the epigraph to

"Atlantis," from Plato's *Symposium*, makes this explicit: "Music is then the knowledge of that which relates to love in harmony and system." Sharp elaborated the context of this epigraph by quoting further from the *Symposium*:

> harmony is composed of differing notes of higher or lower pitch which disagreed once, but are now reconciled by the art of music; for if the higher and lower notes still disagreed, there could be no harmony, – clearly not. For harmony is a symphony, and symphony is an agreement; but an agreement of disagreements while they disagree there cannot be; you cannot harmonize that which disagrees.[8]

What is intriguing is how the first words of the "Proem," "How many dawns," punningly anticipate the dawning of harmony in "Atlantis." Granted that a central theme of *The Bridge* is this oscillation between real and ideal, between accident and essence, between the workaday world of sales and figures and the glittering symbol of Brooklyn Bridge, what could be more appropriate than that this tension should be reflected verbally inside the poem's first three words: "How many dawns" or "Harmony dawns"? The promise of Atlantis, latent inside the quotidian world, is also latent inside the first words of *The Bridge*; and by the time the last section of *The Bridge* has been reached, the harmony inherent in the magic island of "Atlantis" can float to the surface. Again, the pun is a bridge which swings between opposites.

Crane was always interested in ideas of harmony and balance as a bridging of opposites. He wrote to his father in 1917, "There is only one harmony, that is the equilibrium maintained by two opposite forces, equally strong"; and he repeated this theme to Waldo Frank on 19 August 1926: "It is a harmony always with the absolute direction [I] always seek, often miss, but sometimes gain."[9] Frank would have been sympathetic to such ideas, for in *Our America* he had written of how the Indian "prays for harmony between himself and the mysterious forces that surround him: of which he is one. For he has learned that from this harmony comes health." Crane underlined this passage in his personal copy of *Our America*.[10] It might not be too speculative to infer that Crane yearned after harmonic wholeness because this was exactly what was lacking in his own unbalanced and alienated character. Another writer interested in conceptions of harmony was Conrad Aiken, whose *Scepticisms: Notes on Contemporary Poetry* (1919) was also in Crane's library; and here Crane annotated a significant sentence in Aiken's discussion of Jean de Bosschère, where Aiken is analysing the melodic and musical properties of the French poet:

> What is the secret of this amazing magic? It is not verbal merely, nor rhythmic; for it remains in translation. *It springs from the ideas themselves: it is a playing of ideas against one another like notes in a harmony, ideas presented always visually, cool*

images in a kind of solitude. It is not that M. de Bosschère is altogether idiosyncratic in what he does, that he sees qualities that others do not see; but rather that he combines them unexpectedly, that he felicitously marries the lyrical to the matter-of-fact, the sad to the ironic, the innocent to the secular – the tender to the outrageous. He sees that truth is more complex and less sustaining than it is supposed to be.[11]

The lines italicized here were underlined in red ink by Hart Crane. Not surprisingly, for Crane's own *Bridge* is performing this very same "magic," wittily playing off ideas one against other, and marrying "the lyrical to the matter-of-fact" (or, in our idiom, bridging idealism and materialism). In Crane, as in de Bosschère, "truth" is complex and multi-faceted with the "tender" and the "outrageous" jostling side by side, until – "like notes in a harmony" – the secular and transcendental are reconciled, as the elusive hint of harmony in the "Proem" ("How many . . .") blooms into the overt harmony of "Atlantis." Crane marked up only four passages in *Scepticisms*, but another one of these four is on almost exactly the same theme. It comes from the chapter on Maxwell Bodenheim, where Aiken is praising Bodenheim's poetry for its "contemplation of life as a whole" and the "recognition of its items as merely minute sand-grains of that whole":

> For if, like Mr. Bodenheim, he desires that poetry shall be a kind of absolute music, "unattached with surface sentiment" – a music in which sensations are the notes, emotions the harmonies, and ideas the counterpoint; *a music of detached waver and gleam, which, taking for granted a complete knowledge of all things, will not be so naïve as to make statements, or argue a point, or praise the nature of things, or inveigh against it, but will simply employ all such elements as the keys to certain tones –* then truly the keyboard of the poet who uses his brain as well as his sensorium will be immensely greater than that, let us say, of the ideal Imagist.[12]

The passage italicized here was awarded a vertical line in the margin by Hart Crane. And Crane's *Bridge* itself refuses the limitation of "naïve" concrete statement, the poet instead using his brain to manipulate ideas in counterpoint, playfully balancing each against another. In the fallen world, ambiguity becomes the only viable mode of discourse; but "harmony" may possibly be conceived in the "absolute music" of "Atlantis." This perception of the terrestrial world imperfectly echoing a higher harmony is familiar enough in Romantic thought: Crane knew Shelley and Pater, who both contrasted life's many-coloured glass with the white radiance of eternity; and indeed Crane's earliest poetry uses language in a deliberately imprecise way which recalls the implications, evasions and suggestiveness favoured by Pater. But whereas Crane's work before *White Buildings* is a poetry of "waver and gleam" whose ambiguity depends upon vague associations and a withdrawal from specific images, by the time of *The Bridge* Crane's technique of ambiguity had developed into a tougher and more linguistic mode: "How many" reflecting "Harmony." (Although a Neoplatonic interpretation of *The Bridge* might say Crane is merely exploiting these mechanics of Joyceian modernism to relocate within the twentieth century the Paterian quest for ultimate harmony . . .)

In another letter to Frank on 18 January 1926 which accompanied a version of "Atlantis," Crane echoed the conjunction of harmony and symphony which Plato had made in the *Symposium* as he discussed his own desire to create a "symphonic" form for *The Bridge*:

> [The poem] is symphonic in including the convergence of all the strands separately detailed in antecedent sections of the poem – Columbus, conquests of water, land, etc., Pokahantus, subways, offices, etc., etc. I dare congratulate myself a little, I think, in having found some liberation for my condensed metaphorical habit in a form so symphonic (at least so attempted) as this.
>
> The bridge in becoming a ship, a world, a woman, a tremendous harp (as it does finally) seems to really have a career.[13]

So Crane's intention was to assimilate multiple layers of meaning into his *Bridge*. As Crane wrote to Otto Kahn on 12 September 1927, "Thousands of strands have had to be searched for, sorted and interwoven"; and the poem's oscillation between ideal and real, "Harmony dawns" and "How many dawns," could be explained in terms of this polyphonic style which Crane was trying to create.[14] We may recall Crane's 1923 letter to Munson, where he said that to transpose the music of D'Indy, Strauss, Ravel, Scriabin and Bloch "into *words*, one needs to *ransack* the vocabularies of Shakespeare, Jonson, Webster . . . and add our scientific, street and counter, and psychological terms, etc."[15] In this light, all the puns we have seen in *The Bridge* on a "scientific" level (the "whitest Flow-er" of relativity) and a "street and counter" level (the capitalist "sales that cross some page of figures") – all these could be seen as an attempt to unify different areas of American life into a subtle and complicated harmony. The verbal syncopation of the pun imitates the rhythmic syncopation of jazz to produce a slurring or overlapping of meanings; and the musical symphony of *The Bridge* imitates classical composers by integrating these various levels of creation into one harmonic whole. Crane's musical "symphonic form" has its counterpart in visual art, moreover: for the ocular effect of the engineering fact of Brooklyn Bridge is "of a fine tracery of innumerable strands," as Stephen Fender put it; and this parallel image was clearly central to Crane's imagination as he strove to accommodate "innumerable strands" within his own poem. The significance for Crane of the Bridge's visual appearance is demonstrated by the way he made (unsuccessful) attempts to use one of Joseph Stella's Brooklyn Bridge paintings as a frontispiece for his poem, and by his eventual incorporation of three appropriate photographs by Walker Evans into the Black Sun edition. Not only are the Bridge's multiple cables an analogue to Crane's multiple meanings, but an observer's view of the sea through the "Transparent meshes" of these cable strands would also be a visual counterpart to those chaotic ironies which punningly infiltrate Crane's poem. (Crane told Winters in 1927 that he was concerned "Atlantis" "may rely too much on a familiarity with the unique architecture of Brooklyn Bridge.")[16] In this context, it is apposite that one of Evans' three photographs should look down from the bridge into the water below, and that Crane should have insisted this illustration be placed directly after "Cutty Sark," the most overtly aquatic section of *The Bridge*. Evans' other two photographs are also appropriate: in one, the arches and cable strands of the bridge seem to resemble a Gothic cathedral, aspiring towards the open sky beyond; but in the other, our view is from underneath the bridge (with the tracks of the Elevated railway visible) looking across to the grey financial district of Manhattan. One presents an ideal vision, the other a quotidian material vision. Crane's poem, however, strives to reconcile the real (How many) with the ideal (Harmony).[17]

If such harmonic and symphonic form seems too bizarre a literary ambition to be credible, I might anticipate one of my later chapters by recalling that Joyce was writing "Work in Progress" at the very same time, and that Joyce's puns in (what was later) *Finnegans Wake* perform a similar function of integrating different layers of worldly experience into one ideal and timeless work of art. Extolling the "pan-logos" of Joyce's "synoptical prose-poem," Eugene Jolas proclaimed: "We who have watched it grow, hope that there will be ears to hear and rejoice at the fabulous new harmonies of this All-World Symphony!"[18] Jolas was actually praising his friend Joyce, but – if he had read *The Bridge* more closely – he might just as easily have found himself praising the harmonies and symphony of his friend Hart Crane.

9

The new machine and the new word

ACCLIMATIZING THE MACHINE: "AVE MARIA"

Because technology occupied such a central place within their world, many American poets of the early twentieth century saw it as their duty to address themselves to the challenges posed by a changing urban and industrial landscape. Escapist rural idylls became outmoded, and the machine was elevated to a prominent place inside the American poetic consciousness. Most of the machine's champions, however, simply refurbished Whitmanian optimism in contemporary costume. MacKnight Black, for one, published in 1929 a volume actually called *Machinery*, which gazed with open-mouthed admiration at a "Suspension Bridge Pier Under Construction" ("Tall red lily / Beside the dark stream, / Lifting your proud stalk"), and invested "Reciprocating Engines" with a religious aura:

> Now softly, as the great wings of eagles flow through a sky,
> These tons of shaped steel
> Ply through motionless air, how strongly they mesh
> The stillness with a peace of their own.[1]

The content may be of the twentieth century, but the technique is of the nineteenth. Similarly in Harriet Monroe's 1910 poem "The Turbine," in which the turbine itself is personified as a woman who "sits upon her throne / As ladylike and quiet as a nun," there exists what Frederick J. Hoffman has called a "sentimental mecanomorphism," an incongruous wedding of the mechanical and impersonal object to the pathetic fallacies of human form.[2] The problem of the machine was one that greatly concerned Crane, and in his 1930 essay "Modern Poetry" he declared that machinery's "firm entrenchment in our lives has already produced a

105

series of challenging new responsibilities for the poet." Crane went on to say (emphasis in original):

> unless poetry can absorb the machine, i.e., *acclimatize* it as naturally and casually as trees, cattle, galleons, castles and all other human associations of the past, then poetry has failed of its full contemporary function. This process does not infer any program of lyrical pandering to the taste of those obsessed by the importance of machinery; nor does it essentially involve even the specific mention of a single mechanical contrivance. It demands, however, along with the traditional qualifications of the poet, an extraordinary capacity for surrender, at least temporarily, to the sensations of urban life. This presupposes, of course, that the poet possesses sufficient spontaneity and gusto to convert this experience into positive terms. Machinery will tend to lose its sensational glamour and appear in its true subsidiary order in human life as use and continual poetic allusion subdue its novelty. For, contrary to general prejudice, the wonderment experienced in watching nose dives is of less immediate creative promise to poetry than the familiar gesture of a motorist in the modest act of shifting gears. I mean to say that mere romantic speculation on the power and beauty of machinery keeps it at a continual remove; it can not act creatively in our lives until, like the unconscious nervous responses of our bodies, its connotations emanate from within – forming as spontaneous a terminology of poetic reference as the bucolic world of pasture, plow, and barn.[3]

Crane's proposed integration of poetry and machinery depends upon an assimilation of mechanical modes of thought and action into poetic *form*. Simple wonder at turbines or reciprocating engines did not interest Crane. Machine poetry, as he said, does not "essentially involve even the specific mention of a single mechanical contrivance": rather it succeeds in incorporating within its modes of artistic expression a correlative to such mechanical operations as "a motorist in the modest act of shifting gears." The way that *The Bridge* itself shifts gears, punningly oscillates between different layers of meaning, is exactly this *acclimatization* of the machine into the realms of poetry. As "Cape Hatteras" implies, a sudden "flash" jolts the poem onto a different level; and it is no surprise to find that, in an obsolete sense, *flash* is used to denote "a play on words; a quibble":

> A flash over the horizon – shifting gears –
> And we have laughter, or more sudden tears.

Crane sees the machine, "shifting gears," as a twentieth-century manifestation of those fundamental cosmic processes of oscillation described at the beginning of "Cape Hatteras":

> Combustion at the astral core – the dorsal change
> Of energy – convulsive shift of sand . . .

This essential "change / Of energy" is reflected first of all in the ocean-waves, which revolve upon the oscillation of their tides:

> Where strange tongues *vary* messages of surf
>
> Sea eyes and *tidal*, undenying, bright with myth!

But the sea is in turn mirrored by the machines in "Cape Hatteras," which also manifest themselves in dualistic imagery:

> O sinewy silver *biplane*, nudging the wind's withers!
>
> *Two* brothers in their *twin*ship left the dune
>
> Vast engines outward *veering* with seraphic grace

This kind of duality and vacillation works its way into other lines of "Cape Hatteras," so that in this section Crane's whole universe seems to become a force-field turning upon the interaction of opposites:

> . . . until a conch of thunder *answers*
> Cloud-belfries, banging, while searchlights, like *fencers*
>
> O Walt! – Ascensions of thee hover in me now
> As thou at *junctions* elegiac, there, of speed
> With vast eternity, dost wield the *rebound* seed!

And the pun, vacillating between opposite poles, is the natural literary equivalent to this universe of "dorsal change":

> And from above, thin squeaks of radio static,
> The captured fume of space foams in our ears –
> What whisperings of far watches on the main

Those "watches on the *main*" are now watches on the electric main, Americans tuning in to the radio; but the way *main* puns on the great sea, and the analogy the verb *foams* makes between nautical and electrical imagery, serve to demonstrate how sea and machine are both accidents relating back to this same essential process of "Combustion at the astral core." So *The Bridge* does not indulge in uncomplicated paeans to the machine-age, but functions like a piece of new technology in its own right. In Black and Monroe, the mechanical revolution manifested itself in poetic content merely; but in Crane it also manifests itself in poetic form. Whereas Monroe anthropomorphized, Crane moves in the opposite direction, assimilating poetry and the human world itself within a mechanical idiom. To quote again from "Cape Hatteras":

> Seeing himself an atom in a shroud –
> Man hears *himself* an engine in a cloud!

The imagery inside the second stanza of "Ave Maria" provides a good example of Crane's technological techniques at work. Ostensibly couched in the style of late medieval heroism, the verse projects itself forward in time to include complex electrical associations, and to itself function in a quasi-electrical way by an ingenious system of alternating currents. Punning analogies (philosophical bridges) are built between past and present, so that the "Crested and creeping" ocean-waves surrounding Columbus' ships anticipate the oscillating currents ("Crested and creeping") of twentieth-century electromagnetism; but the work of art itself also wavers between opposite poles, for Crane's puns ensure that this "Crested and creeping" action becomes poetically self-reflexive:

> Here waves climb into dusk on gleaming mail;
> Invisible valves of the sea, – locks, tendons
> Crested and creeping, troughing corridors
> That fall back yawning to another plunge.
> Slowly the sun's red caravel drops light
> Once more behind us . . . It is morning there –
> O where our Indian emperies lie revealed,
> Yet lost, all, let this keel one instant yield!

In its guise as a knight's armour, *mail* reinforces the heroic and chivalric theme of Columbus' quest; but taking *mail* back to its etymological origins, we find the Old English *mael* signified a contract, agreement or soldier's pay. "Mail" as soldiers' armour was the physical manifestation of this agreement, but as the word became abstracted it came to mean a small piece of money (especially a silver half-penny at the time of Henry V) or rent and tribute (hence our compounds like "blackmail"). For Ferdinand and Isabella, this is the kind of "gleaming mail" they are particularly interested in, and it points again to the economic merry-go-round which set this enterprise in motion. Of course the *mail* of the knight's armour is a splendid visual analogy to the sun setting over the ocean and the waves glinting in the distance, but the word's more abstract associations are equally important. After Crane's death, E. E. Cummings recalled how his friend used to "thunder there'd always been and would always remain three sorts of people: warriors, priests, merchants"; and this sheds light on these analogical links in "Ave Maria" between covetous Spanish merchants (who subsidized this epic voyage), the warrior-hero Columbus (who executed it) and the poet-priest Crane (who celebrates and sanctifies it).[4]

> Invisible valves of the sea, – locks, tendons

The technical connotations of "valve" transpose the Atlantic Ocean into an elaborate component of Crane's machine-world, technological wizardry foreshadowed in an earlier time. (In Crane's own famous formulation, "to realize suddenly, as I seem to, how much of the past is living under only slightly altered forms, even in machinery and such-like, is extremely exciting.")[5] In electronics, "valve" denotes a contri-

vance "that permits a flow of current in one direction only, used esp. for
rectifying alternating currents"; and so this image becomes poetically
self-reflexive, for the decorous structure of *The Bridge*, like the social
conventions of daily life, allows for only one direction, although all kinds
of other possibilities are bubbling under the surface. Although the *valves*
are *Invisible*, they should not be ignored by the reader alert to the tensions
and suspensions written into Crane's *Bridge*. We also find Columbus here
personifying the sea: for those *valves* can signify a membranous part of
the human anatomy allowing the flow of blood, and *tendons* here may
denote the dense tissue attaching muscle to bone. Similarly, "lock" can
be a "tress, or ringlet of hair" suitable for the medieval warrior; and we
should notice as well how the rings of hair coincide with the rings of his
chain-mail armour. The poem can be bewildering because everything is
defined in terms of everything else: the sea is personified and conceptual-
ized, as we have seen, and the metaphors do actually inter*lock* to produce
closed, self-validating systems. The sea is armour. The sun is a boat.
Objects are denied empirical validity and refracted through the mind of
the maker, who slots the world together with the rigorous logic of a
master-carpenter into a series of mortise and tenon joints. I. A. Richards
in *The Philosophy of Rhetoric* (1936) insisted that, far from being merely an
ornate literary device, metaphor is at the very centre of human modes of
perception and that we explain things to ourselves by analogies. No
object is autonomous, all must be named, and all naming depends upon
comparison with other objects. But if metaphor is a Noble Lie, the
bifocal nature of the pun exposes that lie, for in its swinging between
opposites the pun reveals that every metaphorical imposition can be
contradicted. Metaphor may be necessary, but every metaphor has an
alternative, and so metaphor is a provisional not absolute construction:

> Crested and creeping, troughing corridors

Crested continues the heraldic link (the crests on the helmets of the
medieval warriors), and the word's interaction with *creeping* also gives us
the idea of oscillation and varying depths. "Creep" has all kinds of other
technical uses, mainly concerned with the hindrance of natural or
mechanical processes. For instance, it describes the retrograde movement
on the pulley of a belt as it slides backward "by reason of the contraction
of the belt as the tension is released in passing from the tight side to the
slack side": the general idea is of the *creeping* scepticism of Crane's poem
checking its *Crested* idealism. Electrical images are also central here, for
creeping can be "a variation in the path of an electric current from a direct
line through the conductor," and a "trough battery" (*troughing*
corridors) is "a voltaic battery contained in a vessel divided into cells by
partitions": suggesting that Columbus' transatlantic mission is an

electrical charge leaping across the partitions to form a circuit between Old World and New. Nor are we allowed to forget the economic motives which initiated this voyage, for "Crested and creeping" could analogically refer back to activity at the Spanish court, where politicians in all their finery were obliged to abase themselves to achieve their ends; and in this context the *corridors* of the ocean may punningly relate to secret meetings in corridors of the Spanish palace, without which, in all likelihood, Columbus would never have left Europe.

> That fall back yawning to another plunge.

Crane's "three sorts of people: warriors, priests, merchants" would all find something of interest in this line. The priest would note that, in days gone by, *plunge* was used to mean "to baptize by immersion" – an appropriate image for crossing the ocean to find a New World. The merchant would concern himself more with Webster's slang definition for "plunge": "to bet or gamble heavily and with seeming recklessness; to risk large sums in hazardous enterprises," a fear of overreaching themselves that must have been common to both Columbus and Crane as they started out on their quests. And the warrior would note that, in American military slang, a "plunger" is a cavalryman, thus continuing the epic thread of Columbus and his army riding into battle. In the previous line we were left uncertain whether Columbus is himself *troughing* (subjugating) the *corridors* of the ocean, or whether *troughing* is an adjectival participle leaving Columbus as the passive object bobbing up and down on the *troughing* ocean-waves; and similarly here we do not know whether it is the sea or the men that are doing the "plunging." The men may be heroically exerting their free will and conquering the waves, or merely being manipulated by them: it is a typical Whiteheadian reversal of subject and object. Either the corridors fall back yawning to start another one of their plunges, or the corridors "fall back" (retreat) in deference to the *plunge* of Columbus' task-force.

> Slowly the sun's red caravel drops light
> Once more behind us . . .

A *caravel* in the fifteenth and sixteenth centuries was "a small vessel with broad bows," and Webster specifies that "Columbus had two *caravels* with him on his great voyage." Hence Columbus is visualizing the sun as a ship, another indication of how objects possess no independent life, but must be interpreted by the onlooker. Columbus' interpretation is naturally, as Crane put it, "in the terms of [his] own cosmography": society's practice of mapping out heaven and earth as an extension of its own environment is the necessary fiction underlying this poem.[6] The interlocking metaphors also connect the actions of the sun with the machines of modern America, for "drop" as "a fall of electric potential due to resistance of the circuit" metamorphoses the sun into an exhausted battery. And the way Columbus' apparently absurd mythologization of his surroundings actually mirrors the anthropomorphism of Crane's twentieth-century "myth to God" is further emphasized by the fact that a "drop bar" is "in a suspension bridge, any of the vertical bars connecting the roadway and the chain," because if we reverse subject and object, turning *drops* into a noun and *light* into a verb, we find not the sun dropping light but the sun lighting drops – dawn arising over the vertical bars of Brooklyn Bridge, as we saw in the "Proem."

> . . . It is morning there –
> O where our Indian emperies lie revealed,
> Yet lost, all, let this keel one instant yield!

Columbus, of course, gets it wrong: if he was gazing towards Spain at sunset, it would be morning in Cathay (China) but certainly not in America. And he was well wide of the mark in thinking his quest had eased Spain's passage to her "Indian emperies." His *lie* is *revealed* by the dramatic irony of the poem. The simple narrative meaning of "Yet lost, all, let this keel one instant yield!" is that Columbus fears his voyage will be wasted if the one remaining ship capsizes after two have already been lost. But *keel* had an alternative sense: "a mark made with [red ocher], as at either end of a warp of yarn, to show whether the weaver has used the full length." This is the link between the mariner Columbus and the weaver Crane, for it now becomes possible to see the last phrase as an exhortation: let this tapestry, the poem, reproduce (*yield* as "bear" rather than "relinquish") the "Indian emperies" (the heart of the American continent, as seen in "Powhatan's Daughter"), that culture which historically has been *lost*, but which this fictional poem by its *lie* is able to recapture and reveal. The dramatic irony merges into an example of Crane's formal internal bridging between different parts of his long poem: the "Indian emperies" do not "lie revealed" to Columbus, for Columbus was nowhere near India, but American Indian culture can "lie revealed" to the reader of the skilfully fabricated "Powhatan's Daughter" section of *The Bridge*, where the poet offers to "Lie to us" in order to "dance us back the tribal morn."

Let me attempt to summarize what we have found amongst the complicated cross-currents of this stanza:

(a) Punning analogies between past and present. These are verbal and philosophical bridges indicating Crane's belief in the way different eras mirror each other. The emblems of medieval heroism elide into emblems of twentieth-century technology, just as "Series on series, infinite" (four stanzas later) yokes Roman Ceres with the *series* of ocean-waves and also with a *series* of electrical circuits (currents "in series").

(b) The form of the pun is an expression of this modernistic technology that Crane integrates into his poetry. Ocean-waves, radio waves, electric currents – all operate by alternation, rising and falling. So the oscillations inherent in Crane's poem are a poetic correlative to the inventions of twentieth-century science. Like a radio-set, *The Bridge* itself functions in a "Crested and creeping" manner.

(c) The technological complexity of the poem becomes a means of circumscribing Columbus' heroic free will. Columbus' freedom is balanced by the impersonal machinery of the external world. Is Columbus himself troughing the corridors of the ocean? (The imagery of the medieval warrior would suggest so.) Or is his Romantic subjugation of the world an illusion, is Columbus really dependent for his success upon the favours of the earth's oscillating tides? (All the puns on electric circuits would imply that the sea's "troughing corridors" resemble electricity in that they construct their own self-perpetuating machine which incorporates Columbus as just one more unit inside the system.)

As we have already seen, this kind of relativity whereby active becomes passive and vice versa is an important theme of "Ave Maria." It is a theme Crane made deliberate emendations in his manuscripts to develop, omitting, for instance, a comma after *reel*:

> And biassed by full sails, meridians reel
> Thy purpose – still one shore beyond desire![7]

In this world of perpetual change, where Columbus moves around a world moving in turn around the sun, the Admiral's *purpose* is itself "reeled," for the spinning globe superimposes a dramatic irony upon even his most magnificent efforts. We saw an example of such dramatic irony in this second stanza, where Columbus erroneously assumes he has found the gateway to Spain's "Indian emperies," and in the next stanza he makes an equally mistaken reference to "The Chan's great continent." Columbus originally thought he had landed in China, and his error is synecdochic of the pattern of *The Bridge*, where statements which seem at first sight true turn out to be at least misleading. (Though nowhere near "The Chan's great continent," Columbus was indeed adjacent to what in a later century was to be "The Kahn's great continent," for the financial empire of Crane's patron Otto H. Kahn extended from coast to coast across America. If by a trick-mirror the soft h in *Chan* slides into a hard h, Columbus finds himself magically transposed into modern times. Again, Oriental nobility is punningly redefined within a twentieth-century commercial idiom.) So the ironies of relativity revenge themselves upon a world that can never be entirely self-contained; and Crane's formal links between the various sections of *The Bridge* even manage to associate Columbus' uncertainty about his geographical whereabouts with the uncertainty of the narrator who is confronted by the magic island of "Atlantis":

> – One Song, one Bridge of Fire! Is it Cathay,
> Now pity steeps the grass and rainbows ring
> The serpent with the eagle in the leaves . . . ?
> Whispers antiphonal in azure swing.

"Is it Cathay . . ?" echoes Columbus' question as he set foot on the new-found land; and in these closing lines of the poem, the conception of a further relativity, a world glimpsed but not yet named, looms large. Just as Columbus stumbled upon a New World within the Old, so the reader may find a new world of magical puns within the old literal world of Crane's *Bridge*. The images of magnetism in "Ave Maria" ("A needle in the sight, suspended north") are compatible with this kind of relativity, for the premise of magnetism is a world where objects are not static but flow towards something else. Columbus describes himself as "under bare poles scudding," but he is being moved along not just by the "bare poles" of his own ship, but also by the positive and negative *poles* of the earth's magnetic field. It is a historical fact that the expansion of maritime activity in the fifteenth century was greatly facilitated by the discovery of the polarity of the magnet; but the magnet's production of a world where nothing is motionless, all in motion, leads directly to the dramatic ironies that later undermine the dignity of Columbus. If the world is perpetually rotating, nobody can subjugate this turning world, not even Columbus.[8] Columbus thought he was in "Asia," but the antiphonal whispers punningly swing him back to *azure*, for what Columbus thought was Cathay turns out to be in fact America:

> For I have seen now what no perjured breath
> Of clown nor sage can riddle or gainsay; –
> To you, too, Juan Perez, whose counsel fear
> And greed adjourned, – I bring you back Cathay!

Columbus' hailing of "Cathay" as the one truthful thing beyond the "perjured breath" of language is clearly comic. *The Bridge* is a poem of relativity, and it is designed so that time reveals all things in a new light.

The balance maintained in "Ave Maria" between individual heroism and impersonal systems is consistent with those capitalist themes which are central to *The Bridge*. The invocation in the first line of "Ave Maria" of Ferdinand and Isabella's treasurer, Luis de San Angel ("Be with me, Luis de San Angel, now"), stresses how fifteenth-century Spain, no less than twentieth-century America, turned upon an axis of financial arrangements. Columbus himself was determined to make his fortune by making other people's fortunes, and Ferdinand and Isabella agreed to subsidize his exploratory expedition largely out of mercenary motives. The discovery of America may have been an opportunity for spiritual reflections and an example of human heroism, but it was mercilessly underpinned by economic considerations. The active pioneer was also a passive agent of the money-machine.

AEROPLANES AND PUNS: "TRANSITION"

The most obvious counterparts to Columbus during Crane's lifetime were those aeronautical pioneers who essayed the bridging of land and air. It is noticeable how the exploits of the "Wright windwrestlers" in "Cape Hatteras" are punningly put into a commercial context:

> There, from Kill Devils Hill at Kitty Hawk
> Two brothers in their twinship left the dune;
> Warping the gale, the Wright windwrestlers veered
> Capeward, then blading the wind's flank, banked and spun
> What ciphers risen from prophetic script

Crane's place names always seem magically appropriate, and the *Kitty* (slang for "a pot or pool of money, made up of contributions from several people" (f)) which allowed the Wright brothers' aeroplane to get off the ground was forthcoming largely because of the commercial possibilities of air travel (*Hawk* as to carry about for sale). The way the brothers "*banked* and spun" punningly anticipates the vast amounts of money capitalist entrepreneurs were able to put in their *bank*-accounts when aeroplanes became economically viable, and so the "prophetic script" is also prophetic "scrip" (slang for "a dollar bill" and "money" (f)). As with Columbus' expedition, the pioneering voyage has a commercial *raison d'être* which does not invalidate the pilots' heroism, but objectifies it, and so demonstrates how the lone hero must interact with the impersonal forces of society.

Aviation was in the news all the time during the late 1920s. One endurance record and death-defying feat succeeded another. (James Thurber in *Is Sex Necessary?* (1929) classed aviation with sex as the two subjects whose importance had been greatly overemphasized during the previous year.) However, the most celebrated inhabitant of the skies was Charles Lindbergh, whose solo flight across the Atlantic in 1927 was hailed as a triumph for both Romantic individualism and corporate responsibility:

> Lindbergh was the living symbol of the young, independent American unbound by organization and public pressures. Yet, ironically, his achievement was made possible through the refinements of technology, organization

and industrial finesse. Lindbergh himself gave equal credit to the plane, "that
wonderful motor," and President Coolidge expressed his pride "that in every
particular this silent partner represented American genius and industry."[9]

Columbus and Lindbergh had both bridged the Old World and the New
by a process of heroism working in tandem with mechanical skill, and
Crane himself was determined that his Bridge should follow in their
footsteps. As he wrote to his father in 1927,

> For over a month we haven't heard, read, eaten or been permitted to dream
> anything but airplanes and Lindbergh . . . Time and space is the myth of the
> modern world, however, and it's interesting to see how any victory in that
> field is heralded by the mass of humanity. In a way my Bridge is a manifestation
> of the same general subject. Maybe I'm just a little jealous of Lindy![10]

Again it is not only the theme of Lindbergh's conquering of time and
space that Crane imitates, for Crane's verbal puns – "Giddily spiralled
gauntlets, upturned, unlooping" – are equivalents to the aeroplane in the
way that they defy gravity. The puns themselves leap away from one
sedentary denotation and cavort in the air like aeroplanes looping the
loop. Crane found a poetic technique that was adequate to his advanced
content, for the verbal units are as innovatory as the instruments they
describe. There is none of the banal "sentimental mecanomorphism"
which Hoffman found in Harriet Monroe's turbine. Monroe personified
the machine; but Crane went in the opposite direction, depersonalizing
his poetic world so that the poem itself becomes a magnificent flying
machine, changing gears and spinning dexterously over time and space.
The Twenties was a decade famous for bizarre mechanical inventions,
and *The Bridge* is one of these new toys, a poem that bears the same kind
of relation to nineteenth-century poetry as an automobile does to a horse
and cart. Like all new inventions, *The Bridge* may be imperfect, cranky, at
times unreliable; but it is never dull or complacent, for Crane was
genuinely striving to expand the frontiers of poetic possibility, to
acclimatize machines within the forms of artistic consciousness and so to
harness the energies of American corporate life in the interests of a poetic
"myth to God."

The equation between technological discovery and verbal revolution
was being made most frequently during the late Twenties in the Parisian
magazine *transition*. *transition* often published work by Crane – the
"Cutty Sark," "Harbor Dawn" and "Van Winkle" sections of *The
Bridge* all made their first appearance here – and when Crane visited Paris
in 1929, he found Eugene Jolas, the magazine's editor, ready to act as his
guide. As we shall see later, *transition* was most famous for its serialization
of Joyce's "Work in Progress," later *Finnegans Wake*; but nearly all the
contributors to *transition* were akin to Joyce in so far as they emphasized a

language that transcended national barriers and were dedicated to an eradication of the sense of locality that permeated realistic literature. Jolas's creed was "vertigralism," a combination of *vertical* and *grail* which denoted his attempt to rise above the sluggish material world. Jolas was himself well placed to edit a multilingual magazine, having been born in New Jersey but brought up in his family's native Lorraine, which he left again at the age of sixteen to return to New York. Jolas spoke English, French and German, and under the pseudonym of "Theo Rutra" he tried his hand at writing trilingual poetry. "Dusk" appeared in the November 1927 issue of *transition*:

> Oor forests hear thine voice it winks
> Ravines fog gleamen and the eyes
> When night comes dooze and nabel sinks
> Trowm quills unheard and lize.

Dougald McMillan has patiently explicated this bizarrerie, showing how *lize*, for instance, conflates English *lies* and German *leise* (quietly), while *Trowm* mingles English *down* and *town* with German *Traum* (dream).[11] This is a direct parallel to the multilingual puns Crane (occasionally) employs, as in the "mere toil" of the "Proem" – French *mer*, sea, plus *mère*, mother.

Given such emphasis upon a language that flies by the nets of nationality, it is not difficult to understand how the aeroplane – an emblem of international travel – became part of the iconography of *transition*. Harry Crosby, one of the magazine's joint editors, was a particular devotee of flying, waiting patiently at Le Bourget for Lindbergh in 1927, and proclaiming to his diary that Lindbergh was "the New Christ" and "the New Cross is the Plane." A few months later, Crosby made the analogy between air travel and linguistic revolution by asking himself, "what is the Atlantic to the Oceans Joyce has crossed?"[12] Ezra Pound, who expresses his antipathy towards aeroplanes in Canto 28, exemplifies an exactly opposite literary point of view: Pound implicitly associates Captain Hinchcliffe's fatal attempt to fly the Atlantic with the disembodied idealism of Emerson ("the Sage of Concord / 'Too broad ever to make up his mind'") and sees this as a warning of the consequences of failing to keep one's feet on the ground.[13] But it was largely Poundian attitudes that this time of *transition* was reacting against: Pound's emphasis on the uncluttered image was itself a rebellion against vague Victorian rhetoric; but the *transition* writers were working some fifteen years after the emergence of the Imagists, and they loudly announced themselves to be in revolt against what they saw as Pound's fallacy of misplaced concreteness. Accordingly, *transition* chose to reassert the primacy of language over referent, signifier over signified; and in this context, caps were doffed to Gertrude Stein, who, said

William Carlos Williams, had "found the key with her conception of the objective use of words."[14] Stein manipulated words as if they were objective realities in themselves, selecting them not for "meaning" but for their sound and their formal interrelations. In her "sentences," Stein was attempting to imitate the geometric shapes of Cubist painting, or the abstract necessity of music with words functioning as if formal and autonomous "notes." Elliot Paul, a supporter of Stein, compared her work to Bach's fugues. Eugene Jolas was more lukewarm in his admiration, but he was prepared to open the pages of transition to such a notable personality, and in her contributions to the first issue in April 1927 we can see the basic underlying assumptions Stein shared with the "Revolution of the Word" party. "Halve Rivers and Harbours" plays on and slightly modifies words to suggest the arbitrary correlation between sound and meaning ("you do see that you that you do not have rivers and harbours when you halve rivers and harbours"); and in other pieces Stein continued to weave her elaborate and entirely self-referential verbal patterns:

> Two next.
> To be next to it.
> To be annexed.
> To be annexed to it.[15]

Crane must have seen these pieces by Stein because he wrote to Yvor Winters on 27 March 1927: "The first issue of transition arrived yesterday. It is far better constructed – physically and 'spiritually' than I expected . . . And it so intrigues me that I'm going to send Jolas a number of things."[16] Crane's work was also to appear regularly in transition, but he and Stein were at opposite ends of the magazine's spectrum in that his American side wanted to push these ingenuities through to a moral conclusion, while Stein was content to remain closeted in her studio. Crane and Stein got on well personally, but Crane found her work boring and the most obvious example of that Parisian frivolity he complained to Katherine Anne Porter about.[17]

Nevertheless – and it is a fact of the greatest significance – Crane did sign the "Revolution of the Word" manifesto which appeared in the Spring–Summer 1929 issue of transition. This "Proclamation" declared transition was "Tired of the spectacle of short stories, novels, poems and plays still under the hegemony of the banal word, monotonous syntax, static psychology, descriptive naturalism"; and it accordingly went on to announce:

1. The revolution in the English language is an accomplished fact.
2. The imagination in search of a fabulous world is autonomous and unconfined.
3. Pure poetry is a lyrical absolute that seeks an a priori reality within ourselves alone.

4. Narrative is not mere anecdote, but the projection of a metamorphosis of reality.
5. The expression of these concepts can be achieved only through the rhythmic "hallucination of the word" (Rimbaud).
6. The literary creator has the right to disintegrate the primal matter of words imposed on him by text-books and dictionaries.
7. He has the right to use words of his own fashioning and to disregard existing grammatical and syntactical laws.
8. The "litany of words" is admitted as an independent unit.
9. We are not concerned with the propagation of sociological ideas, except to emancipate the creative elements from the present ideology.
10. Time is a tyranny to be abolished.
11. The writer expresses. He does not communicate.
12. The plain reader be damned.

Among the other signatories were both Crosbys, Jolas, Kay Boyle, Stuart Gilbert, Elliot Paul and Robert Sage.[18] In *Exile's Return*, Malcolm Cowley gave a derogatory account of these proceedings, claiming that although Crane signed the document he was later ashamed of having done so and excused himself on the grounds that he had been drunk.[19] Now, it may well be that Crane felt some unease about the Proclamation's more extravagant claims for the autonomy of the creative imagination: *The Bridge*, after all, was intended to reflect the social and material circumstances of the United States. It may also be that Cowley, who had rediscovered social realism in the late 1920s and who regarded the Proclamation as "portentous," would have encouraged Crane to be flippant about it. But, as Dougald McMillan put it,

> The explanation that he was drunk does not cover the facts of Crane's relation to Jolas and the manifesto sufficiently. He was in Paris for over a month during which time he became close to Jolas and talked frequently with him. Jolas wrote in his autobiography that in these discussions Crane agreed upon each point of the manifesto.[20]

And so we should not dismiss this intriguing fact that Crane's signature is appended to a document which supports the poet's right "to disintegrate the primal matter of words," "to use words of his own fashioning" and "to disregard existing grammatical and syntactical laws." *The Bridge* may not have toed the party-line as far as the "Revolution of the Word" movement was concerned, but it was a poem which had much in common with *transition*'s iconoclastic verbal experiments. In this context, it is appropriate that in his 1924 essay "General Aims and Theories" Crane should have talked of how his poetry was searching for a "new *word*," which he saw as the path to "certain spiritual illuminations" (emphasis in original): "It is as though a poem gave the reader as he left it a single, new *word*, never before spoken and impossible to actually enunciate, but self-evident as an active principle in the reader's consciousness henceforward" – for though in his later poetry Crane seems to take a more agnostic attitude towards these "spiritual illuminations," no such doubts surround the efficacy of the other half of this equation, the "new word" itself.[21]

McMillan emphasized how for these revolutionary *transition* writers the multi-faceted pun had succeeded the image as the best way of presenting "an emotional complex in an instant of time"; and he went on to discuss how the priority Crane apportions to word over image results in his work possessing an open form, a continuous straining to project itself beyond literal levels of experience.[22] In Yeats' "Among School Children," to take a contrasting example, the tensions inside the poem are resolved in the image of the chestnut-tree and the dancer; but in "Atlantis," while we have the visual details of Brooklyn Bridge's "bound cable strands" and so on, there are overt references to the processes of language ("Sibylline *voices*," "labyrinthine *mouths* of history," "death's *utter* wound," "River-*throated*," "myriad *syllables*") – all of which have the effect of divesting the bridge of its status as an empirical object. In Eliot's religious poems, the object of devotion is fixed and imperfect human words revolve uncertainly around that object; but in "Atlantis," inscription precedes description, and language is a means of inventing the world. Time is a "multitudinous Verb" casting and recasting human myths. McMillan thought Crane a more conventional poet than the rest of the *transition* circle, someone who "was content to leave words as he found them . . . but to use them in new and unusual combinations"; but in fact Crane was one of the most radical verbal engineers this time of *transition* produced.[23]

According to his unpublished autobiography, Jolas very nearly decided to call his magazine "The Bridge," a title which in his case would have implied the crossing of national linguistic frontiers that *transition* specialized in.[24] Like aeroplanes, bridges were a common feature of the iconography of *transition*, for both implied the freedom attainable by technological progress in harness with human imagination. In the Spring–Summer 1929 number, Joseph Stella effectively annotated his own Brooklyn Bridge paintings as he discussed "The Brooklyn Bridge (A Page of My Life)." "Brooklyn gave me a sense of liberation," said Stella. "The vast view of her sky, in opposition to the narrow one of NEW YORK, was a relief – and at night, in her solitude, I used to find, intact, the green freedom of my own self." In the same article, Stella described Whitman's poetry as "soaring above as a white aeroplane of Help." And, in the same issue, Harry Crosby celebrated "The New Word" in metallic terms: "the clean piercing of a Sword through the rotten carcass of the Dictionary . . . the girder bridge towards a splendid future . . . the defiance of laws."[25] Bridges, aeroplanes and puns all have a Promethean quality to them: they defy the limitations of a supposedly "natural" world. We have seen how in ancient legend the deities would demand the sacrifice of a human life as recompense for the hubristic business of erecting a bridge over the god–given water, and aeroplanes and puns are similar "vertigralist" attempts to defy gravity.

The hubristic Harry Crosby even decided to live out his theories by taking flying lessons himself, piloting a plane single–handed for the first time just a few weeks before his suicide in 1929; and this kind of machine 'vertigralism' was a mirror of Crosby's belief that "a metaphysical system governs the poet's days, and must be unriddled," and that the artist − necessarily a magician and seer − was the agent who would unravel Man's terrestrial conundrum.[26] For Crosby, as for Crane, words were the precious stones which held the key to a secret world. Crosby's diaries are scattered with coded messages ("harry eagle of the sun," for instance, becomes "rinnu nirln na orn xyz"), and on 23 August 1927 he made a note reminding himself to "study the Code Diary of Samuel Pepys and Poe's Essay on Cryptography." Unlike Crane, Crosby seems to have firmly believed there was a higher spiritual reality which his cryptic wordplay might uncover: "I like dictionaries better than novels," wrote Crosby in 1929, backing up his assertion with a list of the twenty–five assorted dictionaries in his possession.[27] Crane himself became a great friend of Harry Crosby and his wife Caresse, who both provided invaluable psychological and material help which galvanized him into finishing *The Bridge*; and it was the Crosbys' Black Sun Press in Paris which published the first edition of *The Bridge* in February 1930, by which time Harry Crosby had killed himself in a suicide pact with Josephine Bigelow. Whether Crosby or Crane was the more disreputable figure is an issue that has divided commentators, but for our purposes it is important to note that they both mixed in circles where the Revolution of the Word and the Revolution of the Machine were seen to be cognate.

To conclude: Crane assimilated the machine into his poetry through innovation in form rather than content. *The Bridge* itself resembles an electrical instrument functioning on alternating currents, or an aeroplane looping the loop; and the prevalence of the mechanical imagery helps to preserve the conceptual balance in *The Bridge* between individual Romantic heroism and the larger economic and technological worlds which make sure heroism possible. *The Bridge* is certainly a daring and unusual poem, but we should not allow dismissive Johnsonian kinds of "common sense" to circumscribe the possibilities of great literature; and this is especially important in considering art of the 1920s, when, as Hoffman has said, every kind of "natural" limit was being destroyed.

Writers were caught up in the exuberant compulsion of the time to "make it new": "Each major work of literature was unique and *sui generis*. For the first time, perhaps, in modern civilization, all patterns of society and tradition were subjected to fresh, original and outrageous scrutiny."[28]

10

James Joyce

THE DISRUPTION OF REALISM: "ULYSSES"

In the previous chapter we saw how Crane was associated with the Parisian magazine *transition*, and how theorists of the "Revolution of the Word" who congregated around *transition* came to have an important influence on Crane, or at least to reflect his linguistic interests. It is not customary to associate Crane with sophisticated European art: although the presence of Americans in Paris during the 1920s has become legend, Crane is said to represent that native American tradition which viewed with some scepticism what it saw as the cultural high jinks emanating from across the Atlantic. But this dichotomy is itself a critical oversimplification. William Carlos Williams, customarily made to represent a patriotic robustness and realism, appeared in the Parisian magazine *transition* for November 1927 saluting Joyce's "Work in Progress" as "perfectly clear and full of great interest in form and content"; while Sherwood Anderson, the epitome of American purity and romanticism, was on friendly terms with Joyce and Gertrude Stein.[1] Of course there were clashes of personality, but around this time Paris was such an important artistic centre – Pound, Joyce, Picasso, Stravinsky, the Surrealists – that only the most determinedly provincial could afford to ignore the city. Crane was not among them, and he himself spent some six months in France in 1929 when the editor of *transition*, Eugene Jolas, introduced him to notable literary figures. R. W. B. Lewis talked of how "Crane had a deep-rooted suspicion of Europe and resented its attitude toward America," because with his "Romantic American ancestry" Crane had no time for the "cynical contempt" he supposedly found in Europe.[2] This is a half-truth in so far as (like Williams and Anderson) Crane was keen to annex modernist technique in the service of his indigenous content. As an American moralist he disapproved of how some Parisians "were just cutting paper dollies" (as he told Katherine Anne Porter), toying with experimental forms rather than engaging with art's substance.[3] But traditional criticism of Crane has largely tended to ignore his cosmopolitanism and pigeon-hole him as the heir of Whitman without recognizing that one of the bridges Crane was building was a bridge across the Atlantic. Just as Columbus was obliged to involve himself in all kinds of machiavellian intrigues in the Spanish court before his epic voyage could get under way, so Crane's American dream is underwritten by linguistic intricacies worked out in Parisian salons.

The European writer for whom Crane preserved the most constant enthusiasm was James Joyce. In 1918, two years after *A Portrait of the Artist as a Young Man* was published, the nineteen-year-old Crane wrote a defence of Joyce in *The Little Review*, ridiculing the charges of "decadence," "obscenity" and "intellect" brought against the Irishman, and declaring *A Portrait* to be "spiritually the most inspiring book I have ever read."[4] Crane's enthusiasm for *Ulysses*, which he persuaded Munson to smuggle back from Paris for him, was even more marked. In July 1922 he was saying it was "easily the epic of the age," and a month later Charmion Wiegand heard that *Ulysses* "in many ways surpasses anything I have ever read."[5] It was at this time that Crane said Joyce was "the one above all others I should like to talk to," a desire that was never fulfilled because, although the Crosbys knew Joyce well, Crane and Joyce were never introduced.[6] Nevertheless Crane always took Joyce as a model for others to learn from. In August 1922 Crane told Munson: "Frank is so young that he has lots of time to benefit by Joyce and even go further – although I doubt if such will will [sic] be done for a hundred years or more."[7] Malcolm Cowley said that Joyce was the "paramount hero" of this age and that "*Ulysses* came to be revered by the new writers almost as the Bible was by Primitive Methodists"; and Crane was certainly no exception to this, refusing to entrust his illegally imported loose-leaf copy to a bookbinder, and throwing what was even for him a wild fit after he found the novel stolen from his Cleveland bedroom in 1923.[8]

Archibald MacLeish later remembered that in American avant-garde literary circles of the Twenties, *Ulysses*, interweaving actuality with classical myth, "formed the sense of history in which we lived"; and indeed the clearest similarity between *Ulysses* and *The Bridge* lies in the way Crane imitates Joyce's mythological doubling of Dublin. Just as "palladium helm of stars" links Brooklyn Bridge back to the Trojan citadel protected by Pallas Athene, so in the "mocking mirrors" that twin Joyce's novel with Homer's *Odyssey* we find Leopold Bloom and his friends exposed as reincarnations of classical heroes. At the end of the novel, for example, Bloom kisses Molly's backside in a gesture imitating the way Homer's hero kisses the soil of Ithaca.[9] As in all mock-epic, the analogies elevate as well as deflate the apparently bathetic object: if Bloom looks small beside Ulysses, the comparison with Ulysses also grants him refracted grandeur. Hence Eliot's famous essay of 1923, "*Ulysses*, Order and Myth," which argued that, far from celebrating the chaos of modern life, Joyce was in fact rigorously codifying it and so lending his own "myth to God." Joyce, who had covertly invented the phrase "interior monologue" himself, also urged Eliot to circulate "two plane," a phrase they had coined in conversation;[10] and though "two plane" was an expression Eliot was unwilling to take up, Crane's "sinewy silver biplane" in "Cape Hatteras" is summarizing this same principle:

> O sinewy silver biplane, nudging the wind's withers!

Both Crane and Joyce exploited the Rip Van Winkle legend, which is useful in this context because it demonstrates the transmutation of one era into another and so the (often disturbing) affinity between past and present. Crane knew Washington Irving's version of the story, in which Rip wakes up after his "deep sleep" to find the "George the Third" inn renamed "The George Washington," all his old friends dead or gone away and his son "a precise counterpart" of how he himself used to be. "The poor fellow was now completely confounded," reports Irving. "He doubted his own identity, and whether he was himself or another man."[11] There are two references to this legend in *Ulysses*. While watching Gerty Macdowell on the beach, Bloom remembers impersonating Rip Van Winkle during charades at Luke Doyle's house in 1887, and this leads him into a meditation on cyclic time ("The year returns. History repeats itself . . . Names change: that's all. Lovers: yum yum").[12] And in the brothel-scene – with the confused memories of the day rotating around his brain – Bloom himself turns into Rip Van Winkle who on waking up sees a woman he thinks is Molly, only to find she is actually Molly's daughter Milly (p. 494). Crane's "Van Winkle" section disestablishes solid and empirical character in a similar way by reworking the tale on a literal level to show the ancient protagonist sadly adrift on a busy New York street, and on a psychological level to show how the narrator's memories of past time intrude upon and disturb his ability to function within a complicated daily existence. The recognition of "how much of the past is living under only slightly altered forms" could be, as Crane told Waldo Frank, "extremely exciting," but it could also be potentially damaging to an individual's psychological stability, even if the disintegration of such stability was necessary in order to redefine radically the relationship of Man to his environment.[13]

Integral to the decomposition of character and "objective" social realism was the subversion of language. Joyce is this century's most famous punster: on the very first page of *Ulysses*, Buck Mulligan overturns "the genuine Christ" into "the genuine Christine"; but a more significant pun is that on "Rose of Castille" and "Rows of cast steel," which initially forms the basis of Lenehan's riddle ("What opera is like a railway line?" – p. 135) and recurs several times within the novel. This is interesting because it implies a transition from romantic fancy to technological production, the conceptual analogy being mirrored in Joyce's verbal analogy; and it is highly appropriate Lenehan should deliver his joke in the *Telegraph* office surrounded by headlines which the "Rows of cast steel" (newspaper type) have delivered. Joyce chops up this Aeolus section into headlines and paragraphs imitating newspaper layout, and this reflects the dislocation of language into the cheap puns and schmaltz characteristic of the press. Because of his job in advertising, Bloom is always on the look-out for puns as well ("Chamber music. Could make a kind of pun on that" – p. 281); and hearing the strains of evening mass while watching Gerty on the beach, Bloom even makes the kind of Surrealistic comparison between religion and advertising that Matthew Josephson would have been proud of: "Mass seems to be over. Could hear them all at it. Pray for us. And pray for us. And pray for us. Good idea the repetition. Same thing with ads. Buy from us. And buy from us" (p. 375). Punning headlines and advertisements are only an exaggerated version of the pastiche that pervades *Ulysses*: nothing is "real," everything is dependent upon a stylistic mode of perception. In structuralist terms, signifier and signified have only an arbitrary connection. The Victorian rhetoric that serenades Gerty Macdowell is not exactly parody, more a device to show the impossibility of monocular vision, just as in the Oxen of the Sun episode the hospital is perceived through a rotating lens of literary styles and so eludes any clear factual definition.

The problem of this dualism between subject and object finds theoretical expression early in the novel, when Stephen is walking on Sandymount Strand:

> Inshore and farther out the mirror of water whitened, spurned by lightshod hurrying feet. White breast of the dim sea. The twining stresses, two by two. A hand plucking the harpstrings merging their twining chords. Wavewhite wedded words shimmering on the dim tide. (p. 15)

The "mirror of water," like the shaving-mirror in the first scene, symbolizes Stephen's narcissistic impulse to project himself onto the external world, in this case to discover an image of his mother in the sea. The *twining* suggests the twine which Stephen feels binds him to this maternal sea ("The cords of all link back, strand*entwining* cable of all flesh" – p. 43), but as "twin-ing" it also implies the doubling or twinning of subject and object in which Stephen's pathetic fallacy indulges. Also self-reflexive are *feet* and *stresses*, punning upon the processes of artistic composition. As in Crane's "Atlantis," the narrator toys with the idea of "wedding" the brutal namelessness of the sea to the poetic fancy of harp or mother; but just as Crane's "whitest Flower" punningly fractures itself into a "whitest Flow-er," so Joyce's *twining* cables redefine natural object as artistic artefact by punning on the arbitrary "twin-ing" of subject and object that brings this anthropomorphic image into play. The puns of Joyce and Crane reveal the fictive nature of the imaginative objects to which they are attached; and the dualistic process of the pun thereby constructs and deconstructs poetic vision at one and the same time.

GAMES WITH LANGUAGE: "FINNEGANS WAKE"

In the extended pun that is *Finnegans Wake*, Joyce transposes history into forms of burlesque in a way similar to Crane's redefinition of standard American legends in *The Bridge*. Crane's pun on "avail" as profits ("There was a veil upon you, Pocahontas, bride") turns the Indian myth into a comic pastiche; and Joyce's similar equation of history and burlesque is nicely emphasized by the way the Marx brothers squeeze into *Finnegans Wake*. Before their first film in 1929, Groucho and the others made a name for themselves in the vaudeville theatres of New York – after watching one show, Matthew Josephson compared them to European Dadaists.[14] In the first section of "Work in Progress," published in the first *transition* of April 1927, Joyce takes the conflict between Wellington and Napoleon to demonstrate his conception of eternal oppositions and cyclic time, and later on the Iron Duke of Wellington finds himself punningly fused with the mythical Dick Whittington and the already famous jazz musician Duke Ellington ("good Dook Weltington").[15] However, as in "the Willingdone Museyroom" we also find "the three lipoleum boyne grouching down in the living detch," we may recall that three of the Marx brothers featured a sketch about Napoleon in their revue *I'll Say She Is* which ran from 1923 until 1925; and so Napoleon's Marshal Grouchy at Waterloo merges here into Groucho Marx on Broadway. Leonard Lyons of the *New York Post* pointed this out to Groucho many years later, saying the idea originally came from Thornton Wilder, and that "the three lipoleum Coyne" (*sic*) must be a reference to "the Napoleon-type hats" (tricornes) which the Marx brothers wore in their sketch. Groucho himself was incredulous, but the idea of "three young Jewish fellows running around the stage shouting to an indifferent world that they were all Napoleon" was exactly the kind of refurbishing of history as comedy that would have appealed to the Irishman.[16]

Indeed in one of the most interesting essays on "Work in Progress," published in the *transition* of June 1929, Michael Stuart criticized Joyce for his "Martian detachment from the world," and claimed he was so fanatically obsessed with extracting comedy from every situation that his method became escapist. Stuart said that Joyce "shall not walk in the by-streets of the world and note the rags of misery, the wounded dignity of the soul, the insolence of office, nor give ear to the cosmic *Miserere*, but like some Angelic Doctor he shall withdraw into the cloisters of his spirit with a riant dream of a world without travail or sorrow."[17] Stuart stressed the importance of Giordano Bruno's thought to Joyce's work, especially Bruno's belief "that everything can only come to a knowledge of itself through a contrast with its opposite," and he implied that this eternal oscillation between contrary poles prevented Joyce from asserting anything at all.[18] But of course in one sense Stuart was indicting Joyce on entirely unjustifiable grounds: Joyce was writing a Platonic novel which was suggesting not that everything was at all times comic, but that everything at all times contained within itself the potential of comedy. Because Earwicker and Anna Livia function as gigantic archetypes and are the essences of this risible universe, all the warriors and lovers who merge into the text become accidents temporarily assuming the form of their cosmic models. This pulls the rug from under any character claiming more than provisional and ambiguous status, and the destabilizing principle of the pun is reflected by the everlasting conflict between Shem and Shaun which holds all oppositions in perpetual counterpoise. Shem is only the weight on one side of the fulcrum, and must always be balanced by Shaun; Shaun is only the weight on one side of the fulcrum, and must always be balanced by Shem. And Joyce's anagram reveals these patterns as forever reincarnating themselves in slightly different forms: "Time after time. The sehm asnuh."[19]

In this way, we can see that associations between the later work of Crane and Joyce – "the Great Alchemist of the Word," as Harry Crosby called him – are very marked.[20] Joyce, who was openly hero-worshipped in Paris in the late 1920s, used to tell friends puns were "the highest form of humour" and that in the Middle Ages "gatherings of learned men were great festivals of puns, anagrams, leonine verses and so forth"; and Joyce's comments on how he was "working in layers" and how "Some of the means I use are trivial – and some are quadrivial" could have been made by Crane if he had been as garrulous on the subject of *The Bridge* as Joyce was on the *Wake*.[21] The obvious pun in "The

River" on "Thomas a Ediford" is characteristically Joycean – Thomas A. Edison and Henry Ford (inventors of the electric light and of automobile mass production respectively) being modern saints in the mould of Thomas à Becket; but a more specific verbal parallel is the "beating time" pun which Joyce uses in "The Ondt and the Gracehoper," first published in *transition* of March 1928. Here the upwardly mobile gracehoper/grasshopper rebukes the earthbound ondt (ant, plus French *onde*, wave) for failing to transcend the limitations of its physical environment:

> Your genus is worldwide, your spaces sublime!
> But, Holy Saltmartin, why can't you beat time?[22]

The gracehoper is urging the ondt to use his "genius" (pun on *genus*) to "beat time" in a Faustian or religious sense along the lines of Saint Martin ("Holy Saltmartin"). The contradiction of this is that the ondt's worldly *genus* (Latin for "species") is already beating time in a more secular sense, going along with the earth's musical motion and the ebb and flow of its rhythms. From this angle, *Saltmartin* becomes the salty sea (French *marin*, marine or sailor) upon which the ondt bobs up and down. Crane's deployment of this ambiguity occurs in "Cutty Sark," which first appeared in *transition* of June 1927. The old seaman is on the point of renouncing his demonic life of whale-hunting and acquiescing in that Platonic harmony symbolized by the juke-box, "some white machine that sings":

> "It's S. S. *Ala* Antwerp now remember kid
> to put me out at three she sails on time
> I'm not much good at time any more keep
> weak watches sometimes snooze –" his fragile hands
> got to beating time . . .[23]

Defeating time or marking time? It is the same oscillation between romantic transcendence and classical system that we saw in Joyce's poem; and the connotations of *Ala* (Latin *wing*) and *Antwerp* (a Belgian homing-pigeon) provide a further synecdoche of the confrontation inherent in the "beating time" pun, as the wings of epic flight turn into the homeward motion of the pigeon.

Because of the chronology, there is no question of Crane lifting this pun directly from Joyce; but both were involved with the same ideas at the same time, and it is possible that Crane was directly influenced by "Work in Progress" as he went about writing *The Bridge*. Both works were originally conceived in 1923: Joyce's master-plan seems to have been clear from the start, but Crane's early worksheets reveal a more straightforward use of language and suggest he had not yet discovered a

technique fully adequate to the complexity of his theme. On 9 January
1924, however, Crane wrote to Gorham Munson:

> My approach to words is still in substratum of some new development . . . and
> perhaps merely a chaotic lapse into confusion for all I dare say yet. I feel Stein
> and E.E.C. as active agents in it, whatever it is . . . Suffice to say that I am very
> dissatisfied with both these interesting people and would like to digest their
> qualities without being too consciously theoretical about it.[24]

So successful was Crane in his desire to avoid "being too consciously
theoretical" that we never hear any more about this "new development"
or just what it involved. But as Cummings and Stein are allied in Crane's
thought, it is a safe inference that games with language cannot be too far
away. It is extremely clear from the typography of Cummings' work
that he is overthrowing language and grammar, chopping up words and
transforming them into magical puns; and though for various reasons
Crane chose to preserve a more orthodox façade, his verbal ingenuities
are really of a similar order. Not surprisingly, Crane enjoyed parodically
imitating Cummings' verse: a 1923 offering, "America's Plutonic
Ecstasies (With homage to E. E. Cummings)" is reprinted in Crane's
Complete Poems; and another uncollected parody by Crane is appropriately entitled "of an evening pulling off a little experience (with the
english language) by e. e. cummings":

```
                    wrists web rythms
          and the poke-
                    ,dot smile;
          of Genevive


                              talks                   5
          back

          i KNew, kneW my feet
          ?go on) were an applesauce

                              part
          of yoU belching POCHETTEkeepit        10
          upyou, s,uede
          ballbearing

                    celery = grin

          remind of-of la guerre

             UM                                   15
          Trimvirate (creamed dancing bitches)
          corking with Helene, (exactly you make)
          my perpendicularly crowdedPOCKets

                    smilepoke
```

```
    ,,besides: which                           20
    April has
    a
    word to say: classy )eh(!
    while blundering fumbiguts gather    accu
    rate little, O-SO masterbations in/        25
                          to
    fractions of heaven. Hold   tight   bless
    worms trilling rimple flock to
    sad iron

                goats of                        30
              love-
                semi-colon
                piping (dash)
```

(Susan Jenkins Brown gave the date of this parody as 1923 also.) Without needing to analyse this poem in excessive detail, we can see it is a paean to masturbation: starting from those "masterbations" of line 25, we notice the rhythm of *wrists* (line 1); the *ballbearing* of line 12; and the injunction to "Hold tight" (line 27) leading to the climax of *piping* (line 33). Also significant is the thread of puns connecting *poke*, *pocket* and *pochette* (French for "pocket," line 10): we may surmise that the hand in the pocket is indeed "pulling off a little experience." All kinds of punning intricacies are built into this poem: take for instance *Genevive* (line 4), not just a person's name, but also "Gene/vive," vive the gene, long live the sexual hormones that bring about this "experience." It is clear from this parody of Cummings that Crane knew all about the linguistic ingenuities practised by avant-garde writers of his day; and indeed in his 1924 "General Aims and Theories" essay, Crane specifically praised the "calligraphic tricks and slang used so brilliantly at times by an impressionist like Cummings."[25] Crane's desire, however, was to integrate such technical wizardry within a broader and more ambitious artistic design, wherein the puns remained latent rather than overt.

So Cummings and Joyce were the most famous literary punsters of this time, and both were important influences on Crane. Of course Joyce's language, like Cummings', was quite evidently experimental, especially in "Work in Progress," the first excerpt from which was published by Ford Madox Ford's *transatlantic review* in April 1924. On 9 July 1924, Crane complimented Munson on his magazine *Secession* by saying it was "better in its initial contents than several issues of *The Trans-Atlantic Review* that I have seen"; and this suggests Crane had quite probably seen the Joyce extract, because Ford's monthly magazine started up only in January 1924, and so the chances of April 1924 being one of the "several issues" Crane had seen are proportionately high.[26]

Another excerpt appeared in July 1925 in Eliot's *Criterion*, shortly before Crane unsuccessfully submitted "The Wine Menagerie" and "Passage" to that magazine. But all this is speculation. Proof that Crane was familiar with "Work in Progress," at least by the end of the decade, comes with the telegram he sent from New York to Caresse Crosby in Paris on 12 January 1930: "SEND REBECCA WEST BRIDGE VERY IMPORTANT FIND ADDRESS HART." Three days later, Crane wrote to Caresse more fully:

> But I really became greatly excited about an estimate of Joyce's recent work which Rebecca West had just published in the book review of the Herald Tribune. West certainly is an amazing fusion of brains, sensibility and good common sense. I'm sure that she will appreciate the Bridge and hope that you can find some way to get a review copy to her, wherever she is to be reached. I think she is in London at present.[27]

Unterecker suggested Crane must have been drunk when he sent Caresse the initial telegram.[28] But if it had been merely drunken folly, Crane would hardly have written this sober letter to Caresse on the same theme three days later. The article Crane "became greatly excited about" turns out to be a piece entitled "James Joyce and his Followers," published in the *New York Herald Tribune* on that very day of the telegram, 12 January. (The full text of this article is reprinted in Appendix B.) West's essay talked of how

> The distinctive attribute of "Work in Progress" is that it is not written in English, or in any other language. Most of the words that James Joyce uses are *patés de langue gras*. Each is a paste of words that have been superimposed one on another and worked into a new word that shall be the lowest common multiple of them all. These words have been chosen out of innumerable languages, living and dead, either because of some association of ideas or of sound. They are "portmanteau" words such as Lewis Carroll invented when he wrote "Jabberwocky": "'Twas brillig and the slithy toves Did gyre and gimble in the wabe." They are chosen, often but not always, in the sly, punning spirit that looks for disguises by which forbidden things may leer and sidle past the censor . . . There emerges from the text clearly enough not only a superficial pattern of verbal suggestion which is intricate and amusing and occasionally poetically beautiful, but a phantasmagoria of types that represent the main forms thrown up by history. It cannot be read as quickly as ordinary English, just as a cross-word puzzle cannot be read as quickly as the words it contains set up in ordinary form. But that is the only thing against it from the reader's point of view. Granted it will take him ten times as long to read as an equal number of words put into ordinary Anglo-American realist novels, he will get ten times as much entertainment . . . Obviously, he got this idea of the word-paste from the Freudian and Jungian analyses of the puns people make in dreams . . . Can one think of any other writer concerning whose work such interesting considerations arise?[29]

No wonder Crane said it was "very important" for West to see his poem as he was "sure that she will appreciate the Bridge." But he was unlucky: shortly before her recent death, Dame Rebecca West confirmed that she "certainly never received any copy of Hart Crane's long poem *The Bridge* from him or his publishers. Somebody else gave it to me and I admired it, but I do not remember writing about it."[30] Rebecca West was certainly on Caresse's list for the twenty-five copies to be sent "hors commerce," and just what happened is anybody's guess. One possible explanation is that with Harry Crosby having killed himself only a few weeks before, Caresse was by her own account "in limbo" at the beginning of 1930, so stunned that "friends passed before me like automatons upon a moving track." In the circumstances, it is remarkable that she managed to oversee the production of *The Bridge* at all. As for complimentary editions, Rebecca West was not the only casualty: Crane wrote to Waldo Frank on 16 March 1930, "It was reassuring to know that you got your copy of *The Bridge*. Cummings and one or two others didn't – quite inexplicably."[31]

This proposition of affinities between Joyce and Crane is by no means totally original. Readers of the 1940s and 1950s (under the influence of the "New Criticism" of Cleanth Brooks and others who saw the poetic artefact as an autonomous "urn" or "icon") tended to perceive Crane as a lyric rather than epic poet and to emphasize his work's linguistic intricacy rather than its "philosophical" structure, so that in 1948 Brom Weber was talking of how "Much like James Joyce, he understood that language is connotative as well as denotative, fluid as well as solidified"; and indeed as long ago as 1935, R. P. Blackmur discussed Crane's exploitation of "syllabic interpenetration or internal punning as habitually practised in the later prose of Joyce." As an example, Blackmur quoted a line from "Lachrymae Christi":

> Thy Nazarene and tinder eyes.

Blackmur suggested "that tinder is very nearly a homonym for tender and, *in this setting*, puns upon it." Blackmur italicized "in this setting" because he felt that Crane's use of such verbal ingenuities was too personal, too idiosyncratic, so that the puns remained private property ("tricks which can only be resorted to arbitrarily") rather than becoming the stuff of public idiom.[32] The "success" or otherwise of *The Bridge* is a question we can address ourselves to later, but here I must emphasize how Crane's experiments with language were not *merely* a subjective whim, how they had a clear literary parallel in the work of Joyce (and Cummings) and how this was a parallel Crane himself recognized: as we see once again in his response to the justification of avant-garde literary techniques made by Laura Riding and Robert Graves in their 1927 *Survey of Modernist Poetry*, where the authors defended the unconventional typography and double meanings of poets like Cummings by saying that poetry should be sophisticated, and its readers equally intelligent, in order that art and the human world might constantly be perceived through a fresh lens. Complacent Victorian notions of a "plain reader" were derogated here, as was the "dead movement" of Georgianism ("as simple as a child's reading book"); and Shakespeare himself was cited as an example of a witty and difficult writer whom plain readers were prone to domesticate into anthologized blandness. Riding and Graves did not decry classical themes, nor did they pretend that novel puns and jokes could be sufficient in themselves, but they did greatly admire the kind of modernist craftsmanship practised by Joyce and Cummings:

> It must be admitted that excessive interest in the mere technique of the poem can become morbid both in the poet and the reader, like the composing and solving of cross-word puzzles. Once the sense of a poem with a technical soul, so to speak, is unriddled and its patterns plainly seen, it is not fit for re-reading; as with the Sphinx in the fable, allowing its riddle to be guessed is equivalent to suicide. A poem of this kind is nevertheless able to stave off death by continually revealing, under examination, an unexpected reserve of new riddles; and as long as it is able to supply these it can continue to live as a poem.[33]

After reading this *Survey* Crane urged Cummings to purchase a copy, saying, "It has more gunpowder in it than any other book of contemporary criticism I've ever read."[34] So while on the surface Crane appears to be a typographically conventional poet, his actual commitment to the aesthetics of literary radicalism seems indisputable; and the structural principles underlying *Finnegans Wake* and *The Bridge* are very similar: the pun as an emblem of cyclic time ("good Dook Weltington," "palladium helm"); and the pun as an emblem of balance and eternal contradiction (Shem versus Shaun, "How many dawns" versus "Harmony dawns," "beating time" in two different senses). Despite the many and obvious differences between the two works, *The Bridge* is the greatest poem to come out of the "Revolution of the Word" movement, just as *Finnegans Wake* is acknowledged as that movement's greatest novel.

11

La Révolution Surréaliste

According to the historian of *transition* magazine Dougald McMillan, when Joyce wrote in an advertisement for the Faber edition of "Haveth Childers Everywhere" – an extract from the *Wake* – that HCE was the "granddada of all rogues," the Irishman was implicitly recognizing his own kinship with the Dada experiments in Paris earlier in the 1920s.[1] Dada's iconoclasm and exuberant disintegration of the stale conventions of logic and grammar helped clear the ground for more ambitious writers like Joyce and Crane later on; and Crane learnt more from the techniques of Dada and Surrealism than at first meets the eye.

Crane was excited by European culture long before he actually sailed eastwards late in 1928. Of course, the years immediately after the First World War were a time when European intellectuals previously thought irredeemably decadent became increasingly accepted in the United States: the most obvious case being that of Nietzsche, whose praises were sung by Randolph Bourne, H. L. Mencken and Crane himself in a short essay written in 1918. Crane also told Caresse Crosby that it was his "early enthusiasm" for the Italian painter Giorgio de Chirico which had inspired the title "White Buildings" for his first collection of poems.[2] Matthew Josephson retrospectively aligned de Chirico with Dostoyevsky as "the two patron saints of Surrealism": de Chirico sought to dislocate the visible world, to undermine "all usual logic and sense" (as he said in 1927) so that objects are removed from orthodox modes of perception and reappear anew, "as if lit for the first time by a brilliant star."[3] De Chirico's determination to reveal new or hidden worlds endeared him to the Surrealists, who saw his white towers and enigmatic landscapes as the invasion of a Freudian dreamworld upon the banal circumstances of everyday literalism. Many of de Chirico's early paintings were actually called "Enigmas" (*The Enigma of the Oracle*, 1910, *The Enigma of the Hour*, 1912, and so on); he was an artist who specialized in the uncanny, in mystery, in reversing the real and unreal. De Chirico foreshadowed Crane in his frequent disruption of concrete time: in the 1913 painting *Ariadne's Afternoon*, for instance, the antique sculpture of Ariadne is juxtaposed with a medieval tower, an industrial chimney and a modern train. Our "windows," wrote de Chirico in 1919, "are open to Homeric dawns and to sunsets pregnant with tomorrow."[4] Like his mentor Apollinaire, de Chirico placed much faith in the technique of "surprise," jolting his audience into awareness of the co-existence of past and present by these apparent incongruities.

It was Apollinaire who "discovered" de Chirico, and also Apollinaire who coined the term "Surrealism," first using it in 1917 in a review of Cocteau's ballet *Parade*. Like de Chirico, Apollinaire thrived on paradox, distortion, distant associations. Laughter, said Apollinaire, was Man's great virtue ("Le rire: c'est la bonté des hommes"), and his poetic world was a droll celebration of modern technology, often expressed in the fragmented pattern of advertising layout.[5] Crane wrote to Munson praising "the beautiful metaphysics of Chirico," but about the Frenchman he professed himself more doubtful ("just *why* is Apollinaire so portentous a god? Will radios, flying machines, and cinemas have such a great effect on poetry in the end?" (emphasis in original)). Crane also heard all about Apollinaire from Matthew Josephson in Paris, and despite his reservations he recommended *Calligrammes* and *Alcools* to Charmion Wiegand on 6 May 1922.[6] We know that the idea of the calligramme, which thematically exploits the typographical appearance of poetry, had a strong influence on Crane, for he wrote to Yvor Winters in 1926 about the erratic design of "Cutty Sark": "Third page is pure calligramme, and I shan't allow it to be printed in any detail other than the mss designates, – line-end word divisions and all have an organic purpose."[7] But the calligramme also works its way into other sections of *The Bridge*, for, from *Alcools*, Crane purloined one of Apollinaire's most famous felicities. The one-line poem "Chantre" goes:

Et l'unique cordeau des trompettes marines

Cordeau (string) puns on "cor d'eau" (trumpet of water), and "trompettes marines" can be either "marine trumpets" or "wooden stringed instruments." The significance of this is that although the poem has only one line (just as the marine trumpets have only one string), the singer (*Chantre*) is too inventive to be confined to one solitary (*unique*) note; as Jonathan Culler put it, "the fundamental ambiguity of language allows the poet to make music with a single line of verse."[8] Crane transfers *cordeau* into *cordage*, which in "Atlantis" describes Brooklyn

Bridge itself ("And through that cordage, threading with its call"), and which in "Ave Maria" refers to Columbus' ship as it returns from America ("Some Angelus environs the cordage tree"). Webster gives *cordage* as "ropes or chords, collectively; esp., ropes in the rigging of a ship"; so we have here one of Crane's familiar transmutations whereby the Bridge becomes a ship, the ship anticipates the Bridge, and both have overtones of the "cordage tree" Christ was crucified upon. This serves to illuminate the spiritual status of both Columbus' expedition and Crane's Brooklyn Bridge: for the poet is surreptitiously suggesting how ship and Bridge are indeed each "cor d'age," the trumpet of their age, the reconstitution of divine light inside a later era. The pun here implies the sacramental substance latent within the material fact of Brooklyn Bridge, as "cor d'age" is latent within *cordage*; and it also suggests the visual imagination Crane shared with Apollinaire, the concern in both cases that readers should pay attention to the arrangement of letters on the page. But what in Apollinaire was merely self-referential, a proposal of poetry's manifold possibilities, has become in Crane this unification of Surrealist method with ethical assertion and value-judgement.

Crane's friends Matthew Josephson and Gorham Munson were his direct links with the Parisian fashions, but Dadaist ideas had infiltrated New York itself after the 1913 Armory Show, that epoch-making exhibition of modernist art. At its purest and most theoretical, Dada was opposed to everything, including itself; but in its more general manifestations, Dada centred on a rebellion against desiccated forms of life and art and upon the propagation of that primitivistic vitality it found within the technological world. Dada in this vulgarized model had certain affinities with Futurism. In *Skyscraper Primitives*, his analysis of "Dada and the American Avant-Garde," Dickran Tashjian argued that the camera played a crucial rôle in this reaction against the idea of fine art and in the introduction of mechanical forms of expression. The photographer Alfred Stieglitz published Apollinaire's writing in his magazine *291*, and Stieglitz also printed the work of Francis Picabia, who – with Marcel Duchamp and Man Ray – formed part of the trio later identified as "New York Dada." In 1915, Picabia created a series of portraits for *291* where the human subject was reduced solely to a machine: Stieglitz to a camera, Picabia himself to a car-horn ("blowing his own horn") and so on; and in Picabia's *Portrait d'une jeune fille américaine*, the girl was depicted as a spark-plug whose brand name, "Forever," commented on the commercial packaging of American romance. These prototypes of comic dehumanization were followed up by Duchamp, who arrived in New York in 1915 already equipped with the notoriety his *Nude Descending a Staircase* had produced at the Armory Show. Duchamp ridiculed what he saw as the "adoration" of classic art ("as old-fashioned as the superstitions of the religions"), praised New York City itself as "a complete work of art" and keenly welcomed what he saw as the abstract, cold and scientific spirit of the twentieth century. When he presented his infamous urinal (*Fountain*) to a 1917 exhibition, Duchamp justified his product on the grounds that "The only works of art America has given the world are her plumbing and her bridges," and he claimed he was creatively illuminating this "ordinary article of life."[9] In 1920, Duchamp renounced the stigma of individual expression attached to the word "artist" by declaring himself an engineer.

Poets in the American grain around the early 1920s often had an ambivalent attitude towards Dada, rejecting its purely cerebral and frigid game-playing, but welcoming its iconoclastic spirit and overturning of institutionalized European pessimism. Robert Coady's magazine *The Soil*, begun in 1917, anticipated Josephson in its eulogies to baseball, skyscrapers and steam-shovels, and extolled the robust vitality of American life as an antidote to the effete genteel tradition. "Our art is, as yet, outside of our art world," said Coady. *Contact*, started by William Carlos Williams and Robert McAlmon in 1920, similarly found the extravagance of Dada opposed to their sympathies with what was localized and realistic, but Dada's explosion of the hermetically sealed world of high art had affinities with McAlmon's derogation of the "intellectual sterilities" of writers like T. S. Eliot. Eliot, said McAlmon, had remained "too long within his library," with the result that he "continually relates literature to literature, and largely overlooks the relation of literature to reality."[10] Waldo Frank later found himself forced to admit that his country's grotesque and bizarre energy meant "America *is* Dada" ("Dada spans Brooklyn bridge; it spins around Columbus Circle; it struts with the Ku Klux Klan; it mixes with all brands of bootleg whiskey"); but Frank thought that while this was admirable as an antidote to dry and dull rationalism, the exuberance of Dada nevertheless required assimilation within a system of "integrating thought."[11] Here Frank was mirroring the criticism made of Dada by the Surrealists; for although chronologically the movements ran into one another and had many of the same personnel, Dada was much more nihilistic than fully fledged Surrealism, Surrealism sharing many of its predecessor's *bêtes noires* but enjoying its own social and visionary ideals.

Crane himself knew all about these experiments, but at first took a most unfriendly attitude towards them. He wrote to Josephson from Cleveland on 14 January 1921:

> I hear "New York" has gone mad about "Dada" and that a most exotic and worthless review is being concocted by Man Ray and Duchamp, billets in a bag printed backwards, on rubber deluxe, etc. What next! . . . I cannot figure out

> just what Dadaism is beyond an insane jumble of the four winds, the six senses, and plum pudding.[12]

Crane found out more about Dada when Josephson and Munson took off for Paris later in 1921, there to become embroiled in their oft-recounted *Broom/Secession* controversy. Crane's comments in his letters show that he was alternately attracted and repelled by the lives his friends were leading. He wrote to Sherwood Anderson from Cleveland in December 1921 that Josephson and Munson wrote him "letters that made me foam at my moorings";[13] and though in April 1922 he criticized Munson for "following the primrose path of the magazines," he added that the two copies of *Secession* Munson had sent over had been "immediately and doubly devoured." Commenting on what he had read, Crane praised a piece by Aragon, dismissed a poem by Tzara as "perfectly flat" and suggested that Josephson, who had contributed "Apollinaire: Or Let us Be Troubadors" – an invective in favour of a "fun-loving disposition" – would benefit from more matter with less art: "All this talk of Matty's is quite stimulating, but it's like coffee – twenty-four hours afterward not much remains to work with. It is metallic and pointillistic – not derogatory terms to my mind at all, but somehow thin, – a little too slender and "smart" – after all."[14] Crane's justifiable opinion was that, for all his talk of celebrating American billboards and industry, Josephson was unable to match practice to theory. Josephson's hymn to Henry Ford in *Broom* of 5 September 1923 was composed of phrases derived from advertising copy, but the end product was no more impressive for that:

> Here is a town, here is a mill:
> nothing surprises you old horse face.
> Guzzle-guzzle goes the siren;
> and the world will learn to admire and applaud your concern
>   about the parts, your firmness with employés, and your
>   justice to your friends.
>   Your pride will not be overriden.
>   Your faith will go unmortified.[15]

Some of Josephson's French friends (notably Philippe Soupault) were fascinated by America's urban civilizations and popular culture, but Crane kept his distance from indiscriminate reverence, saying there was "Technique" in advertising, "but such gross materialism has nothing to do with art."[16] On 16 May 1922 he wrote to Munson, "People like you, Matty and I belong here. Especially Matty, who was doing better work last summer before he got in touch with the Paris crowd"; but Crane also expressed confidence that Josephson's "present crazes" were "just a phase which will be a practical benefit in the end."[17]

This analysis of Dada as a means towards a more constructive end is crucial. It was foreshadowed by Josephson himself who wrote to Malcolm Cowley in December 1921: "My claim is that these young men, when they break away from the rubbish of Dada, will be the big writers of the next decade."[18] Josephson and Cowley accordingly returned to the United States in the mid-1920s, and their subsequent social awareness could be seen as an attempt to insert Dadaist iconoclasm into a political context. Crane similarly rejected Dada's purely self-indulgent side, but he too maintained a fascinated interest in the movement's more bizarre and avant-garde techniques, and *The Bridge* is in some ways a verbal *trompe-l'oeil* equivalent to Duchamp's *Why Not Sneeze Rrose Sélavy* (1921) – a bird-cage filled with trick sugar cubes made out of marble – or the early films created by Duchamp and Man Ray, which delighted in ingenuities such as slow-motion, reversing the action and superimposing different images. Like Cowley and Josephson, Crane was attempting to build a bridge between the innovatory aesthetics of Europe and the traditional ethics of America.

SURREALISM AND WORDPLAY

One of the weapons of the Dadaists and Surrealists in their campaign to strip the world of its familiar garments was the breaking down of both "logical" grammar and the verbal unit itself. Paradox and pun were intended to undermine the rational structure of bourgeois society. Like Crane, Tzara was a devotee of the unabridged dictionary, and in 1922 he advised Josephson: "Read Littré, the big Littré dictionary. There is an admirable work of the highest art. I keep it at my bedside; begin reading at Z and go backward."[19] The fact that Dada was founded upon a pun ("the word for a hobby-horse, a children's nurse, a double affirmative in Russian and Roumanian") seemed entirely appropriate to Tzara, who refused to make value-judgements discriminating between objects as he believed "everything is equal and unimportant" and that "life is a play on words."[20] From Lautréamont to Apollinaire through to Paul Eluard, the pun was one of the trademarks of the Surrealists and their heroes.

In a December 1922 *Littérature* article entitled "Les Mots sans rides," André Breton proclaimed:

> We began to be wary of words, we suddenly came to realize that they needed to be treated other than as the small auxiliaries for which we had always taken them . . . in short it was a question of liberating them. To the "alchemy of the word" had succeeded a true chemistry which was at first employed to disestablish the proprieties of these words of which only one aspect, the sense, was specified by the dictionary. It was a question, 1: of considering the word in itself. 2: of studying as far as possible the reaction of words upon each other.

> Only at that price could we hope to restore to language its full purpose, which
> . . . was to make a great step towards knowledge, to ennoble life all the
> more.[21]

The etymology of a word was described by Breton as "son poids le plus
mort," its deadest weight, while syntax was "médiocrement utilitaire"
and associated with the kind of "wretched conservatism" which had a
"horror of the infinite."[22] However, with their preference for automatic
inspiration rather than literary grind, the Surrealists tended to rely upon
the supposedly "magical" puns they were able to extract from language,
finding this more to their taste than the labour of exploiting words'
etymological ambiguities in a willed and conscious way. In the October
1922 *Littérature*, for instance, Marcel Duchamp took time off from his
beloved chessboard to create his "Rrose Sélavy" sequence of word
games: "SA ROBE EST NOIRE DIT SARAH BERNHARD" is a fair example of
Duchamp's offerings.[23] Breton commented on "Rrose Sélavy" in "Les
Mots sans rides," saying two things had particularly struck him about
Duchamp's work: "on the one hand their mathematical rigour
(displacement of letters inside words, exchange of syllables between two
words etc.), on the other hand the absence of any comic element which
previously passed as an inherent part of the genre and which resulted in
the genre being undervalued."[24] Breton's aim was to show that words
had an autonomous existence, that they were the "creators of energy"
and could henceforth "command thought." The bandwagon quickly
began to roll, and in December 1922 Robert Desnos delivered more of
the same: "Rrose Sélavy demande si les Fleurs du Mal ont modifié les
moeurs du phalle" (Rrose Sélavy asks whether the *Fleurs du Mal* have
changed phallic habits).[25] In May 1923 Desnos grew more ambitious,
and dedicated to Duchamp a "poem" based upon a network of
homophones:

> Mes chants sont si peu méchants!
> Ils ne vont pas jusqu'à Longchamp
> Ils meurent avant d'atteindre les champs
> ou les boeufs s'en vont léchant
> les astres
> désastres[26]

The poem turns on felicities like "dés/astres," literally disasters,
implicitly a pun yoking together dice and the stars. The literary merit of
these experiments was clearly minimal, but they were symptomatic of a
revised attitude to language which Joyce and Crane were able to
capitalize on later.

After *Littérature* had been superseded by *La Révolution Surréaliste* in
December 1924, these purely linguistic enterprises became more scarce,

because the new magazine was directed more towards the social consequences of Surrealism. Room was found, however, for Michel Leiris, who in a series entitled "Glossaire: J'y serre mes gloses" produced lists of words with punning and anagrammatic aphorisms to define them. Thus *Verbiage* was "herbage des mots sans vie" (pasture of words without life); *mélancolie* "collier de lances qui me lie" (ring of spears which binds me); *révolution* "solution de tout rêve" (solution of every dream). And as for *vie*, life, "un dé la sépare du vide" (a die, or d, separates it from the void).[27] The first appearance of this "Glossary" in April 1925 was followed by a harangue from Leiris against dictionaries, etymologies and conventional uses of words, and in favour of everyone dissecting words "selon le bon plaisir de son esprit" (as his fancy takes him), because then "we discover their [words'] most hidden virtues and the secret ramifications which are spread through all language, wired by underground associations, forms and ideas. Then language is transformed into an oracle, and we have (however tenuous it may be) a thread to guide us, in the Babel of our spirit."[28] As we see, Leiris was straining towards an idealistic justification for his wordplay. The linguistic alchemy of his glossaries was intended to break through the stereotyped conventions of language and affix verbal significances which, although arbitrary and subjective, would have the validity the Surrealists attached to an individual's dream in so far as the dream was rearranging the world in accordance with human free will. If Leiris's definitions had been quite meaningless, they would have only bolstered the assumption that God had created language by divine fiat and Man had better not meddle; but there is just enough plausibility about these glossaries to make the reader stop and wonder about exactly how human language came about and the part Man's unconscious might have played in creating affinities between words. In *La Révolution Surréaliste*, Leiris's work tended to be followed by aphorisms from de Chirico about the need to "rid art of all its stale familiarity" so that the world could be reilluminated in a new way, and all this was part of the Surrealists' plan to understand the hidden workings of Man's brain and so gain control of human destiny.[29] It was a psychological equivalent of the Marxists' ambition to uncover and so bring into harness latent economic forces. Louis Aragon in his *Traité du style* of 1928 justified the idea of "automatic" writing on the grounds of the production of homologues in the subconscious mind which modify the customary usage of language and so provide a key to the mysterious workings of the brain. Words, said Aragon, "contain meanings [portent sens] in every syllable, in every letter"; and so analysis of these minutiae would be fruitful because "the bottom of a Surrealist text carries the greatest significance, it is that which gives it its precious character of revelation."[30]

The Surrealists' conception of language as a magical key to the unconscious anticipated the theories of later linguistic philosophers such as Roman Jakobson, who have interested themselves in the way homonyms are created in the human brain. Leiris's 1925 graphic alignment of AMOUR, MOURIR and MIROIR suggested how the proximity of the sound of these three words reveals the links between them in Man's unconscious; and this is very close to Jakobson's work on paronomastic and mythopoeic connections, the way in which verbal patterns reflect human patterns of belief.[31] The theory of the unconscious, however, is not one I wish to pursue here. More important for my purposes is the comic aspect of Surrealist wordplay, and the fact that the existence of such wordplay was known to Hart Crane. Just as Crane consciously built psychoanalytical theories into *The Bridge*, so he consciously exploited these Parisian games with language to add an extra dimension to his long poem. *The Bridge* wittingly sports with theories of the unwitting, in a way not unlike some aspects of Dada's nonsense poems, which were designed (as Richard Sheppard has shown) "to celebrate, through the creation of verbal analogues, the infinite plenitude of the nonsensical, elusive, contradictory flux of Nature."[32] And the Dadaists' insinuation of comic exuberance (and sexual licence) into the familiar and realistic world ran parallel to their disruption of orthodox codes of language: Sheppard associated the Dadaist poets with the spirit of carnival, the world turned upside down, and also with Jung's image of the Trickster, a protean and subversive figure who "enjoys malicious pranks, sly jokes, reversing hieratic orders and changing his shape." Sheppard asserted that several members of the Dada movement were attracted to Jung's work, and that the Dadaists, like Jung's archetypal Trickster, were "forcibly reminding civilized Western man of those primitive, bestial and chaotic sides of himself which he would rather forget." In Dada, the spirit of carnival and the energy of sexual desire pose a constant threat to pompous and frigid social figureheads such as Love, Honour, Country. The problem with the Dadaists, as Sheppard admitted, was that – by the fallacy of imitative form – they attempted to express a meaningless world through meaningless verse: "Precisely because of its experimental nature, this poetic gave rise to much work which is, frankly, very tedious."[33] Eugene Jolas, the editor of *transition*, found himself caught in a similar dilemma: approving of much Dadaist theory, he nevertheless found Dada's end product unappetizing.

In his 1929 essay "Notes on Reality," printed in *transition*, Jolas accordingly attempted to reconcile the conflicting claims of rational and irrational. He called Dada "one of the greatest movements in modern times," and declared that he was all in favour of a descent "into the night-side of life" as part of the effort to "disintegrate and help batter down the present structure of a pathological civilization."[34] But Jolas believed that liberated instincts and Dadaist destruction were, in themselves, merely a first stage; and he called for a "synthesist reality," the amalgamation of conscious and unconscious, social reconstruction and erotic liberation, into a mythological totality:

> The new creator is out to make the alliance between the dionysian-dynamic and the nocturnal realities. He is out to discover the unity of life. Conquering the dualism between the "it" and the "I," he produces new myths, myths of himself in a dynamic environment, myths of new machines and inventions, fairy tales and fables, legends and sagas expressing a hunger for beauty that is not passive and gentle like that of former ages, but hard and metallic like the age towards which we are going. He brings the fabulous again within our reach. Cause and effect are transposed. The distances of the earth are vanquished, past, present and future disappear in a unity, there remains a time-space stream which is homogeneous. *The new composition is polyphonic and on many planes. It is as exact as possible and tries to produce harmonic unity by balancing the negative and positive.* It is the static point produced by the balancing of the dynamic representations of the world with the spontaneous movement of the dream.[35]

This is exactly the area Crane's *Bridge* is dealing in. *The Bridge* is just this kind of "polyphonic" attempt to counterpoint private sexuality with public mythology, and so produce "harmonic unity" ("Harmony dawns") by working on many different levels at once. Crane's poem preserves its respectable social face, but at the same time, like Jung's satanic Trickster, it punningly changes its shape to become a celebration of licentious sexuality.

CRANE AND THE ANAGRAM

"Van Winkle," itself first printed in *transition*, provides a good example of this constant Dadaist threat to decorum:

> Macadam, gun-grey as the tunny's belt,
> Leaps from Far Rockaway to Golden Gate.
> Listen! the miles a hurdy-gurdy grinds!
> Down gold arpeggios mile on mile unwinds.[36]

"Mac" is "a prefix, in names of Scotch Gaelic and Irish origin, signifying *son*"; and so the poem presents us with a whopper to start with, "Mac/Adam" (*Macadam*), son of Adam. Jack C. Wolf noticed this pun in his 1972 Buffalo University thesis on Crane, and he pointed out that "son of Adam" is "a fitting emblem for the bridging of a new country which had been hailed by William Blake and others as the new 'Garden of Eden.'"[37] Of course the surface meaning of these lines denotes the building of a macadamized roadway across the United States, and so in that sense

Wolf was right to say Crane is celebrating America as the new happy land (as Crane himself chirped to Otto Kahn, "one has the impression of the whole continent – from Atlantic to Pacific – freshly arisen and moving").[38] But Adam was also noted for indulging in illicit sexual activity, and in a deeper sense Crane is the son of Adam because his poem hides confessions about forbidden fruit. "Hurdy-gurdy grinds" is our clue: *grinds* is suggestive of love-making (the *grind-organ* that comes up a few lines later has the double-meaning of "penis"); and with *hurdy* punning on "hurdies" (slang for "the buttocks; rump"), the homoerotic connotations here become clear. (Eric Sundquist has referred to the "thicket of Crane's typical sexual puns" in this passage.)[39] This "Mac/ Adam" *Leaps* ("to copulate with") over his prostrate lover in the same way as the roadway covers the American continent.

The "tunny's belt" develops this theme by working on three levels. It is an apparently innocuous simile comparing the surface of the road to the grey skin of a tunny, a fish of the mackerel family; but there is also a pun on *tunny* and "tonneau," an early kind of automobile in the United States, which of course turns *belt* into the mechanical belt the car operates by. All of this is a most appropriate allusion to the new modes of travel the macadamized surface was helping to produce. But Crane's final rabbit out of the hat is "tonneau" as "a light two-wheeled vehicle with square or rounded body and *rear entrance*," a word that later came to denote the rear section of a motor-car body in more general terms. So here Crane is externalizing his homosexuality into an automatic image reminiscent of Picabia transforming his young American girl into a spark-plug.

This stanza also contains the kind of anagram Leiris would have admired. The reader might think that the repetition of *mile* in the last two lines is slightly clumsy. Having given us "the miles a hurdy-gurdy grinds," surely Crane could have thought of something different for his next phrase rather than "Down gold arpeggios mile on mile unwinds." However, if we "unwind" *mile*, who should we find but "Emil" – Emil Opffer, Crane's long-standing Danish lover and the man for whom the *Voyages* sequence was written. The image of *arpeggios* is an apt way to describe how the anagram functions, because in music an arpeggio is "the production of the tones of a chord in rapid succession, as in playing the harp, and not simultaneously; a chord thus played"; and so in verbal terms this implies the letters of *mile* should be apprehended as separate "notes" and not conflated into one word. In normal reading, of course, we ignore the individual letters and take notice only of what the word as a whole signifies, but Crane was trying to jolt his audience out of such blunt conventionality. That the *arpeggios* are *gold* is especially apposite because Susan Jenkins Brown recalled "Goldylocks" was Hart's "teasing name for Emil Opffer, who as a young man had very yellow hair with a long forelock that tended to fall over his forehead."[40] And with *Winkle* being a synonym for penis, and *Van* suggesting the Dutch "from," this poem's title, "Van Winkle," could be redefined in Dadaist terms as "from the penis," thus uniting the external bridging of the American continent with the bridging (or coming together) of the lovers in amatory revelry. This of course does not invalidate the poem's mythological connotations, but it demonstrates — in Jolas's formula — the "harmonic unity" derived from a balance of public and private interests.

A less exuberant use of proper names in anagram form occurs in Crane's 1927 poem, "O Carib Isle," again first published in the Parisian *transition*. Very broadly, the theme of this poem (written in the West Indies) is how the conventional urban ego collapses into anonymity under the pressures of a tropical environment. This is the central concern of the *Key West* collection: the failure of human art when confronted by the obstinate tarantulas and air plants of an inhuman landscape. In "O Carib Isle" the poet's magic wand has failed him, and the paltry artefact he has created is ironically overturned by the omniscient ocean:

> You have given me the shell, Satan, – carbonic amulet
> Sere of the sun exploded in the sea.

The artistic *shell* is pretty, but hollow, for the *amulet*'s charm is *Sere* (withered, dried up); and *Sere* itself puns on the poetic "seer," whose typewriter carbon ("carbonic amulet") cannot save him from the vengeance wreaked by an all-destroying sea. Of this poem, Eric Sundquist has written,

> "O Carib Isle" . . . is also a poem consumed by the notion of poetry as a magical relic whose protection is itself threatened. Here beneath the palsied eucalyptus, where "Brutal necklaces of shells" frame the graves in a "white sand" to which the poet spreads "a name, fertile / Albeit in a stranger tongue" – here "syllables want breath." Against this lack of breath, of clear articulation, "O Carib Isle" is a tribute to the blasphemous deceiver, "Satan" – at once "the Captain of this doubloon isle" and also "the blue's comedian host," the joking god and sacrament to whom the poet offers himself – who provides for the poet the "shell" of the poem, the "carbonic amulet" whose *empty* magic poses as a protection against death, a purchase against ravishing time.[41]

The empty magic of this joking, satanic god is exemplified by the way Hart Crane's own name is continually being anagrammatized within the poem. The theme of the poem, the collapse and death of the ego, is mirrored inside the poem's verbal patterns:

> The tarantula rattling at the lily's foot
> Across the feet of the dead, laid in white sand

> Near the coral beach – nor zigzag fiddle crabs
> Side-stilting from the path (that shift, subvert
> And anagrammatize your name)

In the first version of "O Carib Isle," printed in *transition*, Crane had written, "the small and ruddy crabs / Flickering out of sight, that reverse your name"; and his strengthening of this into "anagrammatize your name" serves to accentuate the clue offered to us here.[42] Anagrammatize "Near the coral"? H-A-R-T C-R-A-N-E. The *o* and *l* are left over, but slightly imperfect anagrams were frequently being perpetrated at this time by Leiris and the Surrealists. It is as if "Hart Crane" had himself been "beached" or shipwrecked on a coral reef, for his disintegration into "Near the coral" is the linguistic equivalent of this. Like Cummings, Crane seems to have been fascinated by the new-fangled machinery of the typewriter: this "carbonic amulet" of "O Carib Isle" is exposed more fully in the last *Key West* poem, "By Nilus Once I Knew . . .," described by its author as "An able text, more motion than machines / Have levers for"; and, being a mediocre typist himself, part of Crane's interest in anagrams may have derived from the way a typewriter can give the illusion of developing a life of its own, rearranging the letters of the alphabet in an order to suit itself rather than the human creator. In "O Carib Isle," we see this typographical reversal again a few lines later:

> And yet suppose
> I count these nacreous frames of tropic death,
> Brutal necklaces of shells around each grave
> Squared off so carefully. Then
>
> To the white sand I may speak a name

Just as the living human being has been inverted into this nacreous necklace of shells, miserable metonymy of death, so CRANE has been transposed into *nacreous*. (That "*tropic* death" is also the death of poetic tropes: the demise of art and of human life become commensurate.) And again:

> Each daybreak on the wharf, their brine-caked eyes;
> – Spiked, overturned

The eyes (or I's) have indeed been "overturned." CRANE is lurking within *brine-caked*, but his egocentric pretensions have been "Spiked" by the remorseless motion of the earth. And yet again:

> Slagged of the hurricane – I, cast within its flow

The poet is cast within the flow of the hurricane verbally as well as thematically: CRANE is disintegrated inside *hurricane*. Human character is diminished to alphabetical fragments, a series of letters scattered across the page. CRANE undergoes the indignity of constant metamorphosis.

These artistic sleights of hand are an attempt to incorporate the ironic explosions of the sea within the framework of art itself. But, as Sundquist said, the jokes and magic remain empty, and know their emptiness. The monolithic ocean will not be bought off with anagrams.

In *The Sound Shape of Language*, Roman Jakobson discussed Saussure's work on anagrams in ancient Latin writers, and he pointed out that anagrams occur frequently in mythopoeic contexts, the names of saints being repeated in descriptions of seasonal agricultural tasks and so on. Jakobson attributed this "play on proper names" – "a play which the individual inventiveness of children and adults shares with folklore" – to the analogies made in Man's unconscious mind.[43] If we subliminally associate God with harvest-time, we may subliminally anagrammatize God in the words we use to describe the harvest. As we have shown, this is not far removed from the linguistic theories of Surrealists like Aragon and Leiris; but, as with psychoanalysis, it is surely the basic concept of verbal ambiguity that Crane had assimilated and which he exploits here for his own purposes. "O Carib Isle" demonstrates a conscious mind imitating at one remove the patterns of the unconscious. Crane had imbibed various ideas of wordplay from Parisian writers, and in his poetry he manipulates these ideas to become himself the satanic Trickster and blasphemer against poetic decorum. Once again, Crane has invested Surrealist techniques with unusual ethical purpose.

12

Surrealism and madness

I discussed in the previous chapter how Crane's verbal dislocations into pun and anagram are a correlative to Dadaist iconoclasm; but the protoplasmic nature of Crane's verbal units also mirrors the theme of terrestrial metamorphosis which is built into *The Bridge*. As we have seen, relativity usurps Brooklyn Bridge's claims to be at the centre of its world: the "whitest Flower" flows away into nothing. The evanescence of art (like the evanescence of all human constructions) was a favourite conception of the Dadaists, who saw art's necessary intermingling of creation and destruction as an antidote to Man's pompous gesturings towards immortality. In "The Importance of Being 'Dada,'" the final chapter of his *Adventures in the Arts* (1921), Marsden Hartley claimed Dada's exhilarating nihilism stemmed ultimately from Nietzsche, its basis being a celebration of "fluidic change," "the element of life itself," with the result that the impermanence inherent in Dadaist art was "the nearest I have come to scientific principle in experience."[1] This echoes the theories of the Dadaist Hans Arp, who described how the energy of the physical world was to invade the ossified structures of civilization: "the artist was himself to become an agent, or force of Nature, creating 'pure movement,' or rivaling Nature in working out the beautifully erosive effect of chance or accident in the processes of Nature!"[2] This could be a direct justification of the first stanza of the "Proem":

> How many dawns, chill from his rippling rest
> The seagull's wings shall dip and pivot him,
> Shedding white rings of tumult, building high
> Over the chained bay waters Liberty –

We have seen how the last line presents us with the "bay waters" of New

York harbour being *chained* to allow *Liberty* to flourish, the superimposition of order on chaos. But, by a Whiteheadian syntactical reversal, this optimism has a negative underside: *waters* may become a verb, suggesting that Liberty will be gradually eroded, watered away into nothing. (*Liberty* is of course the Statue of Liberty, a symbol of the American constitution.) This throws new light on the previous line's "Shedding white rings of tumult," for, besides symbolizing imagination, the bird could be performing the more mundane natural function of *Shedding* its feathers. The poem's landscape seems to consist of hard abstractions, but it is actually underwritten by more pulpy physical substances: rings *of tumult*, soft [yo]u m[o]ult (moult: "to shed or cast off the hair, feathers, outer layer of skin, horns, or the like, the cast-off parts being replaced by new growth"). And we also notice an ambiguity about the grammatical position of "moult." Apparently it is the bird who is doing the moulting. But the phrase could project forward to address itself to the Statue – soft you moult, building high – which would fit in with the watering away of this proud symbol in the fourth line and with the opening of the next stanza, where the Statue becomes *apparitional*. Even without realizing the subtleties of elision, Gregory Robert Zeck said the "unfortunate contiguity of the [seagull] metaphor with the verb "Shedding" calls to mind the indecorous notion of a moulting bird"; but this constant shattering of decorum is an essential part of the poem, and not, as Zeck thought, a result of Crane's "incoherence."[3]

   This gives some idea of the nihilistic tendencies within Crane's work. The poem itself is an organism constantly casting off its outer layer of skin. The Statue offers itself as an emblem of American freedom and political liberty, while at the same time confessing itself and everything it stands for to be part of an insubstantial pageant. In the poem's perpetual oscillation between proposal and disposal we see what Hartley called the "scientific principle" of Dada at work. The pretensions of social systems and historical perfectibility did not impress the Dadaists: Dada's aim was to imitate time by simply eroding everything into nought, and it took pleasure in such extravagant annihilation. All art, said Tzara, is temporary because it is an imposition upon time: "Lying is ecstasy – which lasts longer than a second – there is nothing that lasts longer."[4] Crane was following Tzara's kind of Dadaist paradox when he wrote to Waldo Frank in 1923 of "Faustus and Helen" (emphasis in original): "The last part begins with *catharsis*, the acceptance of tragedy through destruction (The Fall of Troy, etc., also in it). It is Dionysian in its attitude, the creator and the eternal destroyer dance arm in arm."[5] So the opposing stresses incorporated within Crane's *Bridge* are presaged by the "mounted, yielding cities of the air" in "Faustus and Helen" – that *yielding* in two senses, of course: bearing fruit, but also giving way. As Crane's letter implies, the conflict inherent in his wordplay is analogous to the way Nietzsche (in *Birth of Tragedy*) yokes together the "creator" Apollo with the "eternal destroyer" Dionysus. (Hence the importance of Nietzsche for the Dadaists.) Crane's stresses also bring to mind *Le Paysan de Paris* by the Surrealist Louis Aragon, for Aragon similarly disestablished the solidity of objective fact and propagated an aesthetic of radical ambiguity by describing the city as a mirror where every man defines only himself. Aragon asserted that in the absence of objective truth "A philosophy cannot possibly *succeed*" (emphasis in original), it could only hope to achieve greatness through the nobility of its own subjective purpose, and it would retain "this borrowed greatness only in the context of its own failure."[6] In the same way, the ideals of Crane's *Bridge* cannot possibly *succeed*, because the potential for their reversal is built into these ideals themselves; but *The Bridge* can nevertheless retain a temporary grandeur even as it acknowledges its own fallibility. Aragon said that whereas "Reality" was "the apparent absence of contradictions," the "marvellous" was "the eruption of contradictions within the real"; and he declared that "Nothing could be more gallant than a suspension bridge" which incarnates these principles of tension and suspension within the visible world.[7]

THE QUIXOTIC DILEMMA

The sanctity allotted by Aragon to a Surrealist's private vision brings in the whole question of whether *The Bridge* is based on subjective fantasy or objective fact. This, indeed, was Crane's central quandary. For the insouciant Surrealists, the criminal or outcast was a genius who saw further than other men: hence their reverence for Dostoyevsky and Sade, with their brilliant reversals of bourgeois morality. Hence also André Breton's invocation of Columbus as a Surrealist hero who had demonstrated how an apparently ludicrous fantasy could be conjoined with hard material fact: "Christopher Columbus should have set out to discover America with a boatload of madmen. And note how this madness has taken shape, and endured."[8] Crane's transgression against language might be seen as an analogue to the Surrealists' transgression against social decorum; but in the "Proem," Crane seems to express a more ambivalent attitude towards the visionary–madman:

> Out of some subway scuttle, cell or loft
> A bedlamite speeds to thy parapets,
> Tilting there momently, shrill shirt ballooning,
> A jest falls from the speechless caravan.

Note the medieval imagery here: the bedlamite is *Tilting*, as if a knight in joust; that *caravan* may be a medieval company of merchants or pilgrims organized for a long journey; and the *jest* then becomes a "geste," the sort of tale these travellers would tell amongst themselves to cheer everyone up on their long trip. In this reading, the bedlamite is central to the society he inhabits (perhaps even the original son of Mary of Bethlehem, Jesus Christ?). But, as things stand, the *bedlamite* (or lunatic) is peripheral: a man alienated from the *caravan* of traffic across Brooklyn Bridge, traffic which is *speechless* because it can have no communication with an outcast such as he. Now the medieval caravan's socially important gestes have degenerated into nothing better than a lunatic's hollow jests; and the bedlamite is no longer a man who wins the applause of society by tilting in battle, but instead one who tilts from the Bridge in private misery, on the brink of suicide. What is crucial is the emphasis in this stanza upon oscillation: "cell or loft," high or low, geste or jest. The meanings themselves are "Tilting there momently," swinging to and fro (*momently* as not just "momentarily," for an instant, but also as the tendency to produce motion – the "moment force" – about a point or axis). In conceptual terms, this stanza epitomizes the conflict between "Romanticism and Classicism" summarized by T. E. Hulme in his famous essay published in 1924. Hulme criticized Romantic thinkers for being excessively ego-centric in their unfettered flights of imagination, and he said that poets ought to objectify their own visions by acquiescing in socially accepted systems of thought. If Crane's *bedlamite* is an alienated madman, his jest is no more than a solipsistic romantic dream; but if he were a medieval knight, then this "geste" would be a classical celebration of the world around him, and so an example of what Waldo Frank in 1920 called "the Bridge which all true artists seek, between themselves – expressers of a world – and the world that they express."[9]

Bearing this in mind, we can look back to the first stanza of the "Proem" and see how it too vacillates between romantic quest and classical harmony:

> How many dawns, chill from his rippling rest
> The seagull's wings shall dip and pivot him,
> Shedding white rings of tumult, building high
> Over the chained bay waters Liberty –

Played in the key of "Harmony dawns," these lines suggest that *Liberty* is the omniscient paradigm of earthly things around which the seagull dips and pivots longingly. But *Shedding* is a dangling participle: for we do not know if it is the Statue of *Liberty* which is emanating "white rings" of Platonic order ("Harmony dawns") or whether it is the *seagull* (symbol of the romantic imagination) which is leaving white trails as it circles in mid-air in search of its own *Liberty* ("How many dawns"). Nassar pointed out this pun on *Liberty*, which refers to either the classical Statue or the romantic seagull.[10] So nothing could be more appropriate than that Webster should give for the noun *Shedding*, in an obsolete sense: "a parting; division; separation; also, usually *pl.*, the intersection of two or more roads, a crossroads"; for – among its other meanings – *Shedding* is poetically self-reflexive, and the crossroads indicate the alternative directions a reader may take.

We have, then, a battle here between romantic and classical readings. Classically, *building* must be a noun: the Statue of Liberty is a high building which exists prior to this poem. But romantically, *building* becomes a verbal participle: it is Crane's work of art itself which must accept the burden of constructing a myth *ex nihilo*. As Sherman Paul and others have said, the seagull is an emblem of the freedom of the poet's imagination; but the deeper question posed by Crane is to what extent this creative imagination can or should be self-contained inside an unresponsive world. We may remember his letter to Waldo Frank on 20 June 1926 (about a month before he delivered this "Proem" to Frank) where Crane pessimistically declared that "The bridge as a symbol today has no significance beyond an economical approach to shorter hours," and therefore accused himself of "playing Don Quixote in an immorally conscious way." But this self-doubt is built into the poem: *chill* is an obsolete English form of "I will," and *rest* puns on "wrest" ("to turn from truth; to twist from its natural or proper use or meaning by violence"). So is the poet extorting his symbol from a *rippling* environment that is in a constant state of flux and so resistant to such dogmatic impositions? In this case the poet is as forlorn a figure as the seagull: while the bird hovers round the Statue seeking physical sustenance, the poet similarly forages for emotional sustenance. Maybe he is indeed a "see/gull," a gull that sees, a dupe whose visions are no more than self-deception. (We know Crane used "gull" in this way because in one of his drunken rages he spurned the portrait of himself by David Siqueiros, saying he wouldn't be "gulled into buying that piece of junk.")[11] In this "see/gull" reading, the *rings* would then become the anguished "wrings" ("a wringing; writhing. *Obs.*") of tumult experienced by the poet as he martyrs himself for the sake of his race, attempting to wring his epic myth out of a fluctuating and uncooperative landscape. On the other hand, if this epic poet is the laureate of an organized society, he may feel himself entitled – like the Ancient Greek poets – to wear on his head a *chained* (interlinked) *bay* ("an honorary garland or crown bestowed as a prize for victory or excellence, anciently consisting of branches of the laurel"). This last image of poetic triumph is one Crane employs frequently: compare "Some splintered garland for the seer" (*Voyages* VI) and "To argue with the laurel" ("Passage"). And in this case *rest* would pun on the verb "wrest" in its obsolete sense of "to move the strings of (the harp) in playing": thereby implying how the poet reveals the "harp and altar" of Brooklyn Bridge to be an image of Platonic harmony.

To reiterate: in the Platonic reading, the symbol of the Bridge would pre-exist and be external to the poet; in a conventional Romantic reading, the Bridge is seen as a viable product of the poet's imagination; but Crane's secret concern is that the Bridge may be simply the consolatory fantasy of an alienated "bedlamite." We have already mentioned Crane's "Don Quixote" letter, and it is worth quoting more fully:

> Emotionally I should like to write *The Bridge*; intellectually judged the whole theme and project seems more and more absurd. A fear of personal impotence in this matter wouldn't affect me half so much as the convictions that arise from other sources . . . [if] I had what I thought were authentic materials that would have been a pleasurable-agony of wrestling, eventuating or not in perfection – at least being worthy of the most supreme efforts I could muster.
>
> These "materials" were valid to me to the extent that I presumed them to be (articulate or not) at least organic and active factors in the experience and perceptions of our common race, time and belief. The very idea of a bridge, of course, is a form peculiarly dependent on such spiritual convictions. It is an act of faith besides being a communication. The symbols of reality necessary to articulate the span – may not exist where you expected them, however. By which I mean that however great their subjective significance to me is concerned – these forms, materials, dynamics are simply non-existent in the world. I may amuse and delight and flatter myself as much as I please – but I am only evading a recognition and playing Don Quixote in an immorally conscious way.
>
> The form of my poem rises out of a past that so overwhelms the present with its worth and vision that I'm at a loss to explain my delusion that there exist any real links between that past and a future destiny worthy of it. The "destiny" is long since completed, perhaps the little last section of my poem is a hangover echo of it – but it hangs suspended somewhere in ether like an Absalom by his hair. The bridge as a symbol today has no significance beyond an economical approach to shorter hours, quicker lunches, behaviorism and toothpicks . . . If only America were half as worthy today to be spoken of as Whitman spoke of it fifty years ago there might be something for me to say.[12]

The intrusion of this ironic scepticism into *The Bridge* itself has by now become a familiar idea in Crane criticism. For example, Eugene Paul Nassar pointed out how in the line from "Atlantis"

> Now while thy petals spend the suns about us, hold –

the inference to be made is that "the everlasting Flower's petals [are] sustaining the poet only for 'now.'"[13] The logical extension to this which I wish to make is that Crane's irony is built into his ambiguous words as surely as it is built into his ambiguous grammar. When "Atlantis" describes the Bridge as

Tall Vision-of-the-Voyage, tensely spare –

we can say it is *spare* not only in the sense of "taut," but also in the sense of "redundant." The Quixotic poet punningly recognizes that, despite all his mythopoeic symbolism, the idealistic pretensions of the Bridge may remain superfluous as far as workaday America is concerned: a *Tall* story, in fact ("unusual; incredible; as, *tall* stories. *Colloq.*"). By the same pattern, in the "Proem" the Bridge is personified as "Sleepless" ("O Sleepless as the river under thee") while "Atlantis" silently retracts this mythic claim:

O Thou steeled Cognizance whose leap commits

"Cognizance whose leap," Cognizance who sleep. In the syncopated elision, the fraudulence of this anthropomorphic endeavour is slyly exposed. Myth is proposed and disposed of in the same breath. We may recall noticing a similar kind of trick in the "Proem":

And Thee, across the harbor, silver-paced
As though the sun took step of thee, yet left
Some motion ever unspent in thy stride, –

"As though," as Nassar would say, as though. For, as we saw in Chapter 6, the syncopations inside "motion ever unspent" suggest that the sun does not orbit around the Bridge but in actual fact "never runs." And in this Quixotic context, "thy stride" is the idealistic counterpart to the bridge's bathetic offer of the "hy st/ride" (*thy stride*), the High St ride. This is another of Crane's highly ingenious calligrammes: trains on the New York Elevated Railway ran over Brooklyn Bridge until 1944, and the loop on the Brooklyn side ended up at a station called "High Street Brooklyn Bridge."[14] So the Bridge may be a religious symbol, or it may be simply a convenience of transportation, "an economical approach to shorter hours" as Crane put it, for in the 1920s one would "spend" a "sum" (*Some*) of money for the *motion* of a "ride" on the El across the Bridge to Brooklyn High Street:

Some	motion	ever unspent	in	thy	stride
Sum	motion	[never runs] spent	in	the high	st ride

The ironic complexities involved in Crane's symbol of the bridge are clearly set out in his short poem "The Bridge of Estador," which again plays off the dualism of real against ideal:

Walk high on the bridge of Estador,
No one has ever walked there before.

> There is a lake, perhaps, with the sun
> Lapped under it, – or the dun
> Bellies and estuaries of warehouses,
> Tied bundle-wise with cords of smoke.
>
> Do not think too deeply, and you'll find
> A soul, an element in it all.

If you "Do not think too deeply," it becomes possible to reconcile the smoke and warehouses into an essential "element." If you do think too deeply, it doesn't.

If we were to describe the arc of Crane's career, we might suggest four main phases: the wistful solipsism of his early poems, with their "white milk, and honey, gold love" (to quote from "The Hive") where exquisite aesthetic experiences are preserved in an "Interior" away from the world's "jealous threat and guile"; a conflict between that solipsism and the external world in *White Buildings*; the effort to insert the poet's uncertain voice into a public context in *The Bridge*; and the abdication of the ego and triumph of an obdurately inhuman landscape in *Key West* and the Mexican poems. Crane starts by enclosing all the world within a little room, and ends by disintegrating all the little rooms that claim to enclose the world. As a poetic technician, Crane was extremely conscious of these problems of perception and distortion and the way in which the finite world circumscribes the infinite yearnings of the Romantic seer. Perhaps the clearest example of such awareness is the 1923 poem "Recitative," published in *White Buildings*. There the theme of dualism is explicit in the mirror-image of the first two lines:

> Regard the capture here, O Janus-faced,
> As double as the hands that twist this glass.

Janus was the Roman god of doors, and here he is in his familiar pose of looking two ways; hence the *double*, which introduces the question of alternative perspectives around which "Recitative" revolves. Eventually the poet's subjective imagination comes to be reflected in the external world of New York skyscrapers ("And gradually white buildings answer day": surely no coincidence that an ecclesiastical "gradual" is "an antiphon or responsory"); and the final stanza finds these opposing strands resolved into one vision ("In alternating bells have you not heard / All hours clapped dense into a single stride?"). Without going into the detailed intricacies of the poem, it is apparent that the reader is involved here with questions of the nature of perception, the ways in which a poet can apprehend or distort the world, and the fragmentation of objects into chimeras that can be seen from at least two angles. It is a poem of Romantic theory; its conceptual nature was confirmed by Crane in a letter to Allen Tate (emphasis in original):

the poet sees himself in the audience as in a mirror. ALSO, the audience sees itself, in part, in the poet. Against this paradoxical DUALITY is posed the UNITY, or the conception of it (as you got it) in the last verse. In another sense, the poet is *talking to himself* all the way through the poem.[15]

Significantly, in "Recitative" it is "The bridge" which "swings over salvage, beyond wharves" that symbolizes the reunification of the subjective and objective; and so in a long poem actually called *The Bridge* begun less than three years later, it would have been strange indeed if Crane had completely jettisoned his complex theories of perception and produced instead the kind of artless clash of optimism and pessimism that some critics have found therein. Crane's artistic self-consciousness is evident again in such minor works as "To Liberty," where the poet represents himself as a male lover impregnating the landscape by a process of personification and risking the ridicule of an audience who might think he is aggrandizing his object out of all proportion ("They laugh to hear / How I endow her"). The fragment "Hieroglyphic," found among Crane's Mexican papers, is even more succinct in its summary of the poet's familiar Quixotic dilemma:

> Did one look at what one saw
> Or did one see what one looked at?[16]

So we find that the irony inherent in Crane's oscillation between myth and exploded myth may be redefined as the irony inherent in the oscillation between Romantic vision and explosion of that vision. In this sense, "The Harbor Dawn" and "Van Winkle" verge towards being conscious parodies of the rest of *The Bridge*, for they both define the quest in exclusively personal terms:

> Times earlier, when you hurried off to school,
> – It is the same hour though a later day –
> You walked with Pizarro in a copybook,
> And Cortes rode up, reining tautly in –
> Firmly as coffee grips the taste, – and away!

These lines from "Van Winkle" are a *reductio ad absurdum* of the Emersonian idea that one man contains history within himself. The arbitrariness of Crane's version of the history of America in *The Bridge* is exposed by the naïveté of this school copybook, which is really only a reflection in exaggerated form of Crane's own extreme selectivity. The poet's incongruous and Surreal equation of Cortes' endeavour with the taste of coffee re-emphasizes that idiosyncrasy and subjectivism which Crane knowingly employs here; and so does the mention two lines later of "Captain Smith, all beard and certainty" – for that is a further, childish burlesque of the burlesque version of history later to be presented in

"The Dance." (Captain Smith was, of course, an important figure in the Pocahontas legend.) Similarly the "monoplanes / We launched – with paper wings and twisted / Rubber bands" parodically anticipate the aeroplanes in "Cape Hatteras" – which are also equipped with mere "paper wings," being no more than a literary conceit inscribed within the paper of a text. "The Harbor Dawn" is another kind of withdrawal from the public bravado of *The Bridge*, for there the personification of the landscape suggests how the world has become internalized by the lovers in their private idyll. Sherman Paul admitted finding the adjective *blond* "strained" (in "The window goes blond slowly"), but this is only a counterpart to the anthropomorphic description of the world in terms of the lovers' bed ("Soft *sleeves* of sound," "the *pillowed* bay"), and it implicitly comments on the whole business of mythopoeic transpositions of the empirical world:

> – Two – three bright window-eyes aglitter, disk
> The sun, released – aloft with cold gulls hither.

In this world distorted by Romantic longing, the "window-eyes" are said to "disk" and then release "The sun," as though the sun were subservient to the demands of these "Cyclopean towers." But by a typically disillusioning syntactical reversal, the *sun* may in fact be the subject who releases glittering discs in the skyscraper windows, with *disk* moving from verb to noun: "disk (object) The sun (subject) released (verb)." Myth and language attempt to impose themselves upon the world, and their Noble Lies convince the *gulls* or dupes, but Crane the ironist is surreptitiously pointing out the fraudulence of such metaphorical designs; and so the sense of strain Paul found here is conceptually justified – with this strain in "The Harbor Dawn" being a deliberately exaggerated version of the strain between subject and object inherent in the rest of *The Bridge*. Crane himself told Kahn how in "The Harbor Dawn" "images blur as objects only half apprehended on the border of sleep and consciousness";[17] and such ambiguous interaction between internal and external worlds persists throughout this poem, manifesting itself in that verbal blurring or overlapping of meaning inherent in the pun:

> And then a truck will lumber past the wharves
> As winch engines begin throbbing on some deck

That *lumber*, a lumbering motion, has an obsolete commercial homonym: "a pawnbroker's shop or storeroom . . . a pledge, or pawn, or money lent on it" (from its etymology "Lombardy"); but it also carries a sexual homophone "lumbar" – "of, pertaining to, or near the loins," which makes those "winch engines" in the next line phallic, and the *deck* self-reflexive (the poem itself operating on various "decks" or levels). Again, private eroticism is counterpointed with the public world of trade and commerce, so that Crane's puns, chiming in the distance, turn his poem into a wavering trick-mirror which is suspended between the harbour's *buoys* and homosexual "boys":

> . . . eddied
> Among distant chiming buoys – adrift. The sky,
> Cool feathery fold, suspends, distills
> This wavering slumber. . . .

THE DRUNKARD'S DREAM

The possible retraction of *The Bridge* into a private illusion, perhaps even the demented vision of a bedlamite or see gull, is given another dimension by the plethora of alcoholic images concealed inside the poem. Crane, we know, was an alcoholic: Malcolm Cowley said he had "the drunkard's talent for finding hidden liquor and hiding it somewhere else"; and Katherine Anne Porter remembered how this Jekyll and Hyde element in Crane's character was particularly apparent during the poet's last years in Mexico: "Sober, he was friendly, confidential, melancholy, read poetry, wrote letters, worked in his garden or in mine. Drunk, he fell into indescribable obscenity and violence."[18] Crane consciously employed alcohol as a means towards creative inspiration, but in his sober moods he trained an ironic light upon his own performances, expressing doubts about the status of his poetry and fearing it might all be reducible to nothing more than a sad drunkard's dream. In "Cape Hatteras," for example, an explicit analogy is made between inebriation and poetic vision:

> Hermetically past condor zones, through zenith havens
> Past where the albatross has offered up
> His last wing-pulse, and downcast as a cup
> That's drained, is shivered back to earth – thy wand
> Has beat a song, O Walt – there and beyond!

Whitman's poetry is a model of artistic heroism precisely because it operates "beyond" such alcoholic havens, because it does not depend simply upon the flights of fancy associated with this *albatross* (Coleridge's "Ancient Mariner," Baudelaire's "L'Albatros"). When the "cup" of Coleridge or Baudelaire has been "drained," their imagination fails; and the alcoholic puns in *The Bridge* are secretly confessing that their author may be in this same decadent mould, strive as Crane may for that largeness and fecundity associated with the Whitmanian paradigm. So perhaps the image of Brooklyn Bridge in "Atlantis" may be no more

than a cheerful drinking-toast, "Deity's glittering *Pledge*," with the
imagination coursing through "the bright *drench* and fabric" of the poet's
veins as though it were a drench of alcohol. One could infer the
possibility of a pun on *Pledge* here from the way the word is overtly used
in two quite different senses elsewhere in *The Bridge*: as "promise" in
"Indiana" ("you'll keep your pledge"), but as an alcoholic pledge in
"Quaker Hill":

> We, who with pledges taste the bright annoy
> Of friendship's acid wine . . .

If the idealistic claims made for Brooklyn Bridge might be the product of
a drunkard's dream, the speculative mythopoeic visions in "The River"
may be dependent for their efficacy upon bootleg whisky:

> Under the Ozarks, domed by Iron Mountain,
> The old gods of the rain lie wrapped in pools
> Where eyeless fish curvet a sunken fountain
> And re-descend with corn from querulous crows.

In fact America's "old gods" are a *lie*, visible only to a person "rapt in
pools," ecstatically drunk in pools of liquor. These "eyeless fish" have an
urgent wish to drink like fishes: they "covet" (pun on *curvet*) a "sunken
fountain" (the bootleg liquor concealed from public view, "sunk"
beneath the surface). And so these consumers quench their thirst by
purchasing Prohibition *corn* (slang for illegally sold whisky (f)) from the
"querulous crows" who operate on the black market. The crow is
known as the most intelligent and predatory of birds, and it belongs to
the same sinister corvine family as the ill-famed "rook," "a trickish,
rapacious fellow; a cheat": in *Metamorphoses*, Ovid tells the story of how
the *corvus*, originally a white bird, was turned black as a punishment for
treachery. So these fancifully anthropomorphic "old gods" may inhabit
the Ozark Mountains only when they are perceived through a haze of
Prohibition liquor, just as Brooklyn Bridge itself perhaps relies upon the
poet's inebriation for its aggrandizement into an epic national symbol.

The dreams woven by alcohol are especially apparent in Crane's
"Cutty Sark." As Fender said, the title "Cutty Sark" itself is a pun
swinging between the name of a clipper ship and Crane's favourite brand
of Scotch whisky; and the line "rum was Plato in our heads" seems to
drag the poem's quest for Platonic harmony down to an alcoholic
fantasy, with Atlantis degenerating into a drunken image glimpsed in a
South Street dive (emphases in original):

> ATLANTIS ROSE *drums wreathe the rose*

Maybe the rose of Atlantis – or maybe Atlantis becoming associated with
rosé wine. It is also interesting to note how the verbal components of *rum*,

r–u–m, mirror and invert the m–u–r of *mur* ("'Mur/murs": a bilingual pun on French "wall") which "Cutty Sark" associates with its socially validated *Leviathan*:

> Murmurs of Leviathan he spoke,
> and rum was Plato in our heads . . .

Leviathan is the whale this old seaman broods over, of course, but by association with Hobbes' *Leviathan* it also connotes "the organized whole people of a state in their collective capacities"; and Crane's subversive suggestion in these lines is of the alcoholic *rum* overturning the walls of social decorum, thematically, but also linguistically, as r–u–m overturns m–u–r. This fulfils one of the prophecies made in the "Proem":

> Down Wall, from girder into street noon leaks

The literal meaning is of the noon light seeping down Wall Street in New York City; but "Down Wall" also implies that more general disintegration of the walls of social convention which recurs throughout *The Bridge*, and which is particularly apparent in this rum-sodden universe of "Cutty Sark."[19]

An earlier Crane poem, "The Wine Menagerie," even more clearly equates poetry with drink ("when wine redeems the sight"); and in "To the Cloud Juggler," his 1930 tribute to Harry Crosby, Crane's late friend is described as another whose imaginative feats were helped along by alcohol:

> You, the rum-giver to that slide-by-night, –
> The moon's best lover, – guide us by a sleight
> Of quarts to faithfuls – surely smuggled home –
> As you raise temples fresh from basking foam.

A pun on *foam*: not so much "temples" arising out of the foam of the sea (where this poem is set) as artistic *temples* constructed with the aid of the "basking foam" of ale. Crosby is the "rum-giver" and the "moon's best lover" ("moon" or "moonshine" was Twenties slang for bootleg whisky (f)). The imagery of concealment – "slide-by-night," "a sleight / Of quarts," "smuggled home" – suggests the great importance of deception when trading in liquor during the Prohibition era; but it also suggests the deception of the poem, the way bathetic alcoholic puns are secretly undermining the poem's idealistic pretensions. Calling Crosby "The moon's best lover" seems to be a pleasant tribute to his Romanticism until we know that *moon* puns on whisky. The pun does not cancel the spiritual aura associated with Crosby, but it reveals that for him the clouds were indeed "juggled," that an element of trickery and alcoholic illusion was a necessary preliminary to Crosby's transcendent vision. Similarly in *The Bridge*: the alcoholic puns are not satirically reductive, they do not destroy the poem's Romanticism, but they burlesque it, and so provide us with an alternative angle from which to view the poet's concerns. Crosby loves the Romantic moon and moonshine whisky both at once; and the pun, swinging between opposites, allows this constant interpenetration between ideal and real.

The first stanza of "The Harbor Dawn," originally published in *transition*, demonstrates once again this kind of alcoholic pun at work inside *The Bridge*:[20]

> Insistently through sleep − a tide of voices −
> They meet you listening midway in your dream,
> The long, tired sounds, fog-insulated noises:
> Gongs in white surplices, beshrouded wails,
> Far strum of fog horns . . . signals dispersed in veils.

The scene is of two lovers waking up to early morning noises from the adjacent harbour. Not surprisingly nautical imagery is rife, and the "beshrouded wails" are also the "wales" ("the outside planking of a vessel") which support a ship's "shrouds" ("the ropes of hemp or wire leading, usually in pairs, from a vessel's mastheads to give lateral support to the masts"). These shrouds also seem to possess religious connotations, fitting in with *veils*, *surplices* (a priest's vestments) and those *Gongs* which R. W. B. Lewis associated with the bells rung during a Eucharist service.[21] But this spiritualizing of the sea is in fact subtly introduced in the poem's first word, for *Insistently* punningly fractures itself into "In/cist/tent-ly": "cist," from the Greek *kiste*, is in classical archaeology "a box or chest, esp. for sacred utensils"; and "tent" is "a sweet deep red wine . . . used mainly for ecclesiastical purposes," notably Holy Communion. (Hence the sounding of the *Gongs*.) But of course the "tent" of red wine was more often employed by Crane for a profane purpose, and he was less troubled with sacramental cists than with painful "cysts" ("morbid matter") in his bladder. (Crane complained about his "Uric acid" in a letter to the Browns on 7 May 1926.)[22] So "In/cyst/tent-ly" can have an alcoholic as well as a religious context, and Crane's aggrandizement of the harbour into a church altar is punningly held in check by the knowledge that this metaphorical transposition may derive simply from drunken fancy. The "tide of voices" suggests the presence of more than one voice and that, like ebb and flow, they are pulling in opposite directions; and the "signals dispersed in veils" similarly hint at something concealed from public view. As we saw in Chapter 3, those "signals dispersed in veils" also offer punning suggestions of a hard material world which is counterbalancing the narrator's subjective dreams: for the *Gongs* (like the later *sirens*) suggest hooters calling men to work; *veils* puns on "vails," "profit"; *surplices* puns on "surpluses"; and *dispersed* implies the capitalist necessity of consumers "dis-pursing," taking money out of their purses.

So here, as throughout the rest of *The Bridge*, there is a Quixotic oscillation between subjective fancy and objective fact; and the pun, tilting there momently, is the means by which Crane balances his poem between the illusions of alcoholic or bedlamite vision and the disillusionments of empirical reality. Quixote and his creator Cervantes were, of course, Spaniards; and – to make the broadest of generalizations – while French Surrealism in the early twentieth century was essentially comic, Spanish Surrealism tended more towards the grotesque and tragic in its mournful acknowledgement of the old Quixotic discrepancy between ideal forms and inert reality. Crane's poetry combines an element of both: for *The Bridge* is witty and playful in the French mode, but in its solemnization of a mundane High Street ride into "thy stride" typical of a grand anthropomorphic deity, we may sense the pathos and absurdity of Cervantes' hero attempting to joust with windmills. The Quixotic dilemma was a central theme of Waldo Frank's *Virgin Spain*, which Crane knew, where it is put into the context of metaphysical Christianity confronting sensual and sluggish Islam; and in his final months in Mexico, Crane wrestled ever more hopelessly with this perennial struggle to force dark Spanish landscapes through into artistic significance.[23] Crane's final poem, "The Broken Tower," outlines exactly this collision between ideal music and the fragmented material world ("O terraced echoes prostrate on the plain!"); and the same savage irony can be read back into *The Bridge*, whose Surrealistic trick-mirrors are funny, but never merely funny, for in their brilliant shifting of lights they alert us to the necessary madness circumjacent to Crane's Quixotic vision.

13

Psychoanalysis and homosexuality

"Prayer of pariah, and the lover's cry . . ." ("Proem")

PSYCHOANALYTICAL REDUCTION

In simple biographical terms, Crane's homosexuality made him "adept at compartmentalizing his life," as John Unterecker said.[1] Crane did not reveal his sexual preferences to his mother until 1928, and on his nocturnal prowls around the city dockyards in search of sailors he assumed a quite different rôle from that of the sophisticated urban artist. He even changed his name for these expeditions, calling himself Mike Drayton.[2] Crane found himself in the same predicament as Forster and Auden in England and Marsden Hartley in his own circle: the social mores of the time ensured that to some extent the homosexual was necessarily involved in a life of deception. Things were even worse for the American poet because he himself was not at ease with his own personality. Allen Tate recalled how Crane had "none of the characteristics popularly attributed to homosexuality," how indeed he eradicated every trace of effeminate sensibility from his everyday appearance. Said Tate: "The violence of his obscenity (particularly about women) and his intense emotional attachments to women his own age (not to middle-aged women) convinced me even then that he was an extreme example of the *unwilling* homosexual."[3] Philip Horton recounted the story of when Crane finally did get around to explaining his sexual predicament to his mother, how he mentioned

> certain experiences of his adolescence which had conditioned him towards it; he described the years he had suffered from the sense of his difference from other men and the corrosive consciousness of guilt; he told also of his vain efforts to cure himself by attempting normal relationships; and he concluded by insisting vigorously – too vigorously to be convincing – that he was no longer ashamed of it.[4]

Solomon Grunberg remembered that Crane disliked homosexuals and called them "fags."[5] Nevertheless Crane's late poem "Reply" is specifically addressed to his homosexual reader, "dear brother," and it adumbrates the idea of a secret fraternity recognizing each other's trademarks ("Thou canst read nothing except through appetite"). Only through private confession, the poem suggests, can public esteem be achieved: "fame is pivotal to shame." "Reply" talks of "my shame undone," with *undone* punningly denoting both the exposure of the poet's shame to public view, and – as a desired final end – the undoing or eradication of these guilty feelings. Poems like "The Visible the Untrue" (dedicated to Crane's male lover Emil Opffer) have traditionally been seen in a mystical light as epitomizing Crane's contempt for the material world, but it is possible to take the poem in a more immediate sense as an example of Crane's devotion to concealment. The visible must be the untrue because inside society the homosexual poet is obliged to suppress his genuine desires. On account of his homosexuality Crane was being blackmailed intermittently throughout his life, and there is an oblique reference to this in "Quaker Hill":

> Wait for the postman driving from Birch Hill
> With birthright by blackmail, the arrant page
> That unfolds a new destiny to fill . . .

In a recent interview, John Unterecker suggested this autobiographical reference epitomized Crane's attempt to transmute his private misery into constructive public art.[6]

Inside *The Bridge*, one of the significances of Crane's homosexuality was the way it led the author to ask himself whether his poem might be no more than a consolation for sexual failure. The most explicit lines of confession occur in "Van Winkle," where, as Thomas A. Vogler pointed out in *Preludes to Vision*, the poet wonders if his *Bridge* is really anything more substantial than the product of sublimated Oedipal fixations:

> So memory, that strikes a rhyme out of a box,
> Or splits a random smell of flowers through glass –
> Is it the whip stripped from the lilac tree
> One day in spring my father took to me,
> Or is it the Sabbatical, unconscious smile
> My mother almost brought me once from church
> And once only, as I recall – ?

Vogler said that Crane is asking himself whether the image of Mr Crane senior is an equivalent to Columbus' "Elohim," and so whether the desire of *The Bridge* for a "myth to God" is any more than the subconscious wish for a substitute father. Similarly, the poet wonders whether it was the smile of his own mother that engendered a yearning for the safe bosom of "Atlantis." All this is most appropriate in the context of the Rip Van Winkle legend, the essence of which, as Philip Young has shown, is a man who has "grown old but not up," and which depicts "the self arrested in a timeless infancy," a story appealing to "the child and primitive in everyone that never grow up – and never die in anyone."[7] Young's analysis illuminates Crane's "Van Winkle" in two ways: the survival in the poet of an infantile or pagan irresponsibility gives licence to those puns evoking sexual horseplay that we noted in Chapter 11 (the "grind-organ" and so on); but the images of whipping father and benevolent mother also intimate the perseverance in the narrator of a childish masochism, a regressive refusal to surrender the ethical and metaphysical certainties of his parents' home, with the result that *The Bridge* might become reducible to a pathetic quest to rediscover such a personal heaven-haven. (Hence, as Crane told Kahn, Rip Van Winkle is "the 'guardian angel' of the journey into the past" and "becomes identified with [the poem's] protagonist.") On a slightly more complex level, the analyst Theodor Reik saw masochism as a prolongation of suspense, a refusal to resolve tension; and so the poet may here be asking himself whether his cultivation of literary puns and ambiguities could be traced back to painful childhood experiences which left him with a disinclination for assertion and resolution.[8]

It is possible to see this type of psychoanalytical reduction as working all the way through *The Bridge*; and indeed "Cape Hatteras" explicitly considers how a person's vision of the world may comprise nothing more than an inversion or mirror-image of his past. Crane's "periscope" is an appropriate metaphor for this deterministic process, for while the machine's lens up on high peers towards the future, its actual human operator down below is inexorably bound to a submerged labyrinth of Freudian conditioning:

> . . . while time clears
> Our lenses, lifts a focus, resurrects
> A periscope to glimpse what joys or pain
> Our eyes can share or answer – then deflects
> Us, shunting to a labyrinth submersed
> Where each sees only his dim past reversed . . .

One of the functions of the submersed labyrinth of puns in Crane's *Bridge* is to show how the "low" selfish instincts of the id may be undermining all the "high" mythopoeic pretensions of the ego. Take an example from "The Dance":

> I, too, was liege
> To rainbows currying each pulsant bone:
> Surpassed the circumstance, danced out the siege!

The theme here is, as M. D. Uroff put it, the poet being "burned at the stake as a sacrifice to restore the earth's fertility"; and so it is highly appropriate that *siege* should be, in an obsolete sense, "passage of excrements; stool; fecal matter."[9] For the poet, the dance is a means of overcoming that anal fixation which Freud aligned with repression and infantile sexuality. And the stanza immediately preceding this indicates how the development of a punning consiousness is essential to such a dancing out of the siege:

> Dance, Maquokeeta! snake that lives before,
> That casts his pelt, and lives beyond! Sprout, horn!
> Spark, tooth! Medicine-man, relent, restore –
> Lie to us, – dance us back the tribal morn!

Crane is delving here into the etymological origins of *relent*: Latin *lentus*, tough, slow, sticky; and so *relent* as to melt under the influence of heat, to assume a liquid form. In this way the image of the snake sloughing off its dead skin becomes poetically self-reflexive: the poem metamorphoses in the same way as the snake metamorphoses, and both liquidities are analogous to that mental and physical fluidity which overcomes repressive blocks and which is here associated with psychic health. "Sprout, horn" suggests the advent of a fertile dance (the sailor's hornpipe), also sexual desire (feeling "horny"); but it also implies the double-edged alternatives which persist all the way through the language of *The Bridge*, thus catching the reader on the "horns" of a perpetual dilemma. This admission of a playful ambiguity, the recognition that there are two sides to everything ("Spark, tooth/twoth"), becomes the essential challenge for reader as well as narrator.

A few lines later in "The Dance," we encounter the phrase:

> – Siphoned the black pool from the heart's hot root!

The theme is this section's familiar one of the drawing off of bad blood. The interesting word is *heart's*: John Unterecker has said recently, "I think all the puns on the word 'Hart' in Crane's work are efforts to take his own private mess and give it some kind of lasting form."[10] There seems to be another autobiographical reference in "Quaker Hill," where Hart's personal crack-up becomes equated with the general disintegration of consciousness necessary for admission into "The Tunnel" (and finally into the Platonic harmony of "Atlantis"):

> Yes, while the heart is wrung . . .
> Breaks us and saves, yes, breaks the heart, yet yields
> That patience that is armour and that shields
> Love from despair –

And in "Atlantis" there is a further reference to the *heart* which can be put into an autobiographical context:

> Migrations that must needs void memory,
> Inventions that cobblestone the heart, –
> Unspeakable Thou Bridge to Thee, O Love.
> Thy pardon for this history, whitest Flower,
> O Answerer of all, – Anemone –

The surface idea is of renouncing the past and building a bridge to the future dream-island of Atlantis. But note how the verbal play reduces this to a personal journey: *Migrations* becomes "my Grace shuns" (Grace was the name of Crane's domineering mother, ever a Medusa-like torment to him: in adult life, Crane always addressed Grace by her Christian name). And *must* becomes a noun signifying "a condition of dangerous frenzy, usually connected with sexual excitement; – said of adult male elephants, which become so at irregular intervals"; with *void* denoting the physical process of emission; and memory becoming "me mori," me dying, exploiting the Latin *mori* as a sexual pun on "die" in the Elizabethan sense. In the next line *Inventions* becomes "In/vent/shuns," indicating that the shunning of insertions into a vent (vent as "the anus," zoological) is something which tends to "cobblestone the heart." "Stone" as a verb is "to make like stone; to harden (obs.)"; "cobblers" is given by Wentworth and Flexner as low nineteenth- and twentieth-century slang for "testicles," "cobblers" being short for "cobblers' awls," rhyming slang on "balls"; and so "the heart" puns on the poet himself, Hart Crane, who secretly announces here that abstention from anal intercourse has the effect of turning his cobblers to stone.[11] No wonder, then, the *Bridge* by which Crane approaches his lover is *Unspeakable*: for this love that dare not speak its name must manifest itself in a series of concealed puns, as Crane divulges a need to shun Grace in order to find his erotic freedom, that Atlantean state where must can void the heart. In *cobblestone*, Crane may have been associating his mother Grace with Medusa, one of the three Gorgons in Greek myth accustomed to turn men who looked at her to stone; Crane has an early poem entitled "Medusa" which concludes: "'Behold thy lover, – / Stone!'" Hart did indeed have to flee from his mother to find his sexual liberty: when he was on the run from Hollywood to New Orleans in 1928 to escape her clutches, Crane sent Grace a drunken postcard threatening to take off for the Orient which was signed "Atlantis"; and in this light, the previous section's "Tunnel" – "Umbilical to call" – comes to have overtones of a maternal womb.[12] Eric J. Sundquist recently remarked on how Crane's "family often becomes in his poetry almost a stage prop borrowed from home," and these stage props sometimes work verbally as well as thematically. Crane's "Aunt Sally" Simpson walks quite openly into "The River" (Crane told Mrs Simpson he wanted her in *The Bridge* because she was his "idea of the salt of all pioneers"); but, as we have seen, Grace Crane, Hart Crane and Otto Kahn make covert appearances under the disguise of puns, while Emil Opffer is concealed inside an anagram.[13] Sundquist made some apposite remarks when this pun on *Migrations* was suggested to him: "given the wealth of puns in Crane, and the deep psychological significance they often bear, the possible pun on Grace is not unthinkable. The question then is whether it is good poetry – or simply a private game. Crane walks the line often, and this kind of pun could go either way, I think." While not disagreeing with this, I might add that the problem of whether *The Bridge* might be reducible to "a private game" is one Crane himself kept very much in mind:

> Thy pardon for this history, whitest Flower,
> O Answerer of all, – Anemone –

Crane asks the Bridge's pardon for imposing upon it patterns of objective history, but he also apologizes for imposing the patterns of his own subjective story (*history*: "his/story"). And the flower *Anemone* could also be construed as a private reference, because in Greek mythology Adonis – killed through his association with Aphrodite, goddess of love – was resurrected and immortalized as the Anemone: so while Crane is suggesting how he has immortalized his own homosexuality by transforming it into the mythic Flower of Brooklyn Bridge, the fact that the anemone is, as Mary Jean Butts noted, "a sea animal" not only reinforces "the bridge's connection with the underwater continent, Atlantis," but also suggests how Crane's erotic confessions exist under the surface of his socially respectable poem – just as the author's own homosexuality was concealed under the surface of social life.[14] In this way, "Atlantis" can be seen as perpetually wavering between epic grandeur and autobiographical lament:

> Transparent meshes – fleckless the gleaming staves –
> Sibylline voices flicker, waveringly stream

The voices of the sibylline prophetess? Or the voices of the sibling family (sib: "related by blood; akin")? In the latter reading, those *staves* would become, not musical notes, but rather "a stick; cudgel" – thereby harking back to the threatening parental scene in "Van Winkle." So these "Transparent meshes" of Brooklyn Bridge may also signify "Trans/parent" meshes or snares, that psychological claustrophobia Crane believed his childhood had bequeathed to him. In a letter to Yvor Winters on 29 April 1927, Crane stated that "Atlantis" "contains a metaphysical synthesis of a number of things like aeronautics, telegraphy, *psychoanalysis*, atomic theory, relativity, and what not!"[15] There is no overt imagery of "psychoanalysis" in "Atlantis," so, provided Crane is telling the truth in this letter, the poem's psychoanalytical content must necessarily be concealed.

The family as stage prop reaches its most humorous manifestation in "Cape Hatteras," where, by a bizarre comic-strip of psychoanalysis, the efforts of the Wright brothers' aeroplane to leave the ground become

equated with a child's efforts to leave behind the domineering influence
of its mother:

> There, from Kill Devils Hill at Kitty Hawk
> Two brothers in their twinship left the dune;
> Warping the gale, the Wright windwrestlers veered
> Capeward, then blading the wind's flank, banked and spun
> What ciphers risen from prophetic script,
> What marathons new-set between the stars!
> The soul, by naphtha fledged into new reaches
> Already knows the closer clasp of Mars, –
> New latitudes, unknotting, soon give place
> To what fierce schedules, rife of doom apace!

Crane's place names are rarely chosen at random, and here "Kill Devils
Hill" suggests the poet's own personal *Devils* which he hopes to
expurgate or *Kill* by his act of writing. The "Two brothers" who are
"blading the wind's flank" seem to have overtones of homoeroticism –
"blade" as a dashing young man, *flank* as part of the body – and this act of
mounting makes the soul *fledged*: the child, like the aeroplane, has
acquired its wings for flight. The aeroplane "knows the closer clasp of
Mars" in the sense that air travel has brought the planet Mars
geographically closer – though it has also brought figuratively closer the
prospect of being clasped in war, as we see later in "Cape Hatteras": *Mars*
being Roman god of war. But for the child, this new-found ability to fly
negates or "noes" (a pun on *knows*) the closer clasp of "Ma's" (*Mars*). The
mother or ma's protective clutches have been broken through, and that
unknotting is the untying of the child's umbilical cord. The narrator
depicts his erotic liberation as dependent upon his ability to free himself
from maternal fixations:

> Behold the dragon's covey – amphibian, ubiquitous

The *covey* is an old bird with a brood of young, who is here portrayed as a
repressive "drag/on" (*dragon*) the life of her children, the upshot being
that the narrator urges her, "you be quit of us" (*ubiquitous*), you leave us
to mind our own business. The adjective *amphibian* ("living both on land
and in the water . . . Of a mixed nature, partaking of two natures")
perfectly suggests the dualistic discrepancy between the overt and
concealed halves of Crane's text. And in the next stanza, the battered
child is comically pictured as a plane preparing for flight:

> Wheeled swiftly, wings emerge from larval-silver hangars

The image is reminiscent of Picabia's Surrealistic dehumanization of men
into machines. "Larva" is the immature wingless form into which insects
hatch from the egg. *Wheeled* puns on "wealed," marked with a weal or

whip, which takes up the flailing *bludgeon* in the previous stanza, and hints at the torments of the narrator's childhood ("Is it the whip stripped from the lilac tree . . . ?"). And the aeroplane's *hangars* pun on the child's parents as "hangers," hangmen who have frustrated its easy passage into maturity. Crane himself was never averse to a little amateur dabbling in psychoanalysis in the context of his own problems, and in 1928 he was complaining to his Aunt Zell about "wasteful family problems that have robbed me of my vitality during the last twelve years – unmanned me time and time again and threatened to make me one of those emotional derelicts who are nothing but tremulous jellyfish might-have-beens."[16] And this psychological context is especially apposite if we consider the imagery throughout "Cape Hatteras" revolving around the idea of binding up wounds:

> Power's script, – *wound*, bobbin-*bound*, refined –
>
> *Wounds* that we *wrap* with theorems sharp as hail!

> O, upward from the dead
> Thou bringest tally, and a pact, new *bound*
> Of living brotherhood!

> Thou, pallid there as chalk,
> Has kept of *wounds*, O Mourner, all that sum
> That then from Appomattox stretched to Somme!

> Wherewith to *bind* us throbbing with one voice

Walt Whitman's experience as a nurse during the American Civil War merges into his binding together of the race through poetic myth (a pun on *bind*, of course); and the wounds inflicted during this earlier war elide into the injuries brought about by fighter pilots during the First World War. The aeroplanes' deployment in war is a negative use of machinery which may be redeemed by the "new universe" promised by the "wound, bobbin-bound" spools of the factory's "power house" (a pun on *wound*: wound as injury, but also as the "winding" of the spools). But the poet's psychological traumas are an equivalent to these public wars: the clasp of Ma's and of *Mars* are thematic and verbal equivalents; and so Crane's expurgation of his own personal *Devils* becomes analogous to the process of wound-dressing in the social arena. In this light, Crane's injuries could be seen as a deliberate metamorphosis of psychic scars into sociological and artistic significance, as in the myth of Philoctetes, invoked by Edmund Wilson in *The Wound and the Bow*.

There is, then, a psychoanalytical self-awareness running through *The Bridge*. Monroe K. Spears called Crane "an almost embarrassingly obvious case history for the psychological critic"; but because self-analysis is a concealed but conscious theme of the poem, there is no question of a rational mind being surprised by the machinations of the id. Crane wrote to Yvor Winters on 15 November 1926: "what is 'mythical' in or rather, of the twentieth century is not the Kaiser, the sinking of the Titanic, etc. Rather it is science, travel, (in the sense of speed) – psychoanalysis, etc."; and, as we have noted, in another letter to Winters five months later the poet specifically said that imagery drawn from psychoanalysis had been built into "Atlantis."[17] We can see, then, that Crane is a cunning technician who carefully weaves these regressive biographical strands into his work, and so leaves open the suggestion that his urge to create a "myth to God" may be arising out of nothing more than the circumstances of his own private life. This vacillation between abstraction and autobiography is explicitly discussed towards the end of "Quaker Hill," where the elevated vision of a hawk is contrasted with the bathos of a "worm's eye," as Crane wonders whether the "news" his poem brings might be merely personal and therefore unoriginal:

> So, must we from the hawk's far stemming view,
> Must we descend as worm's eye to construe
> Our love of all we touch, and take it to the Gate
> As humbly as a guest who knows himself too late,
> His news already told? Yes, while the heart is wrung . . .
> Yes, whip-poor-will, unhusks the heart of fright,
> Breaks us and saves, yes, breaks the heart . . .

Here the *heart* puns on himself, Hart Crane, with the "whip-poor-will" – a type of bird – punningly suggesting Crane's masochism. In a "worm's eye" view of *The Bridge*, the ultimate haven of "Atlantis" could be no more than subliminal consolation for the poet's victimization by his father and desertion by his mother, who omitted to bestow smiles upon her son, as "Van Winkle" records.

FREUD AND AMBIGUITY

Crane's concern for "psychoanalytical" revelation would have been inspired by the intense interest in Freud's work which the United States manifested during the 1920s. In this respect Freud resembled Einstein: he became a household name even though few people understood his theories except in their most generalized forms; but in this popularized version psychoanalysis became neatly affiliated to the American belief in self-discovery and self-improvement, and as early as 1915 psychoanalytical "case histories" were appearing in women's journals. According to Frederick J. Hoffman, "The literature of the 1920s offered many examples of the mind's turning in upon itself, examining, explaining, and excusing itself in psychological terms"; and psychoanalysis became so well known that it even found itself turning into a target for *Vanity*

Fair, a New York magazine which specialized in parodies and which offered its readers "Possible Freudian Interpretations of the Aesthetic Appeal of Babe Ruth."[18] So Crane's wry exposition of his own dilemmas was not at all unusual in the context of his time. Freud himself had visited Worcester, Massachusetts in 1909 to deliver a series of lectures which were later published in the *American Journal of Psychology*, and during the following two decades every intellectual faction also had its own version of the master's theories. For the Greenwich Village community, for example, among whom psychoanalysis became a fashionable craze, Freud was a prophet of free love and an ally in the war against bourgeois society. But for James Branch Cabell, Freud provided an excuse to introduce gleeful *double entendres* into his comic romance *Jurgen* (1919), which Crane knew, and which was later suppressed; and it is specifically upon Freud's explanations of this kind of linguistic ambiguity that we need to concentrate here.

In *The Interpretation of Dreams*, Freud stressed the need to analyse dreams in great detail and not to generalize them away into vague themes. Because each dream is of a "composite character," encrusted with layers of "psychical formations," it is essential to examine the dream "as though [it] were a geological conglomerate in which each fragment of rock required a separate assessment."[19] In *The Interpretation*, Freud talked about the old-fashioned desire to decode dreams, treating them "as a kind of cryptography in which each sign can be translated into another sign having a known meaning, in accordance with a fixed key." Such a superstition was now invalid, said Freud, because too much would depend on which particular "key" was chosen as a means of conscripting the "supernatural" into the service of the preferred ideology. Freud claimed greater scientific objectivity, and dispensed with the notion of dream as magic. Nevertheless, he said, the centrality of dreams to these legends was "one of those not infrequent cases in which an ancient and jealously held popular belief seems to be nearer the truth than the judgement of the prevalent science of today."[20] To see dreams as magic was better than seeing them as irrelevant.

Crane said frequently that his poetry was an art of *condensation*, and Freud applied the same word to the process of dreaming, wherein memory and desire are condensed or abstracted into a series of symbols. Hence his now notorious "Freudian symbols," stiff trains being inserted into hollow tunnels. In dreams, words also become objects, and Freud claimed he found cases of verbal disguise the easiest kind of dream to uncover; and *The Interpretation* proceeds to bamboozle the English reader with chains of spectacular German associations which made *The Bridge* look like an example of Augustan decorum by comparison. Freud's point is that a repressed object surfaces in the dream, and that a superficial linguistic association may be the key to a deep actual association. One clear example can be culled from *The Psychopathology of Everyday Life*. Here Freud was discussing waking life, but the same principle applies: the inability of a patient to remember the name Jung is traced back to her having been widowed at the age of thirty-nine, and so wishing not to recall the happiness of her youth (German *Jugend*).[21] In *The Interpretation*, the function of these "verbal bridges" (as Freud called them) is to subvert the quotidian world of the ego by introducing the hidden world of the id, which sneaks its way past the brain's censors as they sleep. Daily logic is transcended; the puns and verbal play express desire as well as inhibition. Said Freud: "The alternative 'either–or' cannot be expressed in dreams in any way whatever. Both of the alternatives are usually inserted in the text of the dream as though they were equally valid."[22] What in *The Interpretation* is a means of recall is in *The Psychopathology* a means of forgetting; in the Jung example quoted above, the pun is a safeguard which represses desire rather than liberates it. These are denominated as "screen-memories," and anticipate *The Future of an Illusion* (1927), where Freud examined how the population requires the image of institutions and gods to defend itself against the terrible licentiousness of nature. The gods are substitutes for a father figure, and (like these words) interpose a screen between culture and nature, ego and id. As we have seen, Crane's cinema-screen performs a similar function in the third stanza of the "Proem."

This brings in Freud's ambivalent attitude towards his "reality-principle." As a therapist, his aim was to reconcile ego and id and to turn his patient into a "mature" and sober citizen; but the author of *Civilization and its Discontents* realized the unsatisfactory nature of the world he was healing the patient for. In *The Psychopathology*, we feel the verbal ambiguities may be a useful psychic defence-mechanism: they are after all examples of things that happen in "Everyday Life," the dramatis personae are generally not classed as neurotics, and the essays testify to Freud's awareness of the relative (not absolute) nature of sanity and insanity; linguistic games are repressive tropes indulged in by all of us. *Jokes and their Relation to the Unconscious*, however, is more uncompromising: there, jokes are described as the psyche's "rebellion against the compulsions of logic and reality."[23] Freud analysed the process whereby the simple pleasure in verbal play is counterbalanced by reason; how the jest then struggles to liberate nonsense from the constrictions of cultural judgement; and how the fully fledged joke, far from being a mere "holiday" from the world, is a direct challenge to reality on behalf of all that reality suppresses. Joke and logic are constantly at war with each other, seeking to undermine the basis on which the other exists: to split "Rousseau" into "roux et sot" (red-haired and foolish) is to gun down the sanctified image of the philosopher and to dismember him by cutting him into separate syllables, as in a charade. On the other hand, as Freud said, "if we undo the technique of a joke it disappears"; when conventional logic has explained the joke to itself, it can allow itself a polite sneer at such childishness.[24]

We find, then, that joke and logic are forever chasing each other in a closed circle: joke constructs, logic deconstructs, logic constructs, joke deconstructs. In one sense, the joke is the parasite, always protesting against a given code upon which it relies for its existence; in another sense it is an integral component of any code, for the area of the joke will expand and contract as the norms of the reality-principle expand and contract. Any social system must have a frontier; and any system must also contain within itself an alternative mode of being perceived, the negative pole to its clearly apparent positive. So joke and logic, apparently mutually antagonistic, are actually as mutually dependent as mortise and tenon. Therefore our attitude to the joker must depend upon our ideological attitude towards the logical reality-principle. The psychologist Ernst Kris, all for the reality-principle, asserted that the perpetual joker is actually manifesting a submerged desire to avoid taking his place in a world he feels incompetent to deal with: "The clown will not remove his cap and bells until he has conquered his anxiety."[25] If we pursue this line, we might see the rebellion against worldly logic and decorous grammar inherent in Crane's punning jests as the emanations of "a disunited personality, disposed to neurotic disorders," to quote Freud on the joker. But if we take a more sceptical line towards ideas of logic and reality, we might be attracted to Jean-Paul Richter's more tranquil attitude that "Joking is the disguised priest who weds every couple" by stressing how jokes are essentially an original way of perceiving familiar things, "making use of a method of linking things up which is rejected and studiously avoided by serious thought."[26] In this latter context, Aristotle's remark that pleasure in *recognition* is the basis of enjoyment in art would embrace *The Bridge*, and in its linguistic ingenuities the poem would be apprehended as a playful and delightfully insouciant enterprise.

In Crane, this conflict between the joke as emblem of neurosis and of freedom can be redefined as the interaction between psychoanalytical reduction and erotic liberation. Sometimes Crane's autobiographical references seem to be dragging the public poem back to the level of maudlin confession ("Prayer of pariah"). At other times Crane's subversive *double entendres* imply how *The Bridge* is secretly a homoerotic idyll ("the lover's cry"), but also how the poet's search for personal freedom becomes equated with America's search for the visionary continent of Atlantis. One man defines the race through defining himself, as Emerson said of Dante; and while Crane was always aware of the possibility that he, like the "bedlamite" in his "Proem," might be imposing an alienated and idiosyncratic vision upon an uncaring world, he nevertheless aspired to make *The Bridge* a true "Song of Myself," an amalgamation of private vision and public responsibility. (This tilting between positive and negative polarities is of course synecdochic of the other vacillations built into *The Bridge*.)

AUTOBIOGRAPHY IN COLOSSAL CIPHER

As an example of how Crane integrates public and private myths, let us examine three stanzas from "The River" which have already been investigated in a capitalist context:

> Down, down – born pioneers in time's despite,
> Grimed tributaries to an ancient flow –
> They win no frontier by their wayward plight,
> But drift in stillness, as from Jordan's brow.
>
> You will not hear it as the sea; even stone
> Is not more hushed by gravity . . . But slow,
> As loth to take more tribute – sliding prone
> Like one whose eyes were buried long ago
>
> The River, spreading, flows – and spends your dream.
> What are you, lost within this tideless spell?
> You are your father's father, and the stream –
> A liquid theme that floating niggers swell.

I noted in Chapter 4 how there is an equation between "tributary" (the stream) and "tributary" (the cash-payment), and how the *ancient* or chieftain conscripts the "bourne" pioneers into his financial system, "spending" their dreams as though they were items of economic exchange. It is, as we saw, the overturning of romantic free will into corporate system. But "spend" was also a Victorian word for ejaculation, and if we look a little harder we can retrieve the sexual undercurrents in these stanzas. That *spell* in the third stanza can be the erotic magic of love-making which brings about a temporary relinquishment of the ego ("*lost* within this tideless spell"); and, amazingly enough, that *stream* must be the emitted semen itself:

> and the stream –
> A liquid theme that floating niggers swell.

When this "*liquid* theme" is floating, it causes a withering of the male erection or *swell*, now a noun rather than a verb. The crucial word is *niggers*, which moves in the opposite direction, from noun to verb: to "nigger" is "to exhaust (land) by working it without proper fertilization

. . . *Local, U.S."* Here it is the penis which is exhausted, the swell niggered by the floating of its liquid theme; but one of Crane's typical mythological puns between *theme* and the Ancient Greek "Themis" ("a form of the earth goddess viewed, in a moral aspect, as the law and harmony of physical phenomena") indicates the pagan exuberance which is at work here. However, as Webster also notes the Greek etymology of "themis" – "that which is laid down or established by usage, law" – we should bear in mind how Themis herself embodied this conception of propriety in her rôle as the goddess of law and order, the patroness of existing rights; and so we can see how in Crane's poem this conception of sexual harmony merges into that Platonic harmony institutionalized by the bonds of America's capitalist state. Sexual order, or its homosexual variant, becomes analogous to the established civic order. In the second stanza here, Crane's equation of capitalism with sexual inversion becomes even more explicit:

> But slow,
> As loth to take more tribute – sliding prone
> Like one whose eyes were buried long ago
>
> The River, spreading, flows – and spends your dream.

But is a pun on "butt," American for buttocks. One lover is *sliding* submissively beneath the other, *prone* in the sense of lying flat because his *eyes* are *buried* as he presents his buttocks to the other lover like a vassal averting his gaze before the lord. The *River* becomes the active partner who "rives," splits the other's flesh, and ejaculates (*spends*).

In this way, the spending of money and the spending of sexual seed become cognate. The anonymity of capitalism, the way employers oppress their workers by reducing them to statistics on the cash-nexus, is associated by Crane with the facelessness of homosexual love-making; and Crane's private erotic world is extended into a myth of corporate America. Once more the tone is one of equivocation, poised as it is between the painful oppression of capitalism and the pleasurable oppression of homoeroticism. It may be possible to indict capitalism's victimization of its employees as an inevitable counterpart to the absence of mature and potent heterosexual relationships – but this again would depend upon an ideological notion of what constitutes the "reality-principle," and value-judgements do not seem Crane's main concern here. It is also interesting to note that the form (as well as the content) of Crane's punning inversions implies how *The Bridge* is a specifically homosexual poem. As Freud said in *The Interpretation of Dreams*, "I think, moreover, that all these dreams of turning things round the other way include a reference to the contemptuous implications of the idea of 'turning one's back on something' . . . It is remarkable to observe, moreover, how frequently reversal is employed precisely in dreams arising from repressed homosexual impulses."[27] "Southern Cross" is interesting in this light, for, in the context of Freud's equation between inversion and homosexuality, we can see that the parodic overturning of ideal romance into the sexual travesty of "Southern Cross" is commensurate with the crypto-homosexual imagery within that poem. "With reversal, everything becomes demonic," as Sherman Paul said of "Southern Cross":[28]

> Furrow of all our travel – trailed derision!
> Eyes crumble at its kiss. Its long-drawn spell
> Incites a yell. Slid on that backward vision
> The mind is churned to spittle, whispering hell.

In Crane's "backward vision," sexual reversal becomes analogous to the conceptual reversal which overturns heaven into "hell" and churns the mind to "spittle." In "Southern Cross," this homosexuality is bathetic and destructive ("Prayer of pariah"); but when the quest reaches "Atlantis," erotic liberation can work in tandem with social myth ("the lover's cry").

That there is a certain amount of latent homosexual imagery in *The Bridge* is not open to dispute, for the manuscripts of "Atlantis" reveal how the poem became less conspicuously homosexual as it developed. This is evident from an early draft sent to Crane's friends the Rychtariks in July 1923:

> Yet, touch its cloudy buried throat where light
> Is branched like prayers unspoken that await
> Your deepest thrusting agony for answer: strike
> Its breast precipitate, its lust-forbidden flanks,
> Sleek with your sweat's erosion, – til we hear
> The sound of waters bending and astride the sky:
> Until, as though an organ pressing doom
> Should set this nave of time atremble[29]

The word *nave* makes the *organ* overtly ecclesiastical; but, given the preceding imagery of "lust-forbidden flanks," *organ* must almost certainly be a conscious pun on the lover's penis. Gregory Robert Zeck's work on these manuscripts has shown how Crane gradually abstracted "Atlantis," making the poem denser and more Metaphysical, less like Shelley and more like Donne; and part of this process involved a refraction of the poem's more obvious homosexual connotations. As Zeck pointed out, the *throat* in the first line of the above passage was evicted to "The Harbor Dawn," where it came to have an apparently heterosexual context (*"my tongue upon your throat"*).[30] Too genteel a reading of Crane can create problems for the interpreter: in *Voyages* III

occurs an image – "And so, admitted through black swollen gates" –
which earlier critics have explained away with vague generalities such as
"dark and swelling waves," but which, as Robert K. Martin recently
pointed out, in fact means the anus.[31] Clearly Crane did not intend single
referents in *The Bridge*, but his personal experience underpins this poem
as much as it does *Voyages*.

Malcom Cowley remembered that Crane's speech generally included
"a larding of waterfront obscenities," and also that he was inordinately
fond of composing bawdy limericks;[32] and one of the funniest examples
in *The Bridge* of Crane's jesting withdrawals from decorum comes
towards the end of "Atlantis":

> . . . O Thou
> Whose canticle fresh chemistry assigns
> To wrapt inception and beatitude, –
> Always through blinding cables, to our joy,
> Of thy white seizure springs the prophecy

By the black comedy of Crane's burlesque, a visual pun in that second
line gives us: "O Thou whose can [slang for rump] tickle(s) fresh chemise
try ass signs." The *canticle* becomes "can/tickle," and *chemistry* "chemise/
try." Chemise, the woman's undergarment, was still active in the late
1920s – chemises were constantly being advertised in the *New York Times*
by smart lingerie shops – and here Crane sneers secretly but aggressively
at the genteel cleanliness of an orthodox heterosexual world. ("Can," say
Wentworth and Flexner, is "usually used of women only to indicate the
rump as contributing to or detracting from sexual appearance.") So if we
apply the "fresh chemistry" offered by the Bridge to the alchemical
transformations which are a latent potential within the text, we do
indeed "try ass signs" as we look for the signals of concealed
homosexuality which pose a threat to the poem's polite façade – but
which Crane perceives as the gateway "To wrapt inception and
beatitude." The imagery in the rest of this stanza also carries sexual
connotations, as the Bridge undergoes one of its familiar transmutations
into a human body ("a ship, a world, a woman," as Crane disingen-
uously told Frank), with "blinding cables" having overtones of a lover's
veins, and "white seizure" suggesting sexual orgasm.[33]

We can also select a stanza from the "Proem" which contains a more
obvious ambiguity:

> O Sleepless as the river under thee,
> Vaulting the sea, the prairies' dreaming sod,
> Unto us lowliest sometime sweep, descend
> And of the curveship lend a myth to God.

The immediate connotations are of Brooklyn Bridge as a "vault," "an arched structure of masonry," which leaps over the water in a literal sense, and by extension provides a mythical object for the entire United States, even the personified prairies of the Midwest which the Bridge vaults over in a symbolic way. This is to read "the prairies' dreaming sod" as the object of *Vaulting*. But as well as denoting the soil, *sod* can also be "sodomite," suggesting that "the prairies' dreaming sod" may be none other than Hart Crane himself, the imaginative homosexual from Ohio. If this is the case, it may be simply the "dreaming sod" who is "Vaulting the sea," which could make this phrase psychoanalytically reductive, implying this "myth to God" might be brought down to mere autobiography and wish-fulfilment. Robert K. Martin has recently discussed the desire of some homosexual poets, notably Whitman, to conjoin themselves with an objective world which is the same as their subjective beings, in the same way as homosexuals choose lovers of the same sex; and so Crane, always guilty about what he thought of as the failure of his sexuality, is secretly admitting here that this vision of Brooklyn Bridge vaulting over the prairies' dreaming sod may be the product simply of a dreaming sod's desire to annex the world as an extension of his own ego.[34] Does *The Bridge* stem from Crane's inability to acknowledge the differences involved in heterosexual love and heterogeneous worlds? *Vaulting* itself has erotic connotations: Webster says "vaulting house" is an obsolete term for "brothel"; and the first two lines of this stanza seem to be a covert description of homosexual love-making, with the *river* being the active partner, one who "rives" ("to rend asunder; to split") the other's flesh, and "reaming," enclosed in *dreaming*, being American slang for anal intercourse. (Crane knew the word *reamed*, for he uses it openly in "After Jonah," a poem published posthumously: "O sweet deep whale as ever reamed the sky.")[35] This would suggest *The Bridge* is secretly a homoerotic idyll; and *sweep* has an obsolescent meaning of "whip" or "scourge" which would support this, inserting the homosexuality into a specifically sado-masochistic context.

There is another covert description of sado-masochistic practice in "Atlantis":

> O Thou steeled Cognizance whose leap commits
> The agile precincts of the lark's return;
> Within whose lariat sweep encinctured sing
> In single chrysalis the many twain

The "pre*cincts*" and "en*cinc*tured" pun on "cincture" as a belt, from the Latin *cingo*, to gird. A *lariat* is a lassoing rope. A *sweep*, as we saw just now, is an old word for whip. And *chrysalis* – ostensibly a pleasant image of new life burgeoning in the spring – carries as its more sinister underside "cry/salis," a cry from the whip, "salis" punning on Latin *salix*, willow. So, as well as detailing the return of the lark or bird, these lines also celebrate "the larks' return," the re-emergence of pastoral frolics – sexual larks – which push their way up through the apparently epic finale to Crane's poem. The song of praise to Atlantis and "the lover's cry" from the whip become cognate: "love *strikes* clear direction for the helm." This is a metamorphosis of the image of the whip signifying Oedipal oppression, which we saw in "Van Winkle"; and such an oscillation between the whip as symbol of power and cruelty, but also of pleasurable sado-masochistic eroticism, is a fulfilment of the prophecy made in the "Proem": "Prayer of pariah, and the lover's cry." *The Bridge* may be a song of alienation or a song of celebration. These lines in "Atlantis" are reminiscent of Crane's much-loved *Moby-Dick*, which on occasions similarly transfers epic endeavour into sexual play: in *Moby-Dick*, the "vice-bench" in Chapter 108 where Ahab has his lost "leg" replaced is surrounded by "leather straps, pads, screws, and various tools of all sorts"; and, as Harold Beaver has said, there the stage seems set for "scenes of flagellation and other aberrant joys."[36] Textual and sexual aspects are commensurate in the great punsters Melville, Crane and Joyce, because in each author a reluctance to force language through into final and unequivocal meaning is analogous to (and textually associated with) the masochist's tendency to cherish sexual and psychological tension and to evade the certainty offered by climax. Textually and sexually, perpetual suspense is the preferred mode. Joyce's *Ulysses* is permeated with sado-masochism; and as "Henry Flower" thinking of Martha Clifford, Leopold Bloom explicitly conflates linguistic and sexual perversion: "How will you pun? You punish me?" (p. 278). In his study *Adultery in the Novel*, Tony Tanner made exactly this association between verbal and social transgression:

> puns and ambiguities are to common language what adultery and perversion are to "chaste" (i.e., socially orthodox) sexual relations. They both bring together entities (meanings/people) that have "conventionally" been differen- tiated and kept apart; and they bring them together in deviant ways, bypassing the orthodox rules governing communications and relationships.[37]

In *Ulysses*, this deviation is most obvious in the Circe section, where Bloom turns into a woman and becomes involved with a dominatrix Bella, or Bello, also of indeterminate sex. (In 1922 Crane mailed to Wilbur Underwood four pages transcribed from these Night Town episodes, which Crane described as "the most thrilling things intellectu- ally that I ever read.")[38] The sado-masochistic sexuality which perme- ates *Ulysses* and *The Bridge* is, as Tanner would say, an expression of that perversity which prefers sexual play to final orgasmic resolution, and in literary terms prefers an ambiguous open-endedness to the "closed form" which attempts to lay claim to some conclusive reality.

Because of its sexual iconoclasm, *Ulysses* was of course banned in the

United States until 1934, and one good reason for Crane to suppress his poem's sexual implications was that *The Bridge* – published in 1930 – would certainly have been outlawed as well had it become generally known that (for instance) "A liquid theme that floating niggers swell" refers to the contraction of the penis after its emission of semen. But these suppressions were psychological as well as pragmatic: when asked in 1978 about Crane's personality, Emil Opffer's first response was the Danish word "Inderlig" meaning "innerly" or "coming from within," thus suggesting Crane's closeness and secrecy; and in a letter to Malcolm Cowley on 9 January 1932, we find an instance of what might be called Crane's pathological concealment:

> Peggy has probably written you about encounters with Brett, Bynner, King, et al. Lewd limericks were shouted from the rooftops – your collection being more than ever in demand. A mad crowd, though. I had enough Duff (Brett's new name, or nickname) – preferring, as I do, the nautical variety.

Susan Jenkins Brown glossed this letter as follows:

> "Lady Brett" is a chief character in Hemingway's *The Sun Also Rises*, regarded as being based on a real-life Englishwoman, Lady Duff Twysden. In 1932, Duff was married to the American painter Clinton King and was living in Mexico, where the poet Witter Bynner also lived. Hart had either confused the real and fictional names of Hemingway's character or else was juggling them for humor. As to "I had enough duff": Hart had originally typed it lower case; he is punning on the various usages of "duff." One of them is a flour pudding, as in "plum duff," a dessert likely to be found on ships' menus. There is another meaning which makes his pun ribald; it can be found in an unabridged dictionary.[39]

Webster's 1909 dictionary modestly refrains from a ribald definition of *duff*; but Webster's 1961 version duly gives: "slang: Buttocks." So in this letter, Crane is punningly indicating how he has had enough of Lady Duff Twysden, but also how his preference is for nautical duff, anal intercourse. Crane's pun is partly comic, of course; but the tortuous and submerged manner in which these desires are manifested suggests how the repressed puns in *The Bridge* mirror the agonized repression of Crane's own homosexuality. However, like Philoctetes, Crane was attempting to redefine psychological distress as artistic triumph, to turn the wound into the bow.

There is in *The Bridge*, then, a series of concealed sexual puns which may serve to transfigure the world from the banality of logic into the brilliant liquid motion of verbal and sexual play; or alternatively may be no more than a perpetual rebellion from final assertion and resolution. We have seen how jesting wordplay was Crane's speciality, and his friend Samuel Loveman was another who remembered Hart introducing this wordplay into daily life: "riding on the subway was just one holocaust of laughter because he saw double meanings in all the ads, and usually obscene meanings. He claimed that most of them had some sexual or phallic undercurrent of meaning. I doubted that, although very frequently he was right or seemed to be right."[40] Crane exploits these sexual double meanings in *The Bridge*, but is always striving to make them more than simply a form of confession. I noted how Emerson's famous essay on "The Poet" talked of the need to apprehend analogies between past and present as such bridging would boost America's cultural self-esteem by its recognition that "Methodism and Unitarianism . . . rest on the same foundations of wonder as the town of Troy and the temple of Delphi"; and this same Emerson essay may have been one of the inspirations behind Crane's attempt to metamorphose his own private history into the public history of America: "Time and nature yield us many gifts, but not yet the timely man, the new religion, the reconciler, whom all things await. Dante's praise is that he dared to write his autobiography in colossal cipher, or into universality."[41]

14

Paradox and oxymoron

OXYMORON

According to Malcolm Cowley, in the late adolescent years of those literati who were to become famous in the 1920s, "everyone had the sense of paradox . . . the ability to say what was not expected, to fool one's audience."[1] This epigrammatic and paradoxical style carried over into their early creative works. Fitzgerald's 1925 novel *The Great Gatsby*, for one, is suffused with it: Jordan Baker's remark that she likes "large parties" because "They're so intimate" possesses an Alice-in-Wonderland logic despite its ostensible absurdity, for, as Jordan goes on to say, "At small parties there isn't any privacy."[2]

The most extreme kind of paradox is the clean shaft of oxymoron, where contraries are yoked together in an apparently meaningless way; and oxymoron is one of Hart Crane's most notable stylistic features. This predilection was continuous throughout Crane's career, from the 1918 poem "Forgetfulness," through *White Buildings* and *The Bridge*, to "The Sad Indian," which was one of the last poems he wrote. Perhaps it would be best, first of all, simply to list some of these oxymorons with a minimum of comment before proceeding to theoretical analyses. The existence of a pun needs justification in each individual case, but the fact of an oxymoron can speak for itself.

> *Minor Poems*
>
> I can *remember* much *forgetfulness*   ("Forgetfulness")
>
> *Dumbly articulate* in the slant and rise   ("Garden Abstract")
>
> Have you no memories, O *Darkly Bright*?   ("North Labrador")
>
> Of what the *dead* keep, *living* still   ("Praise for an Urn")

That beat, continuous, to *hourless days*   ("Faustus and Helen," I)

       Who shall again
Engrave such *hazards* as thy might controls –
   Conflicting, purposeful yet outcry vain
Of all our days, being *pilot*, – *tempest* too!
   Sheets that mock lust and thorns that scribble hate
Are lifted from torn flesh with human rue,
   And *laughter*, burnished brighter than our fate
Thou wieldest with such *tears* that every faction   ("To Shakespeare")

Sad heart, the *gymnast* of *inertia*, does not count   ("The Sad Indian")

The Bridge

How many dawns, chill from his *rippling rest*   ("Proem")

Shedding white rings of *tumult, building* high   ("Proem")

(The mutability of "tumult" as opposed to the immutability of "building": noticed by Nassar.)[3]

Over the *chained* bay waters *Liberty*   ("Proem")

Then, with *inviolate* curve, forsake our eyes
As *apparitional* as sails that cross   ("Proem")

(Is the curve impregnable or is it evanescent? Again, seen by Nassar.)[4]

Till *elevators drop* us from our day   ("Proem")

Foretold to *other* eyes on the *same* screen   ("Proem")

Implicitly thy *freedom staying* thee!   ("Proem")

Unfractioned idiom, immaculate sigh of stars,
Beading thy path – *condense eternity*   ("Proem")

("Unfractioned" suggests holistic; "idiom" suggests idiomatic, idiosyncratic, from Greek, "idios" – peculiar to one's own. "Condense" implies limits, "eternity" implies something limitless.)

Only in *darkness* is thy shadow *clear*   ("Proem")

(Not quite oxymoronic, but a paradoxical juxtaposition of visibility and invisibility.)

And all the eddying breath between dost search
Cruelly with *love* thy parable of man   ("Ave Maria")

Utter to loneliness the sail is *true*   ("Ave Maria")

(See Chapter 5: pun on sail/sale gives pun on *Utter* as to issue fake money; hence true–false paradox.)

Hobo-trekkers that forever search
An *empire wilderness* of freight and rails   ("The River")

(The civilized order of "empire" as opposed to the disorder of "wilderness.")

What *laughing chains* the water wove and threw   ("The Dance")

Flame cataracts of heaven in *seething* swarms   ("The Dance")

(Triple pun and double paradox, as discussed in Chapter 6. Flame (sight) opposite cataracts (blindness); cataracts (blindness) opposite see/thing (sight).)

Like one white meteor, *sacrosanct* and *blent*
At last with all that's *consummate* and *free*   ("The Dance")

(If something is unique, "sacrosanct," it can hardly be "blent," merged into something else. "Consummate" implies completeness and stasis; "free" implies incompleteness and motion.)

And glistening through the *sluggard freshets* came   ("Indiana")

("Sluggard" suggests lazy, inert; "freshets" suggests lively movement, the rush of fresh water.)

long since somebody's nickel – *stopped* –
playing . . .   ("Cutty Sark")

(An example of pun and paradox combined. Apparently the juke-box has "ceased" playing. But an instrument can only play if it is "stopped," if its pitch is regulated – as in to "stop" an organ. So the juke-box either ceased playing or alternatively is playing precisely because it has been "stopped.")

                    skil-
ful savage sea-girls
that bloomed in the spring . . .   ("Cutty Sark")

("Skilful" implies civilized, "savage" implies uncivilized.)

Those continental *folded aeons*, surcharged   ("Cape Hatteras")

("Folded" suggests limits, "aeons" lack of limits.)

The *gleaming cantos* of unvanquished space . . .   ("Cape Hatteras")

(Another instance of pun and paradox. "Cantos" are the highest vocal part in music, whereas "gleaming" puns on the falconry term "gleam," "to disgorge filth, as a hawk." So the height of "cantos" as opposed to the depths of "gleaming.")

And now, as launched in *abysmal cupolas* of space,
Toward *endless terminals*, Easters of speeding light   ("Cape Hatteras")

("Cupolas" are small enclosed domes, in contradiction to "abysmal," bottomless.)

They keep that docile edict of the Spring
That blends March with *August Antarctic* skies   ("Quaker Hill")

(August implies heat, Antarctic implies cold.)

– Or the muffled *slaughter* of a day in *birth* –
O *cruelly* to *inoculate* the brinking dawn   ("The Tunnel")

("Inoculate" is to render harmless, apparently the opposite to anything "cruel.")

Kiss of our *agony* Thou gatherest   ("The Tunnel")

New octaves trestle the *twin monoliths*   ("Atlantis")

(If something is single, monolithic, it is surprising to find it with a "twin.")

Of *inchling aeons* silence rivets Troy   ("Atlantis")

("Inchling" suggests a short, "aeons" a long period of time.)

Bridge, lifting night to cycloramic *crest*
Of *deepest* day – O Choir . . .   ("Atlantis")

Sustained in *tears* the cities are endowed
And justified conclamant with ripe fields
Revolving through their harvests in *sweet torment*   ("Atlantis")

(See Chapter 7: "tears" puns on "state of being torn; a rent" – the opposite to being "Sustained.")

METAPHYSICAL PARADOX

There are several possible ways in which these paradoxes and oxymorons might be conceptually justified. In the first chapter, we saw how Roger Ramsey has argued that Crane's puns are the verbal equivalent of transubstantiation, pivoting *The Bridge* between mundane reality and transcendental vision; and it would be possible to construct a similarly "metaphysical" explanation for Crane's use of paradox. In "To Shakespeare," cited above, the bard is honoured as embracing all conflicting possibilities within himself – he is both "pilot" and "tempest," order and chaos – with the result that Shakespeare comes to represent an omnipotent prime mover from whom all earthly contradictions originate and within whom all earthly contradictions are eventually reconciled. Shakespearian art is seen as imitating the faculty of God in its ability to "engrave hazards," to celebrate the hazards of chance and movement while at the same time positing an engraved area beyond movement, an area where all motion becomes motionless. In this "metaphysical" sense, paradox is the human condition; for human life in the fallen world must necessarily be contradictory, although all these dichotomies may ultimately be subsumed by some higher authority.

The significance of paradox to Christian philosophy would have been clear to Crane from his readings of John Donne. In 1921, Crane mentioned to Munson his "long-standing friendship with Donne,

Webster and Marlowe" on account of their "verbal richness, irony and emotion"; and in his own copy of Donne, Crane underlined the title of "A Hymn to God the Father," where Donne punningly transposes his own name into an instrument of the divine will:[5]

> But swear by thy self, that at my death thy son
> Shall shine as he shines now, and heretofore;
> And, having done that, thou hast done,
> I fear no more.

Some people call Donne an exhibitionist, just as others accuse Crane of a flamboyant display of neuroses, but in both cases this is to misunderstand the rôle of private confession in their work. In Donne and Crane, the personal is never the merely personal, but embodies the universal. And not by mere chance, because other people's experience might happen to resemble the poet's, but because in a theological sense being or reality is primary and thought only secondary. This is essentially a medieval tradition of thought, excellently expounded by Hugh Kenner in his analysis of *Paradox in Chesterton*. The logic of St Thomas asserted that every man is an image of God, the accident of the divine essence, so that – as Chesterton rephrased it – "Man cannot love mortal things; he can only love immortal things for an instant."[6] Man cannot be an autonomous rational being because on the earthly plane he is blinkered and insufficient. So Crane's puns on "heart" serve a similar purpose to Donne's puns on "done": they transform an insufficient autobiographical self into a vessel refracting divine grace. Kenner said that Chesterton employs language as a "bridge" between the self and the world in a way that reflects the Christian (specifically Roman Catholic) dogma of transubstantiation, because, although earthly objects do not forfeit their internal logic or sensuous immediacy, the pun hints at how this logic and immediacy may be imperfect reflections of a higher state.[7] This kind of duality was indeed a common feature of medieval literature: Bernard F. Huppé has shown how in *Piers Plowman* William Langland continually puns on his first name to illustrate the dissimilarities (and similarities) between errant human will and its divine equivalent.[8] And, mirroring this process, the line from "The Dance" "Siphoned the black pool from the heart's hot root!" makes Crane's personal attempt to overcome sexual repression a microcosm of the fecundity introduced into America by Indian mythology. In both cases, the author admits that the world he creates is larger than himself. *The Bridge* is not merely an extension of Crane's ego, any more than *Piers Plowman* is an extension of Langland's; divine forces enter into both poems, and the writer is the agent of these forces rather than their creator.

So Crane, like Donne and Langland, admits his own lack of authorial omnipotence; and by extension it could be argued that the contradictions inherent in the oxymorons of *The Bridge* are designed to demonstrate the insufficiency of all human systems of art and thought. In this light, the structure of *The Bridge* would be collapsed and the poem revealed as a fragment within a fallen world, an imperfect accident of the Neoplatonic essence. *The Bridge* may propose an *empire*, but its *empire* is a *wilderness*. It may erect *cupolas*, but these cupolas cannot conquer *abysmal* space. It may try to superimpose *terminals* on a chaotic world, but the chaotic world is *endless* and so those terminals are left stranded as no more than provisional terrestrial emblems. The claims of *The Bridge* to logical autonomy are exploded, and this explosion serves to emphasize the punning analogies whereby *The Bridge* is transposed into something beyond its empirical self. For instance, the pun connecting New York's "palladium helm of stars" back to the Greek Pallas Athene is consistent with the oxymoron of "twin monoliths" in "Atlantis," for the duality of the monoliths indicates how what is overtly singular is actually plural, how apparently static objects can be transposed into another order of being, how palladium is twinned with Pallas, how accident is twinned with essence, how human is twinned with divine.

OPEN-ENDED PARADOX

These paradoxes, then, would not contradict the Neoplatonic readings of *The Bridge* expounded by Ramsey, L. S. Dembo and others; but some theorists of paradox in Crane have preferred to delineate a more secular and sceptical context. Eugene Paul Nassar, with his emphasis on the fictional nature of Crane's myth, said of "Atlantis": "the poet realizes always the near-absurdity of his 'transcendental' passages, as he did in his religious addresses to the bridge . . . and his diction, with its ironies, paradoxes and conceits, expresses this poised attitude toward his material."[9] Similarly, Richard Hutson related Crane's paradoxes to the ironic consciousness displayed in many of the *White Buildings* poems, where the "well-meant idioms" of the poetic artefact are constantly being hedged in by the physical encroachments of space and time. "Praise for an Urn" consciously retracts its own artistic pretensions as it turns in upon itself in the last stanza:

> Scatter these well-meant idioms
> Into the smoky spring that fills
> The suburbs, where they will be lost.
> They are no trophies of the sun.

So the earlier oxymoron in this poem, "Of what the dead keep, living still," could be explained in terms of the ironic discrepancy between the immortality of Crane's poem (the well-wrought urn "living still") and the physical expiration of the poem's subject, Ernest Nelson, whose ashes are enclosed in an urn and buried in the crematorium. The man's death irrupts into the formal enclosure of the poem and so suggests how artistic construction must be superimposed upon the destructive forces of time. As Hutson said, the negations built into the poem challenge the autonomy of the poetic artefact, and "This synthesis or mingling of the No and the Yes can be found in all of Crane's poetry."[10] Hutson quoted I. A. Richards' definition of irony – "equilibrium of the opposed impulses" – and he developed his theory of Crane's irony in an analysis of "Lachrymae Christi," demonstrating how that poem's preponderance of prefixes ensures that its "affirmation maintains insistently and openly its dependency upon negation" ("unyielding," "immaculate," "unfended," "innocence," "inaudible," "undimming," "unstanched," "unmangled"). "Lachrymae Christi" turns upon the dichotomy between the "Nazarene and tinder eyes" of Christ and the "Unmangled target smile" of Dionysus; and, as Hutson put it, "Whereas the possibilities of contradiction in 'Praise for an Urn' were mainly tentative and oblique, in 'Lachrymae Christi' they tend to be excruciatingly open, at times even oxymoronic."[11] So paradox and oxymoron are crucial to this poem's structure:

> *Immaculate venom* binds
> The fox's teeth

("immaculate" suggesting purity, "venom" suggesting poison)

> . . . worms'
> *Inaudible whistle*, tunneling

– and so is the pun, for in this conflict between Christianity and Bacchic revelry, nothing could be more appropriate than that the poem's title, "Lachrymae Christi," tears of Christ, should covertly pun on the Italian wine "Lacrimae Christi." "Lacrimae Christi" was a brand which Edmund Wilson, in one of his Twenties notebooks, remarked upon as his own particular favourite drink, "harsh salt fire . . . wrung from the meager grapes of Vesuvius."[12]

From Roger Ramsey's point of view, Crane's ambiguities are eventually comprehensible in terms of the poet's sacramental vision; but Hutson was more impressed by Crane's open-endedness, his "love of things irreconcilable" as the first part of "Faustus and Helen" puts it. From this angle, Crane's is a poetry of perpetual motion, perpetual desire, tension not resolution:

> But that star-glistered salver of infinity,
> The circle, blind crucible of endless space,
> Is sluiced by motion, – subjugated never.   ("Cape Hatteras")

Richard P. Sugg noted the religious imagery here, the *salver* exploiting its Latin etymology of *salvare*, to save; and *crucible* bringing to mind the "round plate held under the mouth of the religious communicant to keep the host from falling to the ground"; so that Sugg read these lines as reaffirming the "unitive impulse" in Crane's poem: "Though 'sluiced by motion' . . . the circle–crucible–eye is 'subjugated never.'"[13] But in fact Crane's suspension Bridge is playing its old Whiteheadian trick on us once more: what is "subjugated never," the *circle* or the *motion*? Either is possible. Again, Crane suspends judgement:

> The apple on its bough is her desire, –
> Shining suspension, mimic of the sun.   ("Garden Abstract")

The suspension bridge is the most apposite of symbols for Crane, because the object of engineering functions in the same way as his poem: on a circuit of self-generating tensions, without any possibility of final climax. The way Roebling's construction of flexible steel incorporates physical stresses is analogous to the assimilation of conceptual stresses within Crane's poem: both Bridges are designed to sway to and fro. In psychological terms, the psychoanalyst Theodor Reik regarded such prolongation of suspense and refusal to resolve tension as characteristic of the masochist; and indeed the paradoxical inversions permeating *The Bridge* ensure that the poem's sexuality is heavily sado-masochistic. Pleasure becomes painful, pain pleasurable, as in the oxymorons of "laughing chains," "sweet torment" and "Kiss of our agony," and as in the Divine Father arraigning his subjects "Cruelly with love." To reiterate: the forms of paradox and oxymoron are the literary correlative of a sado-masochistic sexuality which is creative and destructive both at once, and which refuses final resolution in the same way as paradox refuses fixed and final meaning. This particular use of paradox suggests Crane's affinities with the Decadent poets of the late nineteenth century, his first great literary love: Crane's first published poem, "C 33," which appeared in 1916, took its title from the number of Oscar Wilde's cell in Reading Gaol; and though by 1918 Crane's enthusiasm for Wilde had declined ("after his bundle of paradoxes has been sorted and conned, – very little evidence of intellect remains"), nevertheless Wilde's flagrant disrespect for any kind of literal "truth" was an important influence during Crane's formative years. Wilde's *Picture of Dorian Gray* discusses how "the way of paradoxes is the way of truth," and how "To test Reality we must see it on the tight-rope," for "When the Verities become acrobats we can judge them."[14]

Two stanzas from "The Tunnel" will demonstrate the way Crane's paradoxical mentality is extended into an ambiguous attitude towards the modern world:

> The phonographs of hades in the brain
> Are tunnels that re-wind themselves, and love

> A burnt match skating in a urinal –
> Somewhere above Fourteenth TAKE THE EXPRESS
> To brush some new presentiment of pain –

If *love* here is a noun, then love itself has been degraded into "A burnt match skating in a urinal." But *love* may also become a verb: *fin de siècle* aesthetes in the Toulouse-Lautrec mould were devoted to beauty, but, paradoxically, often found that beauty amidst the ugliness of urban life, which they accordingly came to *love*. Crane is imitating these Decadent artists in the sense that he is not only confronting, brushing up against, pain, but also taking aesthetic pleasure in brushing or painting it ("To *brush* some new presentiment of pain"). This is indeed "a subscription praise" for the modern city, a praise secreted under the writing (literally "sub/scription," beneath the script) which intimates that the poet secretly loves what he affects to loathe, taking pleasure in his sweet torment, kissing his agony. New York City's sordid underworld fascinates the poet in a way that innocent and idyllic gardens cannot:

> You'll find the garden in the third act dead,
> Finger your knees – and wish yourself in bed
> With tabloid crime-sheets perched in easy sight.

A later stanza in the same poem performs the ingenious and purely paradoxical feat of facing two different ways at the same time:

> Daemon, demurring and eventful yawn!
> Whose hideous laughter is a bellows mirth
> – Or the muffled slaughter of a day in birth –
> O cruelly to inoculate the brinking dawn
> With antennae toward worlds that glow and sink; –
> To spoon us out more liquid than the dim
> Locution of the eldest star, and pack
> The conscience navelled in the plunging wind,
> Umbilical to call – and straightway die!

We have already noted the oxymorons *slaughter/birth* and *cruelly/ inoculate*, and their function here is to pivot these lines between a lament for the way urban society represses natural desires and a celebration of sexual potency within the modern world. If industrial technology extinguishes Man's natural urges, then we would read the stanza as follows: the day is slaughtered at birth, the *antennae* (radio aerials, symbols of a consumer culture) *inoculate* the dawn, rendering it harmless, thus destroying Man's affinity with the rhythm of pre-urban worlds which "glow and sink" as the earth turns. The radio antennae *spoon* out *liquid* to the population, feed them with commercial pap which resembles a mother's milk for these infants helpless and passive within a uniform society. Hence the constrictive *conscience* which is *navelled* in the *wind*: the radio airwaves link the population back to the maternal centre of state censorship, and so the radio waves are likened to an *Umbilical* cord because this centralized technological society bears some resemblance to a mother pricking the consciences of her offspring to keep them under control. American conventionality equals maternal domination, and the blandness of this morality extinguishes the children's self-assertive (and sexual) desires, which therefore "straightway die."

But that *demurring* Daemon may also be "de/murring," breaking down these prim social walls (the same bilingual pun on "Down Wall" as we saw in Chapter 12); for in the alternative reading we find a "hideous laughter" intruding upon the conventions of this banal technological world, as Crane's stanza can also become a covert description of love-making. The lovers are slaughtering the birth of day because they do not wish the "brinking dawn" to invade their night-time idyll. Accordingly they strive to *inoculate* the dawn, to ward off its approach, by spooning out more bodily liquid (spoon as slang for "to kiss and fondle" (f) and for the act of making love). Those pointed *antennae* may now be a comically dehumanized phallic image, because from this angle the maternal conscience has not been "packed in" the plunging wind, but rather "sent packing" by it. The pun on *pack* faces both ways; and so does the pun on *die*: for the verb could imply the extinction of sexuality, but, if we recall its Elizabethan meaning of "orgasm," *die* may also indicate how this sexuality is burgeoning healthily. (Crane could hardly have read Donne so assiduously as we know he did and remained ignorant of the potential pun on *die*.)

This ambivalent attitude towards the equipment of the modern world is quite characteristic of Crane's paradoxical poetry, and quite character-istic also of a man whose very name was an oxymoron building a bridge between the romantic and the mechanical: H[e]art Crane. Crane frequently exploited this lucky pun during his lifetime: John Unterecker's biography reproduced a photograph Crane sent to the Rychtariks inscribed "To Charlotte and Richard from the 'Heart'";[15] and it is not to be supposed that a man whose philosophy of life held there to be "only one harmony, that is the equilibrium maintained by two opposite forces, equally strong" could have been ignorant of the paradoxical opposition built into the name he had chosen for himself. (Crane gradually abandoned Harold in favour of Hart, his second name, between 1917 and 1919.)[16] Crane's poetry works on a principle of "Shining suspension," and *The Bridge*, constructed – like Roebling's Brooklyn suspension bridge – out of an infinity of opposing tensions, is the oxymoronic Hart Crane's chief glory. In this context, paradox and oxymoron are compatible with the quite overt images of vibration and vacillation which persist throughout *The Bridge*, and which effectively confirm the remark Crane made to Selden Rodman about how in his long poem he had tried to "break loose" from the "fashionable pessimism" espoused by T. S. Eliot, *without however committing myself to any oppositional form of didacticism.*" Crane went on: "Your diffidence in ascribing any absolute conclusions in the poem is therefore correct, at least according to my intentions."[17] Once again, we might best highlight these images of oscillating ambiguity by simply listing some of them:

Tilting there momently, shrill shirt ballooning	("Proem")
Vibrant reprieve and pardon thou dost show	("Proem")

And kingdoms
        naked in the
                trembling heart –   ("Ave Maria")

                The sky,
Cool feathery fold, *suspends*, distills
This *wavering* slumber. . . .   ("The Harbor Dawn")

And one star, *swinging*, take its place, alone	("The Dance")
a nervous shark tooth *swung* on his chain	("Cutty Sark")
As *vibrantly* I following down Sequoia alleys	("Cape Hatteras")
Whose head is *swinging* from the swollen strap?	("The Tunnel")
Upward, *veering* with light, the flight of strings	("Atlantis")
Sibylline voices flicker, *waveringly* stream	("Atlantis")

Pouring reply as though all ships at sea
Complighted in one *vibrant* breath made cry, –   ("Atlantis")

The vernal *strophe* chimes from deathless strings!   ("Atlantis")

("Strophe," one section of an Ancient Greek choric ode, implies its opposite, the answering antistrophe.)

With white escarpments *swinging* into light	("Atlantis")
Whispers antiphonal in azure *swing*	("Atlantis")

15

Alchemy and the Romantic quest

NOBLE LIE AND ROMANTIC FREEDOM: "MOBY-DICK"

Although *The Bridge* is the greatest poem to come out of the "Revolution of the Word" experiment, just as *Finnegans Wake* is the greatest novel, Crane and Joyce were manipulating the pun in quite different ways: for whereas Joyce made no secret of his technical innovations, Crane's puns are concealed subversions of his "official" text. One glance at *Finnegans Wake* is enough to convince the reader that Joyce was up to something strange; but *The Bridge* insists on decorously preserving its secrets and presenting a false brow to the common world.

One reason for the centrality of the lie to Crane's work was the author's interest in how *The Bridge* might become a socially validated system, a national myth. Hence the image of Plato's cave (transposed into a New York cinema-screen) which we saw in the third stanza of the "Proem": society protects its members by surrounding them with a tissue of useful fictions, Noble Lies. Because of this, the repression of the poem's consciously illusory aspects is necessary for mythopoeic credibility. If Crane had advertised the fact that his "whitest Flower" was really a "flow-er" flowing away into nothing, his poem would have become a satire on human gullibility and an exposure of the naïveté of men's belief in foolish myths. This was not Crane's aim: the subtlety of *The Bridge* is to recognize the importance of these social constructions while gently revealing how time will eventually deconstruct everything, how appearance and disappearance are part of the same process ("Like hails, farewells," as "Atlantis" puts it). The Noble Lie played a crucial rôle in the discovery of America itself, for something which comes across in Columbus' *Journal* is that the Admiral was a firm believer in the end justifying the means, and not averse to various kinds of deviousness to

194

secure his final triumph. In his Introduction to the 1925 edition, which Crane knew, Van Wyck Brooks wrote:

> The Admiral is a very adroit master. He deceives the men, mis-stating each day the number of leagues they have sailed; he cajoles them; he encourages them, and perhaps himself, by pointing out signs and portents indicating that they are always near land – birds that never sleep at sea, whales, crabs, pelicans, creatures of the shore.[1]

The entry for Monday 10 September 1492 is typical: "This day and night sailed sixty leagues, at the rate of ten miles an hour, which are two leagues and a half. Reckoned only forty-eight leagues, that the men might not be terrified if they should be long upon the voyage."[2] This discrepancy between Columbus' pose of public confidence and his own private scepticism is given expression in "Ave Maria":

> A needle in the sight, suspended north, –
> Yielding by inference and discard, faith
> And true appointment from the hidden shoal

The grammar here implies that *inference* is in apposition to *faith*, while *discard* goes with "true appointment." Columbus realizes the ship's true position, but discards or censors this frightening knowledge so as not to disturb his crew, just as Crane represses the "true appointment" of dark irony implicit in the "hidden shoal" of meanings within his *Bridge* in order to preserve the poem's conception as a viable public enterprise. For Crane, as for Columbus, visions of Eden were dependent upon the proscription or enchaining of what was funereal, gloomy, sepulchral:

> incognizable Word
> Of Eden and the enchained Sepulchre

M. D. Uroff criticized the hero of "Ave Maria" for being so keen to prove himself right, and she surmised that the speaker in "Proem" was "more truly devout . . . because he looks upon the symbols of his world with reverence and awe."[3] But this is altogether too simplistic: for if the speaker in "Proem" is possessed of "reverence and awe" he is equipped with a great many more machiavellian devices as well – there is "a lie in" (*align*) his "choiring strings"; and if Columbus had not employed a similar kind of chicanery, he might never have had the chance to experience "reverence and awe" before the new continent. For Columbus, as for Crane, the lie was noble because trickery and wonder went hand in hand.

So the pun, swinging between opposites, pivots *The Bridge* between myth and exploded myth, but also between public and private consciousness. There is a conflict between Columbus' social persona and his private awareness of the ships' position; and this oscillation is typical of *The Bridge*, which is both a public "myth to God" and also a private homoerotic idyll. In this sense, Crane's lies are in the familiar tradition of American Romanticism which takes delight in withdrawing from the social arena and discovering, as Richard Poirier put it, "A World Elsewhere." New England writers such as Thoreau were fond of the pun because the secrecy of puns allowed them to retreat to a private space behind the accepted façades of public language. In *Walden* (1854), the play of language is, as Poirier has said, "designed to subvert the comfortable idioms that unite the communities of finance capitalism or of the 'parlor'"; and the literary form of *Walden* matches its thematic content, because the pun was a linguistic equivalent to Thoreau's overthrow of social decorum and installation of himself in a hut alongside Walden Pond.[4] Thoreau's "I walked over the farmer's premises" means not only that he stepped across land owned by the farmer, but also that he trampled upon the legal *premises* by which the farmer claimed exclusive rights to his property. God's good earth was the possession of everybody, thought Thoreau, and should not be bound by restrictive codes of law. In *A World Elsewhere*, Poirier commented:

> As a fantasia of punning [*Walden*] is excelled only by *Finnegans Wake* . . . Thoreau's genius with language, like Joyce's, is to an awesome degree self-satisfying. Both were apparently willing to go to the grave without having anyone recognize some of their best jokes, thereby confirming their theories about the condition of language in the societies about which each of them wrote.[5]

The transcendentalist's pun on *premises* which creates free space for his soul is reminiscent of Crane's hoboes in "The River," who attempt to disintegrate the formal divisions of land by a series of puns on official boundary terms: "Each seemed a child, like me, on a loose *perch*"; "riding the *rods*"; "From *pole* to *pole* across the hills." Like Thoreau, these hoboes stake their claim to existence by punningly undermining traditional legal codes.

If Thoreau's puns create a world elsewhere for the spirit, many of Herman Melville's puns create a world elsewhere for the body. Melville smuggled all kinds of subversive paganism into the overtly Christian framework of *Moby-Dick*, and, like Crane, he was notoriously cagey about his authorial intentions. Lawrance Thompson has said when Melville remarked in a review of *Mosses from an Old Manse* that Hawthorne's literary devices were "directly calculated to deceive – egregiously deceive – the superficial skimmer of pages," Melville was really commenting on his own techniques. Melville went on: "The truth seems to be, that like many other geniuses, this Man of Mosses takes great delight in hoodwinking the world – at least, with respect to himself."[6] But Melville was always one of Crane's boon companions ("I read *Moby*

Dick between gaps down in Cayman – my third time – and found it more superb than ever," he wrote to Waldo Frank on 19 June 1926) and we know that Crane was alert to the demonic ambiguities latent within Melville's novel because of a letter he wrote to Solomon Grunberg on 20 March 1932:

> A way, way back you asked me a question about what I thought of *Moby Dick*. It has passages, I admit, of seeming innuendo that seem to block the action. But on third or fourth reading I've found that some of those very passages are much to be valued in themselves – minor and subsidiary forms that augment the final climacteric quite a bit . . . In *Moby Dick* the whale is a metaphysical image of the Universe, and every detail of his habits and anatomy has its importance in swelling his proportions to the cosmic rôle he plays.[7]

These details of "habits and anatomy" which interested Crane surely relate to the white whale's elusiveness and duality of vision. The narrator Ishmael says that the whale surveys his surroundings through two eyes which are as far apart as a man's ears: "The whale, therefore, must see one distinct picture on this side, and another distinct picture on that side." But, says Ishmael, the whale's brain is "so much more comprehensive, combining, and subtle than man's, that he can at the same moment of time attentively examine two distinct prospects, one on one side of him, and the other in an exactly opposite direction" (p. 437). (This is the exact equivalent of Crane's "How many dawns" and "Harmony dawns," and of the antiphonal whispers swinging to and fro.) Ishmael goes on to infer that "the extraordinary vacillations of movement displayed by some whales when beset by three or four boats . . . indirectly proceeds from the helpless perplexity of volition, in which their divided and diametrically opposite powers of vision must involve them" (p. 438). Melville's whale is the very incarnation of a pun: it sees more than one thing at once, and loses a sense of firm direction as its body vacillates between conflicting possibilities. And the whale also resembles Crane's *Bridge* in the way it presents a deceptive façade to its audience; for just as Crane's puns are submerged beneath the poem's surface, so Moby Dick can bamboozle its human trackers by spending half its time concealed inside the ocean: "the hidden ways of the Sperm Whale when beneath the surface remain, in great part, unaccountable to his pursuers" (p. 280). Ishmael remarks with admiration "that singular craft at times evinced by the Sperm Whale when, sounding with his head in one direction, he nevertheless, while concealed beneath the surface, mills round, and swiftly swims off in the opposite quarter" (p. 317). Melville's villainous multi-faceted beast proves too wily for its trackers in the same way Crane's long poem skilfully resists any fixed definition.

Of course this imagery of obfuscation was for Melville self-reflexive: it was his novel as much as his whale that contained hidden meanings.

The reference in Chapter 53 to "Noah Webster's ark" links verbal units
with the idea of seafaring vessels, and all the dictionary definitions which
precede Melville's text demonstrate how the whale is a literary conceit as
much as a physical entity: "I have swam through libraries and sailed
through oceans," says Ishmael (p. 230). As Harold Beaver put it,

> Ishmael can at the same moment of time attentively examine not merely two,
> but three, four, or five distinct prospects in exactly opposite directions. He
> scores his prose polyphonically, as it were, via puns, through overlapping
> ranges of meaning, across radiating axes of reference . . . every name is a
> cryptonym; every chapter, a cryptogram; and Ishmael, the supreme
> cryptographer.[8]

As in *The Bridge*, one of the major conflicts in *Moby-Dick* is between a
socially validated ethos, in this case the epic quest for the whale, and a
pastoral or sexual energy which is always threatening to overthrow
epic's respectable framework. Just as the "dreaming sod" in Crane's
"Proem" mocks the Bridge's claim to symbolic grandeur and autonomy, so Melville's (homo)sexual ambiguities may be parodying Ahab's
quest and exposing it as the nonsensical dream of an emasculated
madman. (As Beaver has said, Ahab's lost "leg" is fairly suggestive in
itself.)[9] This transfer of heroic endeavour into sexual play runs all the
way through *Moby-Dick*. In bed with Queequeg in Chapter 11, for
example, Ishmael (a pun on "Is male") ponders "how elastic our stiff
prejudices grow when love once comes to bend them" (p. 149): on the
surface, Ishmael is congratulating himself for overcoming his prejudice
against "dark complexioned" pagans; but more immediately, it is his
penis which is transformed from *stiff* to *elastic* after his act of *love*. (Crane
almost certainly knew this passage well because he remarked to Wilbur
Underwood on "that delightful 'Moby Dick' of Melville's including the
memorable and half-exciting erotic suggestions of dear Queequeg.")[10]
And just as with Crane's work, we never know whether this
homoeroticism is exuberant and fulfilling, or whether it shifts Melville's
novel into a narcissistic and in-turned reverie which can never be forced
through into final meaning – in the same way as homosexual pleasure is
incapable of procreation. Chapter 95 ("The Cassock": ass/cock) is most
unsympathetic to the "mincer" holding his Archbisho-*prick* (p. 531); and
this episode becomes an internal self-parody of the novel's evasions and
inversions, for it brings to mind Queequeg groping at his crotch and
Ahab acting out his sterile fantasies, and so suggests the frigidity which
may be at the heart of the novel. Like *The Bridge*, *Moby-Dick* ends on a
permanent question-mark: it is, as R. W. B. Lewis has said, "the supreme
instance of the dialectical novel – a novel of tension without
resolution."[11]

So whereas the puns of Cummings and the later Joyce tend to operate in a social vacuum, a world enclosed unto itself, the puns of Thoreau, Melville and Crane engage in an ideological struggle with the normative reality-principle. This reality-principle may be necessary, as Plato's cave was necessary; but the American writers' puns strive to discover an extra dimension, a private space, which can grant the Romantic hero some freedom from society's restrictions.

THE MILLENNIAL VISION

The Bridge resembles *Moby-Dick* in its admission of a carefully secreted homoeroticism; and, as we have seen, homosexuality as concealment is a theme persistent throughout Crane's work. The visible must necessarily be the untrue because Crane's society demanded that the homosexual poet suppress his genuine expressions of desire. "The Visible the Untrue" itself, dedicated to Crane's lover Emil Opffer, also introduces the more general theme of millennial triumph which was so important to the poet:

> And it is always
> always, always the eternal rainbow
> And it is always the day, the farewell day unkind.

Homosexuality is trapped in the present "day unkind," but it can look forward to the "eternal rainbow," the day when the magic island of Atlantis will float to the surface and all miseries are alleviated. We may be reminded of the inscription to E. M. Forster's *Maurice*, his novel of homosexual love: "Begun 1913. Finished 1914. Dedicated to a Happier Year."

The millennial way of thinking has been, as Stephen Fender noted, "prolonged in the history of the American imagination," and many American long poems have been enamoured of this kind of apocalyptic prophetic vision: one thinks especially of Whitman and Pound.[12] Of course the most respected America philosophers – Jefferson, Emerson, William James – have also been optimists inciting people to invest materially and spiritually in a better future. The paradigm of the American visionary hero was Columbus himself; and Sundquist regarded "Ave Maria" as the thematic centre of Crane's poem, saying the whole of *The Bridge* turns upon the poet-quester's attempt to imitate Columbus and "bring home the redemptive Word."[13] Columbus was a martyr translated into a hero: the King of Portugal spurned his babbling vision of an alternative trade-route to India, and the Spanish monarchs backed his venture only after much hesitation, but the conquering Admiral defeated all the odds to return home in triumph:

> I thought of Genoa; and this truth, now proved,
> That made me exile in her streets . . .

Columbus was also astute enough to ensure that his extraordinary vision would be preserved even if he himself were to be drowned. While on his way back across the Atlantic after having discovered the New World, Columbus became very anxious that they would all be scuppered by bad weather and that he himself would fail to secure his niche in history. Accordingly he took the precaution of writing an account of the voyage, sealing it in a wooden cask and throwing it into the sea:

> And record of more, floating in a casque,
> Was tumbled from us under bare poles scudding

In fact Columbus managed to arrive home safely and his wooden cask was not needed, but the poet-quester Crane was not so lucky: in his lifetime *The Bridge* met only with bewilderment. Perhaps Crane consoled himself with the thought that one day his message in a bottle would be washed up, and his voyage of discovery turn out to be of greater significance than at first appeared. As if to emphasize his sense of a fraternal bond with Columbus, Crane took the epigraph to "Ave Maria" from Don Fernando Columbus' biography of his father, where Don Fernando quoted these lines from Seneca's *Medea* and proclaimed, "This prediction may assuredly be considered as accomplished in the person of the Admiral":

> Venient annis, saecula seris,
> Quibus Oceanus vincula rerum
> Laxet et ingens pateat tellus
> Tiphysque novos detegat orbes
> Nec sit terris ultima Thule.
>
> (In the last days there will come an age in which Ocean shall loosen the bonds of things; a great country will be discovered; another Tiphis shall make known new worlds, and Thule shall no longer be the extremity of the earth.)[14]

And the analogical mirrors reflect once more, for we can now begin to fulfil Seneca's prophecy in relation to *The Bridge*, just as Columbus fulfilled it in relation to the American continent. The whole of Crane's poem revolves around this question of concealment and rediscovery, revealing (not inventing) a New World, finding the Atlantis latent in quotidian existence. By concealing his artistic intentions, Crane expanded his boundaries beyond the conclusion of his poem, beyond the conclusion of his life, until now – more than fifty years after his death – we can start to glimpse what makes up his new-found land. It is not my intention to make apocalyptic claims for this particular critical work, which in any case does no more than touch the tip of an iceberg, but simply to stress how the notion of delayed triumph was essential to Crane's designs, and part of the integral pattern of *The Bridge*. As Crane's poem "The Phantom Bark" puts it,

> So dream thy sails, O phantom bark
> That I thy drowned man may speak again

   Columbus was the archetypal American discoverer, but the theme of
uncovering a new world is compatible with two other myths which
Crane exploits: the perennial American myth of buried treasure and the
myth of the alchemical stone which can magically transform base metal
into gold. Buried treasure is the context of "Indiana," but it is
foreshadowed in "Van Winkle," where the image of the narrator
discovering snakes hidden under an ash heap symbolizes the snake-like
ambiguities that lie coiled within the "unsuspecting fibre" of Crane's
Bridge:

> the rapid tongues
> That flittered from under the ash heap day
> After day whenever your stick discovered
> Some sunning inch of unsuspecting fibre –
> It flashed back at your thrust, as clean as fire.

In "Indiana," these concealed snakes have been transmuted into the
concealed wealth which Jim, the man on the 1849 gold-trail, had hoped to
mine from the ground:

> In golden syllables loosed from the clay
> His gleaming name.

Crane's puns are exactly this: the loosing of golden syllables from under
the clay of the poem's surface. The image of gold being unloosed finds
another manifestation in "Virginia," where "Cathedral Mary" is urged
to imitate that maiden in the fairy tale "Rapunzel," who, incarcerated as
she was in a tower, let down her long hair so her lover could climb up to
the rescue:

> O Mary, leaning from the high wheat tower,
> Let down your golden hair!

In a literal sense, the narrator is merely seeking to make contact with
Mary, his Saturday date; but in a self-reflexive sense, Crane's poem is
teasingly inviting the reader to pursue the golden threads of concealed
puns which will lead towards the meanings similarly incarcerated within
The Bridge. (In the Grimm brothers' fairy tale, the heroine Rapunzel was
imprisoned by a witch who caused the gallant Prince to tumble down
from the tower he was ascending. The Prince was blinded as he fell; but,
by the tears of Ra-PUN-zel, his eyes were restored to sight.) As for
alchemical metamorphosis, it was a theme very popular with the
Surrealists. Breton talked of how Surrealists were the heirs of the
medieval alchemists, how like them they sought the philosophers' stone
which would enable Man's imagination "to take a brilliant revenge upon

things"; and, as we have seen, in his 1924 *Manifesto of Surrealism* Breton
saluted Columbus as a Surrealist hero who could magically transform
fantasy into glittering fact.[15] The epigraph to "Ave Maria" from
Seneca's *Medea* anticipates the time when "another Tiphis shall make
known new worlds"; and it is appropriate that Tiphis was Jason's pilot on
the *Argo* when the Argonauts set out to capture the ram's Golden Fleece,
because this fable held a special interest for alchemists, believing as they
did that the Golden Fleece contained a parchment which held all the
secrets to their magic craft. Hence Epicure Mammon's lines in Jonson's
play *The Alchemist*:

> I have a piece of Jason's fleece, too,
> Which was no other than a book of alchemy,
> Writ in large sheep-skin, a good fat ram-vellum.
>
> (ii.i.89–91)

This gives us another *raison d'être* for the reference to the Argonauts' story
in "Atlantis": "And you, aloft there – Jason! hesting Shout!" Crane is
imitating Jason's quest to decipher prophetic script and so reveal a new
world. We know how strongly Jonson's *Alchemist* influenced Crane's
imagination because he placed a quotation from the play as his epigraph
to "Faustus and Helen"; and in a complex but convincing analysis,
Robert K. Martin has demonstrated how in that poem Crane employs
images drawn from alchemy to invest quotidian New York life with the
dignity of classical myth. Examining these lines, for instance, from Part
II:

> O, I have known metallic paradises
> Where cuckoos clucked to finches
> Above the deft catastrophes of drums

Martin associated *cuckoos* with Hera, Greek goddess of marriage and
fertility, to whom the cuckoo was sacred as messenger of spring, and to
whom Zeus made love while posing as a cuckoo; *finches*, traditional
symbol of sexual desire, with the goddess of love, Aphrodite; and
"catastrophes of drums" with the goddess of war, Athena. Hence the
dancer selecting partners in this New York roof garden becomes equated
with the Trojan hero Paris trying to decide among these three goddesses,
Hera, Aphrodite and Athena, in that legendary beauty contest which was
to plunge the ancient world into war. In this way, Crane employs
Faustian alchemy ("metallic paradises") to metamorphose base reality
into glittering myth: "Know, Olympians, we are breathless," boasts the
poem's sanctified reveller. Crane was suggesting his alchemical methods
when he wrote to Louis Untermeyer of "Faustus and Helen" on 19
January 1923: "Practically all of the current images used have their
counter equivalents 'of ancient days,' yet at the same time they retain
their current colour in the fusion process."[16]

In *The Bridge* images of alchemy tend to carry vaguer and more abstract connotations of heightened worlds; but the retrieval of a new-found land and discovery of some kind of philosophers' stone to convert base metal into gold is a constant theme of Crane's longer poem, and so the revelation of the text's buried linguistic magic is compatible with its more overt thematic pattern. Columbus introduces a new idiom as well as a new continent:

> Witness before the tides can wrest away
> The world I bring . . .

And the Admiral's quest is:

> . . . to the far
> Hushed gleaming fields and pendant seething wheat
> Of knowledge, – round thy brows unhooded now

That "*seething* wheat / Of knowledge" is indeed verbally *pendant* (hanging suspended) because it puns on "see/thing," the *knowledge* that is invisible within everyday life, just as "see/thing" is literally invisible within *seething*. So this journey to awareness is in a sense the decoding of a mystery ("round thy brows unhooded now"). Similarly in "The Dance" the mythical "winter king" holds the magical key to the Indian continent which the poet is trying to uncover as the basis of modern America:

> And in the autumn drouth, whose burnished hands
> With mineral wariness found out the stone
> Where prayers, forgotten, streamed the mesa sands?

In "Cape Hatteras," Whitman is described as a "Vedic Caesar" – *Vedic* denoting the Vedas, the sacred Hindu scriptures written in Sanskrit which surrendered their recondite secrets only after they had lain dormant for many centuries; and Whitman's poetry, like *The Bridge*, is said to be invested with a similar kind of secret millennial vision:

> Thou hast there in thy wrist a Sanskrit charge
> To conjugate infinity's dim marge –
> Anew . . . !

(Crane wrote to Malcolm Cowley on 28 March 1926: "I have been reading the philosophies of the East until I actually dream in terms of the Vedanta scriptures.")[17] So the words of the seer Whitman which gleam out from cryptic tablets are an indication of the world's latent promise:

> . . . your eyes, like the Great Navigator's without ship,
> Gleam from the great stones of each prison crypt
> Of canyoned traffic . . .

And Walt Whitman's magic "wand" is said to operate "Hermetically past condor zones":

> Thou, there beyond –
> Glacial sierras and the flight of ravens,
> Hermetically past condor zones . . .
> . . . thy wand
> Has beat a song, O Walt, – there and beyond!

A *condor* is a very large American vulture found in elevated parts of the Andes and the Rocky Mountains, and ostensibly these lines indicate how, like the aeroplane, Whitman's poetry must be *Hermetically* sealed to survive. Whitman's tropes repress and lie against time in the same way as an aeroplane represses the external atmosphere and guards itself against dangerous flying vultures in order to ensure its own security. But "hermetic" is also the adjective used for anything concerned with alchemy, "hermetic" deriving from the Greek Hermes, god of science and trickery; and so the bird *condor* here puns on Whitman's poetic "con d'or," the gold-plated con or swindle which the wand of the magician Whitman was able to produce. These lines imply that Crane sees Whitman's poetry as imbued with golden secrets which, by the hermetic transformations of alchemy, will be brought to light in a later time. (Presumably Crane was thinking of Whitman's homosexual imagery.) Because Crane is privy to Whitman's vision, Whitman has symbolically risen "upward from the dead," and his words on the page have become the map to the holy grail:

> What ciphers risen from prophetic script

Just as Crane reclaimed Whitman, so we have to reclaim Crane, and by deciphering the secrets of his own magic text uncover the vision of a world where the past and present are in continually interpenetrating harmony. As "Atlantis" says, this enchanted stone will be revealed only to the reader prepared to see the universe in terms of a philosophical joke, a cosmic pun:

> What cipher-script of time no traveller reads
> But who, through smoking pyres of love and death,
> Searches the timeless laugh of mythic spears.

And finally, of course, the very title "Atlantis" indicates a reclamation of submerged land. In May 1926, Crane was reading Lewis Spence's *Atlantis in America*, which makes claims for traces of Atlantean civilization in American Indian culture; and Crane remarked in a letter: "it's easy to believe that a continent existed in mid-Atlantic waters and that the Antilles and West Indies are but salient peaks of its surface."[18] This myth of a sunken island is presented quite overtly at the end of *The Bridge*:

> Atlantis, – hold thy floating singer late!

But the idea of relocating a submerged land is prefigured in "Cutty Sark":

teased remnants of the skeletons of cities

and in "Cape Hatteras":

> While rises in the west the coastwise range,
>   slowly the hushed land

and also in "The Tunnel," where Crane's line

> And Death aloft, – gigantically down

is a conscious echo of Poe's poem "The City in the Sea," a lament for a mysterious and invisible civilization ("While from a proud tower in the town / Death looks gigantically down"). So the social theme of hidden worlds and alchemical transformation, clear enough inside *The Bridge*, is mirrored in the way the text itself is renewed by Crane's linguistic metamorphoses.

THE MARTYR'S TRIUMPH

This notion of alchemy's millennial triumph could be seen as an inversion and secularization of the Christian belief in final reward. Alchemy may blasphemously propose an earthly Atlantis, but, as T. S. Eliot said, genuine blasphemy is a way of affirming belief, and in *The Bridge* the typically Christian images of martyrdom and purgatorial suffering are very marked.[19] This makes *The Bridge* a Christian poem in form and style if not in content. The narrator stricken by arrows in "The Dance" provides the most obvious example of such martyrdom:

> And buzzard-circleted, screamed from the stake;
> I could not pick the arrows from my side.

But we should notice how, by one of Crane's formal or internal bridges, this suffering becomes aligned with the pain of the failed questers in "Indiana":

> A dream called Eldorado was his town,
>   It rose up shambling in the nuggets' wake,
> It had no charter but a promised crown
>   Of claims to stake.

The men on the gold-trail *stake* their *claims* to wealth; but, by an ironic punning reversal, the disintegration of their mission increases their *claims* to the *stake* of martyrdom. The puns, verbal bridges, link the *stake* of "Indiana" back to the *stake* of "The Dance"; and now the "promised crown" becomes a crown of thorns rather than the gold crowns of unlimited wealth. This quest may be either a valid experiment or an exercise in self-destruction, and Crane's puns pivot the reader's interpretation between these two possibilities: in mining, *shambling* is the operation whereby successive platforms are raised one above another so as to bring the ore to a higher level – but *shambling* may also imply the general incompetence of the miners, just as *nuggets*, the lumps of gold, has overtones of "nugatory" (futile, trifling, inoperative). And there is a similar verbal inversion a few lines later:

> Bent westward, passing on a stumbling jade
> A homeless squaw –

Whereas the gold-diggers were previously intent on discovering, *stumbling* upon, *jade* (the precious mineral stone), this has now been modified into the weary *stumbling* of a *jade* which is no more than a worn-out horse. The punning reversal mirrors the poem's thematic reversal of miner into martyr.

In his essay "Magic, Lies, and Silence in Hart Crane," Eric J. Sundquist associated Crane's interest in prophetic concealment with the suffering of the visionary genius as outlaw. Sundquist traced Crane's affiliation of himself with Christ, Whitman and Charlie Chaplin, the oppressed clown of Crane's 1921 poem "Chaplinesque":

> We will sidestep, and to the final smirk
> Dally the doom of that inevitable thumb
> That slowly chafes its puckered index toward us

As R. W. B. Lewis said back in 1963, *index* puns on "the prohibition, or turning thumbs down upon, the publication and the reading of certain books, as in the Catholic Index." Lewis noted that at the time of writing this poem, Crane was outraged at the reported censorship of Chaplin's film *The Kid* ("What they could possibly have objected to, I cannot imagine").[20] Crane believed that because society is bent upon outlawing the radical truths spoken by certain artists, those artists are obliged to work by evasion and sleight of hand, "signals dispersed in veils." Thus the evasive clown Chaplin merges into the evasive clown Crane; and in "Cape Hatteras" Crane similarly admires the *aureole* around his comrade Whitman's head, an aureole – in Roman Catholic theology – being a crown for those who have been in conflict with the world. Here the aureole is a symbol of delayed triumph, the consigning of final revelation to a future era:

> . . . O joyous seer!
> Recorders ages hence, yes, they shall hear
> In their own veins uncancelled thy sure tread
> And read thee by the aureole 'round thy head

"Recorders ages hence" is the title of one of Whitman's own poems in the *Calamus* collection, and in *The Bridge* Crane makes a valiant attempt to embrace Whitman's optimistic vision of the future:

> "Recorders ages hence" – ah, syllables of faith!

In "Quaker Hill," Crane looks forward to the new life that will be granted to his epic poem when all its secrets have been unloosed:

> Who holds the lease on time and on disgrace?
> What eats the pattern with ubiquity?

What is the ubiquitous pattern within the poem, the figure in the carpet which will allow *The Bridge* to imitate Christ and rise from the dead?

> Shoulder the curse of sundered parentage,
> Wait for the postman driving from Birch Hill
> With birthright by blackmail, the arrant page
> That unfolds a new destiny to fill. . . .

The "*arrant* page": shameless, roguish (*arrant* was originally the same word as "errant," an outlaw, roving thief). Crane's "arrant page" will indeed unfold a "new destiny" when its subversive criminal undertones become visible: the exposure of these dark ambiguities will grant *The Bridge* new life. Just as "sundered parentage" is autobiographical – Crane's parents were divorced – so the blackmail reference reminds us that Crane was himself blackmailed throughout his life on account of his homosexuality; and this would doubtless have given him pause for thought about the unacceptability of arrant outlaws and the disguises elicited by the demands of social conformity.

To reiterate, this social conformity is an important component of *The Bridge*. The poem's public and mythopoeic status depends upon the abnegation of ambiguous counter-currents. Nevertheless, as in Melville, the author's linguistic dexterity suggests to the alert reader other paths the poem may take, and the theme of homosexuality is a significant alternative direction which Crane's poem simultaneously raises and represses. While reflecting the social conditions of capitalist America, *The Bridge* is also in the millennial tradition of American long poems which anticipate a final triumph, a better future; and in the case of *The Bridge* this vision is actually concealed within the words on the page themselves. The last lines of "Atlantis" suggest revelation is hovering on the brink of intelligibility: "Whispers" are swinging to and fro, and "Is it Cathay . . . ?" echoes Columbus' words as he first set foot on the New World, but before he had understood just what that New World meant. The sunken island of Atlantis is about to break the surface, but the poet is a martyr because he has accepted the necessity of displacing his final artistic vision into an unknown future. The poet realizes that his vision may not be comprehended within his own lifetime. (It should be obvious that if Crane had gone about meticulously explicating his poem's ambiguities, he would have rendered this millennial aspect of *The Bridge* quite redundant.)

Of course this kind of masochism and self-aggrandizement through suffering might be seen by some readers as less heroic than pitifully adolescent, but it was the kind of suffering Crane unquestionably chose to glory in. In "Southern Cross," the constellation in the heavens becomes associated with the body of the lover, but also with the Cross upon which Christ died, so that the narrator's act of love-making turns into a self-lacerating gesture:

> I wanted you . . . The embers of the Cross
> Climbed by aslant and huddling aromatically.

R. W. Butterfield similarly noticed how, in "The Tunnel," the martyred figure of Poe ("Whose head is swinging from the swollen strap?") is associated both with the crucified Christ and with the persecuted poet, Crane himself.[21] And in the "Proem" ("And Thee, across the harbor, silver-paced"), the Bridge is described as not only crossing the harbour but also harbouring a cross ("a cross the[e] harbor"), taking the burden of America upon its shoulders. Just as Christ redeemed the fallen world, so Crane saw himself as a mythopoeic hero who would transmute the base metal of America's industrial world into gold. Emotionally Crane loathed certain aspects of commercialism, but intellectually he was obliged to recognize that a heroic Saviour must move among His fallen people; and so, solipsist that he was, Crane set himself the task of mythologizing and thus "redeeming" the world he inhabited. "The commercial aspect is the most prominent characteristic of America, and we must all bow to it sooner or later," declared Crane in 1919; and of one of his own unhappy and temporary attempts to bridge poetry with life in the business world, he remarked: "it is like being put up on a cross and divided."[22] In this context, it is appropriate that Crane imitated his divine master by killing himself in his thirty-third year (with "drunken statements in his last year of life that he was Christ");[23] and it is also appropriate that the poet should have secularized the Christian symbol of the *star*, which signalled the birth of Jesus to the wise men from the East at the Epiphany, and which is blasphemously employed in *The Bridge* to suggest how the saviour Crane intends himself to be born again:

> Under the mistletoe of dreams, a star –
> As though to join us at some distant hill –
> Turns in the waking west and goes to sleep.

The way this conclusion to "The Harbor Dawn" aligns the star with *mistletoe*, traditionally associated with Christmas, confirms the religious imagery at work here. This star signifying a new dawn is found once more in "The Dance":

> And one star, swinging, take its place, alone,
> Cupped in the larches of the mountain pass –
> Until, immortally, it bled into the dawn.

And the image occurs again in "Indiana," this time in a specifically homosexual context, the eyes of an Indian woman said to be "like twin stars" which are "Lit with love shine" as they "shun the gaze / Of all our silent men" and fix instead on the poem's female narrator. Crane himself suggested "a tiny star" be placed underneath the title on the cover of *The Bridge*'s New York edition; and although this plan did not materialize, we can see how Crane's cast of mind favoured that combination of martyrdom and millennial triumph which was so beloved of the contemporary Surrealists.[24] Indeed, Crane's mysterious star finds a counterpart in the enigmatic key and moon which appeared on the cover of the first issue of *Le Surréalisme au Service de la Révolution*, the Parisian magazine which superseded *La Révolution Surréaliste* in 1930: for although *Le Surréalisme* prided itself on being more politically realistic than its predecessor, this strange key and moon served to conceal the magazine's actual title, which was inscribed in phosphorescence and so visible only in the dark. However, this enigma was deemed by the editors to be a microcosm of Surrealistic politics: extraordinary secrets were somewhere aglow, and the faithful should be initiated into the ability to decipher the world's mysterious hieroglyphs, before discovering those magical properties latent within social life which would accordingly enable them to pass from cryptography into concrete revolutionary action. So we can see that the Christ-complex, revolving upon its axis of suffering and redemption, was not unfamiliar among those Surrealists who cast themselves in the rôle of visionaries; and, like them, Crane was also a great admirer of Dostoyevsky's *Crime and Punishment* – a cult text for the Surrealists – where the Christ-fixated hero Raskolnikov plans to redeem all the injustices of society by the perpetration of a perfect crime.[25]

Value-judgements on the nature of this complex are not our concern here. The essential thing is that *The Bridge* as Saviour moves among America's humble folk, a mythic symbol even for the farms of the Midwest ("the prairies' dreaming sod"), while at the same time maintaining within itself – like Christ – the spark of divinity and millennial prophecy. In this bizarre urge towards the prophetic glamour of crucifixion, Crane's combination of ambition and self-destruction also bears some resemblance to the Faustian paradigm; and indeed Caresse

Crosby, who remembered Crane as "young and cocky," recalled as well how her doomed friend was particularly fond of declaiming the Epilogue to Marlowe's *Doctor Faustus*:

> Cut is the branch that might have grown full straight,
> And burned is Apollo's Laurel bough,
> That sometime grew within this learned man:
> Faustus is gone, regard his hellish fall,
> Whose fiendful fortune may exhort the wise,
> Only to wonder at unlawful things,
> Whose deepness doth entice such forward wits,
> To practise more than heavenly power permits.[26]

16

Conclusion

EVIDENCE OF INTENT

Two questions confront us finally. Is it true that the pun is the structural principle behind *The Bridge*? And if it is true, how should we read the poem today?

The strongest case for the pun is made by the empirical evidence of the text, and the consistency with which certain patterns of verbal play repeat themselves. Some critics would say this renders biographical proof of "intention" obsolete. Nowhere in his letters does Crane say, "Today I wrote ten puns into my long poem *The Bridge*," but that should not prevent us relating the words Crane uses to a verbal, social and intellectual context, and so attempting to synthesize his poem's "meaning." We may remember Ezra Pound's controversial translation of *Homage to Sextus Propertius*, where Pound rendered the line "gaudeat insolito tacta puella sono" as "And in the mean time my songs will travel / And the devirginated young ladies will enjoy them." The justification made by Pound was that *tacta* literally means "let her be touched," but *intacta* means "intact," hence in its feminine form "virgin"; and so "insolito tacta" gives us the virgin *intacta* being invaded by the word *solito*, "to be much accustomed." The linguistic pattern of invasion, according to Pound, mirrors Propertius' thematic intentions: the virgins are much accustomed to being sundered. "If this sequence of phrases is wholly accidental," remarked Pound, "and if the division of 'in' and 'tacta' is 'wholly' accidental, then Propertius was the greatest unconscious ironist of all time."[1] We may be tempted to add that if Crane was ignorant of the triple pun and double paradox within "Flame cataracts of heaven in seething swarms" (Flame/cataracts, cataracts/see-thing, blindness/vision) – then Propertius would have had a rival for the title. The reader of a poem must read the words as they appear on the page before

211

him and try to make sense of what they say – not rely on the poet's own explications, which will tend to be cast in the most general terms. Just as the great enemy of Propertius (and Pound) was the army of pedantic classical scholars trying to domesticate the scurrilous Latin poet, so Crane has suffered from the disservices of anthologists and cultural critics who have tended to pigeon-hole him as the "heir of Whitman" and "son of industrial society" without paying attention to the intricacies built into his actual poems. As Eugene Paul Nassar has shown, too many readers have taken a "metacritical" attitude towards Crane, often simply repeating the strictures of Allen Tate and Yvor Winters who were distorting Crane to provide fodder for their own ideological cannons on the battlefields of Romanticism and Pantheism. Tate's use of Crane as a cautionary tale to demonstrate the dangers of untutored Romanticism has developed into a weary nostrum masquerading as critical judgement.

A little caution, however, is doubtless necessary. The contention of this work is that Crane was largely aware of the ambiguities within *The Bridge*, and so it is to be hoped that the argument rests upon more solid grounds than the purely subjective and impressionistic reactions of one reader. But the idea of puns in *The Bridge* is not new. Nassar has written about how they ironically yoke together creation and destruction ("time cannot raise" in the "Proem" punning on "time cannot raze"); Roger Ramsey, Eric J. Sundquist and Stanley K. Coffman have produced articles setting Crane's puns in different theoretical contexts; Alan Trachtenberg has discussed how "Like Pater and Joyce [Crane] teases meanings from etymologies"; and Richard P. Sugg, R. W. B. Lewis, Herbert Leibowitz and Sherman Paul have all emphasized the importance of wordplay in their books on Crane.[2] John Unterecker said he thought "all the puns on the word 'Hart' in Crane's work are efforts to take his own private mess and give it some kind of lasting form," and Unterecker's biography reproduces a photograph Crane sent to the Rychtariks inscribed "To Charlotte and Richard from the 'Heart.'"[3] Crane made play with other people's names as well: Laura Riding, for instance, became "Laura Riding Roughshod," while an unfavourable review of *White Buildings* was dismissed as "Kay Boyle's explosive boil";[4] and, as we saw in Chapter 6, a bilingual pun turned Kenneth Burke into "beurre queue" or "Butter-Tail." In Crane's letters, Miami was transposed into "My ammy" while Palm Beach became "Pam Bitch";[5] and Malcolm Cowley specifically commented on the stream of puns Crane would produce at parties (see Chapter 1), with Samuel Loveman also recalling the sexual *double entendres* he was fond of making in response to subway advertisements (Chapter 13). We know as well that Crane kept lists of unusual words in his vocabulary notebooks, and that both Cowley and Susan Jenkins Brown remarked upon Crane's habitual use of an unabridged dictionary (Chapter 1).

All this is consistent with the circumstantial biographical evidence, the kind of authors and ideas that we have proof Crane was interested in. We know he was conscious of the assimilation of psychoanalytical theory into "Atlantis" because he said so in a letter to Yvor Winters, and it would not have been lost on him that puns which people make in dreams are crucial data for Freudian analysis (see Chapter 13). We know Crane read Whitehead's *Science and the Modern World* because he said so in a letter to Munson; and we know he incorporated Whitehead's kinetic idiom within his creative work, because in a letter to Harriet Monroe discussing "At Melville's Tomb," Crane stated (emphasis in original): "This little bit of 'relativity' ought not to be discredited in poetry now that scientists are proceeding to measure the universe on principles of pure *ratio*" (Chapter 2). We know Crane admired Ouspensky's propensity for finding analogies between one era and another, and we know Ouspensky's belief in cyclic time was congenial to Crane because he remarked to Waldo Frank on how exciting it was to discover the past living under only slightly altered forms (Chapter 2). We know Crane was aware of the Don Quixote myth and the consequences for his own work of Quixote's ironic oscillation between ideal grandeur and banal fact because he said so in another letter to Waldo Frank (Chapter 12). We know Crane was fond of burlesque theatre; we know burlesque theatre was based upon puns; and we know Crane made a list of punning song-titles designed for a comic opera about Indians (Chapter 5). We know Crane was fascinated by *Moby-Dick* because he read it at least three times, and we know he was alert to the complex implications of the whale's ambiguous anatomy because he said so in a letter to Solomon Grunberg (Chapter 15). We know Crane was familiar with the Surrealists' artistic experiments because he explicitly commented on them in his letters (Chapter 11); and also with the wordplay of E. E. Cummings, whose poetry he enjoyed parodying (Chapter 10). We know Crane was excited by the paradoxes and conceits of Metaphysical poets like Donne (Chapter 14). We know he specifically stated his interest in musical symphonic form whereby many strands are integrated into one artistic unit; and that he underlined a passage in one of his library books where Conrad Aiken talks about poets playing "ideas against one another like notes in a harmony" (Chapter 8). We know Crane frequently contributed to the Parisian *transition*, which looked upon punning as a moral imperative; and we know he signed the 1929 Revolution of the Word manifesto in that magazine (Chapter 9). And, most significant of all, we know Crane sent Caresse Crosby a transatlantic telegram instructing her to send *The Bridge* to Rebecca West, after having read a newspaper article in which West commended the "sly, punning spirit" of Joyce's "Work in Progress" and declared that Joyce "Obviously . . . got this idea of the word-paste from the Freudian and Jungian analyses of the puns people make in dreams" (Chapter 10). Crane wrote his publisher a longer letter three days later affirming West to be "an amazing fusion of brains, sensibility and good common sense" and saying "I'm sure that she will appreciate the Bridge." Both the West telegram and the Revolution of the Word manifesto have been dismissed by biographers on the grounds that Crane must have been drunk at the time, but such explanations are not sufficient.[6]

We also know that Crane often amended the punctuation of *The Bridge* between manuscript and printed versions, apparently with a view to increasing the complexity of his ambiguity. He extracted the punctuation between "meridians reel" and "Thy purpose" (Chapter 2). He added a hyphen in "The sea's green crying towers a-sway" (Chapter 2). And the 1929 typescript of "Cutty Sark" which Crane sent to Harry Crosby has the appearance of being a good deal more grammatically conventional than the final published text, whose plethora of dashes was evidently inserted at the last moment to help disrupt logical sequence and give the poem more of a sense of being a continuum, a creation whose stylistic components revolve in a constant interpenetration. (Crane told Winters the lack of punctuation was "intended to present the endless continuum of water motion").[7] It is the function of the pun to say everything at once, and the anti-grammatical flow of "Cutty Sark" reflects this all-at-onceness.

Several further clues to the innermost workings of Crane's mind are provided by those books from his library which have been preserved at Columbia University. In his copy of Donne, Crane marked the poem "At once, from hence, my lines and I depart," and underlined especially the eighth line, "My verse, the strict map of my misery." This suggests how Crane, like Donne, saw the basis of his art as autobiographical: *The Bridge* too is secretly a confessional poem. Another intriguing volume is Nietzsche's *Human, All-Too-Human: A Book for Free Spirits*, and here Crane has annotated paragraph 113, where Nietzsche praises the ironic art of Lawrence Sterne. Nietzsche admired Sterne's elusiveness, the way he was continually rebelling against the imprisonment of form and so escaping from the threat of finality:

> Sterne is the great master of *double entendre*, this phrase being naturally used in a far wider sense than is commonly done when one applies it to sexual relations. We may give up for lost the reader who always wants to know exactly what Sterne thinks about a matter, and whether he be making a serious or a smiling face (for he can do both with one wrinkling of his features; he can be and even wishes to be right and wrong at the same moment, to interweave profundity and farce) . . . his maxims contain a satire on all that is sententious . . . So in the proper reader he arouses a feeling of uncertainty whether he be walking, lying, or standing, a feeling most closely akin to that of floating in the air . . . to

be equally ambiguous throughout is just the Sternian super-humour . . . a
carnal and spiritual hermaphroditism.[8]

The word "sententious" was especially underlined by Crane. Nietzsche
had similar praise for Socrates, lauding the Greek's "merry style of
seriousness" and "wisdom of sheer roguish pranks" as being "the best
state of soul in a man," and certainly greatly preferable to the ponderous
didacticism of Christ: Crane underlined "merry style of seriousness."[9]
Crane also annotated paragraph 119 where Nietzsche considered "the
primary germs of the artistic sense," the kinds of pleasure which art
might engender "as, for example, among savage tribes." First among
these, and heavily marked by Crane, is "the joy of understanding what
another means." Nietzsche goes on, "Art in this case is a sort of
conundrum, which causes its solver pleasure."[10] Also revealing in this
context is Crane's Cambridge edition of the complete Shakespeare, for
not a great many pages are marked – 59 out of 1264, to be exact – but
some of those annotations seem to have a direct reference to Crane's own
work. For instance, he underlined "Gargantua" in *As You Like It* ("You
must borrow me Gargantua's mouth first"), and used the word himself
in "Praise for an Urn" ("And, of Gargantua, the laughter"). He marked
an exclamation of Iago in *Othello* – "By Janus, I think no" – which may
have been the origin of the double-edged "Janus-faced" mirror in
"Recitative." So with such concrete consequences of the noted passages,
it would perhaps not be unreasonable to infer a special interest in
ambiguity from Crane's heavy underlining of part of the Porter's speech
in *Macbeth*: "Faith, here's an equivocator, that could swear in both the
scales against either scale."[11]

Why, then, the silence on Crane's part? Well, it was not a complete
silence. His acknowledgement of his own metaphorical "condensation,"
his justification to Harriet Monroe of poetic "*inflection*" of language" and
his discussion in "General Aims and Theories" of how "the terms of
expression employed are often selected less for their logical (literal)
significance than for their associational meanings" are all consistent with
this notion of the pun accumulating disparate associations and bursting
through the weary husks of traditional logic and grammar.[12] Crane
talked more specifically about *The Bridge* in letters to his generous patron
Otto H. Kahn, but it would be a mistake to rely too heavily upon these
communications for notice of Crane's intentions. According to Matthew
Josephson, Kahn did not understand the poem he was subsidizing and
disliked to hear about its development; and so Roger Ramsey is surely
correct to say these letters "are not to be trusted as guide or gloss." Indeed
Kahn's letters back to Crane make comical reading, with the rich banker
pleading "overwhelming demands" on his time to wriggle out of the
critical judgements an importunate Crane would require of him.[13] Of

course Crane would try to couch his account of the poem's progress in the most simple terms when he wrote to Kahn, and although the letters are not entirely without value, it is not difficult to see Crane is keeping something back:

> There are so many interlocking elements and symbols at work throughout *The Bridge* that it is next to impossible to describe it without resorting to the actual metaphors of the poem. (18 March 1926).

> I am really writing an epic of the modern consciousness, and indescribably complicated factors have to be resolved and blended. (12 September 1927)

Crane's missives to Kahn resemble nothing so much as his letter of application for a Guggenheim Fellowship: polite, conventional and vague. The simplistic notions expressed in these letters do not do justice to the artistic complexity of Crane's poem.[14] Conversely, when thanking Herbert Weinstock in 1930 for his review of *The Bridge*, Crane mentioned that "*The Bridge* is at least as complicated in its structure and inferences as *The Wasteland* [*sic*] – perhaps more so"; and as he added that a full understanding of *The Waste Land* had taken him "nearly five years, with innumerable readings," Crane was clearly hinting to Weinstock that it would take some time for all the complexities of his own poem to be revealed: "It is pertinent to suggest, I think, that with more time and familiarity with *The Bridge* you will come to envisage it more as one poem with a clearer and more integrated unity and development than was at first evident."[15] As I noted in my Introduction, there is no question that Crane's poems use puns to some extent, and the fact that this talismanic word "pun" does not appear once within the author's essays and letters about his own work must lead us to infer he was being less than forthright about his artistic designs. After the publication of *The Bridge*, Paul Rosenfeld suggested that the author himself might like to write a critical explication of it; but this plan came to nothing, and within twenty-six months of the poem's appearance Crane was dead, allowing the juggernaut of criticism to roll on its way unaided. As the 1930s proceeded, economic depression ensured that social realism increasingly became the approved literary mode, and Crane's Surrealistic and Joycean intricacies would not have interested the American cultural establishment of that time even if they had perceived them.

Crane was not the first American writer to remain reticent about his work. Melville was not exactly garrulous on the subject of *Moby-Dick*; and, as we have seen, the preservation of social decorum and the prospect of a final, millennial triumph would have been two inducements towards taciturnity. If Crane had pointed out the ironies in *The Bridge*, the poem might have seemed merely ingenious, a rather silly clockwork toy; whereas because these ironies come to light in a later time, the poem becomes more like a Faustian bid to defy the restrictions involved in being confined to one particular era. For us in the 1980s, *The Bridge* is a poem quite different from the way it appeared in the 1930s; and when more work has been done to elucidate its fantastic complexities, the poem will change its shape yet again. Joyce once said of *Ulysses*, "I've put in so many enigmas and puzzles that it will keep the professors busy for centuries arguing over what I meant, and that's the only way of insuring one's immortality" – and Crane's zest for immortality seems to have been of a similar kind.[16] Allen Tate said Crane had "an incapacity to live within the limitations of the human condition," while Cowley remembered he "had a greater thirst for fame than the rest of us," and Josephson that he "was determined at all costs to make himself the Great American Poet."[17] *The Bridge* is certainly a poem *sui generis*, but it is the work of an enormously ambitious writer, and it may expand our ideas of what is possible inside literary creation. A letter from Crane to Munson in 1923 leaves us in no doubt about the poet's Faustian ambition, nor about the fact that he saw his artistic conception as both brilliant and original:

> I am too much interested in this *Bridge* thing lately to write letters, ads, or anything. It is just beginning to take the least outline, – and the more outline the conception of the thing takes, – the more its final difficulties appal me . . . it may be too impossible an ambition. But if I do succeed, such a waving of banners, such ascent of towers, such dancing, etc., will never before have been put down on paper![18]

But there was also a less respectable side to Crane, a side that verged towards paranoia and schizophrenia. Harold Bloom called Crane "a kind of American Marlowe" in his love of the rhetorical Sublime, and so indeed he was, but Crane also resembled Marlowe in his tavern-haunting, homosexuality and general offensiveness to polite society: the poet Roy Campbell, who was unwise enough to play host to Crane for two weeks in 1929, subsequently denounced his guest as "a disgrace both intellectually and morally, a howling, ugly-looking, lachrymose devil, like nothing that I have ever seen before."[19] So it is not by pure chance that the epigraph to *The Bridge*, taken from the Book of Job, is an utterance of Satan's (epigraph emphasized):

> And the Lord said unto Satan, Whence comest thou? Then Satan answered the Lord, and said, *From going to and fro in the earth, and from walking up and down in it.*

Nor is it coincidental that Crane was adept at imitating Satan's trick of metamorphosing his identity and appearing to different people in different guises. Philip Horton reported how Crane often used to reel down the streets of Little Italy shouting, "I am Christopher Marlowe," and on his night-time sexual forages he was accustomed to call himself

Mike Drayton.[20] Crane would also talk about his "strenuous" poetic career to his businessman father ("strenuous" was one of Mr Crane senior's favourite words), just as he would assure his mother he was "as much interested as ever" in Christian Science while writing concurrently to Bill Wright that he was "at present . . . not a Christian Scientist."[21] Along the same lines, in 1977 the *Hart Crane Newsletter* printed a newly discovered letter to Crane's father written shortly after the young poet had arrived in New York in 1917, which cheerfully admitted that "any writing has got to stop now, when I am so occupied in studies." Crane's father thought he was studying for entry to Columbia University, but in fact Crane never had any such intention, and as the *Newsletter* wryly commented, "It is interestingly apt . . . that he composed the letter on April Fool's Day."[22] The maxim of the eighteenth-century double-agent Richelieu was "I talk to everybody in his own way," and Crane was adept as well at the art of telling different people just what they wanted to hear. There was something in him of the hoaxing confidence-man, something also of the advertising-agent he had been trained as, and of the salesman's temperament which takes pleasure in arranging images to suit particular circumstances. Applying for a job with the Thompson advertising company in 1923, Crane jazzed-up his credentials by bogusly describing himself as a graduate of Western Reserve University. At the same time, he went to great lengths to conceal from his father his dismissal from the Patno advertising agency in Cleveland; and when he set off for New York, the official explanation was that he was undertaking a business-trip to explore new markets for Patno. All Crane's friends were sworn to secrecy.[23] Later on, after the rupture with his mother in 1928, Crane was to go to even greater lengths to keep his address secret from his insufferable parent.

Without wishing to delve deeply into psychoanalytical explanations of this deviousness, it is apparent that the arguments and eventual divorce of his parents contributed to the formation of what Unterecker called the "underground man" in Crane.[24] His attempt to express affection for each parent individually when Grace and Clarence were hardly on speaking terms with each other must have engendered fragmentation within his personal life. Even back home in Cleveland in 1927 he found himself changing names every time he changed his interlocutor: he was always "Harold" to his father and "Hart" to his mother. With all these conflicting pressures, it was hardly surprising Crane should write to Munson in 1920: "Of course I am utterly alone, – want to be, – and am beginning to rather enjoy the slippery scales-of-the-fish, continual escape, attitude . . . I am learning, just beginning to learn, – the techniques of escape."[25] Peggy Guggenheim was hinting at Crane's schizoid tendencies when she recalled how in 1927 she had stayed in the house in Connecticut where Hart was boarding: he "lived an extremely monastic life up there," said Guggenheim, "seeing nobody for months on end." Indeed, such were the elaborate divisions of Crane's life that long after the poet's death Waldo Frank recalled, "There are sides of his character which I never saw";[26] and Frank's comment was taken up by the editors of the *Hart Crane Newsletter* in May 1977 (emphasis in original):

> Early in our research into Hart Crane's life and art we were struck by the poet's chameleon mirroring of, and for, his acquaintances. John Unterecker's interviews for the film "In Search of Hart Crane" strengthened our impressions. Near the end of that presentation, for example, Waldo Frank wonders if various stories about Crane's tantrums and antics could possibly have been true, asking if they had been verified.
>
> We asked artist Peter Blume whether Crane had *consciously* attempted such mirroring responses and whether the poet's Rabelaisian antics might be taken in part as reflections of the complex humour of a social satirist and comedian who was also determined to partake of the realities that were plunging by.

Blume, who had been a friend of Crane's, responded:

> It is, of course, impossible to make a definitive characterization of anyone as volatile as he was. It is not surprising therefore that there are many versions of his personality coming from different people. However, Hart did not sow these seeds of confusion deliberately for his own amusement, like a mischievous sprite. He would not have played that silly game.[27]

But it was not so much a "silly game" as the willing exchange of life in the world for an existence in the millennial realms of art. Final triumph in art would depend upon initial concealment in life. The *Newsletter's* question has been raised and not conclusively answered; and the feeling remains that there is something odd about Crane's life and work. In 1962, Kay Kenney, a girl Crane knew in Cleveland, said, "The great laughter which was Hart's most distinctive and charming feature has never, to my knowledge, even been touched." And in 1978, Emil Opffer recalled that Crane was keen on pranks and indeed "something of a practical joker."[28] The practical joke can be a vindictive device, and Crane certainly took a most hostile attitude to the American literary establishment, enthusiastically derogating what he saw as the upper-class inanities of Edmund Wilson and telling himself he could not "expect anything but shit" from the *New York Times*; and it may be that in his solipsistic inner rage Crane took a secret pleasure in the thought of revenging himself upon an unfeeling world.[29] Crane the Mad Provincial Poet became something of a curiosity in smart New York circles, but this was not a rôle the author himself was happy with. In 1964 Samuel Loveman recalled that Crane "mistrusted many of his so-called intimates" because "they were gossiping," and, said Loveman, Hart "confided to me that he wanted to shake them all."[30] Crane seems to have experienced various insecurities both about the status of poetic endeavour in America and about the ability of himself, an uneducated Midwesterner, to fulfil a poet's rôle; and he may have embraced the complexities of Whitehead, Plato, Joyce, the Surrealists, partly in a pugilistic spirit: as if to stick up a derisory finger at the cultural world, saying, "You didn't think I was smart enough, well, here's your sophisticated poem – in spades." It is, nevertheless, terrifying to think of the strain that must have been involved in writing *The Bridge*. Even *Finnegans Wake* is less complicated in certain respects, for Joyce was content to leave his text as an opaque experimental fiction, whereas Crane managed to weave all his fantastic complexities into the shape and structure of an apparently conventional poem. As we have seen, Cowley recalled how Crane would produce streams of puns when intoxicated with red wine, and the poet must have deliberately drunk for creative inspiration, sacrificing his body in the interests of art. (Cowley remembered also one of Crane's typical drunken rages where "Hart was gasping between his clenched teeth, 'You can kill me – but you can't – destroy – *The Bridge*. It's finished – it's on the *Bremen* – on its way – to Paris.'") So *The Bridge* is a work of instability and excess, no less than its author's life was. Small wonder Crane's hair was grey by the time he was thirty. Recounting the orgies of drink and destruction in Mexico that made up the last few months of Crane's life, Philip Horton's witnesses recalled how at this time the poet seemed to be hugging some private jest to his bosom:

> And yet, there were moments, sometimes even in the midst of his outbursts, when he would make some pun or Rabelaisian remark, that would send him off in gales of apparently genuine merriment, to the utter mystification of his companions. To many of them he seemed poised on the brink of insanity.[31]

But we will almost certainly never know the poet's exact motives, because Crane jumped into the Caribbean Sea in 1932 and took his secrets with him. It is equally unlikely we shall ever be able to prove with absolute certainty that Crane was a great punster; we can only hope, like the lawyers, to prove it beyond all reasonable doubt. Moreover, it is not essential to our argument to insist that Crane was necessarily conscious of every pun inside *The Bridge*. This is not an attempt to evade the issue at the last moment: the chances of Crane not being aware of the general Bridge-as-pun principle seem minimal, and it is equally improbable that he was ignorant of the punning oscillation between "How many dawns" and "Harmony dawns," for instance. But given the fragmentation and schizophrenic tendencies within his personal life, it is possible that Crane's facility for making puns may often have come to him instinctively. This split in his mind could have made it relatively easy for him to split up words and transform them into puns. For the "normal" person, the production of puns requires enormous effort and ingenuity, and such effort does not ordinarily seem worthwhile; but for Crane – in some moods – puns may have been a matter of natural course. W. R. Bion has pointed out how the pun is one of the emblems of schizophrenia, because the schizophrenic rebels against the reality-principle embedded in traditional verbal logic (which he sees as one of the contributory factors to his pain) and so splits words into syllables, and syllables into letters. The schizophrenic fragments external objects, including language, as an accompaniment to his fragmentation of the ego. Bion described schizophrenia as "the outcome of a determination which can be expressed verbally as an intention to be as many people as possible, so as to be in as many places as possible, so as to get as much as possible, for as long as possible – in fact timelessly."[32] This schizophrenic tendency was part of Crane's make-up for good as well as bad, and if it caused him unhappiness in his private life it also helped him to write *The Bridge*, which manipulates puns to enclose within itself a multiplicity of possible meanings. In its "intention to be as many people as possible," *The Bridge* is the literary equivalent to Bion's schizophrenic human being. William Empson's *Seven Types of Ambiguity* was published in 1930, the same year as *The Bridge*, and in Empson's terms the schizophrenic pun is his seventh or last type of ambiguity, "when the two meanings of the word, the two values of the ambiguity, are the two opposite meanings defined by the context, so that the total effect is to show a fundamental division in the writer's mind." Freudian theories of the unconscious clearly influenced Empson here – the poems of Crashaw, for instance, were said to be susceptible of "two interpretations, religious and sexual . . . such as would interest the psycho-analyst."[33] As a fervent rationalist, Empson was never quite at home with Freudian jargon, and his interest in Freud diminished as he grew older; but even in 1954, Empson was still boldly declaring (of a controversial reading of Hopkins): "to assert that the half-conscious pun is impossible is to ignore well-known facts about what strange things the mind can do."[34] So although the elaborate wordplay of *The Bridge* seems on the whole to be carefully arranged, some of the imagery – particularly the ubiquitous sexual imagery – may be unconscious emanations from a fragmented mind. One thinks of the ascending escalator in "The Tunnel," which appears to merge into an ascending penis that "Bursts suddenly in rain"; or of the subway train in the same stanza which "humps; then / Lets go" in a way more than faintly suggestive of coition. ("Much of the language of 'The Tunnel,'" as Unterecker has said, "is crawling with sexual overtones.")[35]

"THE BRIDGE" TODAY

The Bridge is such an extraordinarily complex poem that one is left with the frustrating feeling of having merely scratched its surface. What we need in due course is the kind of minute, line-by-line attention which annotators have paid to *Finnegans Wake*, so that we can appreciate more of the subtleties that must lie hidden in the text. *The Bridge* is witty, ironic, sacrilegious and erotic. It is a Surrealist poem, a capitalist poem and a poem of Relativity. It is an epic endeavour which confesses to having a mock-epic or burlesque underside. It is a poem of the criminal 1920s, the Prohibition era, when disguise and deception were all the rage. It is a secret homoerotic idyll which psychoanalytically questions its own sexual assumptions. It is a city poem, a poem about the urban fragmentation of identity; and it operates itself like a piece of new technology, assimilating the machine into its actual forms of expression. But above all, it is the second great work of the Revolution of the Word movement, the nearest thing to *Finnegans Wake* that we have – and indeed the publication of *The Bridge* pre-dated the complete published version of *Finnegans Wake* by nine years.

The Bridge is a poem open to many different interpretations. A Neoplatonic version would see Crane's fragmented puns as emblems of a fallen world where terrestrial word and absolute Word, "How many" and "Harmony," are always striving to become cognate. Other critics might judge *The Bridge* to be no more than a bravura self-referential performance, an "empty trapeze" (to quote from "National Winter Garden") which – like a Houdini trick – leaves the audience with nothing to take away at the end. (Although, as Edmund Wilson said after Houdini's death in 1928, "It is exhilarating, even in a juggler, even in a trapeze performer, to see some human skill or faculty carried to its furthest point, to a point where its feats seem incredible.")[36] But I would prefer to see *The Bridge* not simply as virtuoso acrobatics, but as a poem of radical scepticism where every proposition is susceptible of contradiction as the pun swings eternally between opposites. In this way, Crane's words seem to dance together in a gleeful circle of equivocation, liberated from the moralistic business of sedentary denotation. And from this point of view, light may be thrown on *The Bridge* by some of the comments in *Love's Body* (1966), a classic text of polymorphous perversity by the one-time guru Norman O. Brown. Brown invoked Dionysus, "the mad god" who "breaks down the boundaries . . . and abolishes the *principium individuationis*"; but he cleverly pursued the consequences of this dissolution in terms of psychology and language: "normality," he said, "is split-minded; in schizophrenia the false boundaries are disintegrating . . . Schizophrenics are suffering from the truth."[37] The pun was for Brown a weapon in the battle against his particular *bête noire*, Protestant literalism, where word and object meet. In puns, said Brown, following Bion, "two words get on top of each other and become sexual"; and he was also sympathetic to the Delphic Oracle who spoke in riddles and ambiguities and "never gave a straight answer, in the upright Protestant way":[38]

> Enigmatic form is living form; like life, an iridescence; an invitation to the dance; a temptation, or irritation. No satisfying solutions; nothing to rest in; nothing to weigh us down.
>
> Meaning is in the play, or interplay, of light. As in schizophrenia, all things lose their boundaries, become iridescent with many-colored significances. No things, but an iridescence, a rainbow effect. *Am farbigen Abglanz haben wir das Leben.* [Goethe, *Faust* II, I.] An indirect reflection; or refraction; broken light, or enigma.
>
> No things, but an iridescence in the void. Meaning is a continuous creation, out of nothing and returning to nothingness. If it is not evanescent it is not alive. Everything is symbolic, is transitory, is unstable. The consolidation of meaning makes idols; established meanings have turned to stone.
>
> Meaning is not in things but in between; in the iridescence, the interplay; in the interconnections; at the intersections, at the crossroads. Meaning is transitional as it is transitory; in the puns or bridges, the correspondence.[39]

"Meaning is transitional . . . in the puns or bridges." Pun becomes bridge, bridge becomes pun.

In a 1981 television interview, the English actor Ian McKellen discussed how American productions of Shakespeare tend to be long on energy and "vibrancy" and short on textual subtlety. "A pun of course is in the very heart of Shakespeare," said McKellen, quoting a speech of Macbeth ("and catch, / With his surcease, success") as a "brilliant use of two words which are almost the same sound, but have absolutely opposite meanings." "Irony," McKellen went on, "is not Americans' strong suit and . . . the pun is a form of comedy which is almost totally unrecognized in America."[40] It is perhaps not accurate to say the pun is this rare in the United States (witness Brougham and burlesque), but certainly most American interpreters of Crane have taken little heed of the ironies built into his work. Perhaps "highbrow" American culture, of which literary criticism is a part, has tended to abhor the pun as the provenance of gimcrack commercialism and stand-up comedians: in *The Wine of the Puritans* (1909), Van Wyck Brooks talked of how the "flash" – "juggling with words, double meanings, conundrums" – was typical of low American comedy, "a humor of the pure intelligence, so harsh that if it expressed an enduring mood it would be cynical."[41] Brooks, of course, disapproved of what he saw as this tinpan wit, contrasting it with the wise humour of a mature civilization that finds "true incongruities only in the deep, underlying facts of life."[42] But it might be argued that *The Bridge* is a poem which seeks to reunite the ethical commitment traditionally inherent in American "highbrow" culture with the irony and cynicism more typical of its "lowbrow" mode. And at any rate, it would be true to say that the "suspension of disbelief" involved in the ironic appreciation of a literary work is characteristic of our modern critical temper, highbrow or lowbrow. Margaret Drabble said in 1980 that *The Pilgrim's Progress* invariably brought tears to her eyes even though it was impossible to put faith in a single word Bunyan said as "true," and that this was typical of late twentieth-century reading where the emotions can give allegiance to works which the intellect deconstructs and exposes as naïve.[43] Irony is not so much a negative retraction of belief as a Nietzschean jubilance which allows art and life to exist without ultimately being believed in. Deprived of this appreciation of how human fictions work, we could only ever read works which conform to our own social prejudices. But because we recognize *The Pilgrim's Progress* as morally specious, we can be exhilarated and moved by imagining ourselves into the text, knowingly and temporarily assuming Bunyan's mask. If we were determined to read Bunyan for his "message" alone, he would never get an airing outside nonconformist churches. This is not to claim that art has no ethical content, nor that we should abrogate our responsibility of criticizing it according to the best ethical lights of our day; but we should remember that our reactions to Bunyan must themselves be influenced by the fictions of our time, and are liable to appear as outmoded as Bunyan himself within a few years. *The Bridge* combines moral exertion with ironic self-awareness, and its canonization of Brooklyn Bridge not only proposes a myth to God but sheds light on how all such myths function. It is because we know the myth is not true that we can believe it.

Appendix A
"Proem: To Brooklyn Bridge"

This analysis of the whole of the "Proem" does not pretend to be complete or final, but does at least start to give some idea of the complexities involved in *The Bridge*. Every section could be subjected to a similar analysis. The basic tension here is between the capitalist imagery, which seeks to give the symbol of the Bridge an impersonal validity, and a puncturing scepticism which would reduce this grandiose vision to the demented dream of a "bedlamite." The poem tilts between these opposites.

The following abbreviations, not used in the main text, are employed here: *n.*, noun; *vb*, verb; *adj.*, adjective; *subj.*, subject; *obj.*, object.

```
HOW  MANY   DAWNS,   CHILL   FROM   HIS   RIPPLING   REST
                     (a) cool (adj.)
                     (b) I will (vb, obs.)------------wrest
                                                      (a) distort
Harmony (n.)     dawns (vb)-----------------------(b) "move the
                                                      strings of (the
                                                      harp) in
                                                      playing" (obs.)
                                                      (c) "tune with a
                                                      wrest, or key"
                                                      (obs.)


THE  SEAGULL'S   WINGS   SHALL   DIP   AND   PIVOT   HIM,
     (a) bird      s--wings                   (a) pivot himself,
     (b) see/gull  (swings: poem swings       seagull - self-reflexive
     (dupe)        between opposites)         verb
                                              (b) seagull, like poem,
                                              "pivoted" between
                                              opposite meanings
```

225

SHEDDING   WHITE   RINGS   OF   TUMULT,   BUILDING   HIGH

(a) emitting— — — — — — — — — — —s— —of— —tumult   noun or
                                   soft you moult (seagull)   verb

(b) *shed*: "to   (a) rings,
divide (the   trails
warp) so as to   (b) wrings
form a shed"   of anguish
(Bridge as loom)
(c) "to separate;
to divide" (obs.)

OVER   THE   CHAINED   BAY   WATERS   LIBERTY —

(a) bay of NY harbor
– chain bridge is
another name for
suspension bridge – – –(a) noun– – –(a) Statue of Liberty
(b) water chained or   (b) Liberty of
imprisoned by poet– –(b) verb –   seagull in free
(c) chained bay   Liberty   flight
laurel wreath as   waters away
garland for seer

THEN,   WITH   INVIOLATE   CURVE,   FORSAKE   OUR   EYES

(a) sacred and   (a) curve beyond human sight
unbroken– – – – – –(a) curve   (spiritual)
                   of bridge,
                   curve of
                   seagull's
                   flight
                   (b) curve
                   of sales-
                   graph– – – –(b) renounce our eye/I –
                               abnegation of ego
                               (material)
(b) secure from
violation, not
capable of being
violated – Bridge
resists poet's
designs

AS   APPARITIONAL   AS   SAILS   THAT   CROSS

(a) poem as series of   (a) sails (nautical) – subject of *cross*
deliberate illusions   (b) sales (commercial) – object of *cross*
(b) (astronomy) – "first   (c) poem's meanings *cross* or intersect
appearance of a star . . .   (on page of figures)
after having been
invisible or obscured"
(Bridge as epiphany)

SOME   PAGE   OF   FIGURES   TO   BE   FILED   AWAY

page – man of humble status: *file* (n.) – artful person
so "page of figures" is (sl.); "rascal; cheat"
office-clerk (n., subj.), (obs.); – (vb) to pick
page of figures crossing off sales pockets, steal money
  (obs.)

figure – deviation from plain form
of statement – poem itself as
"page of figures"––––––––––––– poem as sleight-of-
  hand trick

TILL   ELEVATORS   DROP   US   FROM   OUR   DAY

(a) until(a) office elevators our––-day
(b) cash-register–––––––––––––––––––-oday, cash, money (sl.)
  (f)
cash-register's levers   part   us   from   oday

I   THINK   OF   CINEMAS,   PANORAMIC   SLEIGHTS

  (a) panorama of (a) sleight-of-hand
  cinema-screen trick (of cinema
  (b) cinemas as and poem)
  panoramic or (b) pun on "slights":
  ubiquitous slightness or
  throughout USA triviality of
  (c) continuous cinematic fictions
  revolving land-
  scape of poem

WITH   MULTITUDES   BENT   TOWARD   SOME   FLASHING   SCENE

  (a) bent in (a) transitory,
  prayer (cinema evanescent
  as cathedral) –––––––––(a) toward
  (b) "having very cinema
  little money;
  nearly broke"
  (sl.) (f) ––––––––––––––––––––––––(b) *flash*: "pertaining
  to thieves"; "dishonest.
  Underworld use" (f);
  "attractive or gaudy
  merchandise" (f) –
  cinema as capitalist
  trick

  (c) drunk
  "most pop.
  c. 1925" (sl.) (f) –––––––(b) to ward
  off–––––––––––(c) *flash* (n.) – "a play on
  words; a quibble" (obs.)
  – hence subversive
  punning

NEVER   DISCLOSED,   BUT   HASTENED   TO   AGAIN
                              (a) hurried———————(a) once more
(Cinema-audience trapped in cycle of illusions. Full meaning of cinema – and of poem – never
revealed to audience. Forbidden secrets of world outside Plato's cave)
                              (b) promoted—————(b) a/gain
(Cinema-owners exploit audience for profits)

FORETOLD   TO   OTHER   EYES   ON   THE   SAME   SCREEN;
(a) prophesied
(b) Four/told   her———eyes———on
(Four cables of   horizon
(Brooklyn Bridge)
Four told   to the   horizon   the   same   screen

AND   THEE,   ACROSS   THE   HARBOR,   SILVER–PACED
                   (a) linking Brooklyn with   (a) human pace:
                   Manhattan   personifying Bridge
                   (b) a/cross (n., obj.)
                   thee (n., subj.) harbor (vb)
                   (Bridge, like Christ,
                   harbouring a cross) ————————(b) *pace*: raised platform
                                                around religious altar
                                                (c) *pace*: device to
                                                maintain tension on
                                                warp (Bridge as loom)
                                                (d) silver-paste
                                                (tawdry cinematic prop)

AS   THOUGH   THE   SUN   TOOK   STEP   OF   THEE,   YET   LEFT
(Admission   (a) Bridge as sundial
of fiction)   (b) son: Bridge as Universal Father

SOME   MOTION   EVER   UNSPENT   IN   THY   STRIDE, —
                   (a) movement: sun revolves around Bridge
                   (b) change of
                   pitch in
                   successive
                   tones (music)
                        n— —ever———uns   hy———stride
                        never runs: sun is   hy st/ride
                        static
sum (of money) ——————————— spent
                        (money) ————— High St ride

IMPLICITLY   THY   FREEDOM   STAYING   THEE!

implicit not   (a) supporting
explicit   (b) *stay* (engineering) – a
                                      part in tension which holds the structure
                                      together. Here, a technical term for the cables that
                                      keep the roadbed from twisting

OUT   OF   SOME   SUBWAY   SCUTTLE,   CELL   OR   LOFT

                          (a) (n.) – hole in   bathos   or   idealism
                          sidewalk leading
                          down to subway   sell   lofty,
                          (b) (vb) – to   (capitalism)   aloof
                          overthrow: Romantic
                          bathos of   poet
                          subway scuttles
                          poem's idealism

A   BEDLAMITE   SPEEDS   TO   THY   PARAPETS

(a) lunatic (from
Mary of Bethlehem
hospital)– – – – – – – – – – – – – – – – – – –(a) low wall at edge
(b) son of Mary of   of bridge
Bethlehem, Jesus Christ   (b) wall for soldiers'
                                      protection (medieval
                                      imagery)

TILTING   THERE   MOMENTLY,   SHRILL   SHIRT   BALLOONING,

(a) bedlamite   (a) shrill
falling off bridge – – – – – – – – – – – – – –cry – – – – –(a) mad-
(b) medieval   (a) momentarily   man's shirt   (a) as if in flight
joust   (idealism)
(c) Till-ting,
ring of cash-register – – – – – – – – – – – –(b) shrill
                                      ring of
                                      till – – – – –(b) financial
                                      stake – – – – –(b) expansion or
                                                     ballooning of
                                                     profits for
(d) oscillating – – – – –(b) moment force   entrepreneur who
                         about a point   has put his *shirt*
                         or axis: on a business
                         oscillation   gamble

A JEST FALLS FROM THE SPEECHLESS CARAVAN.

(a) comic
jest—————opposite of
            ballooning –
            downward bathos———————————(a) line of
                                                                        modern
                                                                        cars

(b) medieval
geste, story
of epic
action——————————————————————(b) medieval
                                                                        company of
                                                                        travellers or
                                                                        pilgrims

DOWN WALL, FROM GIRDER INTO STREET NOON LEAKS,

(a) Down Wall   (a) steel girder   (a) 12 noon leaks (vb)
Street   (b) *gird* (vb)
                                           to encircle –
                                           (all-embracing
                                           social construct)——————(b) no (adj.,
                                           (c) knight "girding"   obs., medieval)
                                           himself for battle
                                           (medieval)   leaks (n.) –
                                                                                                         hence "no leaks":
(b) disintegration   preservation of social
of social   edifices: paradoxical
boundaries and   (d) a mocker or   opposite to Down Wall
walls of decorum—————caviller ————————————————(c) urinates
                                                                                                         (sl.) –
                                                                                                         leaks (vb); a rip (n.)

A RIP-TOOTH OF THE SKY'S ACETYLENE;

(a) for citizens on Wall St, small   (a) brilliant
gap where sky appears between   colourless gas
skyscrapers is like gap where   (spiritual grandeur)
tooth has been ripped out of a
man's mouth
(b) *rip*: worthless person,
scamp, debauchee——————————(b) etymology of *acetum*,
(c) *rip*: water made rough   vinegar; hence acetic –
by meeting of opposite   of vinegar (alcoholic
currents (poem pulling   inebriation)
opposite ways)

ALL AFTERNOON THE CLOUD–FLOWN DERRICKS TURN . . .

all———after
all laughter

(a) derrick
crane or
crane——————(a) rotate
(b) Crane him-
self as the
cloud-flown
derrick,
the crane with
its head in the
clouds—————(b) of head or
(c) hanging,   brain, to
gallows (obs.) become giddy or
– poet as   dizzy (alcoholic
outcast   inebriation)
                       (c) poem's
                       meaning turns
                       and turns about

THY CABLES BREATHE THE NORTH ATLANTIC STILL.

(a) cables of
bridge, like
cable-ropes
of ship:
Bridge as ship——————————————————————————(a) motionless
(b) submarine line
containing insulated
wires – (hidden wires
hold hidden meanings)———————————————————(b) even now –
                                                                    i.e., water
                                                                    infiltrates
                                                                    mythic system

AND OBSCURE AS THAT HEAVEN OF THE JEWS,

obscure: "inconspicuous   Jews associated with high finance:
to the sight; indistinctly   Bridge as ideal symbol (or *heaven*)
seen" – capitalist imagery is   of capitalism
concealed within the poem

THY GUERDON . . . ACCOLADE THOU DOST BESTOW

(a) reward
(medieval) ———————(a) embrace to mark
(b) Etymology   conferring of
of German   knighthood (medieval)
widarlon,   (b) in music, brace to
"parts which   join two or more
resist the   staves carrying
pull or strain   simultaneous parts
in drawing a   (symphonic form)
load" (scepticism)————(c) reversed curve in
                              a pointed arch (inversion)

OF   ANONYMITY   TIME   CANNOT   RAISE:

("forsake our eyes")   (a) raise up (from anonymity)
                                                        (b) raze, destroy
                                                        (time cannot destroy poem)

VIBRANT   REPRIEVE   AND   PARDON   THOU   DOST   SHOW.

(a) thrilling   religious
(b) vibrating,   indulgence
oscillating- - -etymology of   (medieval)
          French *reprendre*,
          take back, retract

O   HARP   AND   ALTAR,   OF   THE   FURY   FUSED,

Aeolian harp- - - - - -(a) religious
                      altar- - - - - - - - - - -(a) divine
                                                artistic
                                                furies - - - (a) brought
                      (b) alter,   together
                      alteration,
                      poem's
                      oscillation- - - - - - - -(b) personal
                                                rage of
                                                bedlamite- -(b) broken
                      (c) *alter*: "to   (c) Greek   down – cf.
                      geld" (colloq.)   furies,
                                                angry or   fused electric
                                                malignant   circuit
                                                woman,
                                                avenging
                                                goddess
                                                (Crane's
                                                mother)- - -(c) neutered
                                                             (sexually)

(HOW   COULD   MERE   TOIL   ALIGN   THY   CHOIRING   STRINGS!)
                      (a) nothing
                      but - - - (a) labour - - - - - - - - - - - - - - - -(a) strings
                      (b) *mer*, sea - - - -a lie in - - - - - -quire-ing   of harp
                              (b) web: Bridge
                              Bridge   made out
                              as loom   of quires
                      (c) *mère*,   of paper- - - - -(b) string
                      mother   as hoax,
                      (French)   "stringing
                      cf. *fury*- -(c) net or   along"
                              snare (of
                              jealous
                              mother)

TERRIFIC   THRESHOLD   OF   THE   PROPHET'S   PLEDGE,

threshold
of new era— — — — — — — — — —(a) sage's— — — —(a) promise
                                                              (b) drinking-toast
                                   (b) profits'— — —(c) financial
                                                        guarantee

PRAYER   OF   PARIAH,   AND   THE   LOVER'S   CRY, —

(a) social outcast
(alienation)
(b) large drum
beaten at certain
festivals (celebration)

AGAIN   THE   TRAFFIC   LIGHTS   THAT   SKIM   THY   SWIFT

(a) once
more— — — — — — —(a) road signs— — — — — — — — — —(a) glide
(b) a/gain   over (vb) — — — —(a) rapid
(commercial   (b) trade   illuminates— — — — —(b) (n., obj.)   (adj.)
gain)— — — — — — —(n.)   (vb)   "that which is
                                                    skimmed; hence,
                                                    scum; film;
                                                    also, refuse" —
                                                    skim and *scum*
                                                    are etymologi —
                                                    cally cognate — — (b) (n., subj.) —
                                                                      reel for winding
                                                                      yarn and thread:
                                                                      Bridge as loom

UNFRACTIONED   IDIOM,   IMMACULATE   SIGH   OF   STARS,

fraction: amount less   (a) celestial
than unit of dealing   stars
on stock exchange —   pure, without
hence "Unfractioned"   spots or marks
means "sufficient   (Bridge as
for dealing"   Madonna)— — — — — — — — — — — —(b) "bright spot
                                                               or flaw in the
                                                               surface of steel"
                                                               (paradoxical
                                                               opposition to
                                                               "immaculate")

(Bridge as spiritual as Virgin Mary; but, by a syntactical reversal: Bridge, Unfractioned idiom, lights that skim, redeems the refuse of the business world by investing it with symbolic grandeur)

BEADING   THY   PATH   —   CONDENSE   ETERNITY:

(a) beads of
traffic lights
(b) Christian
rosary-beads
(cf. "immaculate")
(c) bubbles formed
by effervescence
in alcohol– – – – – – –pathos,
              suffering

(a) chemical condensation:
nature refracted into art
(b) *condenser*: device to
transmute web into yarn
(Bridge as loom)
(c) con/dense, eternity can
only be "condensed" by a
dense con-trick

AND   WE   HAVE   SEEN   NIGHT   LIFTED   IN   THINE   ARMS.

(a) alleviated
(b) *lift*: mechanism
for winding on
bobbin
(Bridge as loom)
(c) taken away
dishonestly – – – – – – – –(c) offensive

(a) arms of Bridge
as Virgin Mary
(b) arms of medieval
joust; heraldic
devices

            weapons: hence,
            force of arms

UNDER   THY   SHADOW   BY   THE   PIERS   I   WAITED;

(a) in vicinity
of Bridge
(b) four-cornered
light sail
(Bridge as ship)
(c) reflected image,
unreal, counterfeit:
mythic Bridge as
"shadowy" – – – – – – – – – – – – – –(c) "weighted" down

(a) attended
(b) "waited on,"
courted, serenaded

            with symbolic
            significance
            (reductive)

ONLY   IN   DARKNESS   IS   THY   SHADOW   CLEAR.
          (a) night-time— — — — — — —(a) illuminated
                                    shadow — — — —(a) visible
                                                  (b) out of
                                                  debt

     (b) darkness of
     nihilism
     engenders
     need for
     Bridge — — — — — — — — — — (b) shadow
                                meaning
                                produced by
                                obstruction
                                of light,
                                sound etc.— — —(c) transparent:
                                              Bridge's
                                              symbolic
                                              pretensions can
                                              be seen through
(Paradox: in times of darkness, either the Bridge's shadow shines resplendently, or its sceptical
shadow-meaning is more apparent)

THE   CITY'S   FIERY   PARCELS   ALL   UNDONE,
                    (a) New York's
                    lights— — — — — — — — —(a) brought out,
     fiery: shining brightly
     etymologically
     Old French
     feur (price,
     standard), Latin
     forum (market) — — — —(b) par/sells,
                          selling stocks
                          at par— — — — — — — —(b) undo: "to cover
                                              (a transaction) by
                                              a purchase or sale
                                              with another" (on
                                              stock market)

ALREADY   SNOW   SUBMERGES   AN   IRON   YEAR . . .
     (a) imagery of Christmas and New Year (Christian redemption)
     (b) snow:
     "deceptive,
     exaggerated,
     or flattering
     talk" (sl.) (f) — — — — — — — — — — — silver
                                        coins
                                        (sl.) (f) — —dollar-bill (sl.) (f)
(One shadow-meaning suggests Bridge itself has been dealing on the money-markets and is
clear in the sense of having settled its account with the New York business world)

O SLEEPLESS AS THE RIVER UNDER THEE,

(a) Bridge sleepless as natural
world
(b) Lover is
sleepless— — — — — — — — — —(b) one
                                    who rives
                                    (homoerotic)

VAULTING THE SEA, THE PRAIRIES' DREAMING SOD,

(a) Bridge vaulting
over water— —(a) sod
(b) lover vaulting   of earth
over mate:
e.g. "vaulting house"
is "a brothel" (obs.)— — — — — — — — — — — — — — reaming,
                                         buggering— — — —(b) sodomite

UNTO US LOWLIEST SOMETIME SWEEP,   DESCEND

        (a) meek,
        religious— — — — — — — — — — — —(a) glide
                                      majestically
                                      (b) purify,
                                      sweep clean
                                      (c) "any part
                                      of a ship
                                      shaped in a
                                      segment of
                                      a circle"
                                      (Bridge as
        (b) self-abasing: ship)
        grovelling— — — — — — — — — — — —(d) *sweep* (n.):
                                      whip— — — — — — — — whip descends:
                                      (e) *sweep* (vb):   poet's masochism
                                      "tendency to
                                      settle to
                                      thermal equilibrium
                                      of a substance"
                                      (balancing tensions)

AND OF THE CURVESHIP LEND A MYTH TO GOD.

        (a) Bridge as ship   (a) allow temporary
        (curve*ship*)   custody of (myth
        (b) *ship*: dish   as fabrication)
        used to hold
        religious
        incense (obs.)— —God
        (c) Einsteinian
        curve
        (relativity)
        (d) curve of
        sales-graph— — — — — — —(b) *lend*: let
                                out money from
                                business profits
                                — Bridge as
                                capitalist myth

Appendix B
"James Joyce and his Followers," by Rebecca West

(From the *New York Herald Tribune*, 12 January 1930)

There can have been in the whole history of Europe since the Dark Ages no period so destructive of the serenity which the artist needs if the images proceeding from him shall people the mind of the world. At every other time than this he has been supported by the conviction that man would be saved either by a religious process open to all or by his reason. Never before has he had to look at reality with a more desperate sense that his salvation depends on his knowledge of it and that his intellectual mechanism is determined to betray him by distorting all his perceptions of it. There is, of course, light in the eastern sky in the possibility that psychology, working on its own, will so reveal the nature and cause of those distorting dispositions in the human mind that artist and audience alike will be able to clear them out of the way. In the mean time it is reasonable to regard as the salt of the earth those who can go on functioning artistically in spite of these disadvantageous circumstances. Only through the efforts of such can tradition be truly continuous and civilization pass the present bad break; and it is comical that when one looks round to see who is doing this eminently conservative task, one finds none but those who are regarded as revolutionary writers. It is still more comical that of these the most successful is the most revolutionary.

For, though Virginia Woolf can send out the potent image, she stands alone. She has enough strength to carry her through her round trip to reality, and no more. She has founded no school. Though she seems to be surrounded by the intellectuals of her country, it is impossible to avoid suspecting that this is a device similar to that by which people who want to live in the strictest privacy go to stay in the most vast and crowded hotels. In a tiny cottage on the moors there is the man who leaves the milk every day, there is the woman who comes for the washing every week; hey, presto! there are a hundred calls on one to be radiating ego. In the great hotel where everybody has his preoccupations, one can be the violet beneath the mossy stone. For all the part Mrs. Woolf plays in Bloomsbury not one of her followers shows the slightest sign of writing any the better since she published *Orlando*.

And though D. H. Lawrence can send out the potent image, he walks alone. He has strength to carry him a dozen trips winding snakewise round the globe of reality, but it will not send him one step on the way of a companioned voyage. He, too, has founded no school. He is a lens before the eyes of all our generation; we see certain occasions as he has told us to see them. One or two writers – such as Mr. Edward Sackville-West – are recognizably children of his imagination. But he has talked to us more about life than about art. How he has been able to use literature as a probe to cut deeper into reality than the non-artist can do he has certainly never explained; and perhaps, during the not very long time he has been blown about the earth as a flame-colored wisp, he has never had time to ask. Freedom he asks for art, as every sane man does; but he goes very little further. Which means that, though his own glory is very great, he will not build that glory as firmly into the tradition of letters as if he could deliver a critical exposition of what his own function is.

But that James Joyce has done, as well as sending out the potent image. For if one looks round for the group that is cohering before the peril of the age in a formation that seems most likely to procure survival, one will probably find it in the group that, largely to his honor and glory, runs the magazine *Transition*.

This may seem an astonishing choice for those who want above all things to secure the persistence of tradition, the continuity of art; and it needs a certain amount of justification. It is perfectly true that there is no one in this *Transition* group who has written, or seems likely to write, as good a poem as *The Waste Land*. It is perfectly true that most of the fiction published in its pages is of more naive content than Mr. Huxley would feed as subject to his muse; though there are writers – notably Kay Boyle – to whom this stricture does not apply. But there must be recognized here also the effects of the double function that the artist has at present to exercise. If their creative achievements have not the finish that they might have it is probable that this is because they have spent so much of their energies in research into, or appreciation of, the creative processes in others. They are engaged in transactions on such a large scale that, where they make losses, these seem pretty heavy; but the losses are counterbalanced by the gains, which also are true to the scale. This is so, too, in relation to the creative process in which they are most interested; that is, the workings of Mr. James Joyce's genius.

At present there might be suspected to be a heavy loss sustained in that quarter, because it appears more than possible that in "Work in Progress" he is following – if not a blind alley – for no path along which a genius travels can remain that for long – but an avenue hardly wide enough for the army of his powers. One cannot come to any final opinion on the subject until the whole of the book has been published.

It must be remembered how when only half of *A la Recherche du Temps Perdu* was published the complaint against Proust was that his book had no order and no design; whereas the completed work showed that if he had a fault it was that he had pledged himself from the first to symmetry almost too absolute, and controlled his characters too rigidly to maintain it. (Those who are reading it in English will find that the volume published under the name *The Prisoner*, the recital of the author's tyrannous relationship with Albertine, which seems like a long and rather tiresome fugue, produces quite a different effect when one has read the succeeding volume, in which the author, distraught with grief over Albertine's death, is reduced to panic by a telegram that seems to announce that she is not dead after all. When one has reached this climax of ambivalence one sees that all the cunning twists and turns of his relationship with the girl, his sharp alternations of love and hate, have been designed to tighten up one's nerves for this explosion.)

Quite possibly some features will appear in "Work in Progress" in its completed form, which will remove all the objections that at present rise up against it in the mind of any reader outside the cult. But since his own followers insist on discussing it at the present stage, and since if he does remove these objections, he will practically stand everything that is known about the human mind upside down, it is worth while stating them.

The distinctive attribute of "Work in Progress" is that it is not written in English, or in any other language. Most of the words that James Joyce uses are *patés de langue gras*. Each is a paste of words that have been superimposed one on another and worked into a new word that shall be the lowest common multiple of them all. These words have been chosen out of innumerable languages, living and dead, either because of some association of ideas or of sound. They are "portmanteau" words such as Lewis Carroll invented when he wrote "Jabberwocky": " 'T was brillig and the slithy toves Did gyre and gimble in the wabe." They are chosen, often but not always, in the sly, punning spirit that looks for disguises by which forbidden things may leer and sidle past the censor; so that very frequently by their grossness they recall Leopold Bloom out of *Ulysses*, great embodiment of the repressed side of man. They are sometimes strung together in sequences that do not obey the ordinary laws of syntax.

The common accusation against the result of these processes is that it is incomprehensible. It is nothing of the sort. Unless one's parents brought one up in an unusual state of seclusion from contacts with the classics and the Teutonic and Latin languages, it is hard to avoid finding one's way through it. There emerges from the text clearly enough not only a superficial pattern of verbal suggestion which is intricate and amusing and occasionally poetically beautiful, but a phantasmagoria of types that represent the main forms thrown up by history. It cannot be read as quickly as ordinary English, just as a cross-word puzzle cannot be read as quickly as the words it contains set up in ordinary form. But that is the only thing against it from the reader's point of view. Granted it will take him ten times as long to read as an equal number of words put into ordinary Anglo-American realist novels, he will get ten times as much entertainment.

The main objections that make one, in spite of the fact that one is entertained, wonder whether James Joyce is not misapplying his genius in using this new form are three, and one of them involves this very question of effort and time. Even the youngest child in the nursery who hears the rhyme about the general who marched his troops up a hill and then marched them down again and went home to his tea is conscious that the chances are that this was not a very good general. The movements that sanction those who move in this universe are those that have results. Those that do not are taken as mere dithering spendthrifts of time and therefore discreditable to the doers. But if Mr. James Joyce is to take ten, or twenty, or thirty years packing allusions into portmanteau words; and if his readers are to take twelve (since a cipher takes longer for a stranger to read than for its inventor to write) or twenty-five, or forty years unpacking these allusions out of the portmanteau words, it is impossible to avoid the suspicion that troops have been marched up a hill and then down again. A work of art planned in a medium and then executed in a second medium, which cannot be comprehended by any audience unless they can transport it by mental effort back into the first medium, is a crazy conception, and even Mr. Joyce's most devoted followers do regard it as essential that they should unmake his words into the constituents of which he made them, and should acquaint themselves with his subject matter as it appeared to him before he clothed it in these words.

Another objection, which certainly cannot be resolved until "Work in Progress" is complete, is esthetic. We are all of us familiar with Croce's statement that an allegory from which we have to detach the secondary meaning by a purely intellectual process cannot give complete esthetic pleasure. The diffusion of interest, or rather the difference of value between the drama enacted by the symbols and the relationship between the abstractions they symbolize splits up the attention of the mind, is not in the right state of unity for esthetic perception. It would seem that the intellectual effort required to unmake James Joyce's words into their constituent parts would perpetually be splitting up the attention and breaking up the state of unity in which the mind must be to accept, say, his personification of the life of a river, the stream of creation. One remembers that there was in *Ulysses* a curious demonstration of Mr. Joyce's failure to appreciate the effect on the mind of simultaneous presentation of objects on different planes. The parallelism between *Ulysses* and the odyssey which James Joyce carefully contrives by sending Stephen Dedalus through incidents that correspond with the Odyssean wanderings is justified by him and his followers as being designed to afford a contrast between the Manichean spirit manifested by Joyce and the Greek spirit manifested in Homer. But it does nothing of the sort, because there can be no real contrast between its esthetic rendering of the Manichean spirit and its purely factual references (through these correspondences) to the Greek spirit, of which the intellect is invited to remember as much as it can, but which is never esthetically recreated. The two are almost as widely divided in their appeal to the attention as the printing on the page and the page numbers. At present "Work in Progress" seems to be invalidated by more diffused addiction to the same error; but we shall see.

There are two other objections, which both have reference to psychology. It is impossible to discuss James Joyce without frequent references to psychology, since nearly all of his recent subject matter and much of his technique he derives from his knowledge of Freud and Jung. The first point on which one would like to be satisfied is whether the main function he is trying to make the word perform is not one which is properly performed by the image in the mind for which the word is only a counter. "Work in Progress" is largely founded on the philosophy of Giambattista Vico, a late seventeenth-century early eighteenth-century Neapolitan who was popularized by Croce in one of his most charming books, and is a pet of the psychoanalysts because his philosophy of history accords with their conclusions. To condense his teaching, he saw that humanity invents its myths and advances through the world of action making life square with those myths, and therefore creates itself. This reciprocal movement between humanity and nature, the rhythm by which alternately the necessities of birth and maturity and death control man and man controls birth and maturity and death, give Vico his doctrine of reflux. Man was always freeing his will, and then being thrust down to helpless sensation again, and then rising again to a state of free will; and so on. It is Joyce's theory that if words are so handled as to recall meanings they had in the past we will go back into the experience of the race in these bygone phases, and revitalize the words and ourselves by knowledge of these eternal and recurrent processes. But this does not seem to be necessary, if, as Freud and Jung hold in their different ways and to different degrees, the mind of man inherits in his unconscious the collective mythos of mankind and is perpetually in touch with it. That view cannot be considered irrelevant in this connection, because James Joyce has himself accepted it. The aim of this book is to make the unconscious conscious; and it represents the unconscious as a storehouse of primitive myths. It appears clumsy and uneconomical, then, to use obsolete words in order to bring the past to the present when an image spontaneously springing up from the unconscious will do the same thing with much more dynamic force.

The other objection to "Work in Progress" concerning the word has also to do with James Joyce's psychological sources. Obviously, he got this idea of the word-paste from the Freudian and Jungian analyses of the puns people make in dreams. These are resolved into their constituents when the dreamer practices free association on them. For example, a woman will dream that her hair has grown very long and that some one comes into the room and says: "This is the criminolation form of wearing one's hair." The patient, talking at random round the word, will be reminded of the words "crinis," Latin for hair, and crinkly, the fact being that there is an ancient rumor of black blood in the family, which would "incriminate" her if it were known. The word "crinoline" also comes to her, and she remembers that the garment was invented by the Empress Eugenie to conceal the arrival of the Prince Imperial; and since she has a strong sense of guilt about sex, motherhood seems as "incriminating" as black blood. So on the detective work goes, until it uncovers some complex in the unconscious. Now, why does James Joyce invent these words? Has he a naive faith that since free association shows the direct connection between such a word and the unconscious the invention of such a word by reversing the process of free association will automatically drive a connection down into the unconscious? Surely not. He must have entirely created the psyche which he is expressing; he must have before him its conscious and its unconscious and be completely aware of its contents and their relationship. Every portmanteau word he invents must have its causal connection in one of the mythological figures he describes. Then why is there no sense of clarity, of the gratification that comes from comprehension, such as pervades an analysis that is successful in coping with its subject matter in the same way, and any work of art, such as *King Lear* or *The Divine Comedy* that has resolved the matter in the terms of its age? Is it because James Joyce feels a disposition, when in doubt, to create an effect of disintegration because the most satisfactory creation of his genius up to this date has been Leopold Bloom, the disintegrator? Or is there some new sort of clarity that will appear in the completion of "Work in Progress"?

I would not myself stake a penny on any of my objections. I state them only because it seems to me of interest to consider what points James Joyce will have to make if he is to quell all resistance in the minds of his age who are looking for the inheritor of art and would like to find it in him. Can one think of any other writer concerning whose work such interesting considerations arise? Do they not make the ordinary naturalist novel by Arnold Bennett or John Galsworthy seem like the very body of death? And his followers, too, in their robust faith in him, are in the right frame of mind. They realize that though the intellect is to be distrusted, there is something else that transacts the holy business of the artist. Theirs, almost alone today, is a religious attitude to art.

(Reprinted by permission of A. D. Peters and Co. Ltd)

Notes

(N.B.: The dates of letters from Hart Crane are supplied only when not given in the text.)

I. BRIDGE AS PUN

1 Hart Crane, "General Aims and Theories" (1924), in *The Complete Poems and Selected Letters and Prose of Hart Crane*, ed. Brom Weber (New York: Liveright, 1966), p. 217; p. 220; p. 217.
2 Ibid. p. 220; p. 219.
3 Ralph Waldo Emerson, "The Poet," in *Essays: Second Series* (1844), vol. III of *The Riverside Edition of Emerson's Complete Works* (London, 1883), p. 40.
4 R. W. Butterfield, *The Broken Arc: A Study of Hart Crane* (Edinburgh: Oliver and Boyd, 1969), p. 184.
5 Ibid. p. 201.
6 Thomas Parkinson, ed., *Hart Crane and Yvor Winters: Their Literary Correspondence* (Berkeley: Univ. of California Press, 1978), p. 79 (29 April 1927); Sherman Paul, *Hart's Bridge* (Urbana: Univ. of Illinois Press, 1972), p. 246; p. 250. The most thorough analysis of these analogies is in Glauco Cambon's *The Inclusive Flame* (Bloomington: Indiana Univ. Press, 1963). Cambon finds that "a thick network of thematic links, recurrences, and developments connects the various parts of the poem, so that its true physiognomy seems to be definable as one cycle of closely related compositions" (p. 123).
7 Brom Weber, ed., *The Letters of Hart Crane 1916–1932* (1952; rpt Berkeley: Univ. of California Press, 1965), p. 353.
8 Allen Tate, "Hart Crane" (1932–7), rpt in *Essays of Four Decades* (London: Oxford Univ. Press, 1970), p. 315.
9 Stanley K. Coffman, "Symbolism in *The Bridge*," *PMLA*, 66 (1951), 72. The theatrical context here was suggested to me in a letter from John Unterecker, 21 Sept. 1983. Mr Mander, of the London Society of West End Theatres, informs me that "Palladium," like "Empire" or "Coliseum," is a stock name for a place of entertainment, and that the New Yorker Theatre, 254 West Fifty-fourth Street, was between 1936 and 1937 called the Palladium.
10 Weber, *Letters*, p. 274 (19 Aug. 1926).
11 Ibid. p. 142 (11 Aug. 1923).

242

12 The title "The Wires of the Acropolis" is evident from a letter of Crane to Stieglitz, 25 Aug. 1923. Ibid. p. 146. The sentence from this essay quoted in the text comes from the fragment which Crane enclosed in a letter to Stieglitz, 15 April 1923. Ibid. p. 132. Stieglitz's reaction is recounted in an unpublished letter from Crane to Charles Harris, 19 April 1923, held in the Department of Special Collections, Kent State University Libraries. For Crane's letter to Stieglitz on 4 July 1923, see Weber, *Letters*, p. 138.
13 Weber, *Letters*, p. 232.
14 Butterfield, p. 211; Helge Normann Nilsen, "Memories of Hart Crane: A Talk with Emil Opffer," *Hart Crane Newsletter*, 2, no. 1 (1978), 10.
15 R. W. B. Lewis, *The Poetry of Hart Crane* (Princeton: Princeton Univ. Press, 1967), p. 380.
16 Joseph N. Riddel, "Hart Crane's Poetics of Failure" (1966), rpt in *Modern American Poetry: Essays in Criticism*, ed. Jerome Mazzaro (New York: David McKay, 1970), p. 283; p. 282.
17 Allen Grossman, "Hart Crane and Poetry: A Consideration of Crane's Intense Poetics with Reference to 'The Return,'" *ELH*, 48 (1981), 850; Weber, *Letters*, p. 274 (19 Aug. 1926).
18 Grossman, p. 850.
19 Roger Ramsey, "A Poetics for *The Bridge*," *Twentieth Century Literature*, 26 (1980), 282; 284; 279; 286.
20 Paul, *Hart's Bridge*, p. 260.
21 Eugene Paul Nassar, *The Rape of Cinderella* (Bloomington: Indiana Univ. Press, 1970), p. 161. For Crane on Hopkins, see Weber, *Letters*, p. 317; p. 319 (4 March 1928). Crane to Winters in Parkinson, p. 69 (19 March 1927).
22 Lewis, *Poetry of Hart Crane*, p. 254; p. 255; p. 260.
23 Richard P. Sugg, *Hart Crane's "The Bridge"* (n.p.: Univ. of Alabama Press, 1976), p. 94.
24 Weber, *Letters*, p. 374 (20 June 1931). Crane also mentioned his "condensed metaphorical habit" in a letter to Waldo Frank, 18 Jan. 1926. See ibid. p. 232.
25 Crane, "General Aims," in *Complete Poems*, p. 221; pp. 222–3.
26 Malcolm Cowley, *A Second Flowering* (New York: Viking, 1973), p. 208.
27 Quoted in John Unterecker, *Voyager: A Life of Hart Crane* (New York: Farrar, Straus and Giroux, 1969), p. 649.
28 Malcolm Cowley, *Exile's Return*, rev. ed. (1951; rpt Harmondsworth: Penguin, 1976), p. 231.
29 Ibid. p. 230; Cowley, *Second Flowering*, p. 207.
30 Kenneth A. Lohf, "The Prose Manuscripts of Hart Crane," *Proof*, 2 (1972), 34; 36; 35.
31 Susan Jenkins Brown, *Robber Rocks: Letters and Memories of Hart Crane, 1926–1932* (Middletown, Connecticut: Wesleyan Univ. Press, 1969), p. 136.

2. RELATIVITY

1 For Ouspensky, see Weber, *Letters*, p. 124.
2 P. D. Ouspensky, *Tertium Organum* (1912), trans. Nicholas Bessaraboff and Claude Bragdon (London: Routledge and Kegan Paul, 1973), p. 63; p. 214.
3 Ibid. p. 108.
4 Ibid. p. 19; p. 137; pp. 108–9.
5 Hyatt Howe Waggoner, *The Heel of Elohim* (Norman: Univ. of Oklahoma Press, 1950), p. 169.
6 Malcolm Haslam, *The Real World of the Surrealists* (London: Weidenfeld and Nicolson, 1978), p. 99.

7 Weber, *Letters*, p. 235; Williams quoted in Mike Weaver, *William Carlos Williams* (Cambridge: Cambridge Univ. Press, 1971), p. 48.
8 A. N. Whitehead, *Science and the Modern World* (1925; rpt New York: Mentor – New American Library, 1948), p. 49; p. 23; p. 59.
9 Ibid. p. 110.
10 Ibid. p. 68; p. 70.
11 Ibid. p. 70; p. 71; p. 87.
12 Ibid. p. 64.
13 William Carlos Williams, *The Collected Later Poems* ([London]: MacGibbon and Kee, 1965), p. 75.
14 This variant reading has been confirmed to me by Marc Simon, editor of a forthcoming variorum edition of Crane's poetry: "in Crane's 'Ave Maria,' document B6 (Lohf, *Literary Manuscripts of Hart Crane*), line 88 reads *asway* with no hyphen. This dates from circa Jan. 1926. No other extant *asway* text, with no hyphen, appears in my survey. All the rest have the hyphenated form." Letter received from Marc Simon, 8 July 1983.
15 Samuel Johnson, "Preface to Shakespeare" (1768), in *The Works of Samuel Johnson*, ed. Arthur Murphy (London, 1816), II, 94; Harvey Gross, *Sound and Form in Modern Poetry* (Ann Arbor: Univ. of Michigan Press, 1964), p. 222; Herman Melville, *Moby-Dick* (1851), ed. Harold Beaver (Harmondsworth: Penguin, 1972), p. 476.
16 Brom Weber, *Hart Crane: A Biographical and Critical Study* (New York: Bodley Press, 1948), pp. 333–4.
17 Ibid. p. 346.
18 Hart Crane, "A Letter to Harriet Monroe" (1926), in *Complete Poems*, p. 239.
19 Crane made this comment about "Ave Maria" in a letter to Waldo Frank, 26 July 1926. Weber, *Letters*, p. 268.
20 Ibid. p. 240; Parkinson, p. 79.
21 Weber, *Letters*, p. 375.
22 Louis Untermeyer, "Einstein and the Poets," *Broom*, 1 (Nov. 1921), 88.
23 Louis Untermeyer, "Rhyme and Relativity" (1921), rpt in *"Vanity Fair": Selections from America's Most Memorable Magazine*, ed. Cleveland Amory and Frederic Bradlee (New York: Viking, 1960), p. 55.
24 Whitehead, p. 141.
25 Herbert A. Leibowitz, *Hart Crane: An Introduction to the Poetry* (New York: Columbia Univ. Press, 1968), p. 97; p. 91.

3. CAPITALISM

1 Weber, *Letters*, p. 268 (26 July 1926).
2 Waldo Frank, *Our America* (1920), rpt as *The New America* (London: Cape, 1922), p. 191.
3 Brooks quoted in James Hoopes, *Van Wyck Brooks: In Search of American Culture* (Amherst: Univ. of Massachusetts Press, 1977), p. 15; Cowley, *Exile's Return*, p. 106; p. 107.
4 Frank, *New America*, p. 192.
5 Matthew Josephson, *Life among the Surrealists* (New York: Holt, Rinehart and Winston, 1962), p. 189; Josephson, "Made in America," *Broom*, 2 (June 1922), 270.
6 For 1919 interview, see Unterecker, *Voyager*, p. 156. Letter to Winters in Parkinson, p. 59. "Recitative" discussed in a letter to Gorham Munson, 10 Dec. 1923, Weber, *Letters*, p. 161.

7 Weber, *Letters*, p. 241 (18 March 1926).
8 For Boston and China tea, see Cowley, *Exile's Return*, p. 29. For the history of *Taeping* and *Ariel*, see Stephen Fender, *The American Long Poem: An Annotated Selection* (London: Edward Arnold, 1977), p. 65.
9 Crane's conceptual and linguistic equation of eye and I was recalled by his cousin, Helen Hart Hurlbert: when Hart presented Helen with a photograph of himself in which only the eyes were visible, the poet stated these were "*the* true index of character, the only visible part of the brain, the *eye* revealing the I" (emphases in original). See Vivian Pemberton, "Poetry and Portraits: Reflections of Hart Crane," *Hart Crane Newsletter*, 1, no. 2 (1977), 4–5.
10 Weber, *Letters*, p. 129 (2 March 1923).
11 Eugene Jolas, "The Kings's English Is Dying. Long Live the Great American Language," *transition*, nos. 19–20 (1930), 146. American slang was also validated and popularized at this time by H. L. Mencken, whose book on *The American Language* went through many editions.
12 Lewis, *Poetry of Hart Crane*, p. 324. For Crane's personal opposition to the First World War, see Philip Horton, *Hart Crane: The Life of an American Poet* (New York: Norton, 1937), p. 39.
13 Ralph Waldo Emerson, "Plato; or, The Philosopher," in *Representative Men* (1850), vol. IV of *The Riverside Edition of Emerson's Complete Works* (London, 1883), p. 61; p. 55.
14 Eric J. Sundquist, "Bringing Home the Word: Magic, Lies, and Silence in Hart Crane," *ELH*, 44 (1977), 391.
15 Weber, *Letters*, p. 236; D. H. Lawrence, *The Plumed Serpent* (1926; rpt Harmondsworth: Penguin, 1950), p. 232; p. 85.
16 Harold A. Loeb, "The Mysticism of Money," *Broom*, 3 (Sept. 1922), 117; 129; 126.
17 See Horton, pp. 115–16.

4. CAPITALISM AND THE UNDERWORLD

1 Quoted in Willoughby Cyrus Waterman, *Prostitution and its Repression in New York City 1900–1931* (New York: Columbia Univ. Press, 1932), p. 136.
2 For Einstein's activities, see John Kobler, *Ardent Spirits: The Rise and Fall of Prohibition* (London: Michael Joseph, 1974), pp. 294–300. Capone quoted in David E. Kyvig, *Repealing National Prohibition* (Chicago: Univ. of Chicago Press, 1979), p. 26.
3 For the Poncino Palazzo, see Brown, *Robber Rocks*, p. 41. Crane quoted in Cowley, *Exile's Return*, p. 231.
4 Parkinson, p. 122. Malcolm Cowley recalled that in the summer of 1928, while living near Quaker Hill, Crane was drinking heavily: "He was paying more and more visits to Wiley Varian, the cashiered army officer who ran a speakeasy on Birch Hill." Brown, *Robber Rocks*, p. 102.
5 Paul, *Hart's Bridge*, pp. 249–50.
6 Butterfield, p. 194.
7 Paul, *Hart's Bridge*, p. 250.
8 John Dos Passos, *Manhattan Transfer* (Boston: Houghton Mifflin, 1925), p. 33.
9 Ibid. pp. 278–9.
10 John Baker, "Commercial Sources for Hart Crane's 'The River,'" *Wisconsin Studies in Contemporary Literature*, 6 (1965), 47.
11 Sugg, p. 52.
12 According to Fender, p. 52.

[13] John Unterecker, "The Architecture of *The Bridge*" (1962), rpt in *Hart Crane: A Collection of Critical Essays* (Twentieth Century Views), ed. Alan Trachtenberg (Englewood Cliffs, N.J.: Prentice-Hall, 1982), p. 91.

[14] Paul, *Hart's Bridge*, p. 211.

[15] Dos Passos uses "spread" in this way in *Manhattan Transfer* (1925): "The day I chipped in with another fellow to spread a thousand dollars over some Louisville and Nashville on margin I wore that necktie. Scored twentyfive points in twentyfive minutes." Dos Passos, p. 147.

[16] The Negro spiritual "Deep River" was a hit record in 1917. See Julius Mattfeld, *Variety Music Cavalcade 1620–1969*, 3rd ed. (Englewood Cliffs: Prentice–Hall, 1971), p. 351.

[17] Parkinson, p. 94.

5. BURLESQUE

[1] See Walter J. Meserve and William R. Reardon, eds., *Satiric Comedies*, vol. XXI of *America's Lost Plays* (Bloomington: Indiana Univ. Press, 1969), p. xiii.

[2] John Brougham, *Po-Ca-Hon-Tas; or, The Gentle Savage* (1855), rpt in Meserve and Reardon, p. 138.

[3] Philip Young, "The Mother of us All: Pocahontas Reconsidered," *Kenyon Review*, 24 (1962), 402.

[4] Lewis, *Poetry of Hart Crane*, pp. 313–14.

[5] Weber, *Letters*, p. 305 (12 Sept. 1927); Vivian H. Pemberton, "Hart Crane and Yvor Winters, Rebuttal and Review: A New Crane Letter," *American Literature*, 50 (1978), 279.

[6] Parkinson, p. 20 (15 Nov. 1926).

[7] Lohf, "Prose Manuscripts," pp. 41–3.

[8] Ibid. p. 41.

[9] For the Katzenjammer Kids, see, for instance, Jade Snow Wong's memories of a childhood in San Francisco: "'As long as I have been in America,' Mamma often said, 'those little mischief-makers (the Katzenjammer Kids) have never grown an inch!'" Jade Snow Wong, *Fifth Chinese Daughter* (London: Hurst and Blackett, 1952), p. 82. For Crane and Maquokeeta, see Parkinson, p. 31 (19 Jan. 1927); p. 60 (26 Feb. 1927); p. 74 (27 March 1927).

[10] Constance Rourke, *American Humor* (New York: Harcourt, Brace and Co., 1931), p. 128.

[11] John Brougham, *Columbus El Filibustero!!* (New York: Samuel French, [1865?]), p. 8.

[12] Weber, *Letters*, p. 274 (19 Aug. 1926).

[13] Brougham, *Po-Ca-Hon-Tas*, in Meserve and Reardon, p. 143.

[14] Brougham, *Columbus*, p. 4.

[15] Ibid.

[16] Grossman, p. 866.

[17] All from Brougham's *Po-Ca-Hon-Tas*. Meserve and Reardon, p. 142; p. 145; p. 146; p. 150; p. 151.

[18] William H. Pritchard, *Lives of the Modern Poets* (London: Faber, 1980), [pp.] p. 253–4.

[19] Weber, *Letters*, p. 262 (20 June 1926).

[20] See Edmund Wilson, *The American Earthquake* (1958; rpt New York: Farrar, Straus and Giroux, 1979), p. 59.

[21] Weber, *Letters*, p. 306 (12 Sept. 1927).

[22] E. E. Cummings, "You Aren't Mad, Am I? Being Certain Observations anent the Extremely Modern Art of 'Burlesk'" (1925), rpt in *E. E. Cummings: A Miscellany*, ed.

George J. Firmage (New York: Argophile Press, 1958), p. 67. In 1926, shortly after beginning work on *The Bridge* in earnest, Crane himself wrote an essay on burlesque for *Vanity Fair*, but the magazine declined to print the piece and it has now been lost. See Unterecker, *Voyager*, p. 427.

23 Edmund Wilson, *The Twenties*, ed. Leon Edel (New York: Farrar, Straus and Giroux, 1975), pp. 234–5.

24 Butterfield, p. 192; Paul, *Hart's Bridge*, p. 248.

25 E. E. Cummings, "The Adult, the Artist and the Circus" (1925), rpt in *Cummings: Miscellany*, p. 46.

26 W. S. Gilbert and Arthur Sullivan, *The Mikado; or, The Town of Titipu* (London: Chappell, 1885), p. 43. According to newspapers of the time, Winthrop Ames' Gilbert and Sullivan Opera Company was continually performing in New York City during the 1920s. *The Mikado*, for instance, was put on at Chanin's Royale Theater, W. 45th Street, in January 1928.

27 Lewis, *Poetry of Hart Crane*, p. 323; p. 322.

28 Weber, *Letters*, p. 307 (12 Sept. 1927).

29 Ibid.

30 Ralph Waldo Emerson, "The Comic," in *Letters and Social Aims* (1875), vol. VIII of *The Riverside Edition of Emerson's Complete Works* (London, 1883), p. 154; p. 151.

6. BRIDGE AS MYTH

1 Tate, "Hart Crane," *Essays*, p. 317.

2 Joseph J. Arpad, "Hart Crane's Platonic Myth: The Brooklyn Bridge," *American Literature*, 39 (1967), 82; R. H. S. Crossman, *Plato Today* (1937; rpt London: Unwin Books – Allen and Unwin, 1963), p. 82.

3 Weber, *Letters*, p. 238.

4 For Kahn and Paramount, see Kevin Brownlow and John Kobal, *Hollywood: The Pioneers* (London: Collins, 1979), p. 258. Crane was acknowledging that he was being subsidized by a pillar of the American establishment when he wrote to Wilbur Underwood (on 25 Dec. 1925) of the "amazing" effects of Kahn's patronage upon his Republican family: "Shakespeare's own endorsement of me wouldn't have counted so much as a banker's, like Kahn's." Documented in Warren Herendeen and Donald G. Parker, "Wind-blown Flames: Letters of Hart Crane to Wilbur Underwood," *Southern Review* (Louisiana State Univ.), 16 (1980), 361.

5 Parkinson, p. 20.

6 Nassar, p. 149; p. 147.

7 Ibid. p. 154.

8 Quoted in Noel Stock, *The Life of Ezra Pound* (1970; rpt Harmondsworth: Penguin, 1974), p. 96.

9 Herman Melville, *Moby-Dick* (1851), ed. with commentary by Harold Beaver (Harmondsworth: Penguin, 1972), p. 131. All further references to Melville's narrative appear in the text.

10 R. W. B. Lewis, "Hart Crane and the Clown Tradition" (1963), rpt in Trachtenberg, *Hart Crane: A Collection of Critical Essays*, p. 99.

11 *The Collected Poems of Hart Crane*, ed. Waldo Frank (New York: Liveright, 1946), p. 159. "The Return" was excluded from Weber's 1966 edition of Crane's poetry on the grounds that it was a fragment. See also Grossman, p. 841.

12 For Crane's French books, see Kenneth A. Lohf, "The Library of Hart Crane," *Proof*, 3 (1973), 283–334. Most of these French books were poetry – by Hugo, Laforgue, Apollinaire, etc. He also possessed a French dictionary (by J. MacLaughlin) and a

Complete French Course (by C. A. Chardenal). Crane's letter of 16 Nov. 1923 in Pennsylvania State Univ. Library is the photocopy of a typed copy made by Kenneth Burke's wife. The original has been lost.

13 Parkinson, p. 21 (15 Nov. 1926).

14 Alan Trachtenberg, *Brooklyn Bridge: Fact and Symbol* (New York: Oxford Univ. Press, 1965), pp. 69–70.

15 Robert Combs, *Vision of the Voyage: Hart Crane and the Psychology of Romanticism* ([Memphis]: Memphis State Univ. Press, 1978), p. 112: "We might say that the mind of the narrator presented in [*The Bridge*] is like a great movie screen on which all tableaux possible in his culture can be seen and eventually seen through." Combs' discussion of Crane's poetry in terms of the Hegelian aesthetic of dialectic and opposition is consistent with this analysis of the pun as the bridge between contraries. Crane himself owned a copy of John Steinfort Kedney's *Hegel's Aesthetics: A Critical Exposition* (1897). See Lohf, "Library of Hart Crane," p. 315.

16 Crane's interest in ancient culture is also shown by some of the books in his library (all in English translation): *The Tragedies of Sophocles*, *The Medea* by Euripides, *The Greek Anthology* selected by W. R. Paton, *Plutarch's Lives*. He also possessed several works by the classical scholar Nietzsche, including *Early Greek Philosophy and Other Essays*. See Lohf, "Library of Hart Crane." For a convincing analysis of the use of Greek myth in another poem, see Charles C. Walcutt, "Crane's *Voyages*, VI," *The Explicator*, 4, no. 7 (1946), note 53. Walcutt sees Crane's lines "Where icy and bright dungeons lift / Of swimmers their lost morning eyes" as related to the myth of blinded Orion, who was beloved by Eos – goddess of dawn – and who recovered sight when the first rays of the rising sun struck his eyes. This is another version of the blindness and vision dichotomy in *The Bridge*. Parallels between ancient and contemporary culture were, of course, commonplace in the Modernist literature of the 1920s.

17 Marcel Detienne and Jean-Pierre Vernant, *Cunning Intelligence in Greek Culture and Society* (1974), trans. Janet Lloyd (Sussex: Harvester Press, 1978), p. 2; p. 299. Edmund Wilson was one intellectual of Crane's time similarly scornful of the "moderation and wisdom" Victorian dons purported to find amidst the "hideous discords" of Greek tragedy. See his novel *I Thought of Daisy* (1929; rpt Harmondsworth: Penguin, 1963), pp. 129–30.

18 Gorham B. Munson, *Robert Frost: A Study in Sensibility and Good Sense* (New York: Doran, 1927), p. 100.

19 The nickname "Phoebus Apollo" is evident from the letter of Hart Crane to Wilbur Underwood, 12 May 1927, held in the Collection of American Literature, Beinecke Rare Book and Manuscript Library, Yale University. Here Crane quoted for Underwood's benefit a letter he had received from this sailor "in the quartermaster's div." Unterecker reproduced this letter (in *Voyager*, p. 495), but omitted the signature – "A Morte, E" – which makes it almost certain that the sailor in question was Emil Opffer. When Opffer visited Washington D.C. six months later, Crane gave him a letter of introduction to Underwood; and a further letter from Opffer to Underwood, regretting their failure to meet, is preserved in the Beinecke Library. This communication of November 1927 is signed unequivocally "Emil Opffer." With Underwood, Crane tended to be less reticent than usual about his emotional affairs because Underwood was himself homosexual.

20 Nilsen, p. 10; letter received from Emil Opffer, 17 Aug. 1983.

21 Yvor Winters, *In Defense of Reason* (1947; rpt London: Routledge and Kegan Paul, 1960), p. 579.

7. ABSTRACTION AND THE CITY

1 Weber, *Letters*, pp. 4–5.
2 Jean Guiguet, *L'Univers poétique de Hart Crane* (Paris: Minard, 1965), p. 113; Weber, *Critical Study*, p. 209.
3 Waldo Frank, *The Re-discovery of America* (New York: Charles Scribner's Sons, 1929), p. 80.
4 Frank, *New America*, p. 97.
5 Jacqueline Fear and Helen McNeil, "The Twenties," in *Introduction to American Studies*, ed. Malcolm Bradbury and Howard Temperley (Harlow: Longman, 1981), p. 205.
6 Combs, p. 162; Cowley, *Exile's Return*, p. 203; p. 201.
7 Cowley, *Exile's Return*, p. 203; p. 201.
8 Thomas Bulfinch, *The Age of Fable* (1855), rpt in *Bulfinch's Mythology* (London: Bodley Head, 1934), p. 108. Bulfinch was for some hundred years the standard American authority on classical myths.
9 Nassar, p. 180.
10 Jack Clifford Wolf noted this verdigris/*verte-di-Grice* pun in his unpublished thesis on Crane, "Hart Crane's Harp of Evil: A Study of Satanism in *The Bridge*," State Univ. of New York at Buffalo, 1972, p. 199.
11 D. H. Lawrence, *Studies in Classic American Literature* (London: Martin Secker, 1924), p. 67.

8. MUSIC

1 Josephson, "Made in America," p. 269; Will Bray, "Apollinaire: Or Let us Be Troubadors," *Secession*, no. 1 (1922), p. 13. "Will Bray" was a pseudonym for Matthew Josephson.
2 Quoted in Sherman Paul, Introduction, *Port of New York*, by Paul Rosenfeld (1924; rpt Urbana: Univ. of Illinois Press, 1961), p. xli.
3 Gorham B. Munson, *Waldo Frank: A Study* (New York: Boni and Liveright, 1923), p. 24; Frank, *Re-discovery*, p. 130.
4 Weber, *Letters*, p. 89 (16 May 1922).
5 Leibowitz, p. 67.
6 Michael Sharp, "Theme and Free Variation: The Scoring of Hart Crane's *The Bridge*," *Arizona Quarterly*, 37 (1981), 201; 211–12.
7 Coffman, p. 75.
8 Sharp, p. 198.
9 Weber, *Letters*, p. 5 (5 Jan. 1917); p. 273.
10 Documented in Trachtenberg, *Brooklyn Bridge*, p. 148.
11 Conrad Aiken, *Scepticisms: Notes on Contemporary Poetry* (New York: Knopf, 1919), pp. 167–8.
12 Ibid. pp. 237–8.
13 Weber, *Letters*, p. 232.
14 Ibid. p. 305.
15 Ibid. p. 129 (2 March 1923).
16 Fender, p. 42; Parkinson, p. 79 (29 April 1927).
17 Crane instructed his publishers about the photographs in a letter to Caresse Crosby, 26 Dec. 1929, Morris Library, Univ. of Southern Illinois at Carbondale. For a fuller discussion, see Gordon K. Grigsby, "The Photographs in the First Edition of *The Bridge*," *Texas Studies in Literature and Language*, 4 (1962), 5–11. Exactly how closely

Crane and Evans collaborated on the photographs is not clear, though both were living on Columbia Heights, near the Brooklyn waterfront, in 1928: "There . . . where [Evans] put in as much time as he could photographing the neighborhood, they saw a great deal of each other, Hart strolling along on photography afternoons." Unterecker, *Voyager*, p. 562.

18 Eugene Jolas, "Homage to the Mythmaker," *transition*, no. 27 (1938), 169; 175.

9. THE NEW MACHINE AND THE NEW WORD

1 MacKnight Black, *Machinery* (New York: Liveright, 1929), p. 54; p. 4.
2 Frederick J. Hoffman, *The Twenties*, rev. ed. (New York: Free Press–Macmillan, 1965), p. 294; p. 299.
3 Hart Crane, "Modern Poetry" (1930), in *Complete Poems*, pp. 261–2.
4 Cummings' recollections of Crane occur in a letter to Howard Nelson, 10 Nov. 1940. *Selected Letters of E. E. Cummings*, ed. F. W. Dupee and George Stade (London: Deutsch, 1972), p. 121.
5 Weber, *Letters*, p. 274 (19 Aug. 1926).
6 Ibid. p. 268 (26 July 1926).
7 See Weber, *Critical Study*, p. 346. This is discussed more fully in Chapter 2.
8 This is a theme William Carlos Williams developed in his essay on "The Discovery of the Indies," where Williams pointed out how, for all Columbus' heroic genius, he was also a "straw in the play of the elemental giants." William Carlos Williams, *In the American Grain* (1925; rpt New York: New Directions, 1956), p. 10. Crane told Waldo Frank on 21 Nov. 1926 that "Williams' *American Grain* is an achievement that I'd be proud of . . . I'm very enthusiastic – I put off reading it, you know, until I felt my own way cleared beyond chance of confusions incident to reading a book so intimate to my theme." Weber, *Letters*, pp. 277–8.
9 Fear and McNeil, p. 207.
10 Unterecker, *Voyager*, p. 506.
11 Theo Rutra, "Dusk," *transition*, no. 8 (1927), 145; Dougald McMillan, *transition: The History of a Literary Era 1927–1938* (London: Calder and Boyars, 1975), p. 115.
12 Harry Crosby, *Shadows of the Sun: The Diaries of Harry Crosby*, ed. Edward Germain (Santa Barbara: Black Sparrow, 1977), p. 146; p. 157.
13 Ezra Pound, *The Cantos* (London: Faber, 1975), p. 134.
14 William Carlos Williams, *The Autobiography* (1951; rpt [London]: MacGibbon and Kee, 1968), p. 241.
15 Gertrude Stein, "An Elucidation," *transition*, no. 1 (1927), 64; 69.
16 Parkinson, p. 73.
17 Unterecker, *Voyager*, pp. 658–9.
18 "Proclamation" (The Revolution of the Word), *transition*, nos. 16–17 (1929), 13.
19 Cowley, *Exile's Return*, p. 277.
20 McMillan, pp. 139–40.
21 Hart Crane, "General Aims," in *Complete Poems*, p. 221.
22 McMillan, p. 123.
23 Ibid. p. 143; p. 140.
24 Ibid. p. 128.
25 Joseph Stella, "The Brooklyn Bridge (A Page of my Life)," *transition*, nos. 16–17 (1929), 86; 87; Harry Crosby, "The New Word," ibid. p. 30.
26 Geoffrey Wolff, *Black Sun: The Brief Transit and Violent Eclipse of Harry Crosby* (New York: Random House, 1976), p. 187.
27 Crosby, *Diaries*, p. 222; p. 154; p. 232.
28 Hoffman, p. 446.

10. JAMES JOYCE

1   William Carlos Williams, "A Note on the Recent Work of James Joyce," *transition*, no. 8 (1927), 154.
2   Lewis, *Poetry of Hart Crane*, p. 349.
3   Unterecker, *Voyager*, pp. 658–9.
4   Hart Crane, "Joyce and Ethics" (1918), rpt in *Complete Poems*, pp. 199–200.
5   Weber, *Letters*, p. 94 (27 July 1922); p. 97 (15 Aug. 1922).
6   Unterecker, *Voyager*, p. 246.
7   Weber, *Letters*, p. 99 (n.d.).
8   Cowley, *Second Flowering*, p. 16.
9   MacLeish quoted in Gorham Munson, "Woodstock, 1924," *Hartford Studies in Literature*, 1 (1969), 170; Hugh Kenner, *Ulysses* (London: Allen and Unwin, 1980), p. 27.
10 Richard Ellmann, *James Joyce*, 2nd ed. (New York: Oxford Univ. Press, 1965), p. 541.
11 Washington Irving, *Rip Van Winkle* (1820: rpt Philadelphia: Lippincott, 1923), p. 55.
12 James Joyce, *Ulysses* (1922; rpt Harmondsworth: Penguin, 2nd ed., 1971), p. 374. All further references to this edition appear in the text.
13 Weber, *Letters*, p. 274 (19 Aug. 1926).
14 Josephson, *Life*, p. 249.
15 James Joyce, *Finnegans Wake* (1939; rpt London: Faber, 1975), p. 371.
16 James Joyce, "Opening Pages of a Work in Progress," *transition*, no. 1 (1927), 13; 14; Groucho Marx, *The Groucho Letters* (London: Michael Joseph, 1967), p. 145.
17 Michael Stuart, "The Dubliner and his Dowdili (A Note on the Sublime)," *transition*, no. 18 (1929), 158; 157.
18 Ibid. p. 153.
19 Joyce, *Finnegans Wake*, p. 620.
20 Harry Crosby, "Observation-Post," *transition*, nos. 16–17 (1929), 203.
21 John Glassco, *Memoirs of Montparnasse* (Toronto: Oxford Univ. Press, 1970), p. 226; Ellmann, p. 559.
22 James Joyce, "Continuation of a Work in Progress," *transition*, no. 12 (1928), 19.
23 Hart Crane, "Cutty Sark," *transition*, no. 3 (1927), 116–17.
24 Weber, *Letters*, p. 167.
25 "of an evening" reproduced in Brown, *Robber Rocks*, p. 23: a few typographical errors have been corrected in accordance with Crane's original manuscript at Brown Univ. Library, Providence, Rhode Island; Crane, "General Aims," in *Complete Poems*, p. 219.
26 Weber, *Letters*, p. 185.
27 Unpublished letters of Hart Crane to Caresse Crosby, Caresse Crosby Papers, Morris Library, Southern Illinois University at Carbondale.
28 Unterecker, *Voyager*, p. 617.
29 Rebecca West, "James Joyce and his Followers," *New York Herald Tribune*, 12 Jan. 1930, sect. 12, p. 6, cols. 1–4.
30 Letter received from Dame Rebecca West, 8 Feb. 1982.
31 Caresse Crosby, *The Passionate Years* (1953; rpt London: Alvin Redman, 1955), p. 261; Weber, *Letters*, p. 349.
32 Weber, *Critical Study*, p. 332; R. P. Blackmur, "New Thresholds, New Anatomies: Notes on a Text of Hart Crane" (1935), rpt in *Language as Gesture* (1952; rpt London: Allen and Unwin, 1954), p. 313; p. 316.
33 Laura Riding and Robert Graves, *A Survey of Modernist Poetry* (London: Heinemann, 1927), pp. 118–19; p. 25. The justification of the pun in Riding and Graves' *Survey* strongly influenced Empson's *Seven Types of Ambiguity*, published three years later.

³⁴ Unpublished letter of Hart Crane to E. E. Cummings, 21 Dec. 1927, Harry Ransom Humanities Research Center, The University of Texas at Austin.

I I. LA RÉVOLUTION SURRÉALISTE

¹ James Joyce, "James Joyce, Ad-Writer," *transition*, no. 21 (1932), 258. See McMillan, p. 210.
² Unterecker, *Voyager*, p. 374.
³ Josephson, *Life*, p. 215; James Thrall Soby, *Giorgio de Chirico* (New York: Arno Press, for the Museum of Modern Art, New York, 1966), p. 42.
⁴ Soby, p. 55.
⁵ Guillaume Apollinaire, "Notes," *Dada*, no. 2 (Dec. 1917), 17.
⁶ Weber, *Letters*, p. 87 (16 May 1922); p. 84 (19 April 1922); p. 95.
⁷ Parkinson, p. 14 (9 Oct. 1926).
⁸ Jonathan Culler, *Structuralist Poetics* (London: Routledge and Kegan Paul, 1975), p. 177.
⁹ Dickran Tashjian, *Skyscraper Primitives* (Middletown, Conn.: Wesleyan Univ. Press, 1975), p. 50; p. 49; p. 55.
¹⁰ For Coady, see ibid. p. 76; for McAlmon, ibid. p. 86.
¹¹ Quoted in Weaver, pp. 131–2.
¹² Weber, *Letters*, p. 52.
¹³ Unterecker, *Voyager*, p. 226.
¹⁴ Weber, *Letters*, p. 84 (19 April 1922); Will Bray, "Apollinaire," p. 10. "Will Bray" was a pseudonym for Matthew Josephson.
¹⁵ Matthew Josephson, "The Brain at the Wheel," *Broom*, 5 (Sept. 1923), 96.
¹⁶ Weber, *Letters*, p. 106 (Nov. 1922).
¹⁷ Ibid. p. 87.
¹⁸ David E. Shi, *Matthew Josephson: Bourgeois Bohemian* (New Haven: Yale Univ. Press, 1981), p. 57.
¹⁹ Josephson, *Life*, p. 103.
²⁰ Tristan Tzara, Manifesto II (1918), rpt in *Seven Dada Manifestoes and Lampisteries*, trans. Barbara Wright (London: John Calder, 1977), p. 4; "Lecture on Dada (1922), ibid. p. 108.
²¹ André Breton, "Les Mots sans rides," *Littérature*, NS, no. 7 (1922), 12. All translations from Surrealist magazines are by the author, unless otherwise stated.
²² Ibid. p. 12.
²³ [Marcel Duchamp], "Rrose Sélavy," *Littérature*, NS, no. 5 (1922), 7.
²⁴ Breton, "Les Mots sans rides," p. 13.
²⁵ Robert Desnos, "Rrose Sélavy," *Littérature*, NS, no. 7 (1922), 14.
²⁶ Robert Desnos, "L'Aumonyme," *Littérature*, NS, no. 10 (1923), 26.
²⁷ Michel Leiris, "Glossaire: J'y serre mes gloses," *La Révolution Surréaliste*, no. 3 (1925), 7; no. 4 (1925), 20; no. 3 (1925), 6; no. 6 (1926), 21.
²⁸ Ibid. no. 3 (1925), 7.
²⁹ Giorgio de Chirico, Notes, *La Révolution Surréaliste*, no. 4 (1925), 21.
³⁰ Louis Aragon, *Traité du style* (Paris: Librairie Gallimard, 1928), pp. 191–2.
³¹ Michel Leiris, "Le Sceptre miroitant," *La Révolution Surréaliste*, no. 5 (1925), 7.
³² Richard W. Sheppard, "Tricksters, Carnival and the Magical Figures of Dada Poetry," *Forum for Modern Language Studies*, 19 (1983), 117.
³³ Ibid. p. 116; p. 118.
³⁴ Eugene Jolas's remark on Dada comes in his note on "Cabaret," by Hugo Ball, *transition*, no. 22 (1933), 10. The other comments are from Jolas, "Notes on Reality," *transition*, no. 18 (1929), 18; 20.

35 Jolas, "Notes on Reality," p. 19; pp. 19–20.
36 Hart Crane, "Van Winkle," *transition*, no. 7 (1927), 128.
37 Wolf, p. 97.
38 Weber, *Letters*, p. 306 (12 Sept. 1927).
39 Sundquist, p. 382.
40 Brown, *Robber Rocks*, p. 90.
41 Sundquist, pp. 393–4.
42 Hart Crane, "O Carib Isle," *transition*, no. 1 (1927), 101.
43 Roman Jakobson and Linda Waugh, *The Sound Shape of Language* (Brighton, Sussex: Harvester Press, 1979), p. 229. Anagrams had a more secular rôle to play in America during the 1920s as the staple fodder of crossword clues. "By 1927 a widespread neurosis began to be evident, faintly signalled, like a nervous beating of the feet, by the popularity of crossword puzzles," recalled F. Scott Fitzgerald in "Echoes of the Jazz Age" (1931), rpt in *The Crack-up* (Harmondsworth: Penguin, 1965), p. 16. Crane's "O Carib Isle" and "Van Winkle" both first appeared in 1927.

12. SURREALISM AND MADNESS

1 Marsden Hartley, *Adventures in the Arts* (1921; rpt New York: Hacker Art Books, 1972), p. 251.
2 Josephson, *Life*, p. 183.
3 Gregory Robert Zeck, "Hart Crane and the Logic of Metaphor," unpublished diss., Univ. of Texas at Austin, 1973, p. 184; p. 185.
4 Tzara, Manifesto VI (1920), in *Manifestoes*, p. 28.
5 Weber, *Letters*, p. 121 (7 Feb. 1923).
6 Louis Aragon, *Paris Peasant* (1926), trans. Simon Watson Taylor (London: Picador – Pan, 1980), p. 208.
7 Ibid. p. 217; p. 193.
8 In Breton's 1924 Manifesto. André Breton, *Manifestoes of Surrealism*, trans. Richard Seaver and Helen R. Lane (Ann Arbor: Univ. of Michigan Press, 1969), pp. 5–6.
9 Frank, *New America*, p. 213. Joyce uses a similar conflation of jest, geste and joust in the *Wake*: "In the beginning was the gest he jousstly says." Joyce, *Finnegans Wake*, p. 468.
10 Nassar, p. 146.
11 For Don Quixote, see Weber, *Letters*, p. 261; in contrast to Paul, *Hart's Bridge*, pp. 178–9. Crane on the Siqueiros portrait quoted by Peggy Cowley in Brown, *Robber Rocks*, p. 164.
12 Weber, *Letters*, p. 261 (20 June 1926).
13 Nassar, p. 188.
14 For Brooklyn Bridge and the Elevated Railway, see David McCullough, *The Great Bridge* (New York: Simon and Schuster, 1972), p. 552. According to subway maps of the time, there were two train systems (run by different companies) which crossed the East River in the 1920s. The Elevated Railway ran over Brooklyn Bridge until 1944, while the subway line ran (and still runs) under the water, as it does in "The Tunnel" ("Taking the final level for the dive / Under the river"). The "High Street Brooklyn Bridge" station was shared by both systems, and still survives today, though now serving only the Rapid Transit Authority (subway line).
15 Weber, *Letters*, p. 176 (1 March 1924).
16 Hart Crane, *Ten Unpublished Poems*, ed. Kenneth A. Lohf (New York: Gotham Book Mart, 1972), no. IX, n. pag.
17 For Paul on "The Harbor Dawn," see *Hart's Bridge*, p. 200; Weber, *Letters*, p. 306 (12 Sept. 1927).

18 Cowley, *Second Flowering*, p. 213; Katherine Anne Porter, letter to Philip Horton, 20 July 1935, Univ. of Maryland Libraries, College Park.

19 For "Cutty Sark," see Fender, p. 62. The wall/*mur* pun is a thread running throughout *The Bridge*; see also: "Your cool arms *murmurously* about me lay" ("The Harbor Dawn"); "like the elemental gist / of *unwalled* winds" ("The River"); "The bearings glint, – O *murmurless* and shined" ("Cape Hatteras"); "Daemon, *demurring* and eventful yawn" ("The Tunnel").

20 "The Harbor Dawn" first appeared (in a slightly different version) in *transition*, no. 3 (1927), 120–21.

21 Lewis, *Poetry of Hart Crane*, p. 291.

22 Brown, *Robber Rocks*, p. 56.

23 Crane praised the "magnificence" of *Virgin Spain* in a letter to Waldo Frank on 20 March 1926; and he added that "'The Port of Columbus' is truly something of a prelude to my intentions for *The Bridge*." Weber, *Letters*, p. 242. "The Port of Columbus" is the last chapter of *Virgin Spain*, and features a conversation between Columbus and Cervantes about the possibility of spiritual order in the United States.

13. PSYCHOANALYSIS AND HOMOSEXUALITY

1 Unterecker, *Voyager*, p. 30.

2 Brown, *Robber Rocks*, p. 69.

3 Allen Tate, "Crane: The Poet as Hero" (1952), in *Essays*, p. 325.

4 Horton, p. 241.

5 Quoted from Leo Hurwitz, dir., *In Search of Hart Crane*, film for National Educational Television, U.S.A., 1966.

6 For Crane's experiences with blackmailers, see Unterecker, *Voyager*, p. 247; Karl T. Piculin, "The Critics and Hart Crane's *The Bridge*: An Interview with John Unterecker," *Hart Crane Newsletter*, 2, no. 1 (1978), 28–9.

7 Thomas A. Vogler, *Preludes to Vision* (Berkeley: Univ. of California Press, 1971), p. 159; Philip Young, "Fallen From Time: The Mythic Rip Van Winkle," *Kenyon Review*, 22 (1960), 569; 571.

8 Weber, *Letters*, p. 306 (12 Sept. 1927); see Theodor Reik, *Masochism in Modern Man* (1941), trans. Margaret H. Beigel and Gertrud M. Kurth (New York: Grove Press, [1957]).

9 M. D. Uroff, *Hart Crane: The Patterns of his Poetry* (Urbana: Univ. of Illinois Press, 1974), p. 31.

10 Piculin, p. 29.

11 For "cobblers," see Wentworth and Flexner, p. 763. Rhyming slang was originally a "secret argot" of the criminal underworld: it has tended to be more common in England, though not unknown in the United States. See Wentworth and Flexner, pp. 606–7. The word "cobblers" would have been much in evidence in the Lime-house pubs of East London, which Crane visited in December 1928. Unterecker, *Voyager*, p. 577.

12 For "Medusa," see Hart Crane, *Seven Lyrics*, ed. Kenneth A. Lohf (Cambridge, Mass.: Ibex Press, 1966), n. pag.; for Crane's postcard, see Unterecker, *Voyager*, p. 568. Crane sometimes justified his erotic activity by associating it with artistic production: "My continence has brought me nothing in the creative way . . . There is not love enough in me at present to do a thing." Quoted in Weber, *Critical Study*, p. 75.

13 Sundquist, p. 377; Weber, *Letters*, p. 303 (4 July 1927).

14 Letter received from Eric Sundquist, 11 July 1983. For Anemone, see Mary Jean Butts, "Art as Affirmation: A Study of Hart Crane's 'Atlantis,'" in *Critical Essays on Hart Crane*, ed. David R. Clark (Boston: Hall, 1982), p. 170.

15 Parkinson, p. 79.

16 Unterecker, *Voyager*, p. 565.

17 Monroe K. Spears, *Hart Crane* (Minneapolis: Univ. of Minnesota Press, 1965), p. 6; Parkinson, pp. 19–20 (15 Nov. 1926); Parkinson, p. 79 (29 April 1927).

18 Hoffman, p. 234; p. 231.

19 Sigmund Freud, *The Interpretation of Dreams* (1900), trans. James Strachey, ed. Angela Richards (Harmondsworth: Penguin, 1976), p. 178; p. 172.

20 Ibid. p. 171; p. 174.

21 Sigmund Freud, *The Psychopathology of Everyday Life* (1901), trans. Alan Tyson, ed. Angela Richards (Harmondsworth: Penguin, 1975), p. 66. Compare Crane's letter to Herbert Weinstock, 22 April 1930, where he talks of "the intentional condensation and 'density' of structure that I occasionally achieve." Weber, *Letters*, p. 350.

22 Freud, *Interpretation*, p. 427.

23 Sigmund Freud, *Jokes and their Relation to the Unconscious* (1905), trans. James Strachey, ed. Angela Richards (Harmondsworth: Penguin, 1976), p. 175.

24 Ibid. pp. 62–3; p. 113.

25 Ernst Kris, *Psychoanalytic Explorations in Art* (London: Allen and Unwin, 1953), p. 216.

26 Freud, *Jokes*, p. 194; p. 41; p. 169.

27 Freud, *Interpretation*, p. 440.

28 Paul, *Hart's Bridge*, p. 245.

29 See Weber, *Critical Study*, p. 428.

30 Zeck, p. 52.

31 Robert K. Martin, *The Homosexual Tradition in American Poetry* (Austin: Univ. of Texas Press, 1979), p. 133.

32 Cowley, *Second Flowering*, p. 196; p. 205. Cowley recalled that one of Crane's typical limericks ran as follows:

> Said the poetess Sappho of Greece,
> "Ah, better by far than a piece
>   Is to have my pudenda
>   Rubbed hard by the enda
> The little pink nose of my niece."

33 Weber, *Letters*, p. 232 (18 Jan. 1926). Peggy Cowley also remembered Crane's obscenity about women; for instance: "Just take a gander at that woman. A typical tart from the word go. Watch her mincing along on her way to a date, swishing her fanny." Brown, *Robber Rocks*, p. 148.

34 For Martin's discussion of the relationship between Whitman's homosexuality and his philosophy of social "adhesiveness," see Martin, *Homosexual Tradition*, pp. 33–47.

35 Hart Crane, "After Jonah," *Hart Crane Newsletter*, I, no. 2 (1977), I. Crane can also be seen punning on *ream* and *realm* in his worksheets for "Ave Maria": "ream? (realm?)." He also toys with the phrase "rudder reams the path" – the rudder being the back part of Columbus' ship, here personified as buggering the ocean. See B6 in Lohf, *Literary Manuscripts*.

36 Beaver, Commentary, *Moby-Dick*, p. 904. There is also an extended discussion of naval flogging in Melville's *White-Jacket*, a work Crane found "delightful." Letter to Gorham Munson, 5 March 1926, Weber, *Letters*, p. 235. Crane was, of course, sexually obsessed with sailors: "They were a fetish," recalled Samuel Loveman. "The minute he saw a sailor, he went over-seas, so to speak." Jay Socin and Kirby Congdon, eds., *"Hart Crane": A Conversation with Samuel Loveman* (New York: Interim Books, 1964), p. 20.

37 Tony Tanner, *Adultery in the Novel* (Baltimore: Johns Hopkins Univ. Press, 1979), p. 53.

[38] Herendeen and Parker, p. 357; p. 359. Crane mailed the *Ulysses* excerpts on 13 Aug. 1922, and made the comment quoted in the text on 30 Oct. 1922.
[39] Opffer quoted in Nilsen, p. 12; Brown, *Robber Rocks*, pp. 134–5.
[40] Quoted in Unterecker, *Voyager*, p. 181.
[41] Emerson, "The Poet," *Works*, III, 40.

14. PARADOX AND OXYMORON

[1] Cowley, *Exile's Return*, p. 21.
[2] F. Scott Fitzgerald, *The Great Gatsby* (1925; rpt Harmondsworth: Penguin, 1950), p. 56.
[3] Nassar, p. 146.
[4] Ibid.
[5] Weber, *Letters*, p. 71 (26 Nov. 1921); the Donne poem documented in Alfred B. Cahen, "Hart Crane's Ghost Written Suicide Notes," *Hart Crane Newsletter*, I, no. 2 (1977), 13.
[6] Hugh Kenner, *Paradox in Chesterton* (London: Sheed and Ward, 1948), pp. 8–9.
[7] Kenner, *Paradox*, p. 42.
[8] Bernard F. Huppé, "*Petrus Id Est Christus*: Word Play in *Piers Plowman*, the B-Text," *ELH*, 17 (1950), 188–90.
[9] Nassar, p. 183.
[10] Richard Hutson, "Exile Guise: Irony and Hart Crane" (1969), rpt in Trachtenberg, *Hart Crane: A Collection of Critical Essays*, p. 136.
[11] Ibid. p. 135; pp. 148–9; p. 147.
[12] Wilson, *The Twenties*, p. 119.
[13] Sugg, pp. 74–5.
[14] Hart Crane, "Joyce and Ethics," in *Complete Poems*, p. 199; Oscar Wilde, *The Picture of Dorian Gray* (1890), in *The Works of Oscar Wilde*, ed. G. F. Maine (London: Collins, 1948), p. 43.
[15] Reproduced between p. 722 and p. 723 in Unterecker, *Voyager*.
[16] Weber, *Letters*, p. 5 (5 Jan. 1917). This name-change was initially inspired by Crane's wish to affiliate himself more to his mother's side of the family, the Harts; but Crane certainly made use of the pun later in his life. A letter of Crane's to Wilbur Underwood (on 14 May 1921) is actually signed with a heart shape instead of Hart's name: "Mes regards à Mme Cooke et à vous – votre ♥ ." See Herendeen and Parker, pp. 352–3.
[17] Weber, *Letters*, p. 351 (22 May 1930).

15. ALCHEMY AND THE ROMANTIC QUEST

[1] Van Wyck Brooks, ed., *Christopher Columbus: The Journal of his First Voyage to America* (London: Jarrolds, 1925), p. vi. Crane mentioned reading this *Journal* in a letter to Munson on 5 March 1926. Weber, *Letters*, p. 235.
[2] Brooks, *Columbus: The Journal*, p. 8.
[3] Uroff, p. 210.
[4] Richard Poirier, *A World Elsewhere* (London: Chatto and Windus, 1967), p. 85.
[5] Poirier, p. 85; p. 87.
[6] Herman Melville, "Hawthorne and his Mosses" (1850), quoted in Lawrance Thompson, *Melville's Quarrel with God* (Princeton: Princeton Univ. Press, 1952), p. 12.
[7] Weber, *Letters*, p. 260; p. 404.

⁸ Beaver, Introduction, *Moby-Dick*, pp. 30–1.
⁹ Beaver, Commentary, *Moby-Dick*, p. 900.
¹⁰ Herendeen and Parker, p. 355 (15 June 1922).
¹¹ R. W. B. Lewis, *The American Adam* (Chicago: Univ. of Chicago Press, 1955), p. 146.
¹² Fender, p. 4. Crane's conception of the visible as the untrue may also have been influenced by the Christian Science religion of his childhood, with its emphasis upon the insubstantiality of the material world.
¹³ Sundquist, p. 376.
¹⁴ Brooks, *Columbus: The Journal*, p. 247.
¹⁵ Breton quoted in Maurice Nadeau, *The History of Surrealism* (1945), trans. Richard Howard (London: Cape, 1968), p. 163.
¹⁶ Robert K. Martin, "Hart Crane's 'For the Marriage of Faustus and Helen': Myth and Alchemy," *Concerning Poetry*, 9 (1976), 59; unpublished letter of Hart Crane to Louis Untermeyer, Univ. of Delaware Library. Brom Weber pointed out that as the lines used in Crane's epigraph are actually spoken by Dol Common, they could be seen as a comic parody by Jonson of Marlowe's *Doctor Faustus*; and so Weber suggested this epigraph contains an "ironic purpose," casting the poet in the rôle of a fake alchemist whose pretensions outstrip his achievement (*Critical Study*, p. 180). This seems quite plausible, but again the irony surely burlesques the poet's vision without entirely negating it.
¹⁷ See Brown, *Robber Rocks*, p. 52.
¹⁸ Weber, *Letters*, p. 256 (22 May 1926).
¹⁹ T. S. Eliot, "Baudelaire" (1930), rpt in *Selected Essays*, rev. ed. (London: Faber, 1951), p. 421.
²⁰ Lewis, "Hart Crane and the Clown Tradition," p. 99. See Weber, *Letters*, p. 65 (1 Oct. 1921).
²¹ Butterfield, p. 203.
²² Unterecker, *Voyager*, p. 143; p. 308.
²³ Weber, *Critical Study*, p. 235.
²⁴ Crane's suggestion for the cover of *The Bridge* was made in a letter to "Pete," presumably an employee of the Liveright Publishing Corporation, on 18 Feb. 1930. Unpublished manuscript held by University of Maryland Libraries, College Park.
²⁵ Dostoyevsky's *Crime and Punishment* "caught me by the throat," said Crane in a letter to Gorham Munson, 9 Nov. 1920. Weber, *Letters*, p. 46. In a letter to his mother on 21 Dec. 1923, Crane wrote: "Suffering is a real purification, and the worst thing I have always had to say against Christian Science is that it willfully avoided suffering, without a certain measure of which any true happiness cannot be fully realized." Thomas S. W. Lewis, ed., *Letters of Hart Crane and his Family* (New York: Columbia Univ. Press, 1974), p. 243.
²⁶ Caresse Crosby, *Passionate Years*, p. 246; p. 249. The Faustian pact also features in Balzac's *Le Peau de chagrin*, which was in Crane's library (in English translation: see Lohf, "Library," p. 300). In Balzac's novel, the hero Raphael has his every fantastic wish granted through the agency of a magic piece of shagreen which, however, shrinks as each spell is performed, and whose eventual disappearance ensures Raphael's death. Crane's early death after constructing his magical *Bridge* might be seen (not least by the poet himself) as a similar kind of Faustian bargain.

16. CONCLUSION

¹ Peter Brooker, *A Student's Guide to the Selected Poems of Ezra Pound* (London: Faber, 1979), p. 162.

2 Nassar, p. 151; Trachtenberg, Introduction, *Hart Crane: A Collection of Critical Essays*, p. 6.

3 Piculin, p. 29; Unterecker, *Voyager*, p. 722.

4 Brown, *Robber Rocks*, p. 40; Weber, *Letters*, p. 321 (27 March 1928).

5 Ibid. p. 251 (7 May 1926).

6 See Cowley, *Exile's Return*, p. 277; Unterecker, *Voyager*, p. 617.

7 Parkinson, p. 14 (9 Oct. 1926).

8 Friedrich Nietzsche, *Human All-Too-Human: A Book for Free Spirits, Part 2* (1879), vol. VII of *The Complete Works*, trans. Paul V. Cohn, ed. Oscar Levy (Edinburgh: Foulis, 1911), pp. 60–2.

9 Ibid. p. 242.

10 Ibid. p. 64.

11 William Shakespeare, *The Complete Works*, ed. William Allan Neilson (Boston: Houghton Mifflin, 1906), p. 221 (*As You Like It*, III.ii.237); p. 937 (*Othello*, I.ii.33); p. 1015 (*Macbeth*, II.iii.39).

12 Crane, *Complete Poems*, p. 235; p. 221.

13 Josephson, *Life*, pp. 297–8; Ramsey, p. 278; letter to Hart Crane from Otto H. Kahn, 19 Sept. 1927. The unpublished letters to Crane from Kahn are held by the Hart Crane Collection, Rare Book and Manuscript Library, Columbia University.

14 Weber, *Letters*, p. 241; p. 308.

15 Ibid. p. 350 (22 April 1930).

16 Quoted in Ellmann, p. 535.

17 Tate, "Crane: The Poet as Hero," p. 327; Cowley, *Second Flowering*, p. 201; Josephson, *Life*, p. 38.

18 Weber, *Letters*, pp. 124–5 (18 Feb. 1923).

19 Harold Bloom, *Agon: Towards a Theory of Revisionism* (New York: Oxford Univ. Press, 1982), p. 253. Campbell expressed his views on Crane in a letter to Wyndham Lewis, June 1929, quoted in Peter Alexander, *Roy Campbell: A Critical Biography* (Oxford: Oxford Univ. Press, 1982), p. 112.

20 Horton, p. 145; Brown, *Robber Rocks*, p. 69.

21 Weber, *Letters*, p. 170 (12 Jan. 1924); Unterecker, *Voyager*, p. 124; p. 125.

22 Hart Crane, letter to Clarence A. Crane, *Hart Crane Newsletter*, I, no. 1 (1977), 5; 4.

23 Unterecker, *Voyager*, pp. 285–90.

24 Ibid. p. 39.

25 Ibid. p. 170.

26 Peggy Guggenheim, *Out of this Century: Confessions of an Art Addict* (London: André Deutsch, 1980), p. 72; Frank quoted from Hurwitz.

27 "A Letter from Peter Blume," *Hart Crane Newsletter*, 2, no. 1 (1978), 17; 18.

28 Unterecker, *Voyager*, p. 201; Nilsen, p. 14.

29 Letter to Wilbur Underwood, 3 Aug. 1926, Herendeen and Parker, p. 364. On the subject of Edmund Wilson, see, for instance, Crane's letter to Yvor Winters, 29 May 1927. Weber, *Letters*, p. 298.

30 Socin and Congdon, p. 13.

31 Cowley, *Exile's Return*, p. 233; Horton, p. 296.

32 W. R. Bion, "Language and the Schizophrenic," in *New Directions in Psycho-Analysis*, ed. Melanie Klein and others (London: Tavistock Publications, 1955), p. 223.

33 William Empson, *Seven Types of Ambiguity* (London: Chatto and Windus, 1930), p. 244; p. 276; p. 275.

34 William Empson, Letter, *Times Literary Supplement*, 1 Oct. 1954, p. 625, col. 2.

35 Letter received from John Unterecker, 13 July 1983.

36 Edmund Wilson, "A Great Magician" (1928), rpt in *The Shores of Light* (London: W. H. Allen, 1952), p. 291.

37 Norman O. Brown, *Love's Body* (New York: Random House, 1966), p. 161; p. 159.

38 Ibid. p. 252; p. 245.

39 Ibid. pp. 246–7.

40 Melvyn Bragg, "Interview with Ian McKellen," *The South Bank Show*, London Weekend Television, 22 Nov. 1981.

41 Van Wyck Brooks, *The Wine of the Puritans* (London: Sisley's, 1909), p. 110; p. 100.

42 Ibid. p. 110.

43 Margaret Drabble, "The Future of the Novel," Oxford Literary Society, Oxford, 22 Oct. 1980.

Works cited

I. WORKS BY HART CRANE

Crane, Hart. "O Carib Isle." *transition*, no. 1 (1927), 101–2.
  "Cutty Sark." *transition*, no. 3 (1927), 116–19.
  "The Harbor Dawn: Brooklyn Heights." *transition*, no. 3 (1927), 120–1.
  "Van Winkle." *transition*, no. 7 (1927), 128–9.
  The Bridge. Paris: Black Sun Press, 1930.
  The Collected Poems. Ed. Waldo Frank. New York: Liveright, 1946.
  The Complete Poems and Selected Letters and Prose. Ed. Brom Weber. 3rd ed. New York:
    Liveright, 1966.
  Seven Lyrics. Ed. Kenneth A. Lohf. Cambridge, Mass.: Ibex Press, 1966.
  Ten Unpublished Poems. Ed. Kenneth A. Lohf. New York: Gotham Book Mart, 1972.
  "After Jonah." *Hart Crane Newsletter*, 1, no. 2 (1977), 1.
  "of an evening pulling off a little experience (with the english language) by e.e.
    cummings." Brown University Library, Providence, Rhode Island.
  Letter to Clarence A. Crane. *Hart Crane Newsletter*, 1, no. 1 (1977), 4–5.
  Letter to Louis Untermeyer. 19 January 1923. University of Delaware Library,
    Newark, Delaware.
  Letter to Charles Harris. 19 April 1923. Department of Special Collections, Kent State
    University Libraries, Kent, Ohio.
  Letter to Wilbur Underwood. 12 May 1927. Collection of American Literature,
    Beinecke Rare Book and Manuscript Library, Yale University, New Haven,
    Connecticut.
  Letter to E. E. Cummings. 21 December 1927. Harry Ransom Humanities Research
    Center, The University of Texas at Austin.
  Letter to Pete [?]. 18 February 1930. University of Maryland Libraries, College Park,
    Maryland.
  Letters to and from Otto H. Kahn. Hart Crane Collection, Rare Book and Manuscript
    Library, Columbia University, New York City.
  Letters to Harry and Caresse Crosby. Caresse Crosby Papers, Morris Library,
    Southern Illinois University at Carbondale.
Herendeen, Warren, and Donald G. Parker. "Wind-blown Flames: Letters of Hart
    Crane to Wilbur Underwood." *Southern Review* (Louisiana State Univ.), 16 (1980),
    337–76.

Lewis, Thomas S. W., ed. *Letters of Hart Crane and his Family*. New York: Columbia
  Univ. Press, 1974.
Lohf, Kenneth A., ed. *The Literary Manuscripts of Hart Crane*. [Columbus]: Ohio State
  Univ. Press, 1967.
  "The Prose Manuscripts of Hart Crane: An Editorial Portfolio." *Proof*, 2 (1972), 1–60.
Parkinson, Thomas, ed. *Hart Crane and Yvor Winters: Their Literary Correspondence*.
  Berkeley: Univ. of California Press, 1978.
Pemberton, Vivian H. "Hart Crane and Yvor Winters, Rebuttal and Review: A New
  Crane Letter." *American Literature*, 50 (1978), 276–81.
Weber, Brom, ed. *The Letters of Hart Crane 1916–1932*. 1952; rpt Berkeley: Univ. of
  California Press, 1965.

II. WORKS IN WHOLE OR GREAT PART ABOUT HART CRANE

Arpad, Joseph J. "Hart Crane's Platonic Myth: The Brooklyn Bridge." *American
  Literature*, 39 (1967), 75–86.
Baker, John. "Commercial Sources for Hart Crane's 'The River.'" *Wisconsin Studies in
  Contemporary Literature*, 6 (1965), 45–55.
Blackmur, R. P. "New Thresholds, New Anatomies: Notes on a Text of Hart Crane."
  1935. In *Language as Gesture*. 1952; rpt London: Allen and Unwin, 1954.
[Blume] "A Letter from Peter Blume." *Hart Crane Newsletter*, 2, no. 1 (1978), 17–19.
Brown, Susan Jenkins. *Robber Rocks: Letters and Memories of Hart Crane, 1923–1932*.
  Middletown, Connecticut: Wesleyan Univ. Press, 1969.
Butterfield, R. W. *The Broken Arc: A Study of Hart Crane*. Edinburgh: Oliver and Boyd,
  1969.
Butts, Mary Jean. "Art as Affirmation: A Study of Hart Crane's 'Atlantis.'" In Clark, ed.,
  op. cit., pp. 156–83.
Cahen, Alfred B. "Hart Crane's Ghost Written Suicide Notes." *Hart Crane Newsletter*, 1,
  no. 2 (1977), 11–16.
Cambon, Glauco. *The Inclusive Flame: Studies in Modern American Poetry*. Bloomington:
  Indiana Univ. Press, 1963.
Clark, David R., ed. *Critical Essays on Hart Crane*. Boston: Hall, 1982.
Coffman, Stanley K. "Symbolism in *The Bridge*." *PMLA*, 66 (1951), 65–77.
Combs, Robert. *Vision of the Voyage: Hart Crane and the Psychology of Romanticism*.
  [Memphis]: Memphis State Univ. Press, 1978.
Dembo, L. S. *Hart Crane's Sanskrit Charge: A Study of "The Bridge."* Ithaca, New York:
  Cornell Univ. Press, 1960.
Grigsby, Gordon K. "The Photographs in the First Edition of *The Bridge*." *Texas Studies
  in Literature and Language*, 4 (1962), 5–11.
Grossman, Allen. "Hart Crane and Poetry: A Consideration of Crane's Intense Poetics
  with Reference to 'The Return.'" *ELH*, 48 (1981), 841–79.
Guiguet, Jean. *L'Univers poétique de Hart Crane*. Paris: M. J. Minard, 1965.
Horton, Philip. *Hart Crane: The Life of an American Poet*. New York: W. W. Norton,
  1937.
Hurwitz, Leo, dir. *In Search of Hart Crane*. Film for National Educational Television,
  U.S.A., 1966.
Hutson, Richard. "Exile Guise: Irony and Hart Crane." 1969. Rpt in *Hart Crane: A
  Collection of Critical Essays*. Ed. Trachtenberg, op. cit., pp. 131–49.
Leibowitz, Herbert A. *Hart Crane: An Introduction to the Poetry*. New York: Columbia
  Univ. Press, 1968.
Lewis, R. W. B. "Hart Crane and the Clown Tradition." 1963. Rpt in *Hart Crane: A*

Collection of Critical Essays. Ed. Trachtenberg, op. cit., pp. 97–110.

The Poetry of Hart Crane: A Critical Study. Princeton: Princeton Univ. Press, 1967.

Lohf, Kenneth A. "The Library of Hart Crane." Proof, 3 (1973), 283–334.

Martin, Robert K. "Hart Crane's 'For the Marriage of Faustus and Helen': Myth and Alchemy." Concerning Poetry, 9 (1976), 59–62.

Nassar, Eugene Paul. The Rape of Cinderella: Essays in Literary Continuity. Bloomington: Indiana Univ. Press, 1970.

Nilsen, Helge Normann. "Memories of Hart Crane: A Talk with Emil Opffer." Hart Crane Newsletter, 2, no. 1 (1978), 8–14.

Opffer, Emil. Letter to Wilbur Underwood. November 1927. Beinecke Rare Book and Manuscript Library, Yale University, New Haven, Connecticut.

Letter to author. 17 August 1983.

Paul, Sherman. Hart's Bridge. Urbana: Univ. of Illinois Press, 1972.

Pemberton, Vivian. "Poetry and Portraits: Reflections of Hart Crane." Hart Crane Newsletter, 1, no. 2 (1977), 4–11.

Piculin, Karl T. "The Critics and Hart Crane's The Bridge: An Interview with John Unterecker." Hart Crane Newsletter, 2, no. 1 (1978), 22–33.

Porter, Katherine Anne. Letter to Philip Horton. 20 July 1935. University of Maryland Libraries, College Park, Maryland.

Ramsey, Roger. "A Poetics for The Bridge." Twentieth Century Literature, 26 (1980), 278–93.

Riddel, Joseph N. "Hart Crane's Poetics of Failure." 1966. Rpt in Modern American Poetry: Essays in Criticism. Ed. Jerome Mazzaro. New York: David McKay, 1970, pp. 272–300.

Sharp, Michael. "Theme and Free Variation: The Scoring of Hart Crane's The Bridge." Arizona Quarterly, 37 (1981), 197–213.

Simon, Marc. Letter to author. 8 July 1983.

Socin, Jay, and Kirby Congdon, eds. "Hart Crane": A Conversation with Samuel Loveman. New York: Interim Books, 1964.

Spears, Monroe K. Hart Crane. Univ. of Minnesota Pamphlets on American Writers, no. 47. Minneapolis: Univ. of Minnesota Press, 1965.

Sugg, Richard P. Hart Crane's "The Bridge": A Description of its Life (Studies in the Humanities, no. 20). n.p.: Univ. of Alabama Press, 1976.

Sundquist, Eric J. "Bringing Home the Word: Magic, Lies, and Silence in Hart Crane." ELH, 44 (1977), 376–99.

Letter to author. 11 July 1983.

Tate, Allen: "Hart Crane." (1932–7) Rpt in Essays of Four Decades. London: Oxford Univ. Press, 1970, pp. 310–23.

"Crane: The Poet as Hero." 1952. Rpt in Essays of Four Decades. op. cit., pp. 324–8.

Trachtenberg, Alan. Brooklyn Bridge: Fact and Symbol. New York: Oxford Univ. Press, 1965.

Trachtenberg, Alan, ed. Hart Crane: A Collection of Critical Essays (Twentieth Century Views). Englewood Cliffs, N.J.: Prentice-Hall, 1982.

Unterecker, John. "The Architecture of The Bridge." 1962. Rpt in Hart Crane: A Collection of Critical Essays. Ed. Trachtenberg, op. cit., pp. 80–96.

Voyager: A Life of Hart Crane. New York: Farrar, Straus and Giroux, 1969.

Letter to author. 13 July 1983.

Letter to author. 21 September 1983.

Uroff, M. D. Hart Crane: The Patterns of his Poetry. Urbana: Univ. of Illinois Press, 1974.

Vogler, Thomas A. Preludes to Vision: The Epic Venture in Blake, Wordsworth, Keats, and Hart Crane. Berkeley: Univ. of California Press, 1971.

Walcutt, Charles C. "Crane's Voyages, VI." The Explicator, 4, no. 7 (1946), note 53.

Weber, Brom. *Hart Crane: A Biographical and Critical Study*. New York: Bodley Press, 1948.

West, Rebecca. Letter to author. 8 February 1982.

Winters, Yvor. "The Significance of *The Bridge* by Hart Crane, or What Are we To Think of Professor X?" In *In Defense of Reason*. 1947; rpt London: Routledge and Kegan Paul, 1960, pp. 575–603.

Wolf, Jack Clifford. "Hart Crane's Harp of Evil: A Study of Satanism in *The Bridge*." Unpublished diss., State Univ. of New York at Buffalo, 1972.

Zeck, Gregory Robert. "Hart Crane and the Logic of Metaphor." Unpublished diss., Univ. of Texas at Austin, 1973.

III. OTHER WORKS

Aiken, Conrad. *Scepticisms: Notes on Contemporary Poetry*. New York: Knopf, 1919.

Alexander, Peter. *Roy Campbell: A Critical Biography*. Oxford: Oxford Univ. Press, 1982.

Apollinaire, Guillaume. *Alcools: Poèmes, 1898–1913*. Paris, 1913.

"Notes." *Dada*, no. 2 (Dec. 1917), 17.

Calligrammes: Poèmes de la paix et de la guerre, 1913–1916. 2nd ed. Paris, 1918.

Aragon, Louis. *Paris Peasant*. 1926. Trans. Simon Watson Taylor. London: Picador–Pan, 1980.

Traité du style. Paris: Libraire Gallimard, 1928.

Balzac, Honoré de. *The Magic Skin* [*La Peau de chagrin*]. Trans. Katharine Prescott Wormeley. Boston: Little, Brown, 1901.

Beaver, Harold. Introduction and Commentary. *Moby-Dick*. By Herman Melville. Harmondsworth: Penguin, 1972.

Bion, W. R. "Language and the Schizophrenic." In *New Directions in Psycho-Analysis: The Significance of Infant Conflict in the Pattern of Adult Behaviour*. Ed. Melanie Klein, Paula Heimann, R. E. Money-Kyrle. London: Tavistock Publications, 1955, pp. 220–39.

Black, MacKnight. *Machinery*. New York: Liveright, 1929.

Bloom, Harold. *Agon: Towards a Theory of Revisionism*. New York: Oxford Univ. Press, 1982.

Bragg, Melvyn. "Interview with Ian McKellen." *The South Bank Show*. London Weekend Television. 22 Nov. 1981.

Bray, Will [Matthew Josephson]. "Apollinaire: Or Let us Be Troubadors." *Secession*, no. 1 (1922), 9–13.

Breton, André. "Les Mots sans rides." *Littérature*, ns, no. 7 (1922), 12–14.

Manifestoes of Surrealism. Trans. Richard Seaver and Helen R. Lane. Ann Arbor: Univ. of Michigan Press, 1969.

Brooker, Peter. *A Student's Guide to the Selected Poems of Ezra Pound*. London: Faber, 1979.

Brooks, Van Wyck. *The Wine of the Puritans: A Study of Present-Day America*. London: Sisley's, 1909.

Brooks, Van Wyck, ed. *Christopher Columbus: The Journal of his First Voyage to America*. London: Jarrolds, 1925.

Brougham, John. *Po-Ca-Hon-Tas; or, The Gentle Savage*. 1855. Rpt in Meserve and Reardon, op. cit., pp. 115–55.

Columbus El Filibustero!! New York: Samuel French, [1865?].

Brown, Norman O. *Love's Body*. New York: Random House, 1966.

Brownlow, Kevin, and John Kobal. *Hollywood: The Pioneers*. London: Collins, 1979.

Bulfinch, Thomas. *The Age of Fable*. 1855. Rpt in *Bulfinch's Mythology*. London: Bodley Head, 1934, pp. 1–295.

Cabell, James Branch. *Jurgen: A Comedy of Justice.* 1919. Introduction by Edward Wagenknecht. Westport, Connecticut: Limited Editions Club, 1976.

Cervantes. *Don Quixote.* Trans. J. M. Cohen. Harmondsworth: Penguin, 1950.

Chirico, Giorgio de. Notes. *La Révolution Surréaliste,* no. 4 (1925), 21.

Cowley, Malcolm. *Exile's Return: A Literary Odyssey of the 1920s.* Rev. ed., 1951. Rpt Harmondsworth: Penguin, 1976.

A Second Flowering: Works and Days of the Lost Generation. New York: Viking Press, 1973.

Crosby, Caresse. *The Passionate Years.* 1953; rpt London: Alvin Redman, 1955.

Crosby, Harry. "The New Word." *transition,* nos. 16–17 (1929), 30.

"Observation-Post." *transition,* nos. 16–17 (1929), 197–204.

Shadows of the Sun: The Diaries of Harry Crosby. Ed. Edward Germain. Santa Barbara: Black Sparrow Press, 1977.

Crossman, R. H. S. *Plato Today.* 1937; rpt London: Unwin Books – Allen and Unwin, 1963.

Culler, Jonathan. *Structuralist Poetics: Structuralism, Linguistics and the Study of Literature.* London: Routledge and Kegan Paul, 1975.

Cummings, E. E. "You Aren't Mad, Am I? Being Certain Observations anent the Extremely Modern Art of 'Burlesk.'" 1925. Rpt in *E. E. Cummings: A Miscellany.* Ed. George J. Firmage. New York: Argophile Press, 1958, pp. 66–71.

"The Adult, the Artist and the Circus." 1925. Rpt in *Cummings: Miscellany,* op. cit., pp. 45–9.

Selected Letters. Ed. F. W. Dupee and George Stade. London: André Deutsch, 1972.

Desnos, Robert. "Rrose Sélavy." *Littérature,* NS, no. 7 (1922), 14–22.

"L'Aumonyme." *Littérature,* NS, no. 10 (1923), 25–6.

Detienne, Marcel, and Jean-Pierre Vernant. *Cunning Intelligence in Greek Culture and Society.* 1974. Trans. Janet Lloyd. Brighton: Harvester Press, 1978.

Donne, John. *The Complete English Poems.* Ed. A. J. Smith. Harmondsworth: Penguin, 1971.

Dos Passos, John. *Manhattan Transfer.* Boston: Houghton Mifflin, 1925.

Dostoyevsky, Fyodor. *Crime and Punishment.* 1866. Trans. Constance Garnett. London: Bantam–Heinemann, 1958.

Drabble, Margaret. "The Future of the Novel." Oxford Literary Society, Oxford. 22 Oct. 1980.

[Duchamp, Marcel.] "Rrose Sélavy." *Littérature,* NS, no. 5 (1922), passim.

Eliot, T. S. "*Ulysses,* Order and Myth." 1923. Rpt in *Selected Prose of T. S. Eliot.* Ed. Frank Kermode. London: Faber, 1975, pp. 175–8.

"Baudelaire." 1930. Rpt in *Selected Essays.* Rev. ed. London: Faber, 1951, pp. 419–30.

The Complete Poems and Plays. London: Faber, 1969.

Ellmann, Richard. *James Joyce.* 2nd ed. New York: Oxford Univ. Press, 1965.

Emerson, Ralph Waldo. "The Poet." In *Essays: Second Series.* 1844. Vol. III of *The Riverside Edition of Emerson's Complete Works.* London, 1883, pp. 7–45.

"Plato; or, The Philosopher." In *Representative Men.* 1850. Ibid. vol. IV, pp. 39–77.

"The Comic." In *Letters and Social Aims.* 1875. Ibid. vol. VIII, pp. 149–66.

Empson, William. *Seven Types of Ambiguity.* London: Chatto and Windus, 1930.

Letter. *Times Literary Supplement,* 1 Oct. 1954, p. 625, cols. 2–3.

Fear, Jacqueline, and Helen McNeil. "The Twenties." In *Introduction to American Studies.* Ed. Malcolm Bradbury and Howard Temperley. Harlow: Longman, 1981, pp. 195–219.

Fender, Stephen, ed. *The American Long Poem: An Annotated Selection.* London: Edward Arnold, 1977.

Fitzgerald, F. Scott. *The Great Gatsby.* 1925; rpt Harmondsworth: Penguin, 1950.

"Echoes of the Jazz Age." 1931. In *The Crack-up*. Harmondsworth: Penguin, 1965, pp. 9–19.

Forster, E. M. *Maurice: A Novel*. London: Edward Arnold, 1971.

Frank, Waldo. *The New America*. London: Jonathan Cape, 1922. [Originally published in the U.S.A. as *Our America*, 1919.]

    Virgin Spain: Scenes from the Spiritual Drama of a Great People. London: Jonathan Cape, 1926.

    The Re-discovery of America. New York: Charles Scribner's Sons, 1929.

Freud, Sigmund. *The Interpretation of Dreams*. 1900. Trans. James Strachey. Ed. Angela Richards. Harmondsworth: Penguin, 1976.

    The Psychopathology of Everyday Life. 1901. Trans. Alan Tyson. Ed. Angela Richards. Harmondsworth: Penguin, 1975.

    Jokes and their Relation to the Unconscious. 1905. Trans. James Strachey. Ed. Angela Richards. Harmondsworth: Penguin, 1976.

    Group Psychology and the Analysis of the Ego. 1921. In vol. XVIII of *The Standard Edition of the Complete Psychological Works of Sigmund Freud*. Trans. James Strachey. London: Hogarth Press and the Institute of Psycho-Analysis, 1955, pp. 69–143.

    The Future of an Illusion. 1927. Ibid. vol. XXI, pp. 5–56.

    Civilization and its Discontents. 1930. Ibid. vol. XXI, pp. 64–145.

Gilbert, W. S., and Arthur Sullivan. *The Mikado; or, The Town of Titipu*. London: Chappell and Company, 1885.

Glassco, John. *Memoirs of Montparnasse*. Toronto: Oxford Univ. Press, 1970.

Gross, Harvey. *Sound and Form in Modern Poetry: A Study of Prosody from Thomas Hardy to Robert Lowell*. Ann Arbor: Univ. of Michigan Press, 1964.

Guggenheim, Peggy. *Out of this Century: Confessions of an Art Addict*. London: André Deutsch, 1980.

Hartley, Marsden. *Adventures in the Arts*. 1921; rpt New York: Hacker Art Books, 1972.

Haslam, Malcolm. *The Real World of the Surrealists*. London: Weidenfeld and Nicolson, 1978.

Hemingway, Ernest. *The Sun Also Rises*. 1926; rpt London: Granada, 1976.

Hoffman, Frederick J. *The Twenties: American Writing in the Postwar Decade*. Rev. ed. New York: Free Press–Macmillan, 1965.

Hoopes, James. *Van Wyck Brooks: In Search of American Culture*. Amherst: Univ. of Massachusetts Press, 1977.

Hulme, T. E. "Romanticism and Classicism." In *Speculations: Essays on Humanism and the Philosophy of Art*. Ed. Herbert Read. 1924; rpt London: Routledge and Kegan Paul, 1960, pp. 111–40.

Huppé, Bernard F. "*Petrus Id Est Christus*: Word Play in *Piers Plowman*, the B-Text," *ELH*, 17 (1950), 163–90.

Irving, Washington. *Rip Van Winkle*. 1820; rpt Philadelphia: Lippincott, 1923.

Jakobson, Roman, and Linda Waugh. Assisted by Martha Taylor. *The Sound Shape of Language*. Brighton, Sussex: Harvester Press, 1979.

Johnson, Samuel. "Preface to Shakespeare." 1768. In *The Works of Samuel Johnson*. Ed. Arthur Murphy. London, 1816. Vol. II, pp. 77–140.

Jolas, Eugene. "Notes on Reality." *transition*, no. 18 (1929), 15–20.

    "The King's English Is Dying. Long Live the Great American Language." *transition*, no. 19–20 (1930), 141–6.

    A note on "Cabaret," by Hugo Ball. *transition*, no. 22 (1933), 10.

    "Homage to the Mythmaker." *transition*, no. 27 (1938), 169–75.

Jonson, Ben. *The Alchemist*. In vol. III of *The Complete Plays of Ben Jonson*. Ed. G. A. Wilkes. Oxford: Oxford Univ. Press, 1982, pp. 223–356.

Josephson, Matthew. "Made in America." *Broom*, 2 (June 1922), 266–70.

"The Brain at the Wheel." *Broom*, 5 (Sept. 1923), 95–6.

Life among the Surrealists. New York: Holt, Rinehart and Winston, 1962.

Joyce, James. *A Portrait of the Artist as a Young Man*. 1916; rpt London: Granada, 1977.

Ulysses. 1922; rpt Harmondsworth: Penguin, 2nd ed., 1971.

"From Work in Progress." *transatlantic review*, 1 (1924), 215–23.

"Fragment of an Unpublished Work." *Criterion*, 3 (1925), 498–510.

"Opening Pages of a Work in Progress." *transition*, no. 1 (1927), 9–30.

"Continuation of a Work in Progress." *transition*, no. 12 (1928), 7–27.

"James Joyce, Ad-Writer." *transition*, no. 21 (1932), 258.

Finnegans Wake. 1939; rpt London: Faber, 1975.

Kenner, Hugh. *Paradox in Chesterton*. Introduction by Herbert Marshall McLuhan. London: Sheed and Ward, 1948.

Ulysses. London: Allen and Unwin, 1980.

Kobler, John. *Ardent Spirits: The Rise and Fall of Prohibition*. London: Michael Joseph, 1974.

Kris, Ernst. *Psychoanalytic Explorations in Art*. London: Allen and Unwin, 1953.

Kyvig, David E. *Repealing National Prohibition*. Chicago: Univ. of Chicago Press, 1979.

Lawrence, D. H. *Studies in Classic American Literature*. London: Martin Secker, 1924.

The Plumed Serpent. 1926; rpt Harmondsworth: Penguin, 1950.

Leiris, Michel. "Glossaire: J'y serre mes gloses." *La Révolution Surréaliste*, no. 3 (1925), 6–7; no. 4 (1925), 20–1; no. 6 (1926), 20–1.

"Le Sceptre miroitant." *La Révolution Surréaliste*, no. 5 (1925), 7.

Lewis, R. W. B. *The American Adam: Innocence, Tragedy, and Tradition in the Nineteenth Century*. Chicago: Univ. of Chicago Press, 1955.

Loeb, Harold A. "The Mysticism of Money." *Broom*, 3 (Sept. 1922), 115–30.

McCullough, David. *The Great Bridge*. New York: Simon and Schuster, 1972.

MacLeish, Archibald. *Einstein*. Paris: Black Sun Press, 1929.

McMillan, Dougald. *transition: The History of a Literary Era 1927–1938*. London: Calder and Boyars, 1975.

Marlowe, Christopher. *The Tragical History of Doctor Faustus*. In *The Works of Christopher Marlowe*. Ed. C. F. Tucker Brooke, Oxford: Oxford Univ. Press, 1910, pp. 139–229.

Martin, Robert K. *The Homosexual Tradition in American Poetry*. Austin: Univ. of Texas Press, 1979.

Marx, Groucho. *The Groucho Letters: Letters from and to Groucho Marx*. London: Michael Joseph, 1967.

Mattfeld, Julius. *Variety Music Cavalcade 1620–1969*. 3rd ed. Englewood Cliffs, N. J.: Prentice–Hall, 1971.

Melville, Herman. *White-Jacket or The World in a Man-of-War*. 1850. Ed. Arthur Humphreys. London: Oxford Univ. Press, 1966.

Moby-Dick. 1851. Ed. Harold Beaver. Harmondsworth: Penguin, 1972.

Mencken, H. L. *The American Language: An Enquiry into the Development of English in the United States*. Rev. ed. London: Jonathan Cape, 1922.

Meserve, Walter J., and William R. Reardon, eds. *Satiric Comedies*. Vol. XXI of *America's Lost Plays*. Bloomington: Indiana Univ. Press, 1969.

Munson, Gorham B. *Waldo Frank: A Study*. New York: Boni and Liveright, 1923.

Robert Frost: A Study in Sensibility and Good Sense. New York: George H. Doran, 1927.

"Woodstock, 1924." *Hartford Studies in Literature*, 1 (1969), 169–80.

Nadeau, Maurice. *The History of Surrealism*. 1945. Trans. Richard Howard. Introduction by Roger Shattuck. London: Jonathan Cape, 1968.

Nietzsche, Friedrich. *The Birth of Tragedy: or, Hellenism and Pessimism*. 1872. Vol. I of *The Complete Works of Friedrich Nietzsche*. Trans. W. A. Haussmann. Ed. Oscar Levy.

Edinburgh: T. N. Foulis, 1909.

Human, All-Too-Human: A Book for Free Spirits, Part 2. 1879. Vol. VII of *The Complete Works of Friedrich Nietzsche.* Trans. Paul V. Cohn. Ed. Oscar Levy. Edinburgh: T. N. Foulis, 1911.

Ouspensky, P. D. *Tertium Organum: A Key to the Enigmas of the World.* 1912. Trans. Nicholas Bessaraboff and Claude Bragdon. London: Routledge and Kegan Paul, 1973.

Paul, Sherman. Introduction. *Port of New York: Essays on Fourteen American Moderns.* By Paul Rosenfeld (1924). Urbana: Univ. of Illinois Press, 1961.

Poe, Edgar Allan. "The City in the Sea." 1845. In *Edgar Allan Poe: Selected Writings.* Ed. David Galloway. Harmondsworth: Penguin, 1967, pp. 71–2.

Poirier, Richard. *A World Elsewhere: The Place of Style in American Literature.* London: Chatto and Windus, 1967.

Pound, Ezra. *The Cantos.* London: Faber, 1975.

Praz, Mario. *The Romantic Agony.* Trans. Angus Davidson. 2nd ed. London: Oxford Univ. Press, 1951.

Pritchard, William H. *Lives of the Modern Poets.* London: Faber, 1980.

"Proclamation" (The Revolution of the Word). *transition,* nos. 16–17 (1929), 13.

Reik, Theodor. *Masochism in Modern Man.* 1941. Trans. Margaret H. Beigel and Gertrud M. Kurth. New York: Grove Press, [1957].

Richards, I. A. *The Philosophy of Rhetoric.* 1936; rpt New York: Oxford Univ. Press, 1965.

Riding, Laura, and Robert Graves. *A Survey of Modernist Poetry.* London: Heinemann, 1927.

Rourke, Constance. *American Humor: A Study of the National Character.* New York: Harcourt, Brace and Co., 1931.

Rutra, Theo [Eugene Jolas]. "Dusk." *transition,* no. 8 (1927), 145.

Seldes, Gilbert. *The Seven Lively Arts.* 1924. Rev. ed. New York: Sagamore Press, 1957.

Shakespeare, William. *The Complete Works.* Ed. William Allan Neilson. Boston: Houghton Mifflin, 1906.

Sheppard, Richard W. "Tricksters, Carnival and the Magical Figures of Dada Poetry." *Forum for Modern Language Studies,* 19 (1983), 116–25.

Shi, David E. *Matthew Josephson: Bourgeois Bohemian.* New Haven: Yale Univ. Press, 1981.

Soby, James Thrall. *Giorgio de Chirico.* New York: Arno Press, for the Museum of Modern Art, New York, 1966.

Spence, Lewis. *Atlantis in America.* London: Ernest Benn, 1925.

Stein, Gertrude. "An Elucidation." *transition,* no. 1 (1927), 64–78.

Stella, Joseph. "The Brooklyn Bridge (A Page of my Life)." *transition,* nos. 16–17 (1929), 86–9.

Stock, Noel. *The Life of Ezra Pound.* 1970; rpt Harmondsworth: Penguin, 1974.

Stuart, Michael. "The Dubliner and his Dowdili (A Note on the Sublime)." *transition,* no. 18 (1929), 152–61.

Tanner, Tony. *Adultery in the Novel.* Baltimore: Johns Hopkins Univ. Press, 1979.

Tashjian, Dickran. *Skyscraper Primitives: Dada and the American Avant-Garde 1910–1925.* Middletown, Connecticut: Wesleyan Univ. Press, 1975.

Tate, Allen. *Essays of Four Decades.* London: Oxford Univ. Press, 1970.

Thompson, Lawrance. *Melville's Quarrel with God.* Princeton, N.J.: Princeton Univ. Press, 1952.

Thoreau, Henry David. *Walden.* 1854. Rpt in *The Portable Thoreau.* Ed. Carl Bode. Harmondsworth: Penguin, 1977, pp. 258–572.

Thurber, James, and E. B. White. *Is Sex Necessary?* 1929; rpt Harmondsworth: Penguin, 1960.

Tzara, Tristan. *Seven Dada Manifestoes and Lampisteries*. Trans. Barbara Wright. London: John Calder, 1977.

Untermeyer, Louis. "Einstein and the Poets." *Broom*, 1 (Nov. 1921), 84–8.

"Rhyme and Relativity: Parodies Showing the Possible Influence of the Einstein Theory on our Contemporary Poets." 1921. Rpt in *"Vanity Fair": Selections from America's Most Memorable Magazine*. Ed. Cleveland Amory and Frederic Bradlee. New York: Viking Press, 1960, p. 55.

Waggoner, Hyatt Howe. *The Heel of Elohim: Science and Values in Modern American Poetry*. Norman: Univ. of Oklahoma Press, 1950.

Waterman, Willoughby Cyrus. *Prostitution and its Repression in New York City, 1900–1931*. New York: Columbia Univ. Press, 1932.

Weaver, Mike. *William Carlos Williams: The American Background*. Cambridge: Cambridge Univ. Press, 1971.

Webster's New International Dictionary of the English Language. Springfield, Mass.: Merriam, 1909.

Wentworth, Harold, and Stuart Berg Flexner. *The Dictionary of American Slang*. 2nd supplemented ed. New York: Crowell, 1975.

West, Rebecca. "James Joyce and his Followers." *New York Herald Tribune*, 12 Jan. 1930, sect. 12, p. 1, cols. 1–3; p. 6, cols. 1–4.

Whitehead, A. N. *Science and the Modern World*. 1925; rpt New York: Mentor–New American Library, 1948.

Whitman, Walt. *The Complete Poems*, Ed. Francis Murphy. Harmondsworth: Penguin, 1975.

Wilde, Oscar. *The Works of Oscar Wilde*. Ed. G. F. Maine. London: Collins, 1948.

Williams, William Carlos. *In the American Grain*. 1925; rpt New York: New Directions, 1956.

"A Note on the Recent Work of James Joyce." *transition*, no. 8 (1927), 149–54.

The Autobiography. 1951; rpt [London]: MacGibbon and Kee, 1968.

The Collected Later Poems. [London]: MacGibbon and Kee, 1975.

Wilson, Edmund. "A Great Magician." 1928. Rpt in *The Shores of Light: A Literary Chronicle of the Twenties and Thirties*. London: W. H. Allen, 1952, pp. 286–92.

I Thought of Daisy. 1929; rpt Harmondsworth: Penguin, 1963.

The American Earthquake: A Documentary of the Twenties and Thirties. 1958; rpt New York: Farrar, Straus and Giroux, 1979.

The Twenties: From Notebooks and Diaries of the Period. Ed. Leon Edel. New York: Farrar, Straus and Giroux, 1975.

The Wound and the Bow: Seven Studies in Literature. Cambridge, Mass.: Houghton Mifflin, 1941.

Winters, Yvor. *In Defense of Reason*. 1947; rpt London: Routledge and Kegan Paul, 1960.

Wolff, Geoffrey. *Black Sun: The Brief Transit and Violent Eclipse of Harry Crosby*. New York: Random House, 1976.

Wong, Jade Snow. *Fifth Chinese Daughter*. London: Hurst and Blackett, 1952.

Yeats, W. B. *Collected Poems*. 2nd ed. London: Macmillan, 1950.

Young, Philip. "Fallen from Time: The Mythic Rip Van Winkle." *Kenyon Review*, 22 (1960), 547–73.

"The Mother of us All: Pocahontas Reconsidered." *Kenyon Review*, 24 (1962), 391–415.

Indexes

I. Index of works by Hart Crane

269

II. Index of people and periodicals

/811.52C891BYG>C1/